POSTCARD HISTORY SERIES

Ocean City's Historic Boardwalk, Beach, and Bay

The Fisher Collection

Robert M. Craig

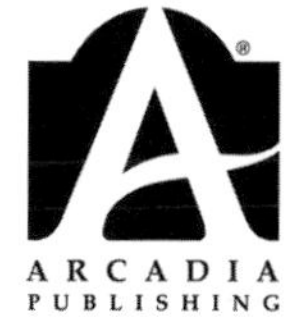

ISBN 978-1-4671-6032-2

Published by Arcadia Publishing
Charleston, South Carolina

Printed in the United States of America

Library of Congress Control Number: 2023933337

For all general information contact Arcadia Publishing at:
Telephone 843-853-2070
Fax 843-853-0044
E-mail sales@arcadiapublishing.com
For customer service and orders:
Toll-Free 1-888-313-2665

Visit us on the Internet at www.arcadiapublishing.com

To Bob and Kathy Fisher, with gratitude for their generous sharing of a lifetime of collecting.

POSTCARD HISTORY SERIES

Ocean City's Historic Boardwalk, Beach, and Bay

The Fisher Collection

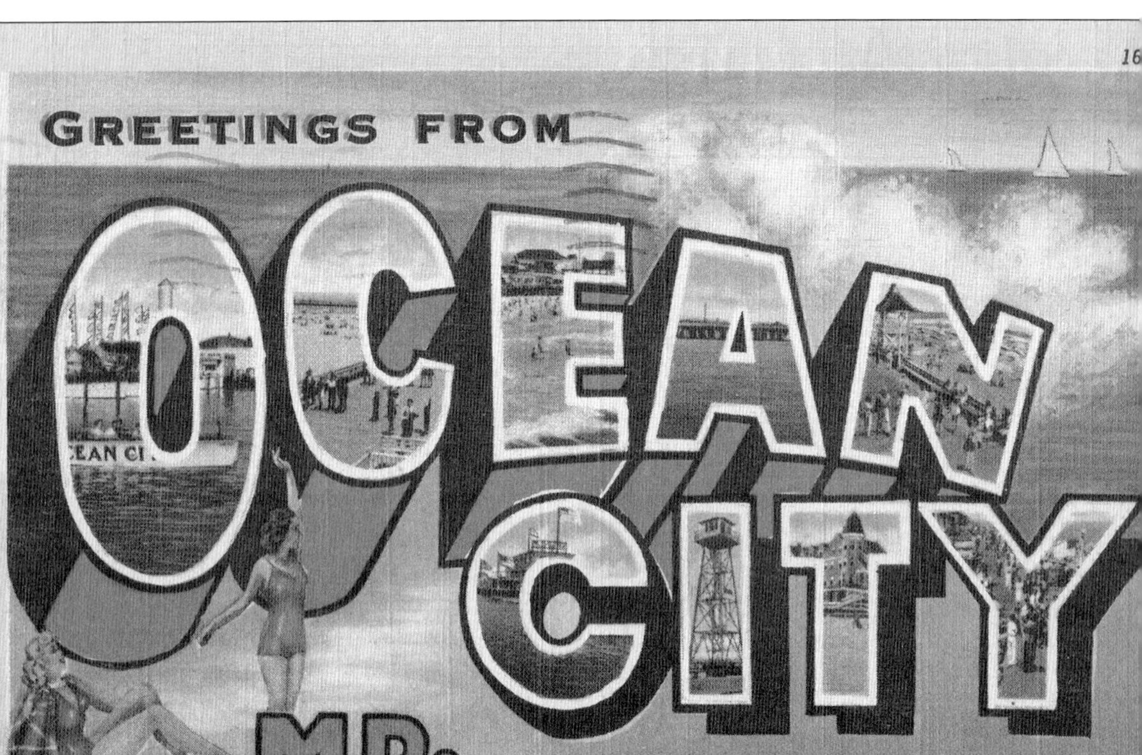

This characteristic Curt Teich & Company "Greetings from" postcard was one of the company's most popular and colorful formats. Large letters spell out the town name forming a stencil within which (in this case) scenes of the boardwalk, beach, and bay are visible. The format promoted cities and towns nationwide. The code on the bottom right of this example translates to an issuance date of 1944, while this Ocean City, Maryland, card in the Fisher Collection was postmarked 1952. (Courtesy of Bob and Kathy Fisher, The Fisher Collection.)

On the Front Cover: An early "white-border" postcard, published by Louis Kaufmann, shows the boardwalk and beach in a view north from the US Life-Saving station tower/pavilion to the pier and pre-1925 convention hall. Narrower private wooden walkways join oceanfront cottages to the boardwalk. The wider ramp in the foreground accommodates the US Life-Saving station's lifeboat. The ramp onto the beach at middle distance illustrates the raised height of the early boardwalk. (Courtesy of Bob and Kathy Fisher, The Fisher Collection.)

On the Back Cover: Three urchins are described as "Bold Adventurer of the Briny Deep" in this undated postcard silhouetting the children against the sea. Like many postcards of the era, the scene is generic and, lacking any particularly local and recognizable features, allowed the postcard to be sold in various markets with the name of the ocean resort town stamped in the border. (Courtesy of Bob and Kathy Fisher, The Fisher Collection.)

Contents

Acknowledgments

Two books have now been developed around the Bob and Kathy Fisher postcard collection, Arcadia's *Historic Lodgings of Ocean City* and *Ocean City's Historic Boardwalk, Beach, and Bay*. Both pay tribute to the Fishers and their preservation of postal images and ephemera and also acknowledge their other contributions to historic preservation and leadership in the Worcester County Historical Society. This book joins *Historic Lodgings* in being dedicated to the Fishers; neither book could have been written without their support.

Arcadia's entire Postcard History Series is indebted to photographers' work in the field, to local and international printers and publishers of the highly popular pictorial postcards, and above all, to Curt Teich. In *Historic Lodgings*, I acknowledged the highly significant role of the Lake County Discovery Museum in preserving the Curt Teich Postcard Archives Collection (the largest in the world), which is now housed at the Newberry Library in Chicago. I now take the opportunity to outline, in the introduction of this companion book, Curt Teich's 80-year history as the premier creator and printer of millions of postcards produced between 1898 and 1978. Many postcards of the Fisher Collection are Curt Teich products, while the Fisher Collection also features work of competitor printers and local photographers.

Recognizing inconsistencies and inaccuracies in website and print documentation of the subjects treated in these books, I have consulted scholars, authors, colleagues, and friends long familiar with Ocean City and its history. Among these, whose information and comments have assisted the writing of this book, are Gordon Katz, Bunk Mann, Diane Savage, and especially waterman Ricks Savage, whose information about head boats, charter boats, and sailboats in the Bay chapter has been particularly helpful. I am also grateful to acquisition editors Katelyn Jenkins and Erin Vosgien at Arcadia Publishing, who have been receptive to my proposals for books in both Images of America and Postcard History Series—this being my fifth book for Arcadia—and who, along with Stacia Bannerman, have stewarded the projects toward successful completion.

My wife, Carole, continues to support my writing, providing services as proofreader and guidance as occasional editor, and takes up extra duties at home allowing me to devote needed time to photography, scanning, research, and writing.

Unless otherwise noted, all images appear courtesy of Bob and Kathy Fisher, The Fisher Collection.

Introduction

Bob and Kathy Fisher are likely the most significant private postcard collectors on the Eastern Shore. Throughout their lives they have participated in one of the world's three-largest collectible hobbies, postcard collecting, a pastime rivaled in popularity only by coin and stamp collecting. Despite the more sophisticated terms applied to these three pastimes (deltiology, numismatics, and philately), the imagery of each can be relatively commonplace, ranging from popular art and the vernacular to landmark imagery known nationally or merely significant locally. While postcards may not be considered "high art," their photography is often meritorious, and the manipulations of content and composition, as well as the tonality of printing, are often notably artistic. Significantly, pictures of local businesses and places, professions, daily activities, and recreational pursuits, as recorded on postcards, provide a visual documentation of history itself.

Herein lies the rationale for Arcadia's Postcard History Series of books. The Bob and Kathy Fisher Collection includes postcards from the earliest years of the 20th century, the pioneer era of postcards when even American companies were distributing imported penny cards, mostly from Germany, and when the postcard culture was becoming epidemic. In the single year, June 1907 to June 1908, for instance, when the population of the United States was less than 89 million, over 677 million postcards were mailed.

By the 1910s, the largest manufacturer of postcards, Curt Teich, & Company, was printing millions of postcards per year. The company founder, a German immigrant named Curt Otto Teich, is said to have accepted every project proposal that passed through the company's door, producing throughout the company's 80-year history, hundreds of thousands of different images and postcard views of historic buildings, famous people, objects of art, celebrations and holidays, streetscapes, landscapes, and seascapes. The Newberry Library's Curt Teich Postcard Archives Collection today contains more than half a million unique postcard images. The subjects extended from coast to coast, and within the Fisher Collection, postcards of Ocean City's buildings, boardwalk, beach, bay, and ocean include substantial numbers of Curt Teich postcards.

Just as the postcard imagery of hotels, motels, and related tourist buildings collected in *Historic Lodgings of Ocean City: The Fisher Collection* provides an architectural history of Maryland's beach resort, so, in this companion volume, the Fisher Collection's postcards of boardwalk views, beach scenes, and picturesque imagery of sailing on the Sinepuxent Bay or the many moods of the Atlantic Ocean offer a visual representation of Ocean City's recreational activities, which were promenading, sunbathing, sailing, fishing, and engaging in water sports like "fanny dipping" and surfing. Postcard styles range from photographic snapshot imagery to hand-colored tonal pictures, to novelty postcards including cartoons and stencil overlays, and to the familiar "Greetings from" series of cards and large-letter stencil postcards, which include views of historical buildings, local businesses, and/or natural landmarks inside big letters that spell out the name of the city or town. Whether the postcard subject is a building, boardwalk, beach, or bay, a well-developed postcard collection, such as the Fisher Collection, serves the cultural historian with an unrivaled pictorial documentation of the past. In these two companion volumes on Ocean City, Maryland, part of Arcadia's Postcard History Series, readers will find a visual history of everyday life of Americans on vacation.

The postcard has its own history. The "postcard" (as opposed to a government's "postal card" containing preprinted postage) is a rectangular (between 3.5 and 4.25 inches high by 5 to 6 inches wide) thin cardboard card intended for writing and mailing without an envelope. When the idea of a postal card originated in Germany in 1865, it was thought improper to mail messages that a servant, or anyone else, could read, but cheaper postal rates made postal cards popular. The US Post Office Department (USPOD) issued America's first postal card (without pictures) in 1873. During the so-called pioneer era, pre-1898 postcards (mostly from New York and other major metro areas) had an address side and filled the reverse side with commercial advertisement. At this time, privately printed postcards were known as souvenir cards, correspondence cards, or mail cards.

The US Post Office issued its first picture postcards in 1893 at Chicago's World's Columbian Exposition, illustrating scenes from the world's fair's "White City." That same year, an 1893 Act of Congress permitted privately printed postcards to be mailed at the same penny rate as the government's 1¢ cost for postal cards issued by the USPOD. As a result, the private production of souvenir cards and the popularity of picture postcards increased substantially. The early "picture side" of even privately printed postcards was given over to mainly advertising, and additional message writing was disallowed on the address and stamp side of the card, though messages were scrawled in the empty border around the imagery on the photograph side. Between 1901 and 1907, the publication of printed postcards doubled almost every six months. European publishers opened American branch offices and imported millions of mostly German-printed postcards, supplying over 75 percent of all postcards sold in the United States by 1907. Most American postcard businesses could not match the quality of German printers. Although production and delivery delayed receipt of cards by six to twelve months, the imported postcards were less expensive.

By the late 1890s, however, Curt Teich, a German immigrant who grew up in the printing trade, had already moved to Chicago where he established his own firm in 1898. Curt's father, Christian, was a printer, newspaper publisher, and book salesman in Western Germany, and in 1893, he and Curt's eldest brother, Max, traveled to the World's Columbian Exposition in Chicago. Max stayed in the Windy City, entering the hotel business, and two years later, Curt joined Max in the United States. After a brief apprentice job in a New York printing house, Curt moved to Chicago and, in 1898, opened his own printing business, partially subsidized by his older brother.

Competition was fierce, and Curt Teich initially projected a broad corporation plan in printing, lithography, publishing, and importing art printing and souvenirs. In an effort to be more competitive, especially in the face of extensive German imports, Teich returned to Germany in 1904. His purpose was to research new lithography and printing methods in hopes of giving his burgeoning printing business an edge with respect to efficiency, quality of product, and marketing. He found in Germany a burgeoning tourist postcard industry where, since the early 1890s, German printers had been producing *Grüße aus* ("Greetings from") postcards. Municipalities and chambers of commerce found in such "Greetings from" postcards a way to feature local tourist attractions and promote a town. Such postcards became a mainstay for the Curt Teich Company, and the Fisher Collection contains many examples extending "Greetings from Ocean City."

When Teich returned to the United States, he embarked on what was to be a formative train trip to solicit postcard orders. It was also a marketing research exercise to provide feedback from businessmen, town leaders, and other potential customers for his postcard venture—what image they sought and how they wanted their businesses and towns represented. Teich traveled by train from Chicago to St. Petersburg, Florida, and then on to the West Coast, disembarking at each stop to photograph businesses on the main streets of small towns, collecting $30,000 (over $1 million today) worth of orders along the way.

Teich began to print his own cards, millions of them, and continued to do so for seven decades. He died in 1974, and the company closed in 1978. Although he printed postcard views of over a hundred countries, the bulk of the Curt Teich postcard output comprised scenes of small-town America, the hotels and stores, churches and public buildings, city views, and landscapes of American vernacular culture. The Curt Teich Company illustrated scenes of over ten thousand cities and towns across the United States. With the rise of the automobile, these small towns became destinations, and in the case of Ocean City, Maryland, virtually every hotel, motel, public building, street view, boardwalk, beach, and bay and ocean seascape became subject matters. When a bridge spanned the Chesapeake Bay near Annapolis in 1952, the number of travelers from Baltimore and Washington, DC, to Ocean City increased, and Ocean City's population of a few thousand residents grew to 300,000 on a summer weekend. Many of these tourists bought postcards to send to friends and family back home.

Curt Teich's success reflected other early developments in postcard history. In March 1907, the format of postcards changed with the "divided backs" now permitted in which the address and message were written on the right and left respectively of the back of the postcard, and the front was given over to imagery of buildings or scenes of everyday townscapes, albeit idealized by developments in tonal printing, hand coloring, and various photographic, textured linen, and painterly manipulations. During the next eight to ten pre–World War I years, the public taste for postcards skyrocketed. Moreover, Curt Teich benefited from the passage in 1909 by Congress of the Payne-Aldrich tariff, which imposed an import duty on all view cards coming in from Germany. Curt Teich increased its growing fleet of offset presses and was soon able to print 100-plus postcards on one sheet and roughly 500,000 cards per day, per machine. He maintained these production levels throughout the 1910s, producing roughly 150 million postcards a year, and many were distributed through such five-and-dime stores as F.W. Woolworth Co. After Curt Teich's introduction of the five-color printing process in 1931, the textured linen finish of his "C.T. Art-Colortone" became the familiar style of Teich postcards well in the 1950s. Airbrushing fluffy pink clouds in sunset skies became almost a signature.

The Curteichcolor process was purchased in 1980 and used by John Hinde, Ltd., an Irish company founded in 1956 by photographer John Hinde. Ten years later, the company was producing 32 million postcards, mostly of scenes of Ireland and the United Kingdom. Hinde images, taken on a large-format camera, were manipulated to produce a retro, color-saturated realism, reminiscent of Technicolor in early-Hollywood films such as *The Wizard of Oz* (1939) and *Fantasia* (1940). Intensifying the color-rich imagery of the Curteichcolor process, Hinde photography is part of an international revival of interest in postcard pictorialism, in which reality defers to an artistic interest in the beauty of subject matter, tonality, and composition. Like a still life painter setting up the objects of a projected work of art, artists like Curt Teich and John Hinde removed and added people, cars, bushes, and other objects from a scene in order to optimize their artistic vision. While casual purchasers of postcards may not be aware of such art consciousness, the artistic merits of postcard scenes were not accidents nor mere "snapshot" photography but carefully orchestrated compositions. Readers of Arcadia's Postcard History Series of books are able to discover this, as notably in evidence in the picturesque, even scenographic, postcards of moonlight sailing on the bay, the magical moods of the ocean, and the perambulations at night on the famed Ocean City Boardwalk.

The Curt Teich Company was purchased in 1976 (two years after Teich's death) by another Chicago firm founded by a German immigrant, the Regensteiner Publishing Enterprises, and the Curt Teich name was no longer associated with new postcards being printed. On the other hand, founder Curt Teich had made a practice of retaining copies of every photograph and postcard the company produced. The family sought a home where this extraordinary archive could be preserved as a single collection, and in 1982, they donated the archive to the Lake County Discovery Museum (in Wauconda, Illinois). According to the *Encyclopedia of Chicago History*, this is considered the largest public collection of postcards in the world, including approximately 2.5 million postcards and more than 360,000 images of 20-century American life and culture, as well as subjects from 115 other countries. In late 2016, the Curt Teich Postcard Archives Collection was transferred to the Newberry Library in Chicago. In the meantime, private collectors nationwide amassed shoebox-loads of postcards of local subjects; bought, sold, and traded cards at flea markets; and compiled notebooks and albums full of postcards depicting local scenes and places of historical interest. Often, as with Bob and Kathy Fisher, these individuals were active in the historical preservation movement, saving local buildings and raising the consciousness of fellow citizens regarding the importance of history in a civilized society. Curt Teich is well represented in the Fisher Collection.

A cursory view through the Fisher Collection, moreover, gives evidence of several contemporaries and competitors to Curt Teich in the postcard business. Louis Kaufmann & Sons operated out of Baltimore and published regional postcard scenes of subjects from Pennsylvania to Virginia, contracting many of their images to be printed by Curt Teich, using his offset printing process. The Fisher Collection includes postcards with borderless painterly pictures of tonal atmospheric imagery, much like the hand-colored postcards widely in evidence before World War I, many of which were locally distributed by Dr. Frank Townsend at his Washington Pharmacy on the boardwalk at Somerset Street. Other Kaufmann & Sons cards had plain-white borders, which not only saved printer's ink but also were increasingly the norm of Curt Teich production cards.

The Albertype Company, founded in 1890 by Adolph and Herman L. Wittemann, employed "new technologies," such as albertype to reproduce photo-mechanical images, and created more than 25,000 prints between 1890 and 1952. Headquartered in Brooklyn, the company gathered photographic negatives from throughout the United States and printed from a gelatine-coated plate using a process invented by German photographer Joseph Albert. The Albertype process employs glass plates, rather than copper or lithographic stone used in collotype printing, in a process that produced about 2,000 prints from each gel/silicate plate. Several postcards from the Fisher Collection are identified on the following pages as Albertype.

Postcards published by the Boston firm Tichnor Brothers, Inc., are also represented in the Fisher Collection. During the 1930s through World War II, Tichnor Brothers published color postcards with linen texture, specialized in American vacation places, and were a significant competitor for Curt Teich. The Boston Public Library's Tichnor Brothers Collection contains about 25,000 office proofs of postcards by the firm, including "Greetings from" cards. The firm offered postcard scenes from across the United States, comic/novelty postcards, and numerous beach and town views of Ocean City, many of which were collected by the Fishers and appear in the pages that follow.

Local photographers and publishers on the Eastern Shore also contributed to the postcard coverage of Ocean City's boardwalk, beach, bay, and ocean attractions. Fred W. Brueckmann's Tingle Printing Company, headquartered in Pittsville, Maryland, produced postcards of Eastern Shore subjects, with Brueckmann's photography supplemented by occasional postcard images during the 1950s by Robert S. Craig (longtime captain of the Ocean City Beach Patrol) and others. Delaware firms HPS of Dover and Marketing Merchandising of Lewes reproduced striking images by R.C. Pulling and Kevin N. Moore, illustrating especially the northern development of Ocean City along the beaches of "Condo Row." By the date of these 1970s, and 1980s architectural developments, postcards were less popular forms of communication. The Curt Teich Company, which had illustrated scenes of over 10,000 cities and towns across the United States, had closed in 1978, and "Greetings from" postcards would soon be supplanted after 1983 by Motorola's mobile phones (1983), flip phones (1996), BlackBerrys (1999), Apple iPhones (2007), and, ultimately, the digital world's answer to postcard communication—Facebook (2004), Twitter (2006), and Instagram (2010).

One

Early Years

Imagine the entire 9.2-mile stretch of the barrier island that is now Ocean City devoid of any development, unpopulated except by native shorebirds, dune grasslands, scrub shrubbery, seabeach amaranth, coastal beach, and with only a sparse bayside landscape of salt marshes and tidewater coves. Much of the coastal barrier isles from Tom's Cove on the Eastern Shore of Virginia north to the Ocean City inlet remains so today, conserved as Assateague Island National Seashore, Assateague State Park, and Chincoteague National Wildlife Refuge. The town of Ocean City, however, has had almost a century and a half of development, from isolated hunting lodges and a hamlet of small fishing shacks to late-Victorian summer cottages and shingle-clad resort hotels, to motels and a "coastal highway" of commercial excess "with no there, there," and, finally, to a dramatic alignment of condo towers on a stretch of sand that 60 years ago was little more than dunes and seagrass.

When Ocean City's development began, a century and a half ago, the coastline from northern Virginia into southern Delaware was isolated and characterized by dunes with seagrass and salt-tolerant weeds with burs, by hillocks of sand serving as barriers to high tide and storm surge overflow oceanside and to bayside flooding along the island's back side, and by wetlands and marsh. Once a coastal wasteland, apparently uninhabitable, the barrier island's isolation was breached early by farmers seeking grazing land and by fishermen finding isolated beaches for surf casting or places between dunes where their boats could be hauled overnight above high tide lines. Duck blinds, hunting lodges, isolated fishing shacks, and lifesaving stations erected by the US Life-Saving Service were the only built works, the first signs of human activity marked by architecture. It took only a few generations of real estate developers and pioneer hotel and cottage builders after 1875 to change the face of the beachscape.

Even as Ocean City developed as a resort town in the late 19th century and built its permanent porch-fronted hotels and gabled and turreted cottages, photographers were keen to record the disappearing dunes, seagrass, and wetlands. Translating photographs to souvenir postcards, printers created picturesque, indeed nostalgic, postcard views of the vacant beaches with their preserved sand dunes and wispy seagrass.

Not infrequently, a ship passing by the barrier island, unable to navigate due to lack of island or mainland lights and few coastal lighthouses, would run aground on the shifting sandbars offshore. Sailors attempted valiantly to swim ashore, sometimes in rough sea. If they survived the shore breaks, they found an uninhabited barrier island with neither food nor human assistance available. Another swim across the bay to the mainland was needed, and even then, farms were sparsely sited, and assistance may not be found. Many shipwrecked sailors were lost, prompting the formation in 1878 of the US Life-Saving Service and the building of lifesaving stations every six to eight miles along the coast. (For more information, please see chapter one of Arcadia's *Maryland's Ocean City Beach Patrol.*) Several such lifesaving stations appeared on the barrier islands along the Delmarva (DELaware, MARyland, and VirginiA) peninsula at the following locations: Indian River, Delaware (1876); Ocean City, Maryland (1878), and Isle of Wight, Maryland (1897); and Green Run, Virginia (1875).

Thus, among the earliest souvenir images of the coastal landscape of the future Ocean City were postcard views of the natural dune-scapes and open seas, showing the ocean in different moods from magical moonlit calm to storm surf. Early also are the postcards of the boardwalk at Caroline Street where the Ocean City Life-Saving Station and its tower were sited—architectural landmarks of the earliest development of the town. In those early days, for practical purposes, the populated beach meant only that short stretch of beach in front of the lifesaving station's tower, where bathers felt safe to enter the ocean for recreational swimming under the watchful eye of lifesaving servicemen (and later Coast Guardsmen) during the years before the 1930 creation of the Ocean City Beach Patrol (the town's lifeguards).

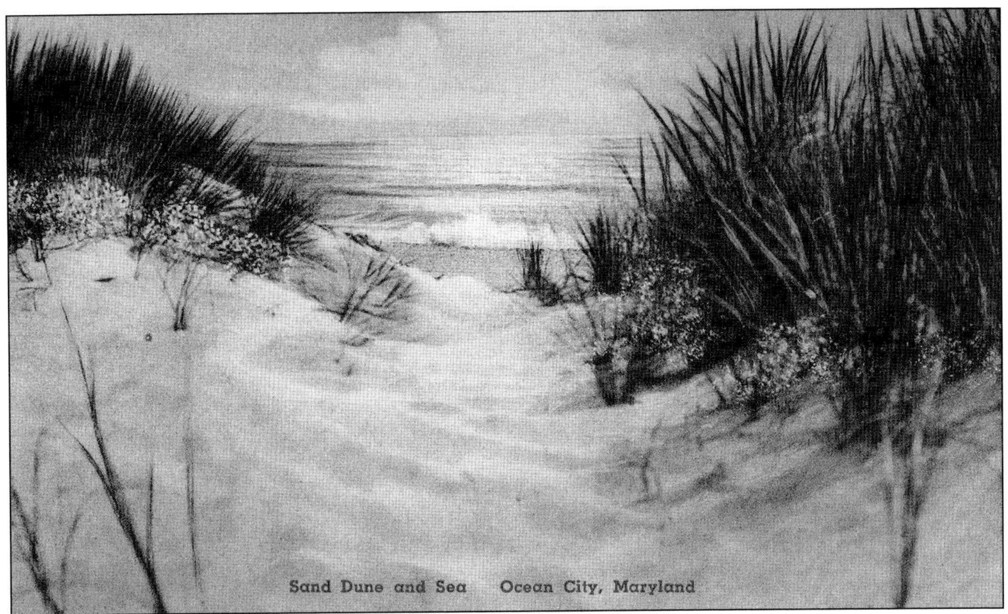

Ocean City dates its founding to the 1875 opening of the Atlantic Hotel, an establishment rebuilt after a 1925 fire and still operating today. This is an early borderless "Atlantic Hotel postcard," one of many images sold as postcards at the hotel. It pictures an unspoiled view of "sand dune and sea," with seagrass framing the view toward low breaking waves, soft clouds, and sunlight highlighting the ocean.

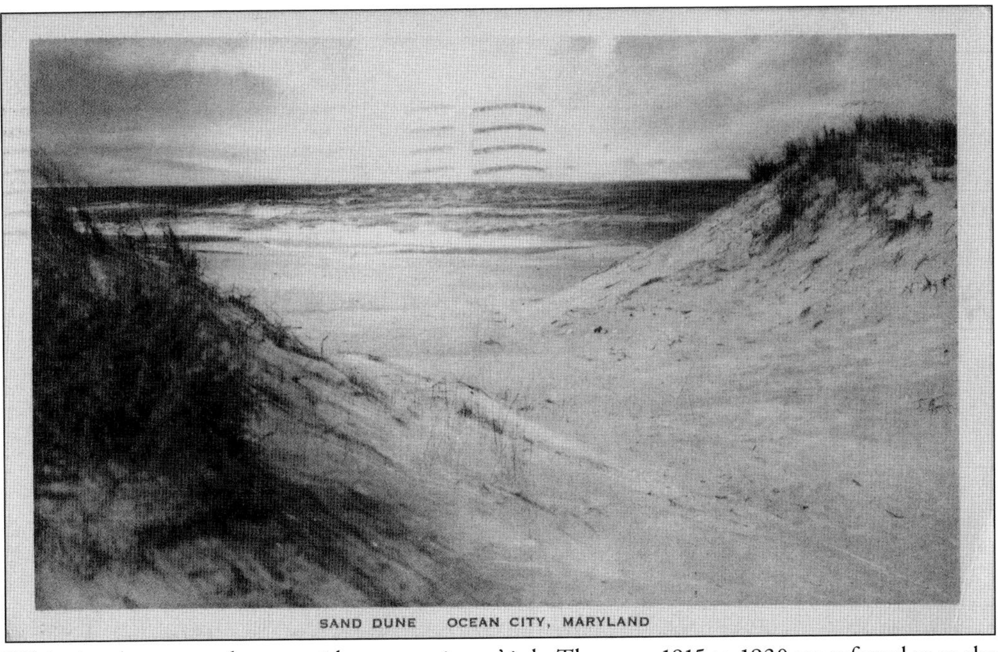

White-border postcards were said to save printers' ink. The years 1915 to 1930 are referred to as the "White Border Period." Please note that the date of this black-and-white view is unknown. Prior to World War I, most postcards were produced by German publishers, importing thousands to the states. The German group IG Farben held patents for most colorants and printing dyes. This card of a "sand dune," postmarked 1937, locates the dune in Ocean City.

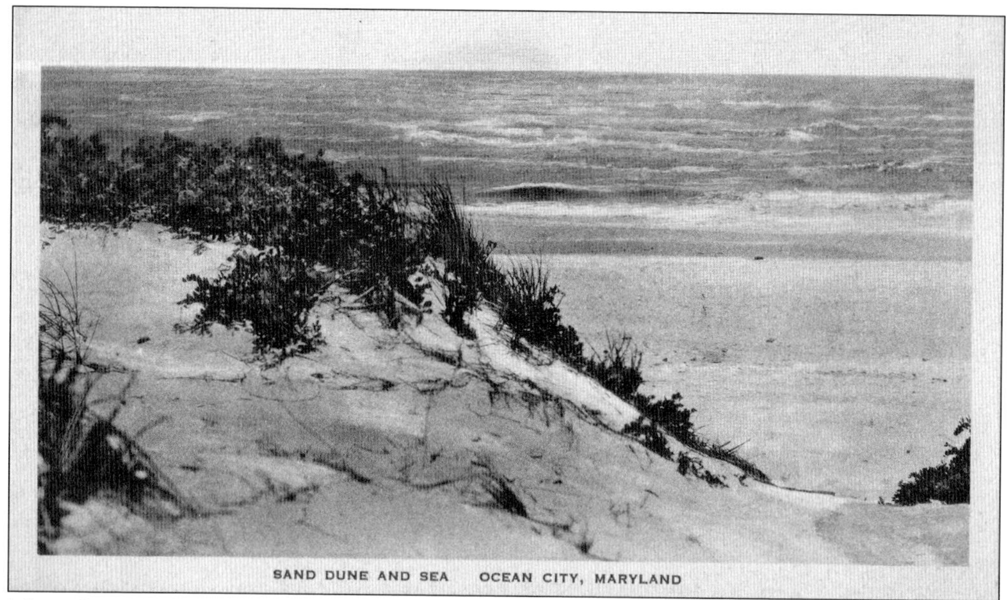

These four black-and-white photographs of dunes and sea on pages 14 and 15 were produced by R.D. Driscoll. The views of unspoiled coastline were typical of undeveloped acreage north of Ocean City's city limits. When those town limits were extended to the Delaware state line in 1965, empty duneland and vacant beaches began to be dotted with cottages, multifamily apartment blocks, and multiple commercial buildings.

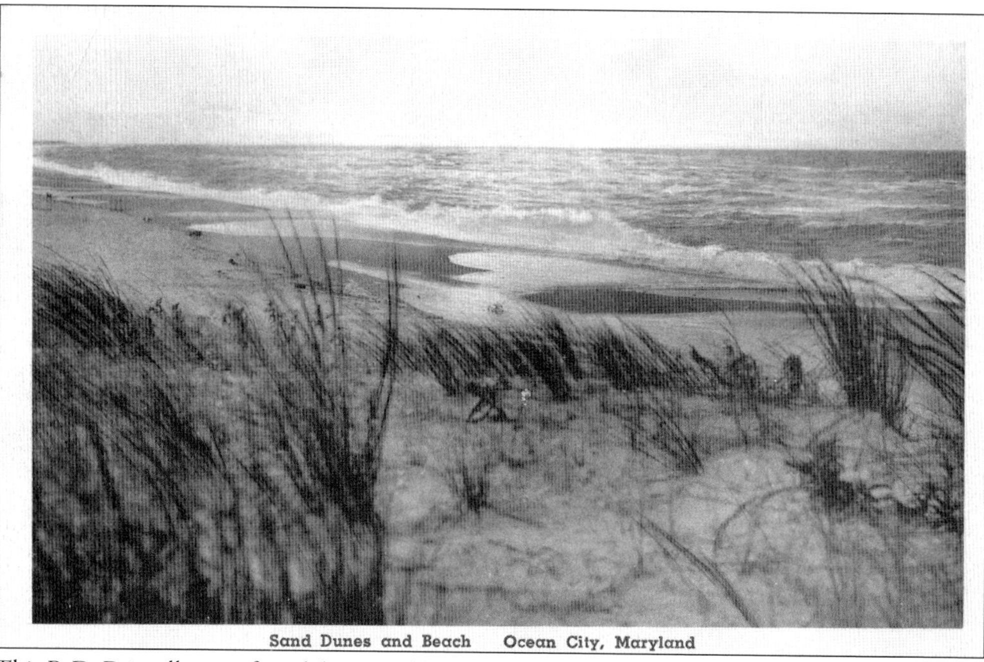

This R.D. Driscoll view of sand dunes and beach is postmarked 1950, a time when only sandpipers, seagulls, and sand crabs populated the landscape. It would not be until the next decade that such vacant beach and ocean would be accented with the silhouettes of surfboards and, at night, the flickering lights of campfires and beach parties. Civilization was creeping north, and such unspoiled seascapes were disappearing.

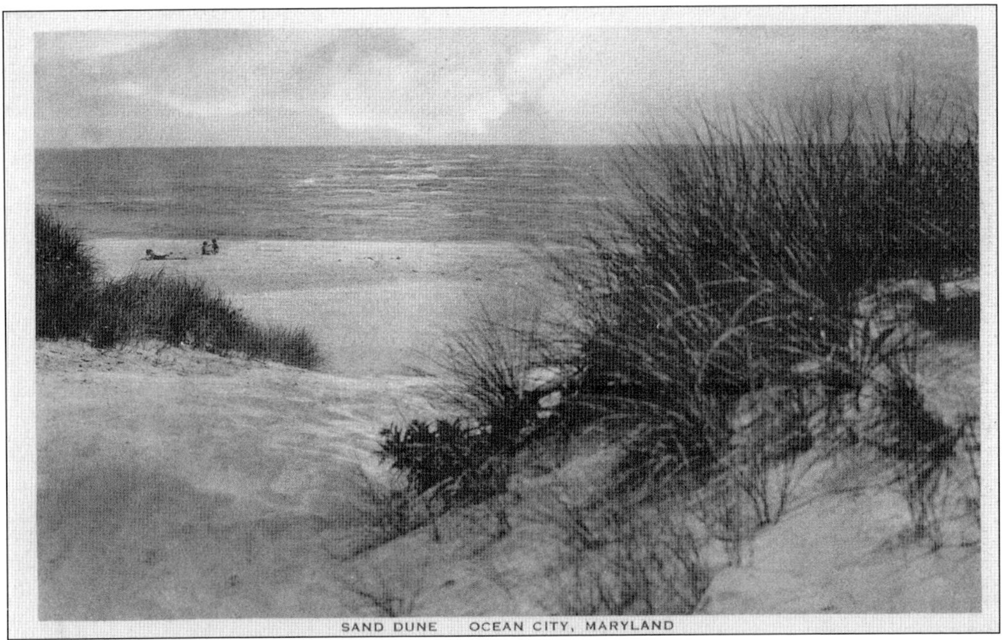

The two children at play and lone sunbather in this "sand dune" postcard view only served to emphasize the otherwise empty and completely natural landscape of north Ocean City. By foregrounding the sloping sand and unkempt seagrass, with a gentle S-curve of space leading the eye to the ocean, where neither swimmers nor boats are in evidence, the photographer records an image of undeveloped shoreline only recalled nostalgically today.

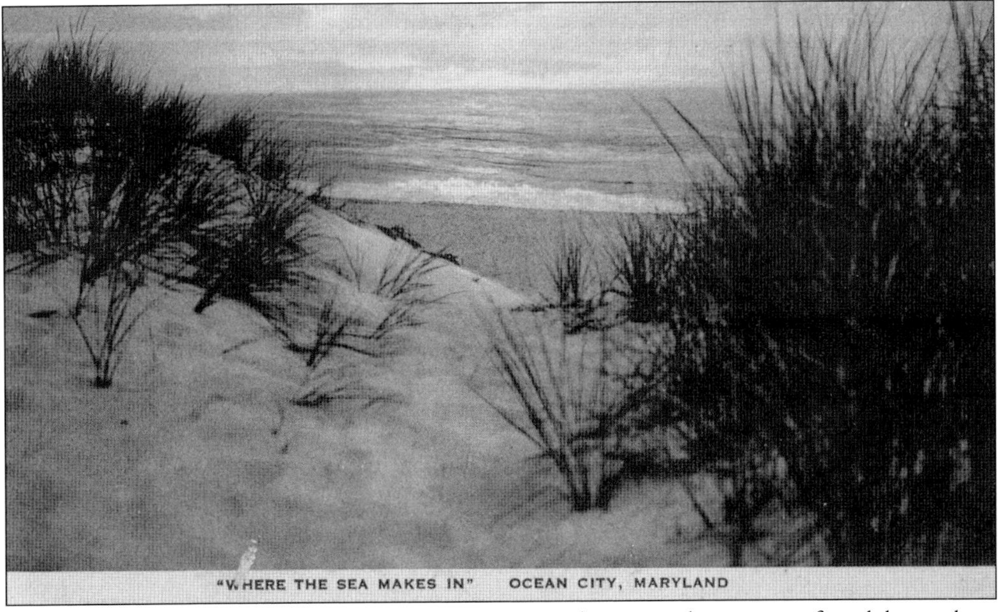

Titled "Where the Sea Makes In," this Albertype postcard suggests the purpose of sand dunes along the coast, which is to serve as barriers against high tides and storm surge. Clumps of grass minimize wind erosion of the sand, and only salt-tolerant plants, such as seabeach amaranth (*Amaranthus pumilus*), survive the harsh environment. Such postcards normally show a calm sea, promoting a more pastoral scene rather than one of untamed storm surf.

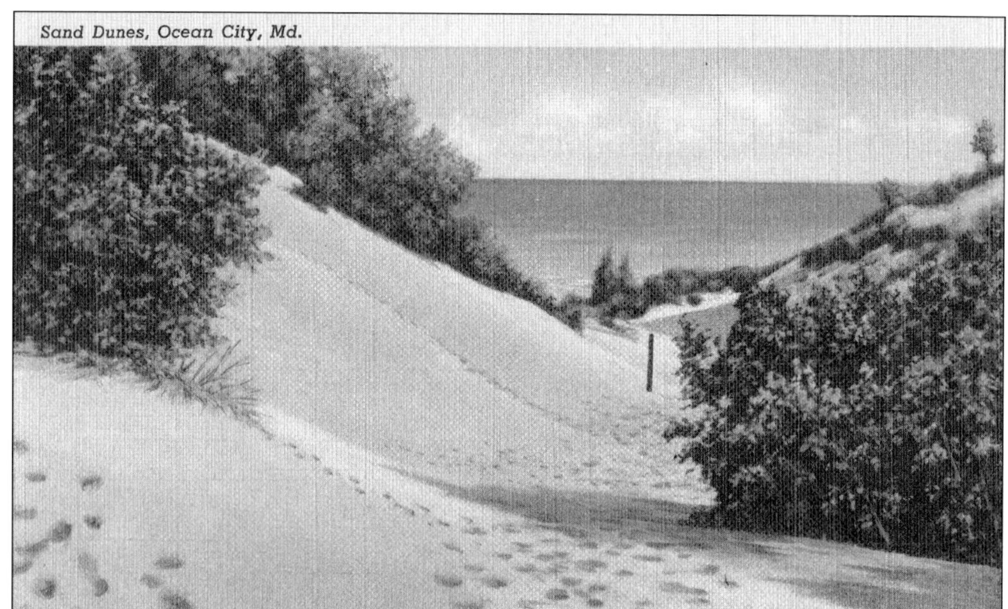

What distinguishes this color view of "sand dunes" at Ocean City are the numerous footprints, indicating the presence of some form of life in the otherwise empty landscape. The photographer gives no hint—is it human, bird, or animal? What remains is a natural dune setting unspoiled by construction. By the 1970s, such northern dunes would be displaced by Condo Row, and soon thereafter, the entire coastline would be crowded with buildings.

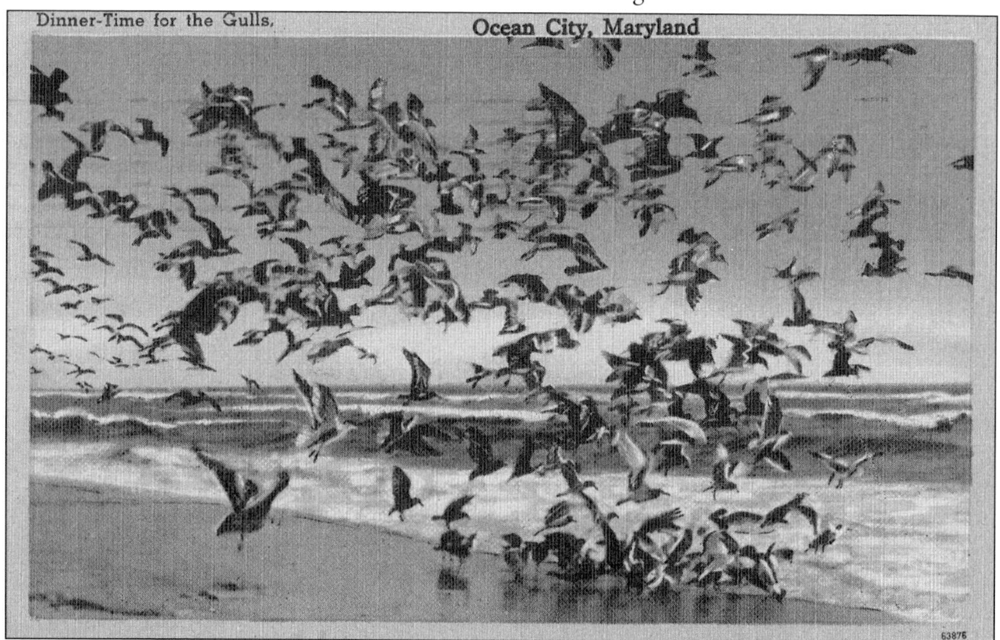

"Dinner-Time for the Gulls" captures a huge flock of squawking seagulls, likely following the lead of a seagull who has discovered a source for food. "Dinner" could be anything from fish to crabs, insects to rodents, even injured seagulls, or, on Ocean City beaches, Thrasher's french fries supplied by humans. Gulls are voracious opportunistic feeders, consuming almost any food they encounter. Found worldwide, seagulls inhabit all seven continents.

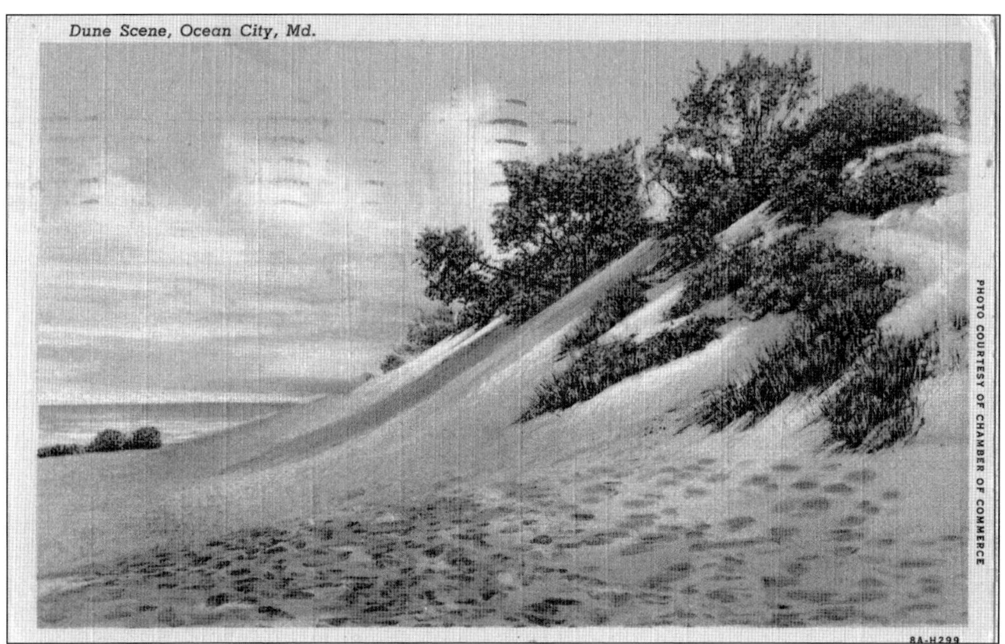

This Curt Teich "Dune Scene" was published in 1938 and credits its photo to the chamber of commerce. Windswept sand rises to scrub bushes and low-clinging foliage in a coastal view that is not site specific. The generic postcard image could be reissued and relabeled as depicting a location most anywhere on the Atlantic Ocean barrier islands.

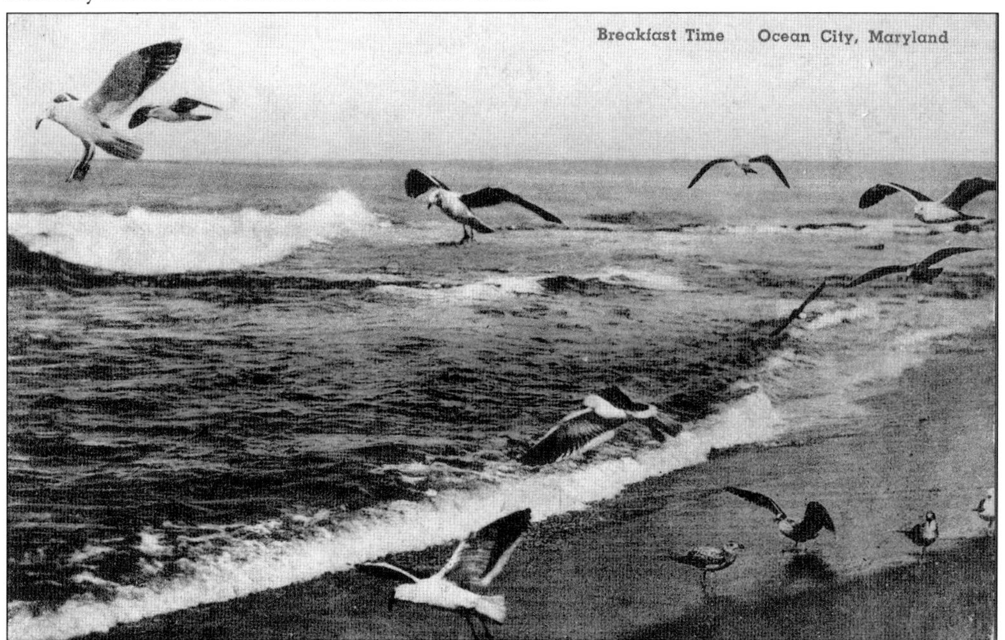

Continuing the theme of "Dinner-Time for the Gulls" (page 16 opposite), this Atlantic Hotel postcard captures hovering seagulls at "breakfast time," as though, like some ocean dolphin show, the feeding had been arranged for the hotel guests and tourists. The scene remains devoid of humans, lending an impression comparable to the sand dune postcards of the still natural setting of the undeveloped oceanfront.

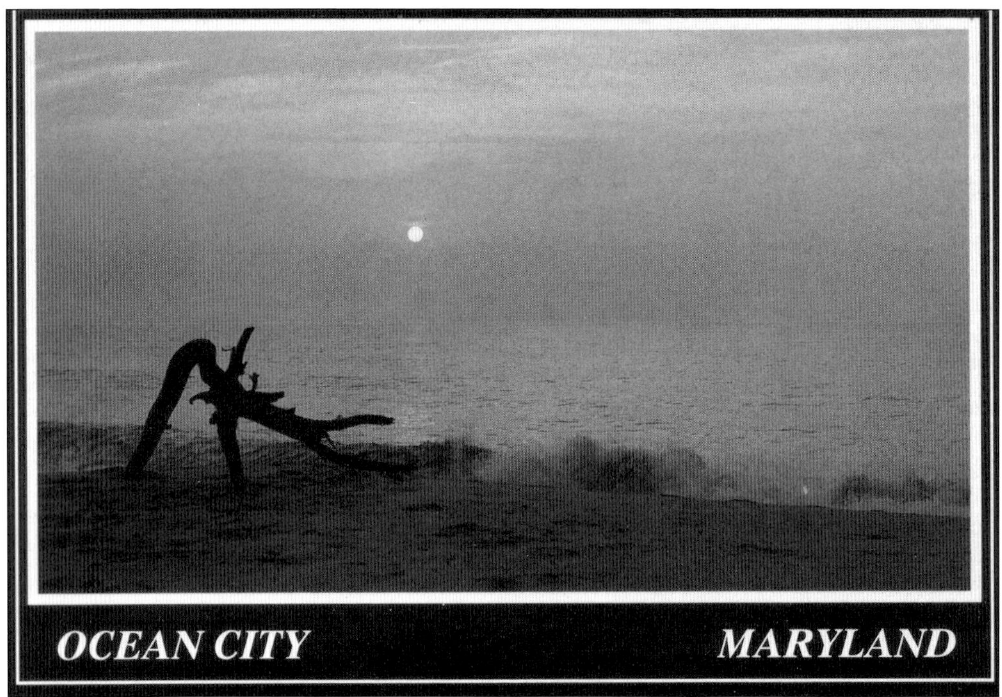

During the latter decades of postcard popularity, after unspoiled sand dunes had been displaced by hotels, condo towers, and apartment blocks, local photographers continued to produce artistic images of discovered driftwood, surviving or reclaimed dunes, isolated seagrass, and snow fences. R.C. Pulling, whose work was frequently distributed by HPS, Inc., out of Dover, Delaware, captured this late-20th-century sunrise.

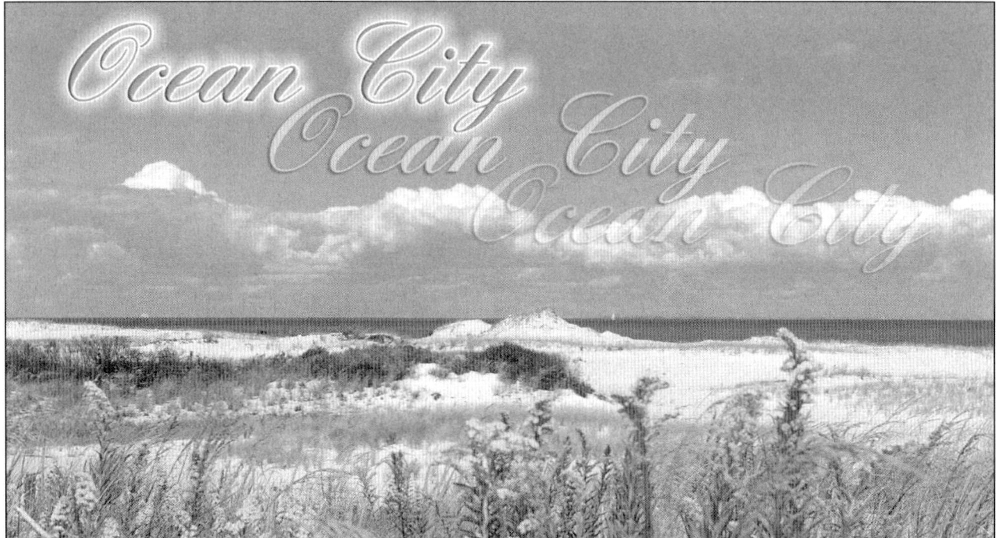

Artistic photographs by Kevin N. Moore were popular in postcard form, as evidenced in this view romanticizing the preserved natural beachscape, as well as in the postcards on page 19. Here, even the lettering identifying Ocean City appears to cascade like a breaking wave, while the crisp foreground of seagrass and yellow flowering weeds offers contrast to the open shoreline and eye-level horizon line where blue sea meets sky.

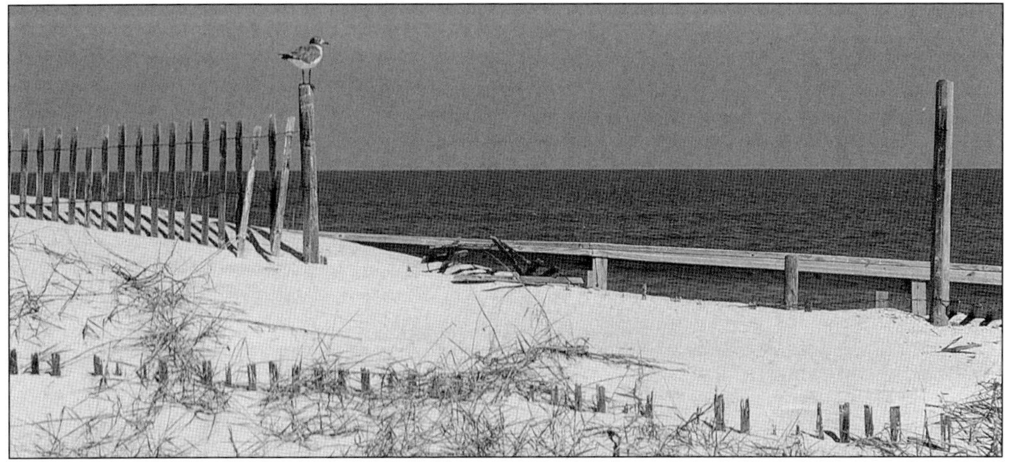

Titled "A Lone Seagull Gazes out at the Beautiful Atlantic Ocean," this postcard by Kevin N. Moore is a study of horizontal and vertical lines, including the hard-edge horizon line of a clear day, the ragged line of broken fencing in the foreground, the rustic vernacular of the ordinary beach fencing at left, and even the feathery abstract lines of the disheveled seagrass.

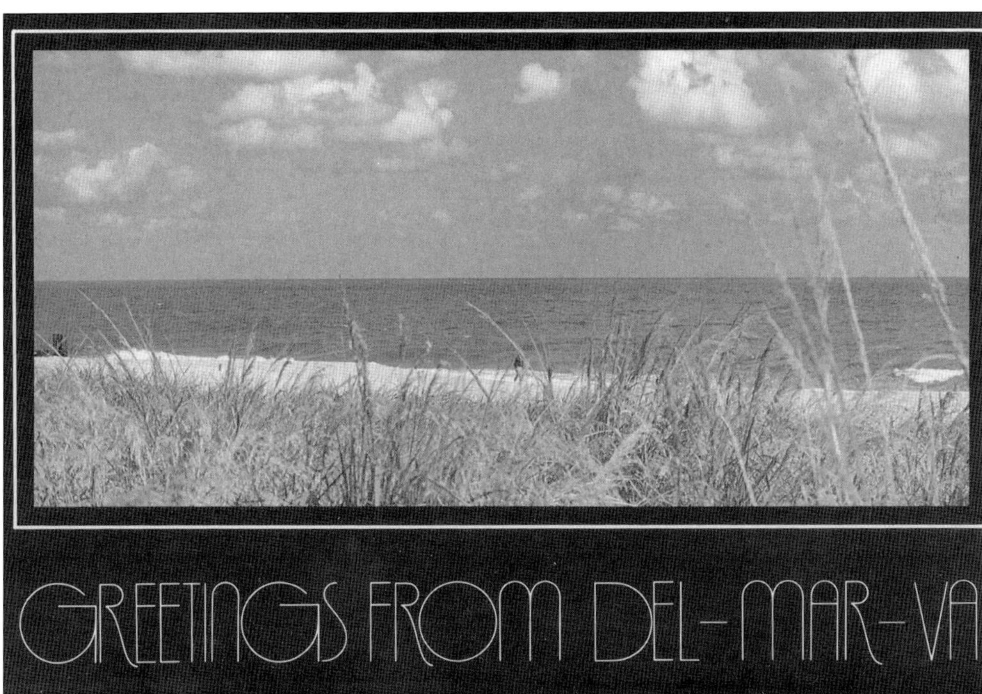

GREETINGS FROM DEL-MAR-VA

Distributed by Marketplace Merchandising out of Lewes, Delaware, Kevin N. Moore's photograph of a lone figure strolling the beach and barely visible beyond the foregrounded yellow-green seagrass could be a scene anywhere along the Delmarva barrier island, as suggested by the "Greetings from Del-Mar-Va" subtitle.

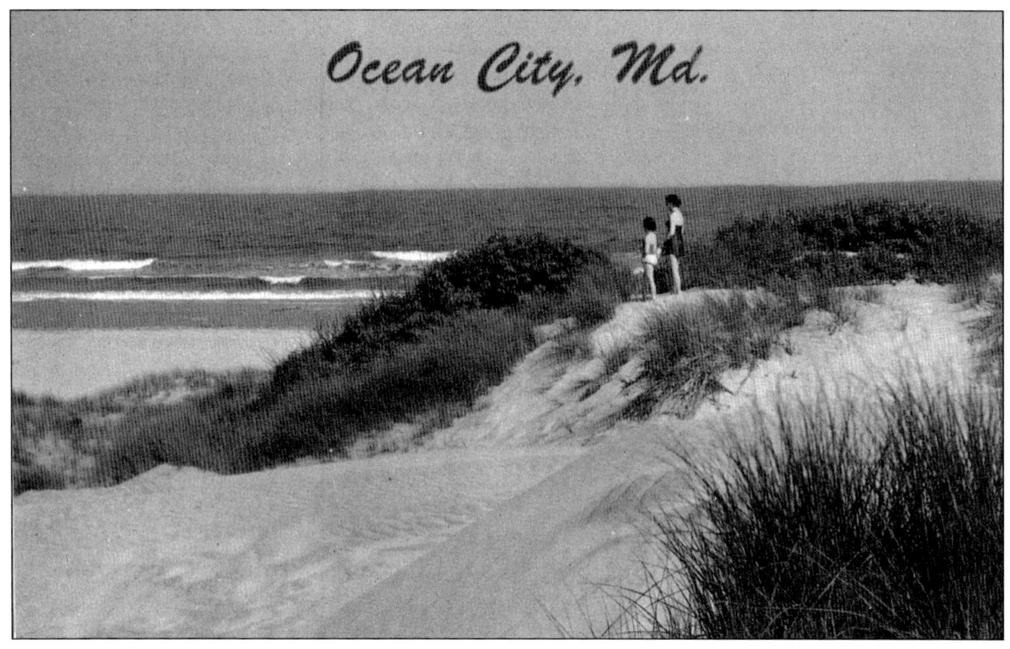

When human figures were introduced to dunes scenes, it was never a crowded beach of sunbathers but rather an isolated figure or two, emphasizing the still-intact and relatively undisturbed landscape. This undated postcard was published by Tichnor Brothers, Inc., of Boston. The Tichnor Brothers Collection at the Boston Public Library contains approximately 25,000 office proofs of c. 1930–1945 textured linen postcards, mostly depicting American vacation places.

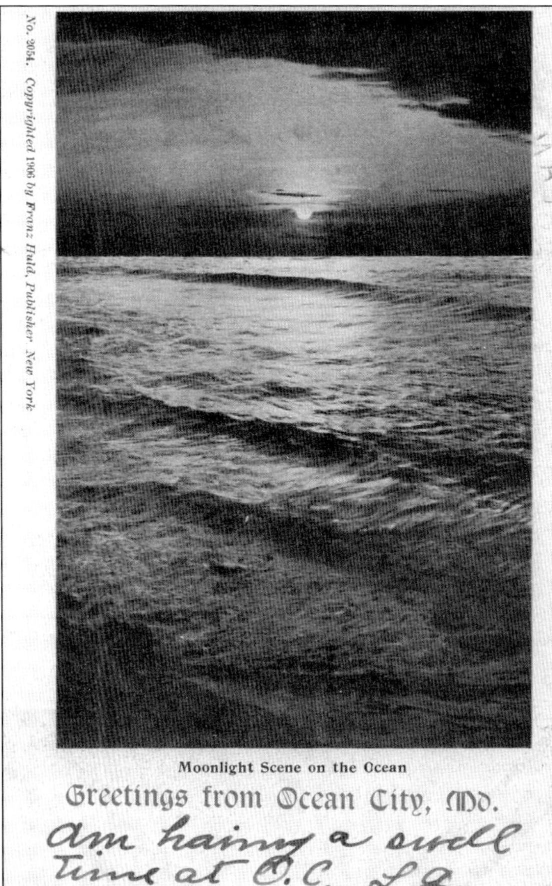

This "Moonlight Scene on the Ocean" was published by Franz Huld (1861–1928), a German immigrant who arrived in New York in 1897 and produced view cards, comics, novelty cards, and holiday greeting cards, before judged bankrupt in 1909. This atmospheric card of the rising moon over the ocean was published in 1906.

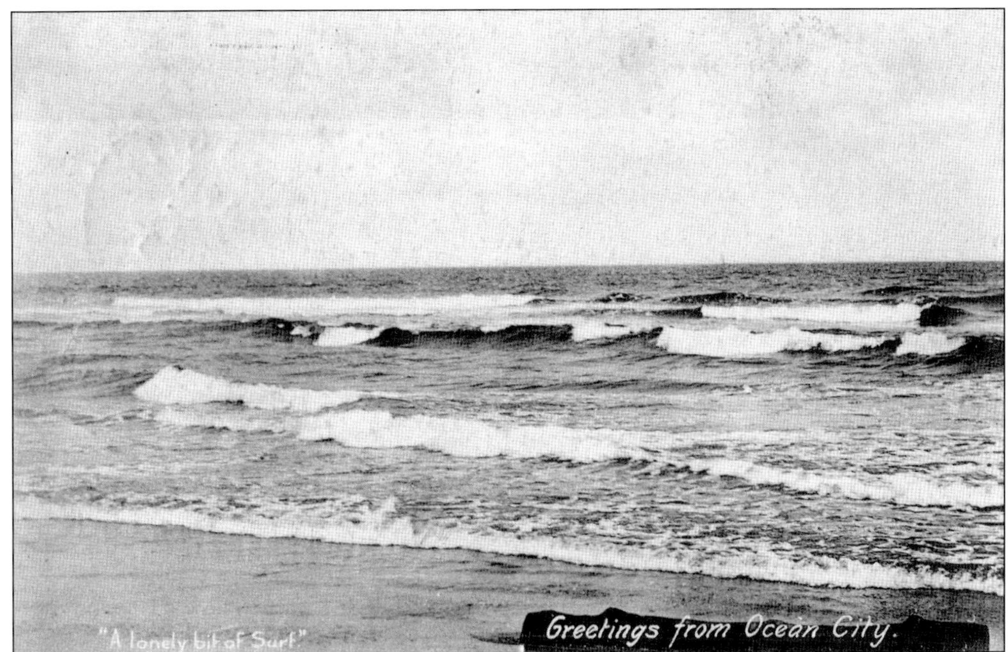

Postmarked 1908, this card shows "A lonely bit of Surf," a scene which in a few decades would be populated by bathers on surf mats or, from the 1960s on, by surfboarders hanging ten, riding the shoulder, or wiping out, but always looking for a perfect day when the "surf's up" with a west wind. A sandbar causes outer waves to break, with a second display of whitewater closer in.

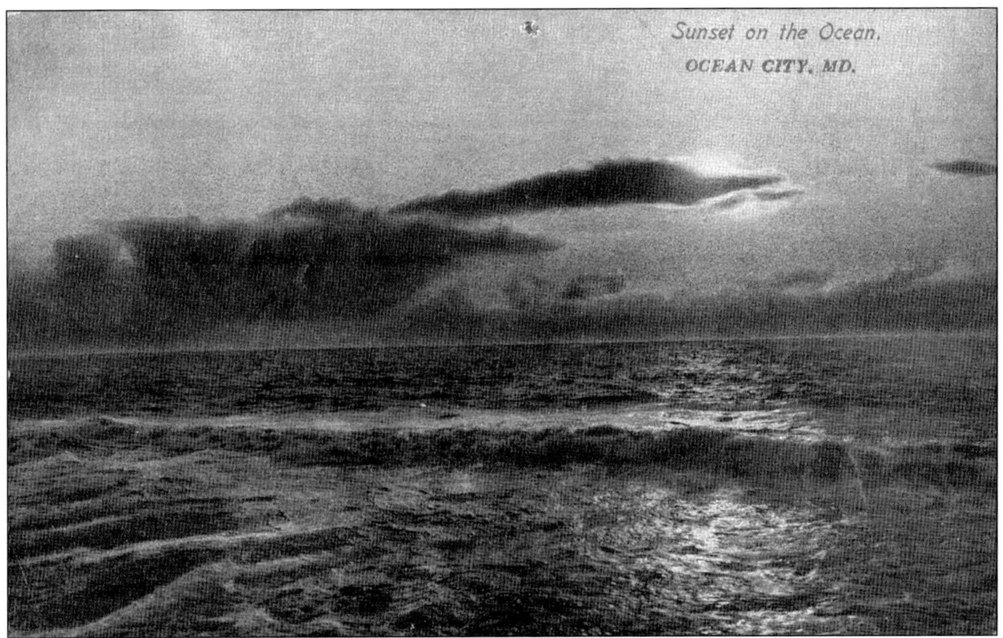

Printed titles can be deceiving. Unless the publisher thinks Ocean City is on the West Coast, this view of a "sunset on the ocean" is more likely a sunrise, or since the photographer is taking the photograph from the beach, as the shallow shore break indicates, it is possibly a view of a rising moon. The distant clouds enhance the sense of depth and emptiness of the relatively calm sea.

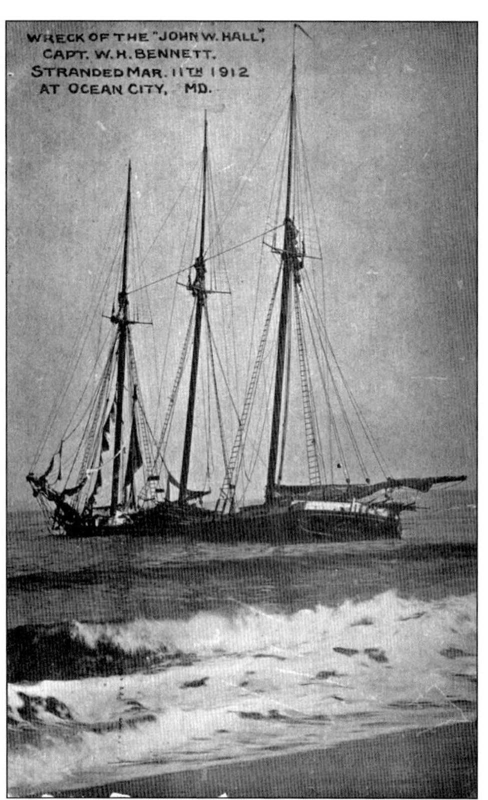

On March 11, 1912, Capt. W.H. Bennett's boat, the *John W. Hall*, was stranded off Ocean City. Shifting sandbars and minimal coastal lighting impaired navigation, and periodically, sailors would misjudge the distance to land and run aground on sandbars invisible just below the waterline. On the other hand, slight differences in the ocean's color and surface texture, with whitewater wave caps in evidence, would be high sand indicators.

Just three months earlier, on December 14, 1911, the Italian ship *Fortuna* was stranded off Fourteenth Street in Ocean City. In this photograph, barely visible off the port bow, is a lifeboat with oars extended, making its way to shore. Breaking waves are already shifting the stern of the three-masted ship toward shore, a circumstance that does not bode well.

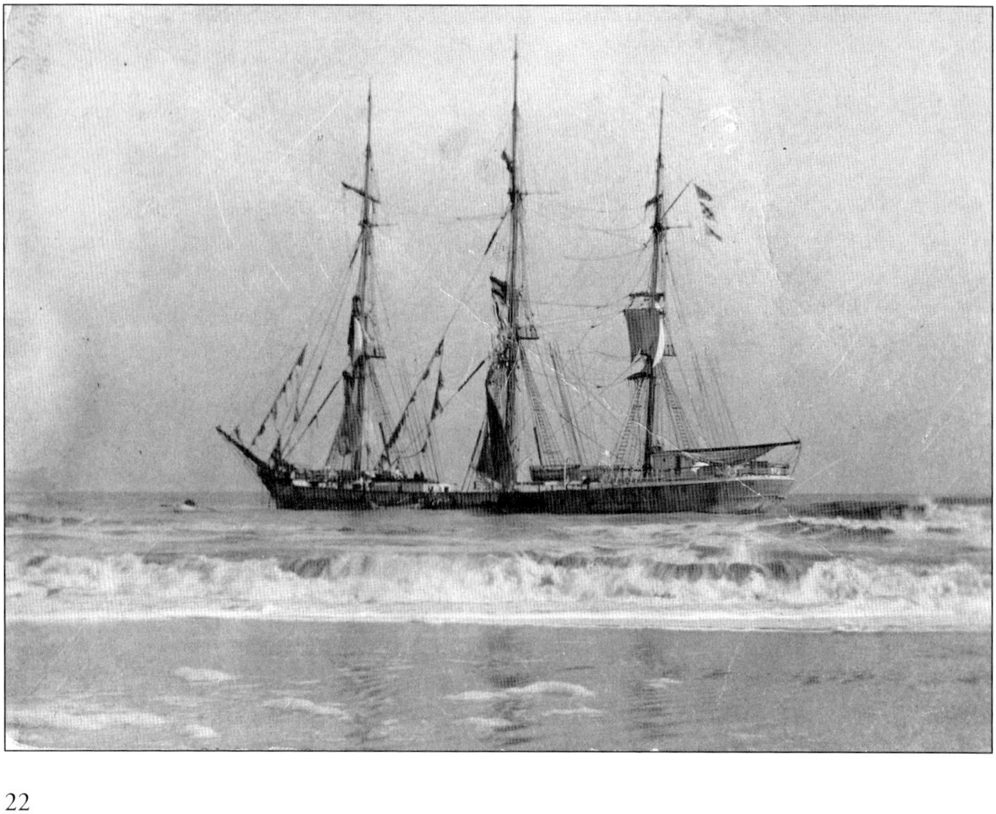

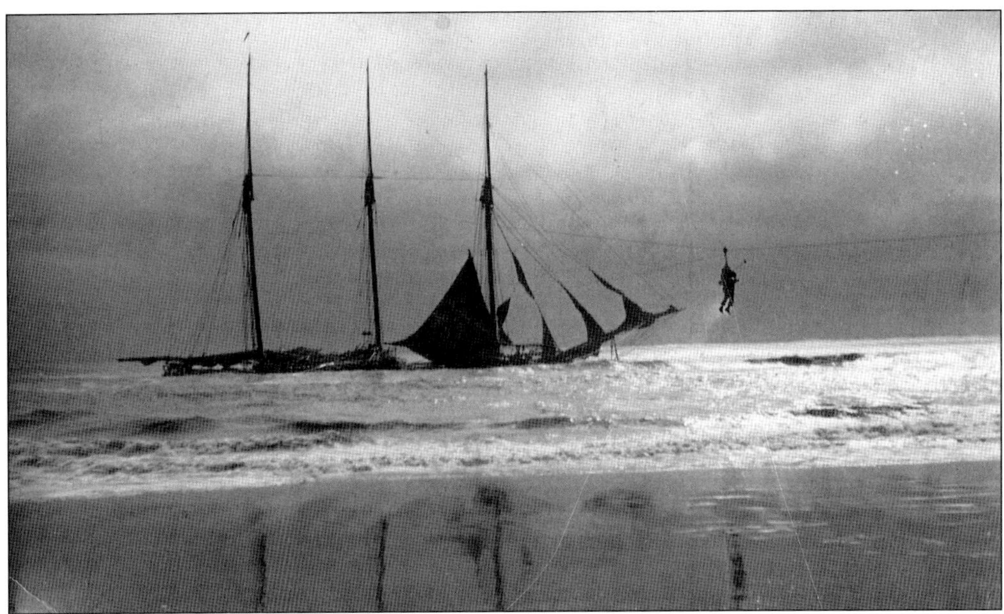

Fortuna sat at the edge of the ocean's breakers, which continued to push her battered hull closer to shore. Taking on increased amounts of water, the ship was photographed at various stages of its floundering. In the image above, a lifeline has been fired by gun out to the ship and attached to a mast. A rescued sailor is visible hanging over the water and being hauled ashore via the lifeline. The later view below shows the sinking ship further battered by waves and lower in the surf. All of this transpired under relatively calm ocean conditions. One of the worst maritime disasters in the United States was the 1956 collision and sinking off Nantucket Island, Massachusetts, of the Genoa-based ocean liner SS *Andrea Doria*, the largest ship in the Italian Line. A total of 1,660 of the 1,706 passengers and crew were rescued, while 46 died.

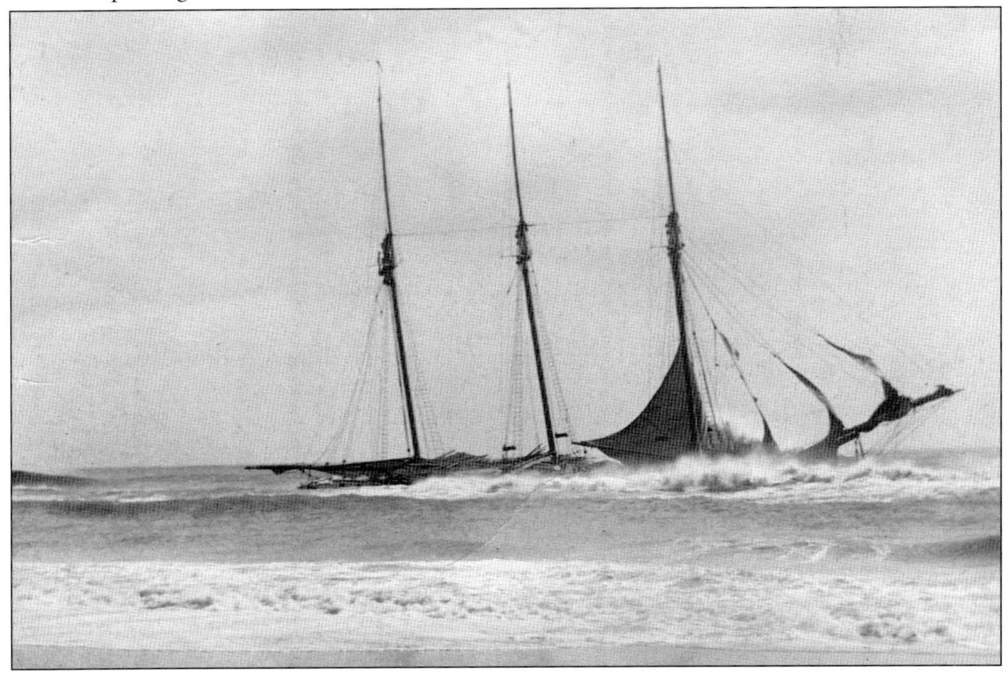

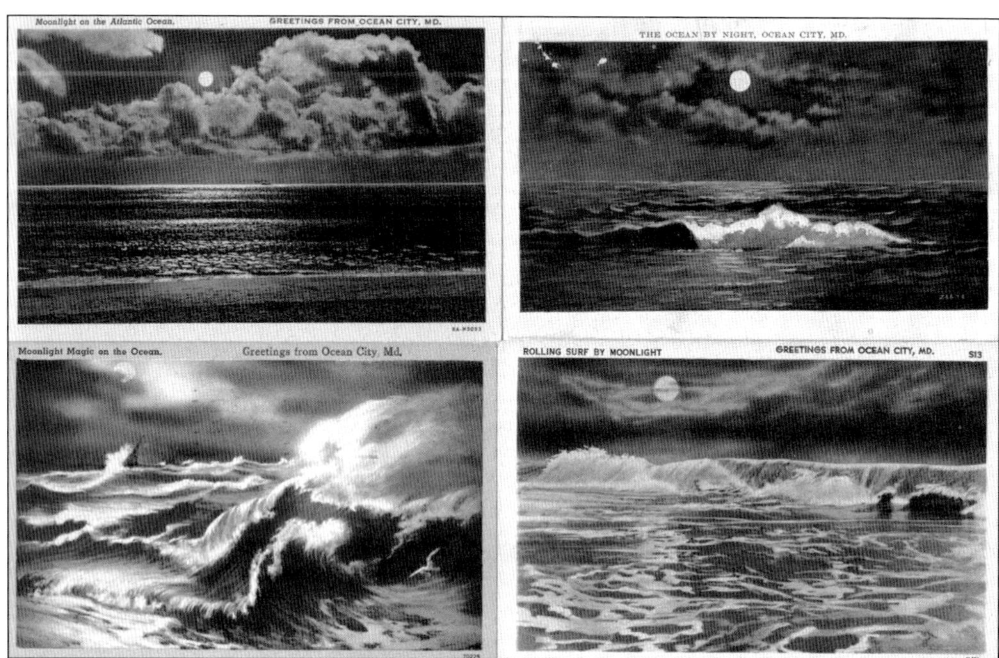

Four postcards (above) illustrate the changing moods of the ocean. "Moonlight on the Atlantic Ocean" (top left) was published in 1938 by Curt Teich and shows a lake-calm sea. A wave breaks in a more accurately observed view, "The Ocean by Night," postmarked 1929 (top right). "Moonlight Magic on the Ocean" (bottom left), a more fanciful, painterly view, is postmarked 1957. "Rolling Surf by Moonlight," possibly an early (c. 1906) Curt Teich card, depicts a long wall of breaking surf appearing like a weir with a foreground of sudsy froth surfacing the shallow ebb-tide shore. The card below, titled "A Majestic Breaker from the Mighty Deep," is neither identified, dated, nor postmarked. Its totally unconvincing wave suggests the work of a landlubber artist who has not looked carefully at either shore breaks or back-wave wind spray, and prefers airbrushing.

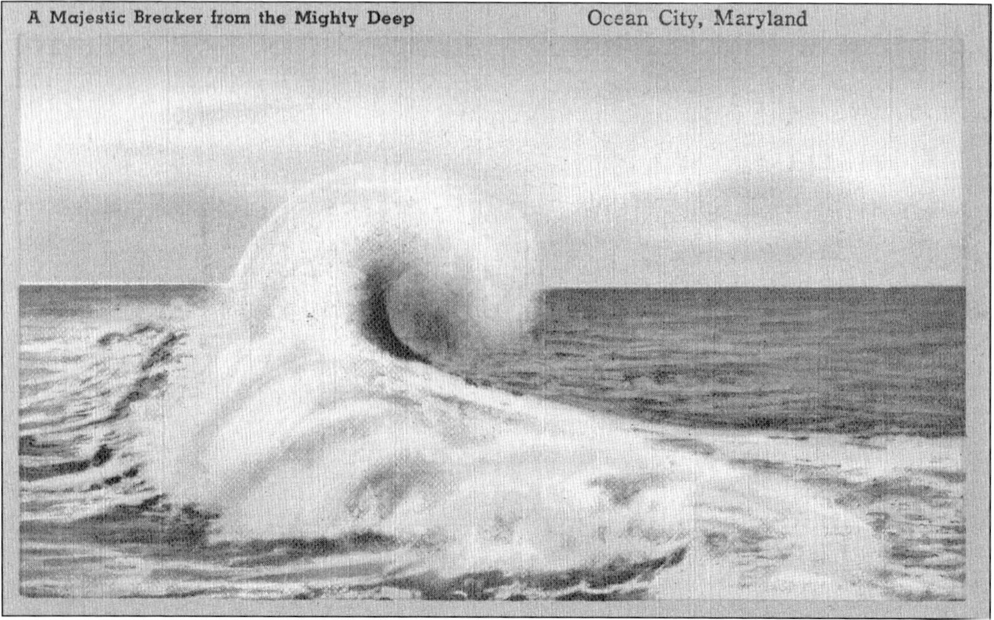

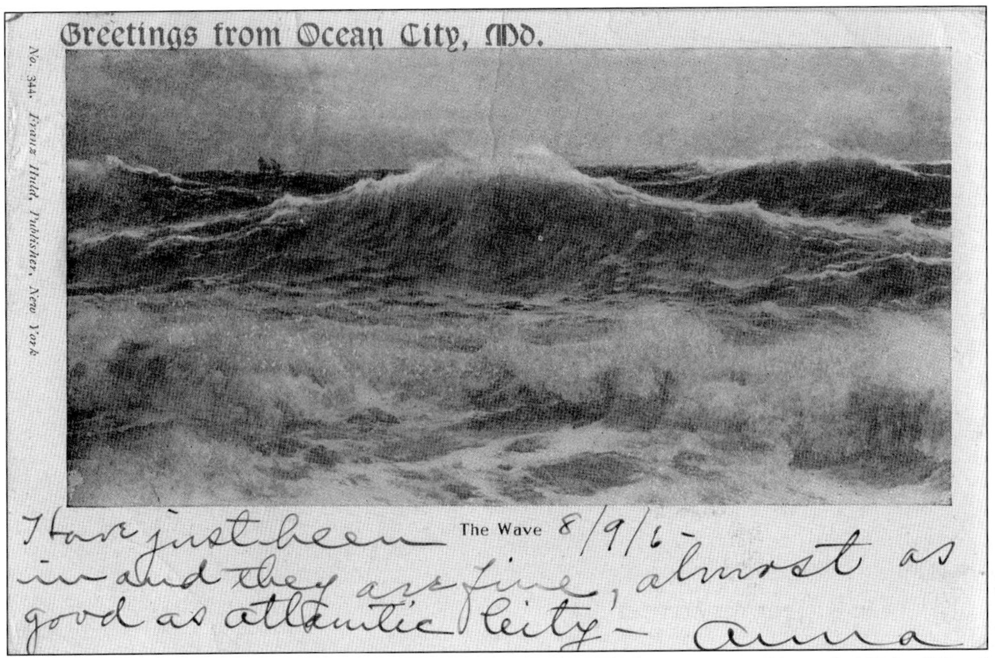

An early postcard (above) by the German-born New York publisher Franz Huld is titled "The Wave" and was mailed August 9, 1906. It sends "Greeting from Ocean City, MD," and depicts a rough sea, which was not likely the state of the surf reported by "Anna" who writes, "Have just been in and they [the waves?] are fine, almost as good as Atlantic City." The image appears predominantly gray in its black-and-white printing with hand-colored touch-ups giving the postcard an atmospheric tonal quality. The color image (below) features airbrushed whitecaps whose painterly transparency below is adequately convincing. Note the clouds building up beyond the flock of seagulls in the distance. The color tonalities are predominantly marine blue-green and gray with white-accented breaking waves.

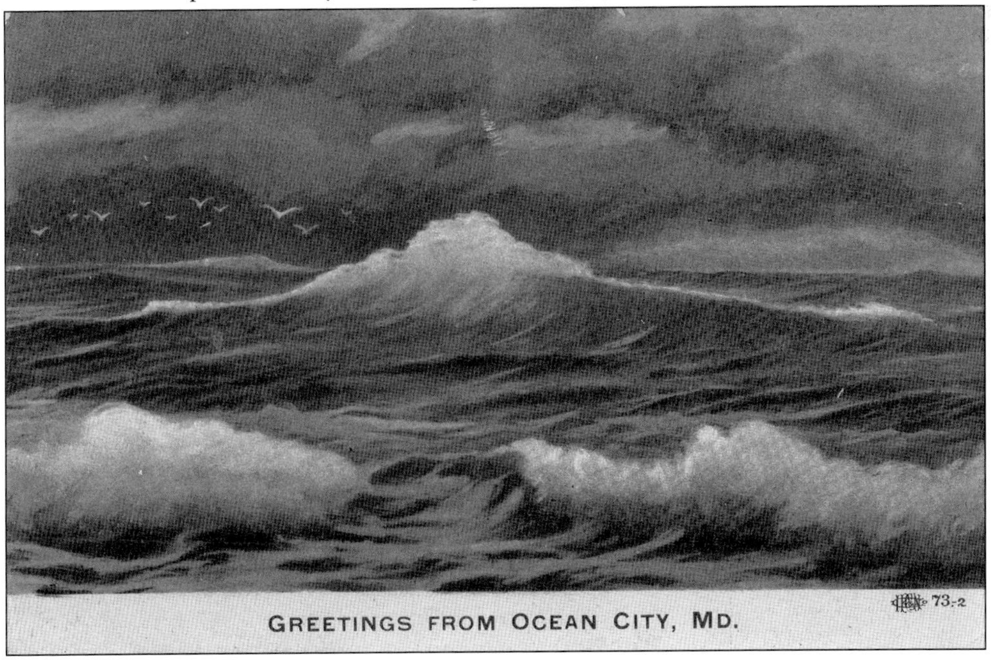

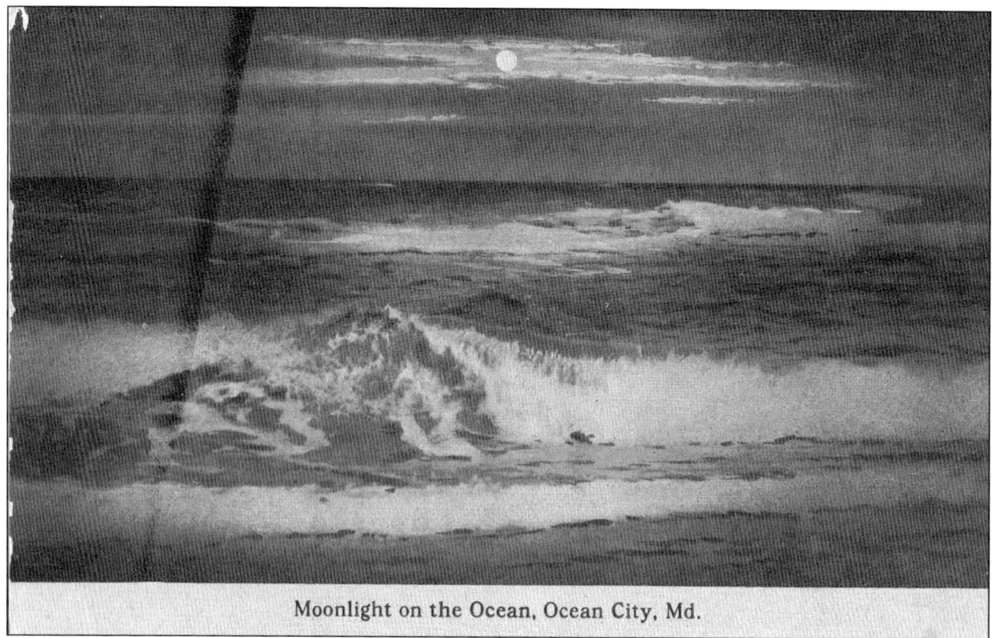

"Moonlight on the Ocean" is postmarked 1918. Behind the shore break in the foreground is a "trough" of deeper water, with whitecaps and an indication of a shallow sandbar in middle distance, and with the deep open sea and horizon line extending beyond. Lifeguards learned to "read" these signs of depth, current, and potential rip currents; although this postcard predates the Ocean City Beach Patrol by a dozen years.

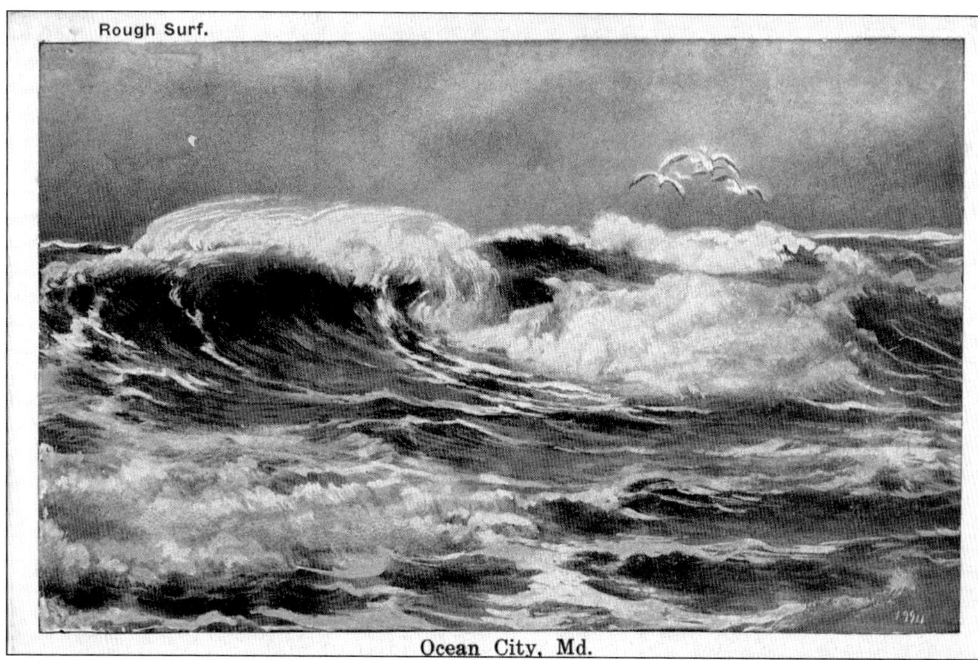

More treacherous "Rough Surf" is depicted as waves build up and then break below storm clouds with surface turbulence in the foreground. A small group of seagulls in flight offers some scale to the threatening size of the waves in the open seascape. The postcard is postmarked 1934.

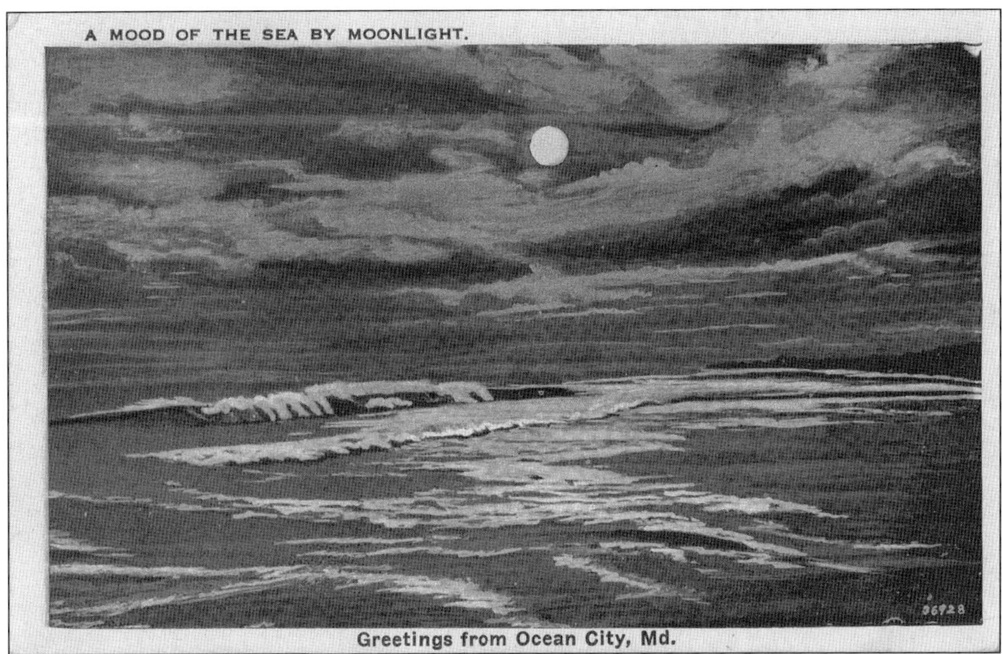

The tonal style of early postcards encouraged moonlight views of the ocean such as "A Mood of the Sea by Moonlight" (above) and "Breaking Waves in the Moonlight" (below), two postcards likely of the interwar period. While these have no postmarks, the pale borders are neither stark white (earlier date) nor bright orange (increasingly evident during the 1930s and after). The first card shows shore breaks at ebb tide, while the below image records a first break as a sandbar's white-water wave that would then pass across a deeper trough to a second break at shore. Both are colorized cards, and the image below has a lot of airbrushing.

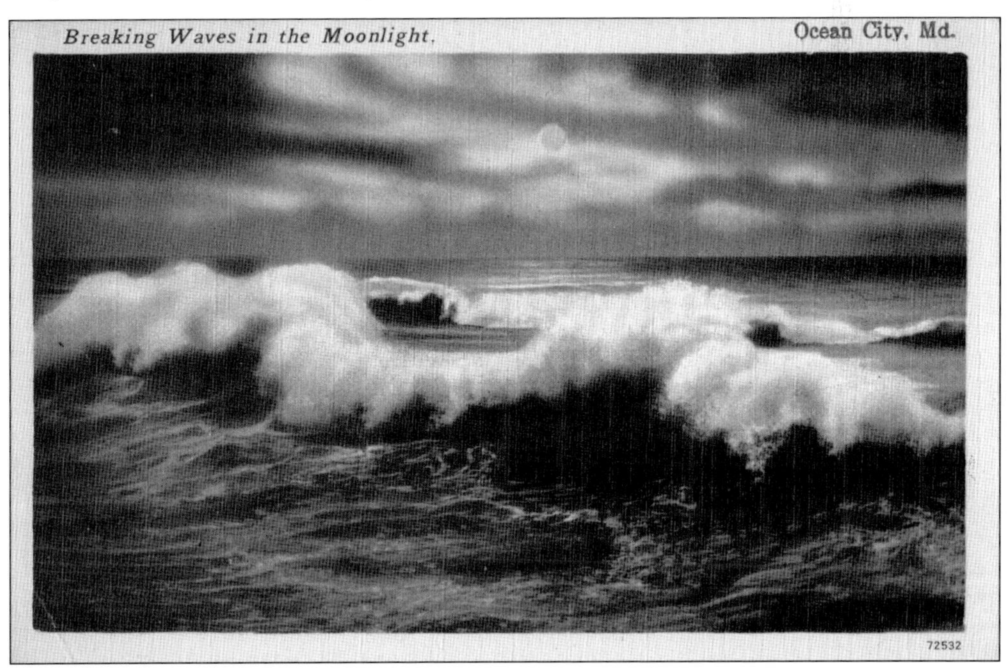

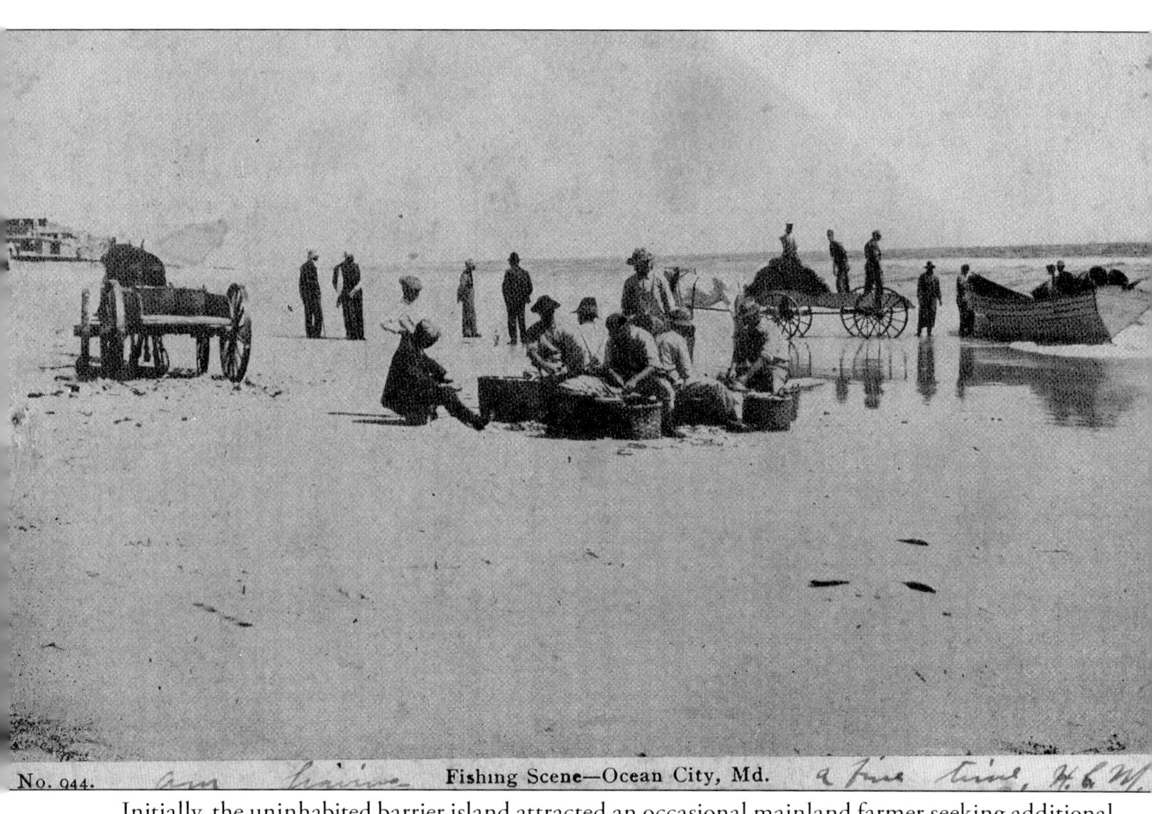

Initially, the uninhabited barrier island attracted an occasional mainland farmer seeking additional grazing lands, but the earliest permanent settlers were fishermen whose small shacks were located in the lowlands where the 1933 inlet was later cut through during a storm. This view, titled "Fishing Scene," shows a daily activity of loading the day's catch on wagons and gathering around baskets to clean fish for icing and shipping to mainland cities. The building at the top left may be the Atlantic Hotel, and if so, this group is considerably south of its location. The card is postmarked 1906, the year before the US Postal Service started allowing divided backs on cards for address and message. Prior to March 1907, the reverse side was for address and stamp only, and messages were crammed into available space on the picture side of the card, where the sender here, identified by initials only, writes, "Am having a fine time."

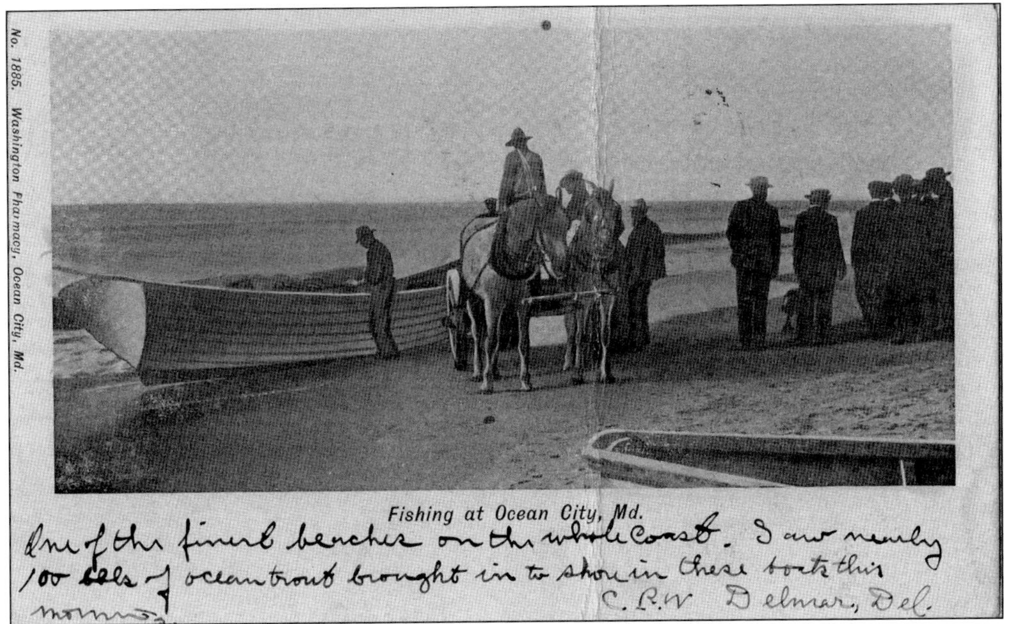

A 1907-postmarked card, published for Ocean City's Washington Pharmacy, is titled "Fishing at Ocean City, MD." It shows a pound boat used to haul the fish ashore from the ocean pound nets. C.R.W. from Dover, Delaware, writes the following below the image: "One of the finest beaches on the whole coast. I saw nearly 100 [barrels] of ocean trout brought in to shore in these boats this morning."

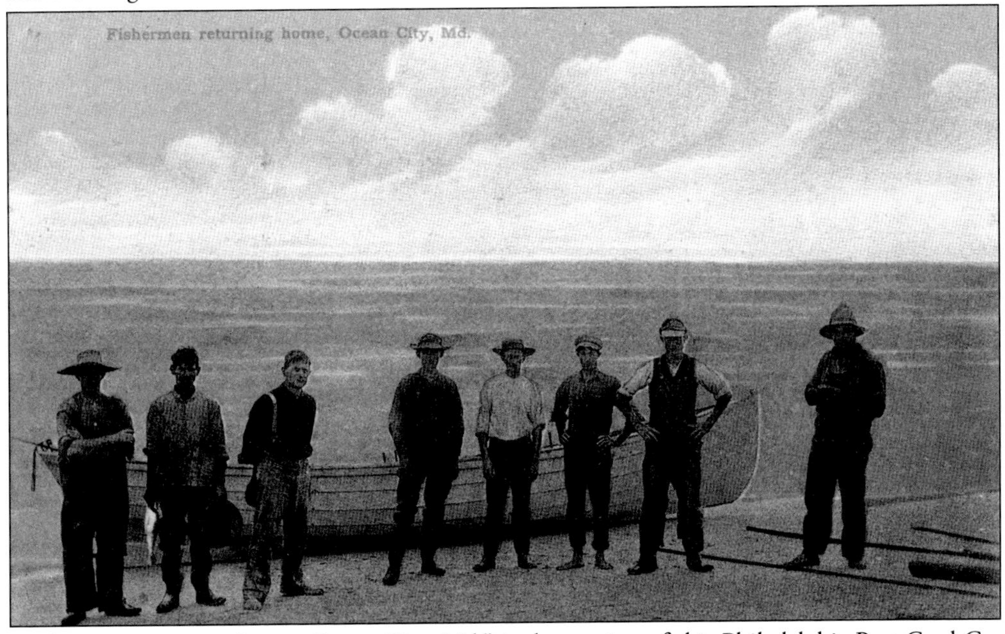

"Fishermen returning home, Ocean City, Md." is the caption of this Philadelphia Post Card Co. pre-1910 image. The skiff in the background, usually 16 to 18 feet long, was used to free up lines in the fishing pounds offshore. Larger pound boats that were 36 to 38 feet long (see the bottom of page 30) were standard vessels for pound fishing, which trapped large quantities of fish in huge nets during the early century.

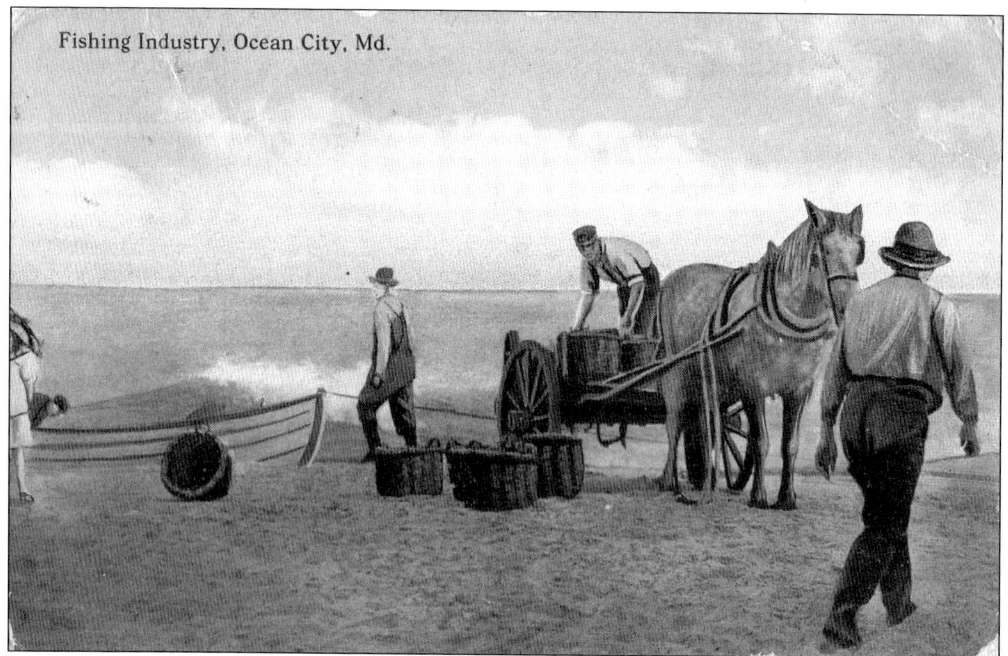

Wicker baskets were used to offload fish to horse-drawn carts where the daily catch would be hauled across the beach, iced, and transferred to trains transporting the fresh catch to hotels in Baltimore; Washington, DC; Wilmington; and Philadelphia. This Louis Kaufmann postcard of the "Fishing Industry, Ocean City, Md." is postmarked 1913.

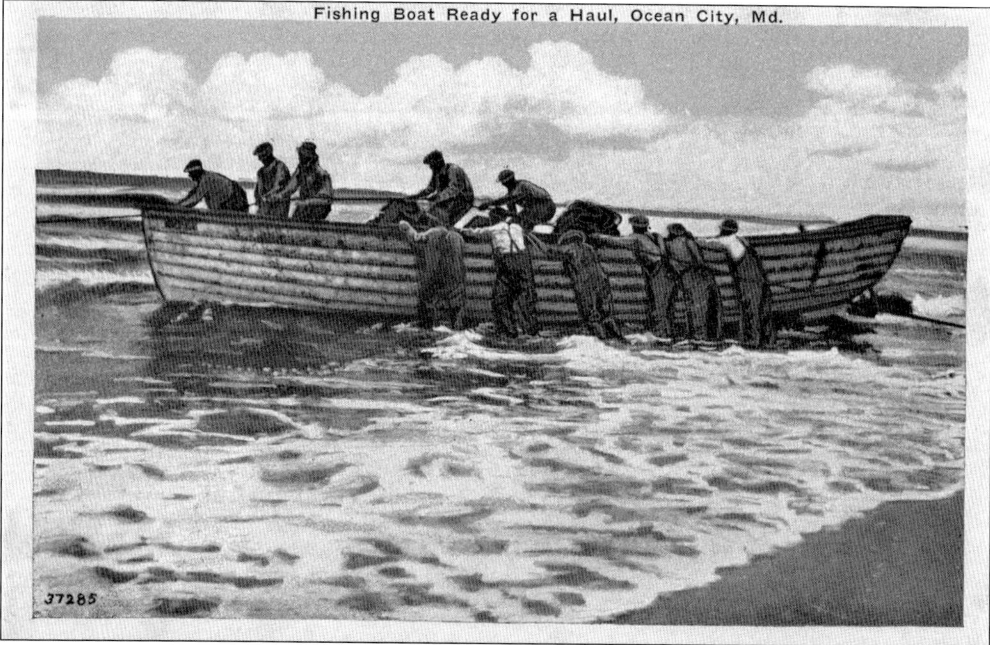

It was all hands on deck when the deep-sea fishing boats were to be hauled ashore and the fish unloaded for transport to restaurants in the Delmarva and Chesapeake area. While the men in the boat were the crew for this vessel, additional help from shore was needed to drag the loaded pound boat to awaiting wagons and rollers to store the boat overnight above high tide line.

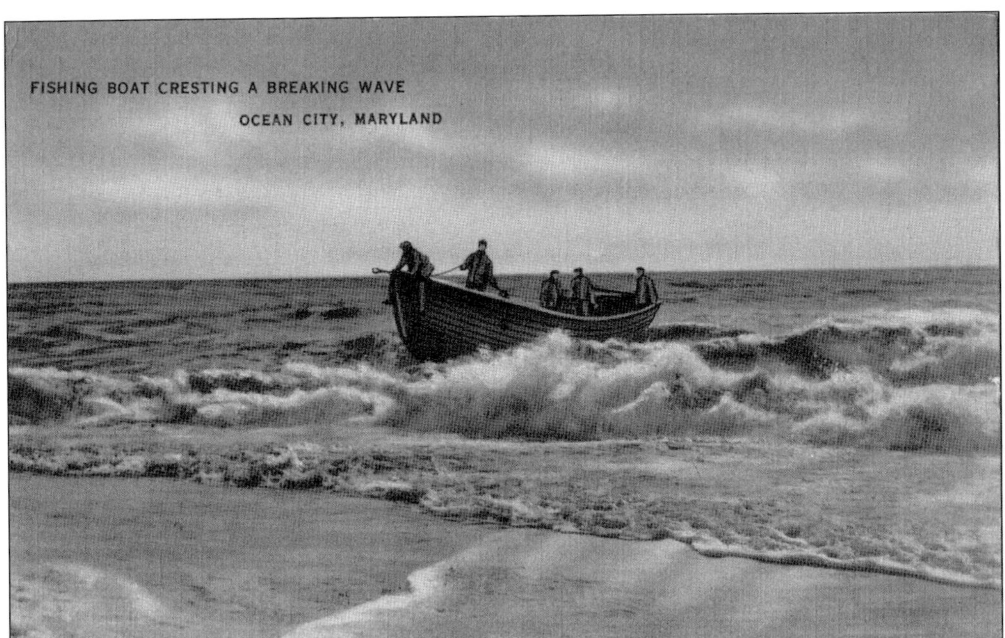

In this Tichnor Brothers postcard, a crew of five is depicted negotiating the difficult maneuvers of landing a loaded fishing boat through breaking surf. While these waves are relatively benign, conditions often changed from the early-morning departure in calm seas to the rough surf and high breakers that shifting winds from the west and high shore breaks could create by day's end.

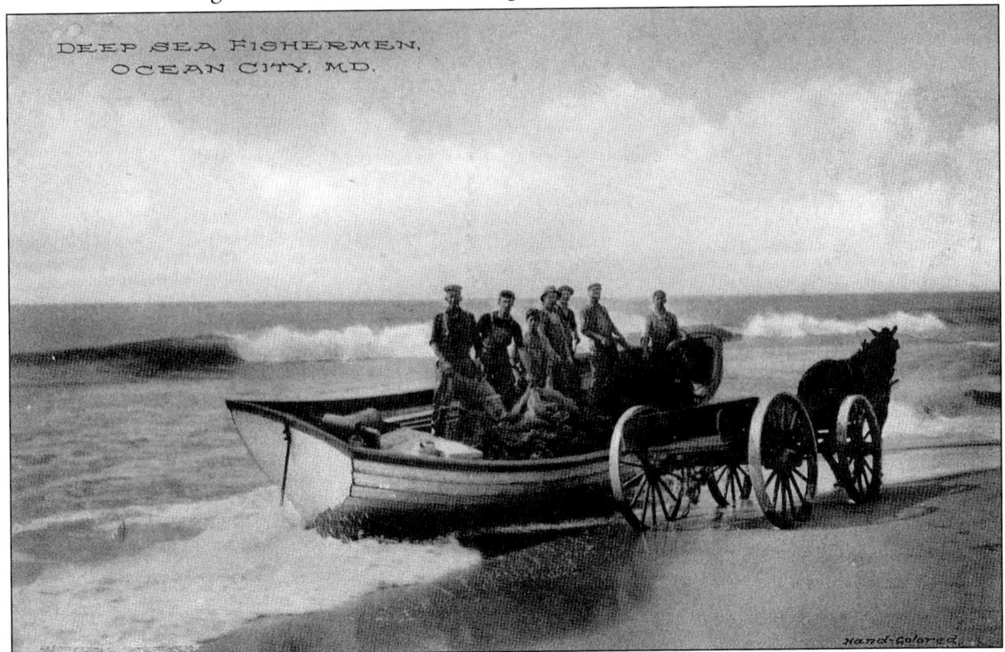

Seven fishermen hold up a net full of the day's catch in this hand-colored Washington Pharmacy postcard, sent in 1920. The horse-drawn wagon awaits the fish, and once off-loaded, the boat will be dragged beyond the dune line. The fishermen will then retire to their shanties and small cottages in the fishermen's enclave, located at the south end of town; today, the site is under the water of the inlet.

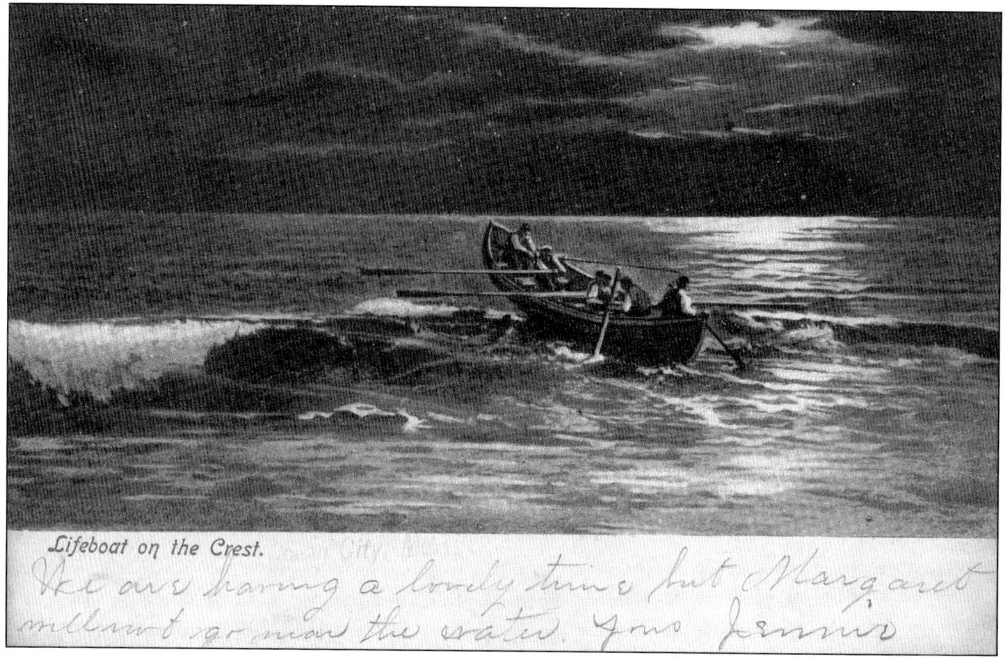

A second group of watermen active during the years prior to major development of the town of Ocean City was the lifesaving servicemen, whose arduous job was ill paid and, at times, not paid at all. Prior to 1900, lifesaving stations were manned by full-time crews only from April to November when shipwrecks were most likely. Many of the servicemen turned to fishing for livelihood. The postcard above, titled "Lifeboat on the Crest," resembles the fishing boatsmen in the postcard "Cresting a Breaking Wave" (pictured on the top of page 31), but in fact, it illustrates a lifesaving servicemen's drill. For years after the 1915 merger of the US Life-Saving Service with the Revenue Cutter Service to form the Coast Guard, servicemen continued similar drills. In the postcard below, "oars up" indicates shallow water as a Coast Guard crew negotiates the shore break.

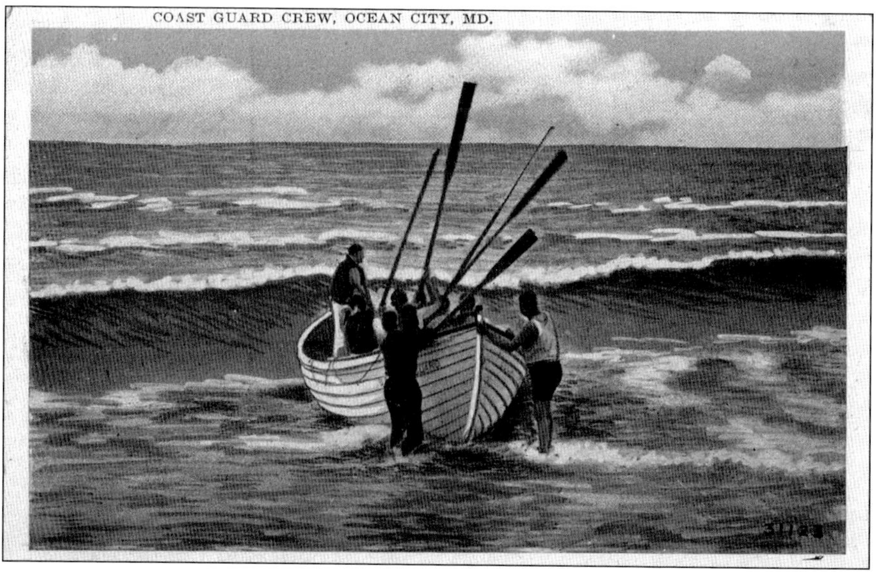

The first Ocean City Life-Saving Station, built in 1878 of the "1874 type, second variation," stood isolated on the dunes at the north edge of the original town plat (beachfront at Caroline Street, just south of North Division Street). The building was replaced in 1891 by an enlarged station, pictured here. Also wood framed, the 1891 station provided more space to house both crew and boat and a lookout rooftop cupola; the first station had an open crow's nest on the gable ridge. The 1891 station was clapboarded on the ground floor with board-and-batten siding above and featured open structurally expressive framing at the several gable ends. The Chessler Company, Baltimore, postcard below of the "Life Saving Station, Boats, and Crew" with a detached tower at boardwalk's edge is here postmarked 1919 but remained available for many years.

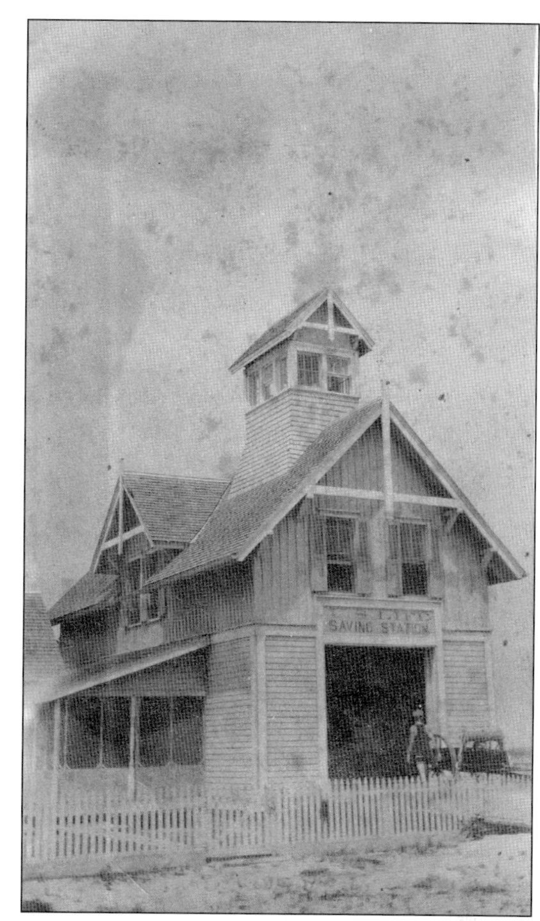

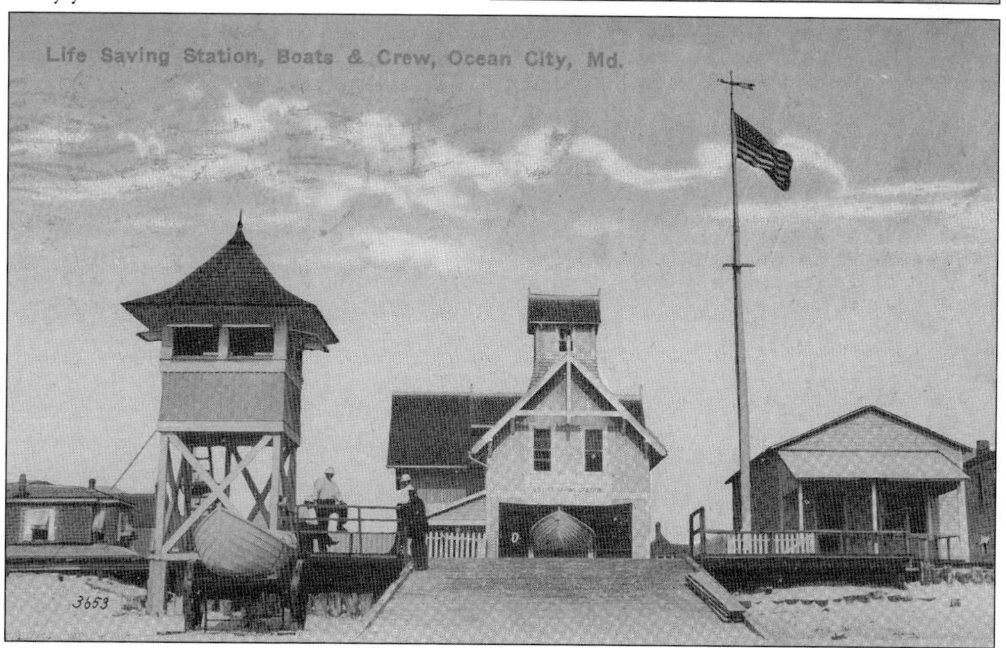

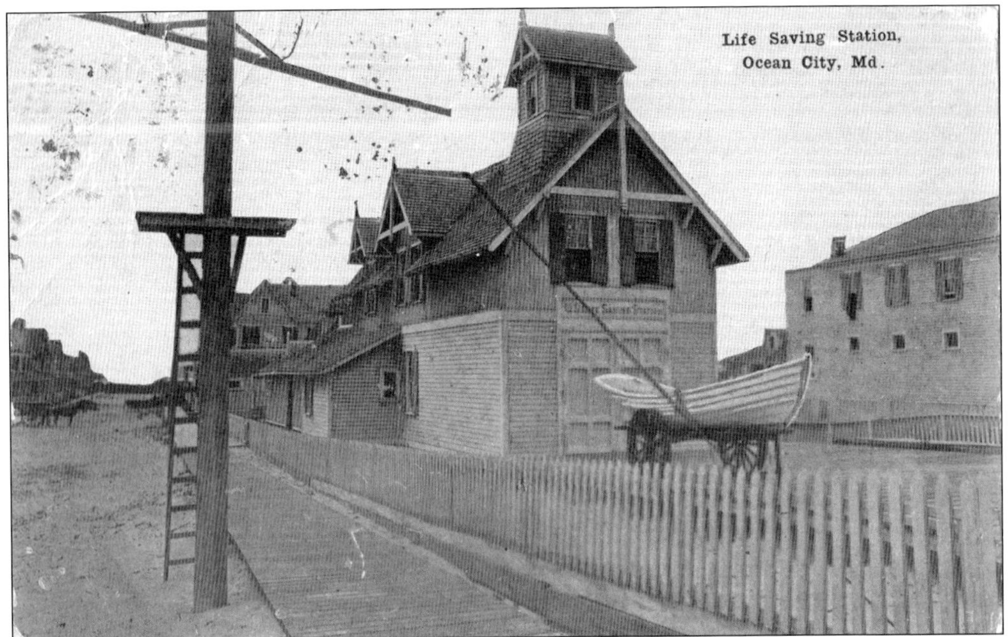

Capt. William T. West, the first keeper of the Ocean City Life-Saving Station, maintained a handwritten daily logbook between December 25, 1878, and January 22, 1880, recording weather conditions, shipwrecks, rescues, patrols along the beach, and lifesaving drills conducted by the servicemen. Many such exercises were recorded in popular postcards of the later years. Both these postcards, for instance, show what appears to the modern eye to be telephone poles along Caroline Street but are actually poles between which are stretched lifelines for practicing breeches buoy rescues. In real shipwreck rescues, a canon would fire a lifeline to the ship (see pages 23 and 35–38), ends would be secured on a ship mast and anchor pole ashore, and individuals harnessed and attached to the connecting rope would be pulled ashore.

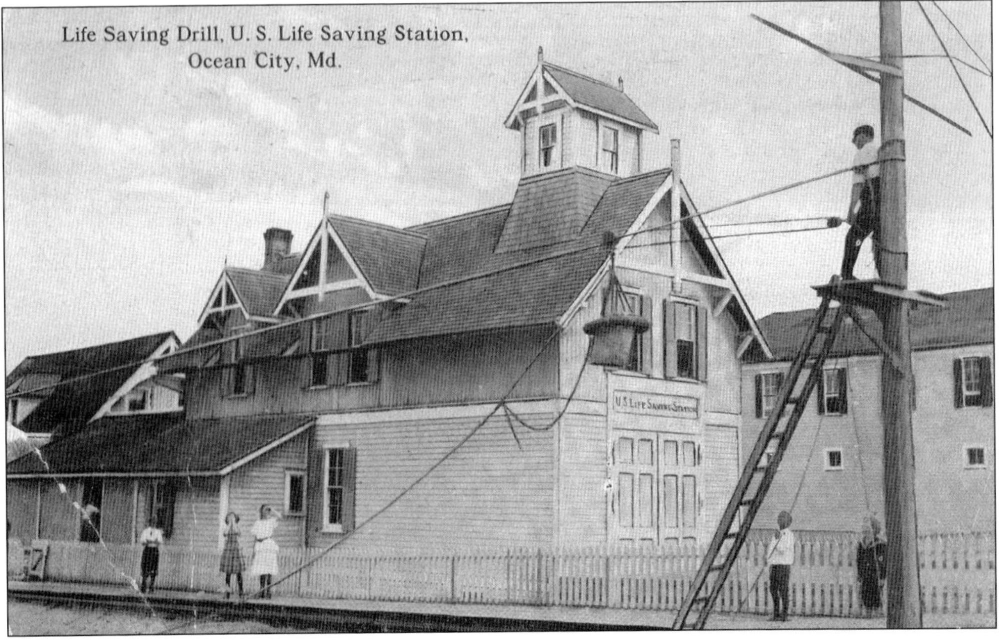

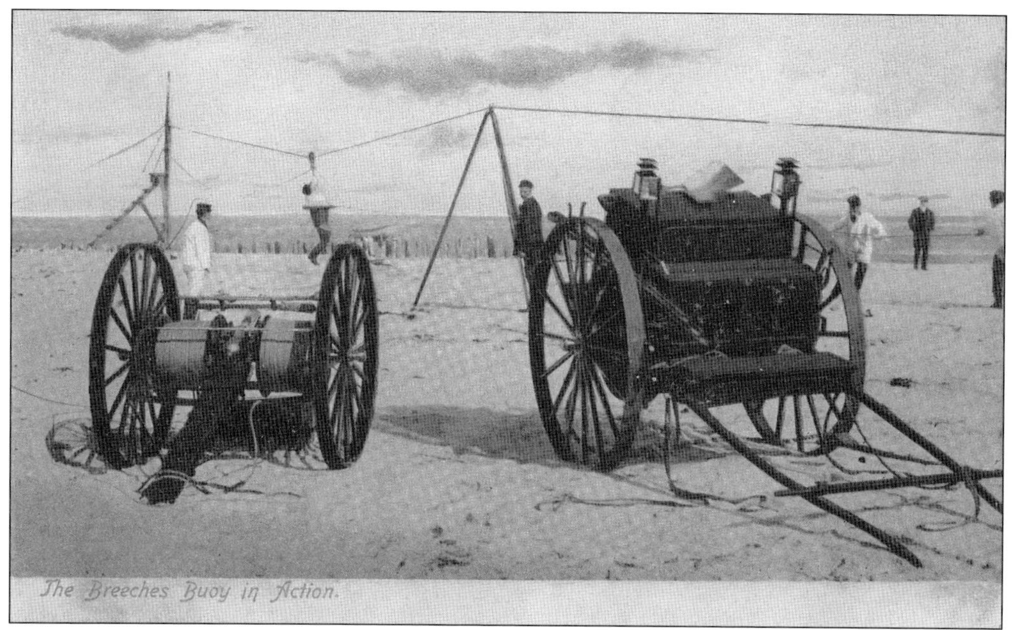

An Illustrated Post Card Co., New York, card shows "The Breeches Buoy in Action." Beyond the rope caisson and two-wheeled carriage, poles and A-frames support a rope from which a harnessed practice victim is pulled along in a simulated rescue. Although the card is undated, postcards with similar composition illustrating lifesaving drills bear postmarks between 1906 and 1910.

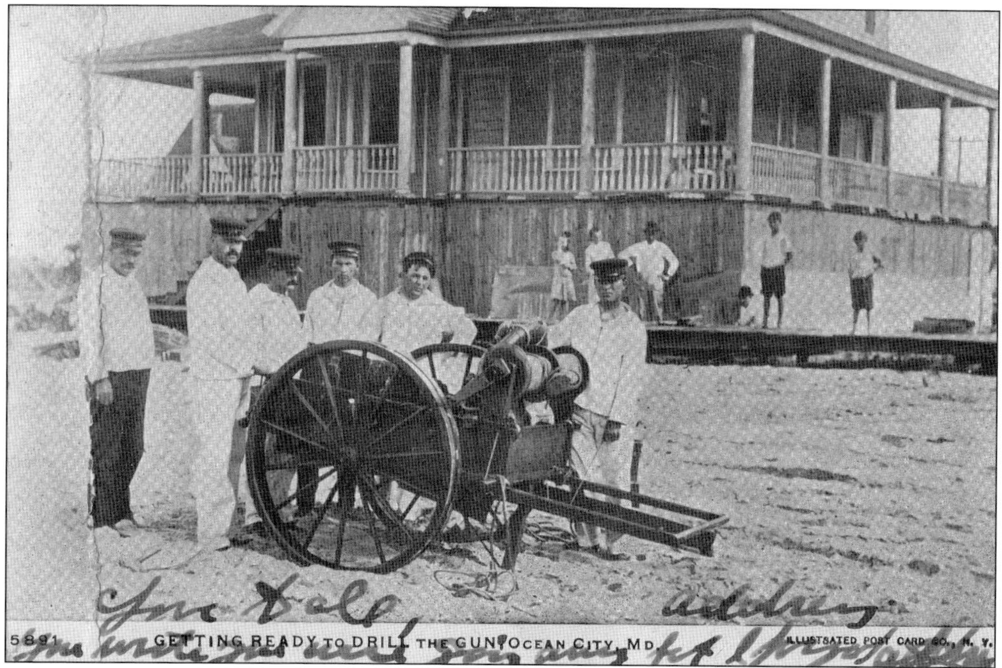

From the same Illustrated Post Card Co., New York, this "Getting Ready to Drill" card is postmarked 1910. The beach cottage in the background is of the raised cottage type built along the boardwalk; today, a notable surviving example, the 1911 Walker House, is on Seventh Street and Baltimore Avenue and is known as Romarletta.

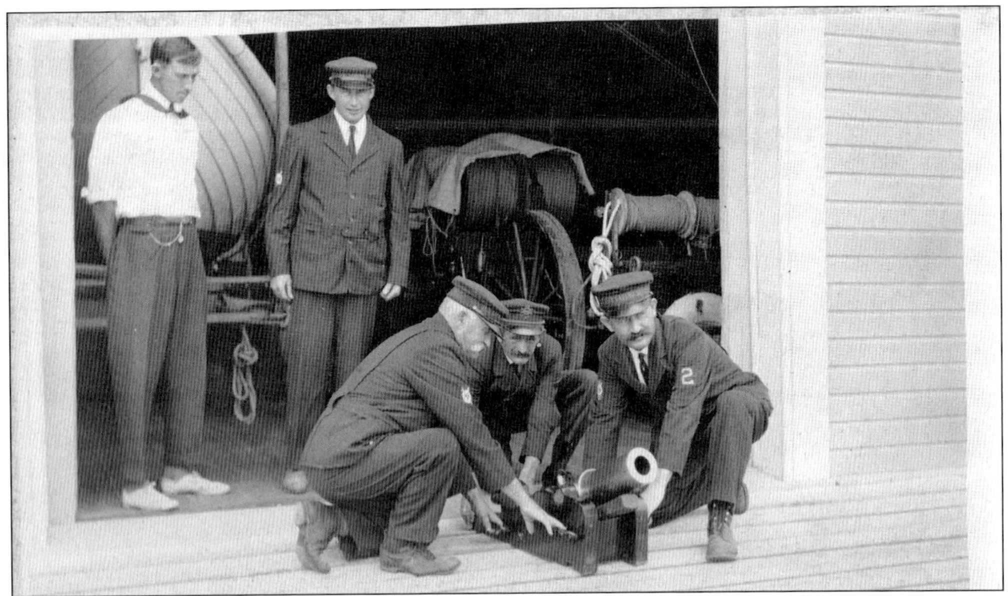

The original sepia photograph of Coast Guardsmen setting up a life rope canon shows the storage garage for the lifeboat, rope caissons, and other equipment behind five men identified as the cook, James Quillen, Bill Quillen, Henry Richardson, and Capt. William Purnell.

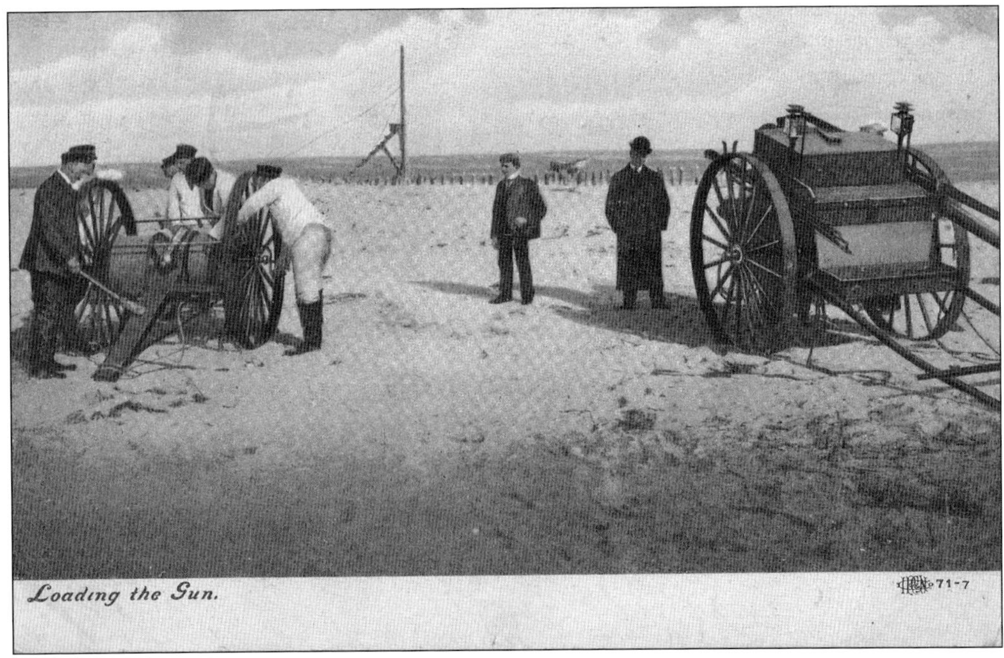

A series of photographs, from the Illustrated Post Card Co., records various lifesaving exercises of the US Life-Saving Service specifically linked to firing a lifeline to a stranded ship. The 1909 postcard is captioned "Loading the Gun." Others on page 37 document other phases of the lifesaving procedure, including rescue boat exercises.

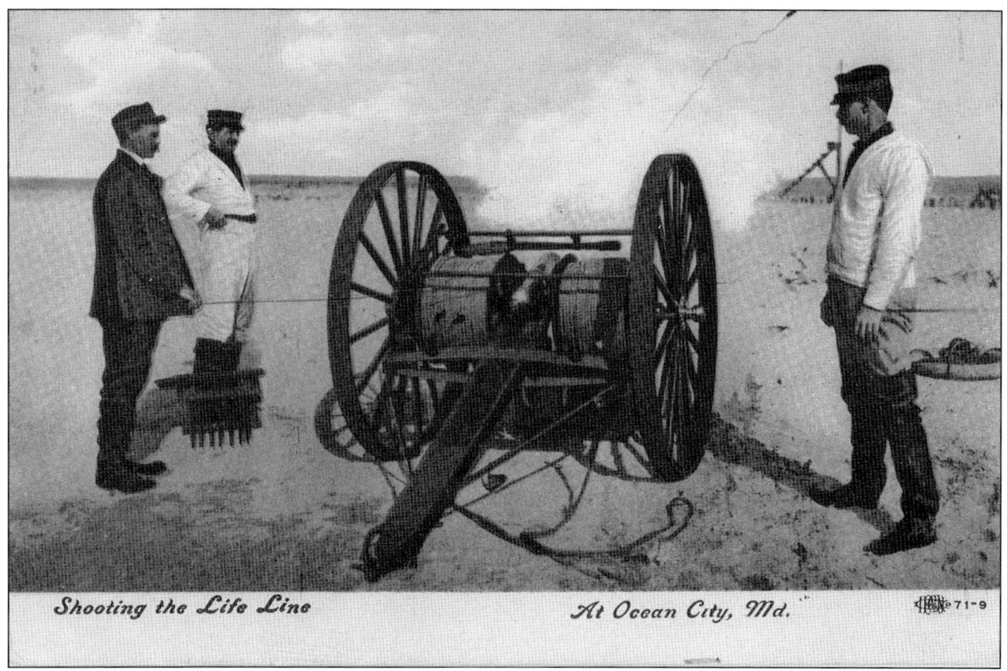

Two postcards representing the same action of launching a lifeline are captioned, "Shooting the Life Line," postmarked 1908 (above), and "Firing the Lifeline," postmarked 1906 (below). In both, the photographer positions the cannon, composes the scene, and then airbrushes the explosion emerging from the cannon's mouth and draws a squiggly line skyward at the end of which a weight/projectile is indicated. In the 1908 card (above), the rope unwinds from a caisson; in the 1906 card (below), the rope emerges from the open box at the right.

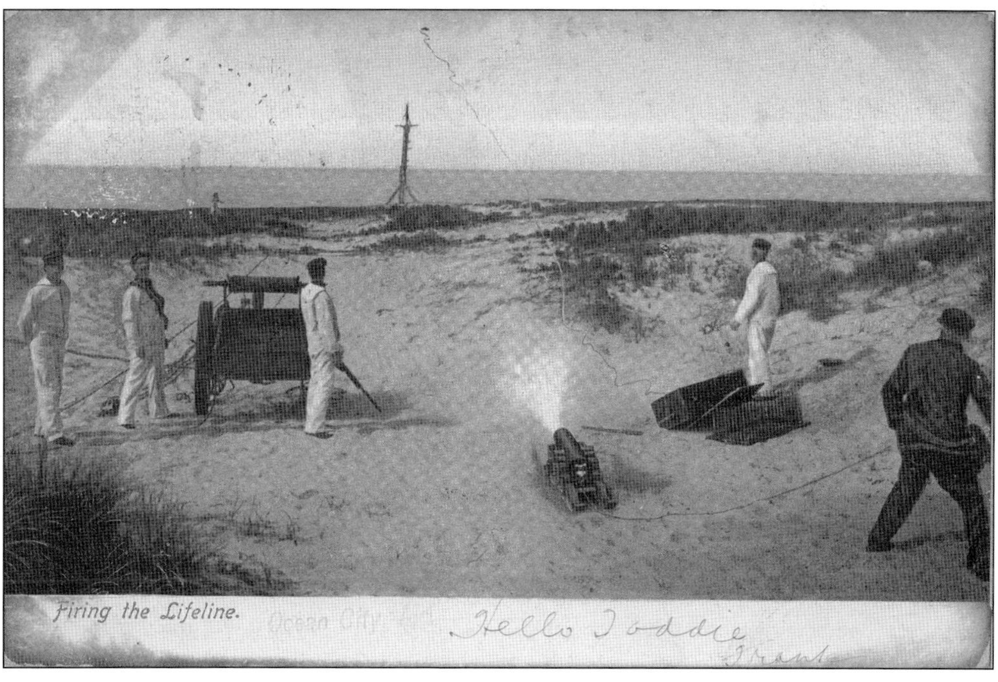

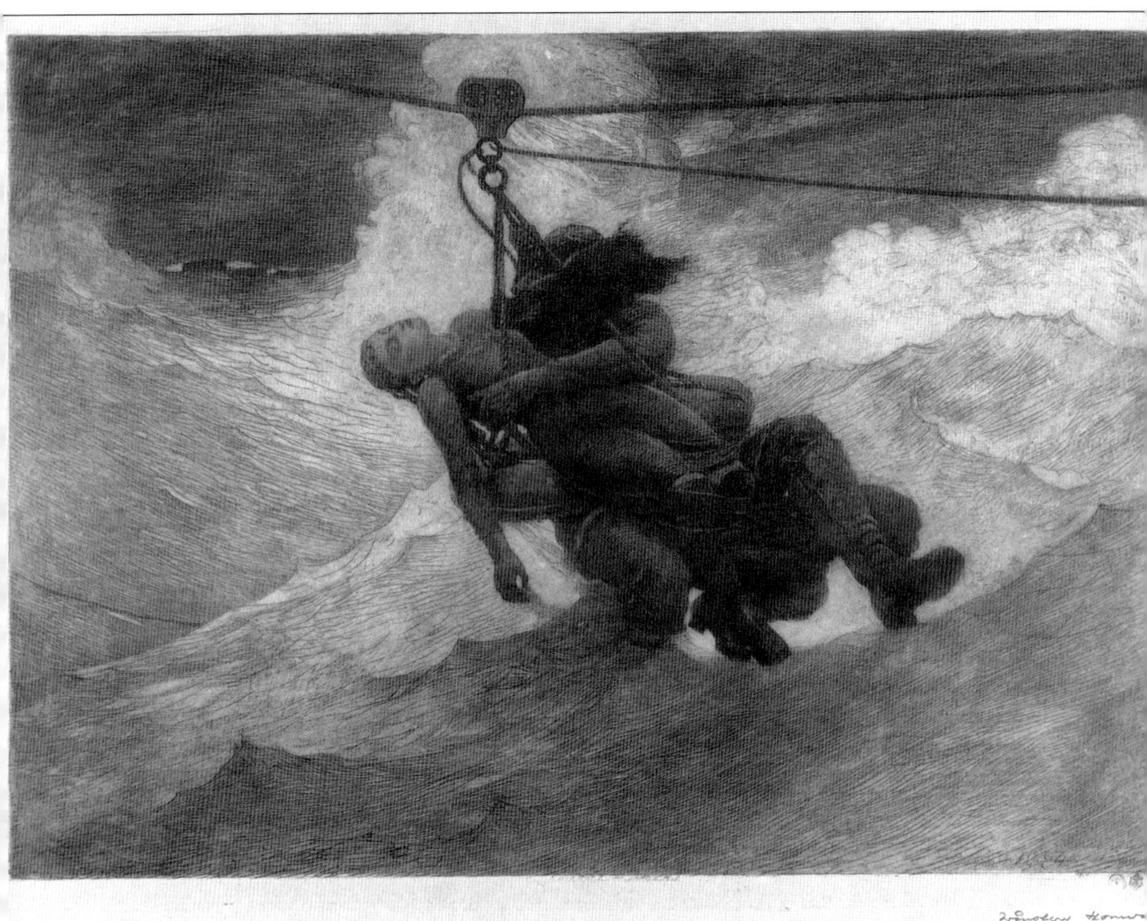

Winslow Homer's 1884 oil-on-canvas painting *The Life Line*, now in the Philadelphia Museum of Art (The George W. Elkins Collection, 1924), is the source for this etching in the collection of the Metropolitan Museum of Art, New York (Harris Brisbane Dick Fund, 1941), printed by Charles S. White. The scene shows a rescue in progress in which the lifeline, shot from a Lyle gun, and ship's pulley serve to transport sailors from a floundering or shipwrecked vessel to shore. The original painting dates from the active years of the US Life-Saving Service, six years after Ocean City's first lifesaving station was built in 1878. (Public domain.)

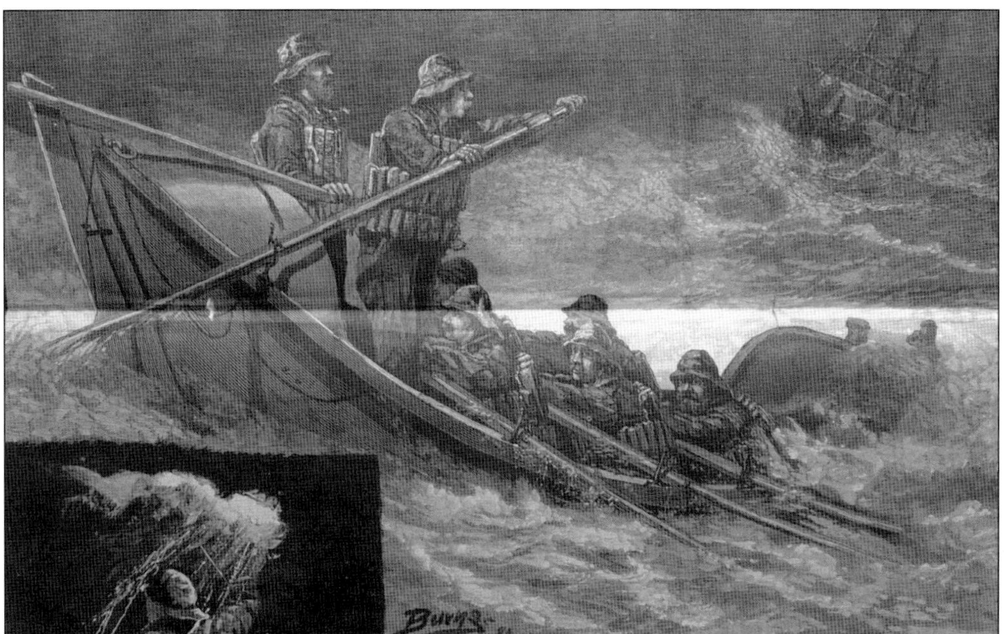

In 1881, *Harper's Weekly* published an illustrated article on the US Life-Saving Service with illustrations captioned "Perils of the Coast—The Life Saving Service." The image "Off to the Wreck" shows a rescue boat with oarsmen struggling against the strong waves and itself almost floundering as the distant ship awaits assistance. (Courtesy of the Indian River Life-Saving Station Museum.)

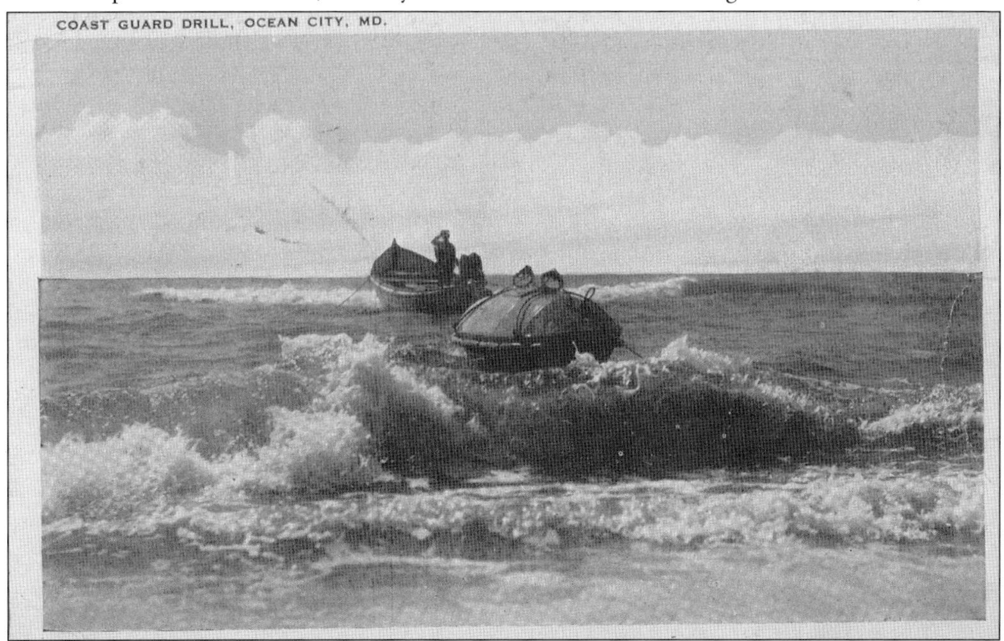

Open and closed rescue boats were also used for surf rescues as illustrated in this 1927-postmarked Tichnor Brothers, Inc., postcard. The enclosed vessel behind the oarsmen can be dragged to a wreck and, despite potential claustrophobia for the rescued victim, provides protection from seawater, rough weather, and strong winds. As waves topple the vessel, it evidences higher watertight integrity as shown here in a "Coast Guard Drill."

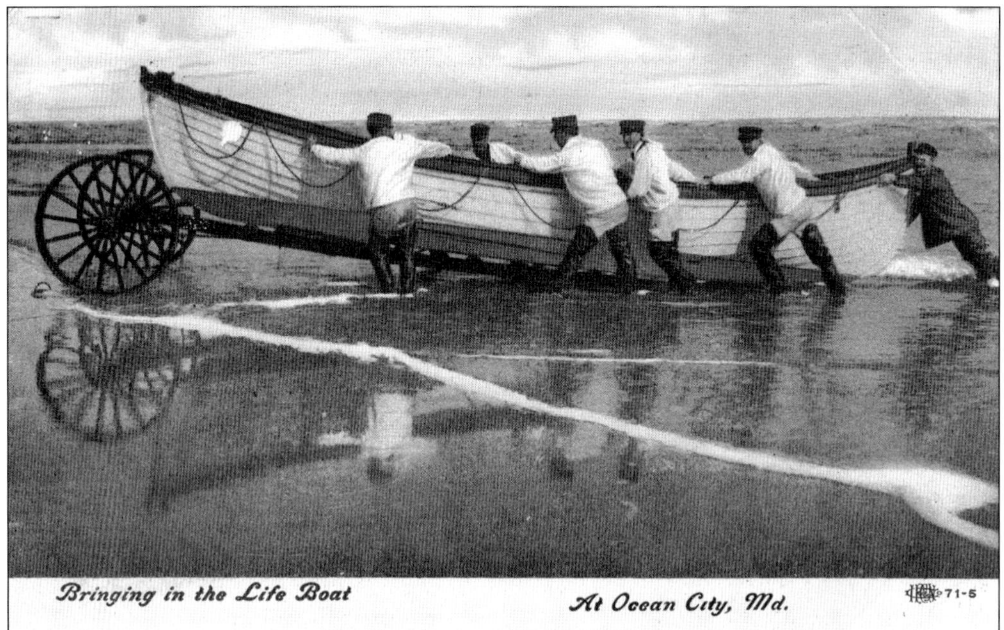

The "Bringing in the Life Boat" postcard (above) and "Return of the Life Boat" (below) are postmarked 1908 and are part of the series of Illustrated Post Card Co. depictions of rescue operations of the US Life-Saving Service. Here, crewmen are hauling the rescue boat ashore and onto a trailer where it would be wheeled to the station after an exercise drill.

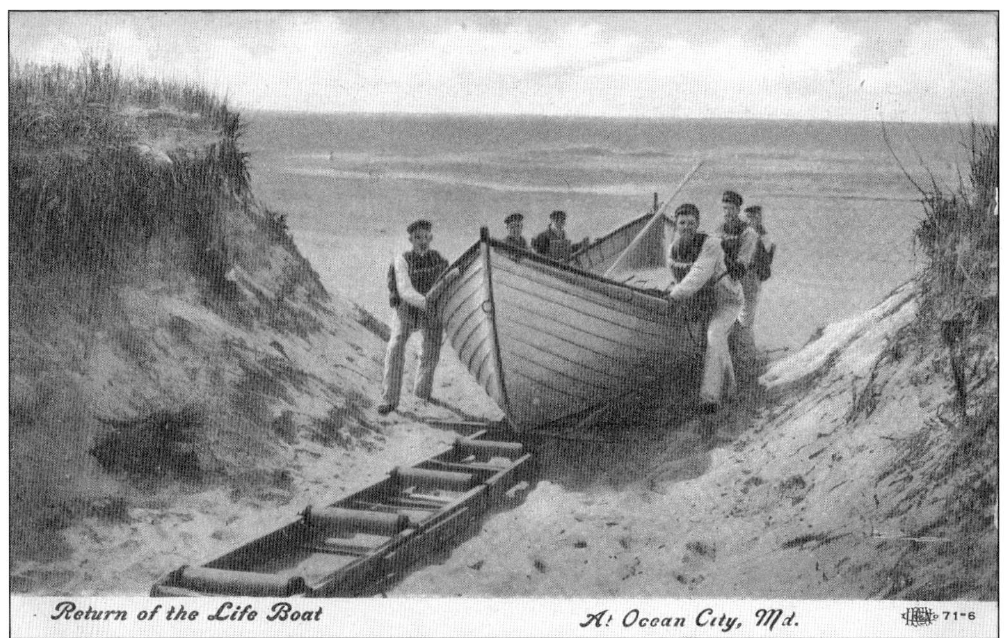

Lifesaving servicemen use rollers here to transport the rescue boat between two sand dunes where it would be protected against high tides. The use of oar-powered rescue boats by the US Life-Saving Service continued until motorized vehicles supplanted them. For a short period of time, rescue boats were also employed by the Ocean City Beach Patrol; although torpedo buoys, introduced in 1947, were found to be more efficient.

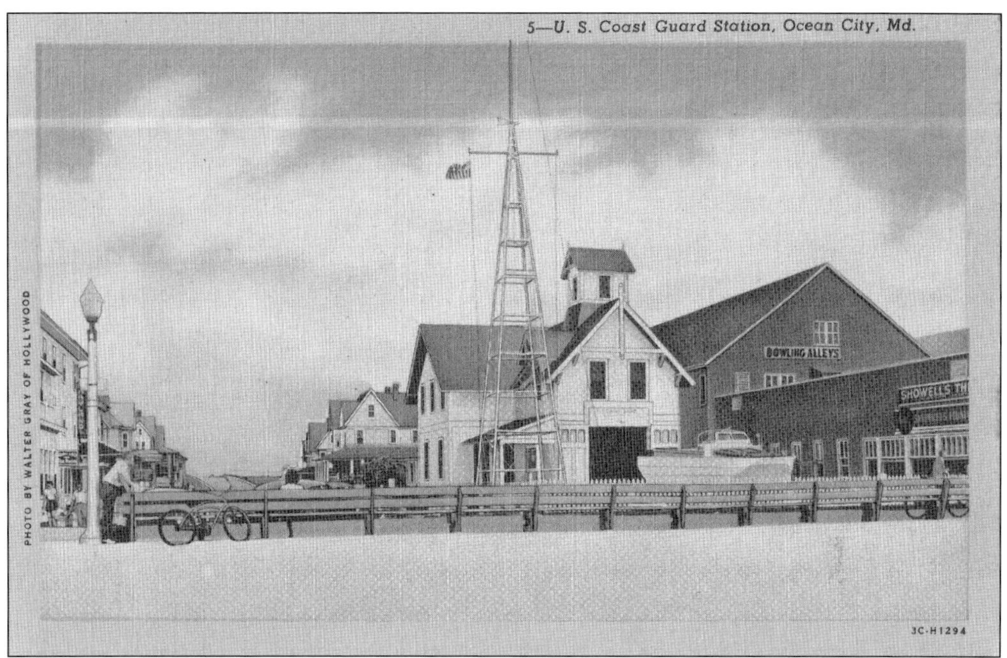

The 1953 Curt Teich postcard shows the Coast Guard station with a "duck," or DUKW, parked outside. The DUKW, used by the military in World War II, was a six-wheel-drive amphibious vehicle used for rescues and able to drive 50 miles per hour on land and operate at 5.5 knots (6.3 miles per hour) at sea. The nomenclature "DUKW" derives from the GMC nomenclature D (1942), U (utility), K (front wheel drive), W tandem rear axles, both driven.

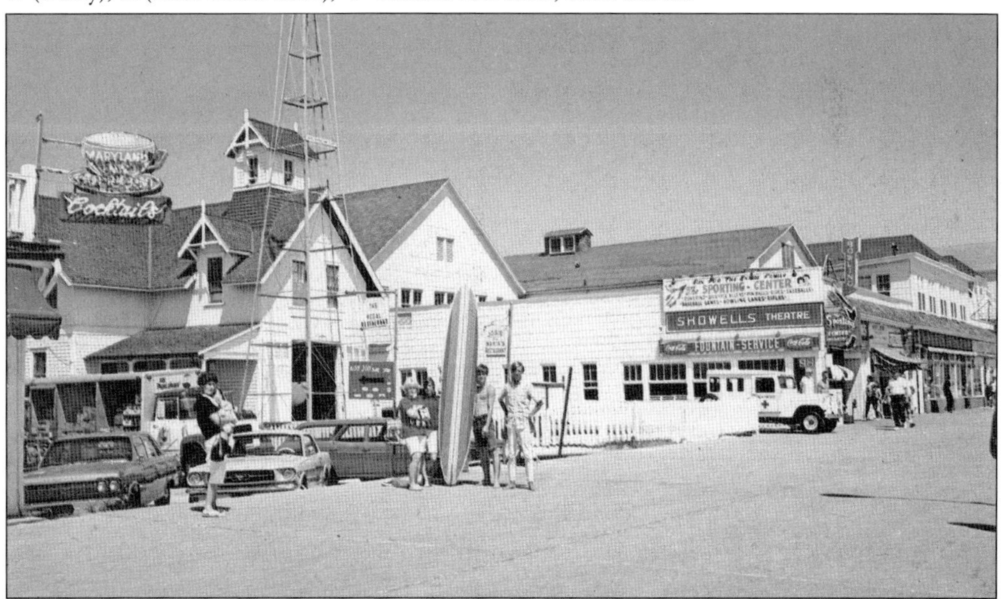

In 1964, a new Coast Guard station was commissioned bayside, and for a few years, the historic US Life-Saving station on Caroline Street was used as the headquarter of the Ocean City Beach Patrol (OCBP). In this postcard of the period by Fred Brueckmann, OCBP captain Robert S. Craig (left) and assistant to the captain George Schoepf (right) are seen standing next to the white beach patrol jeep at the far right.

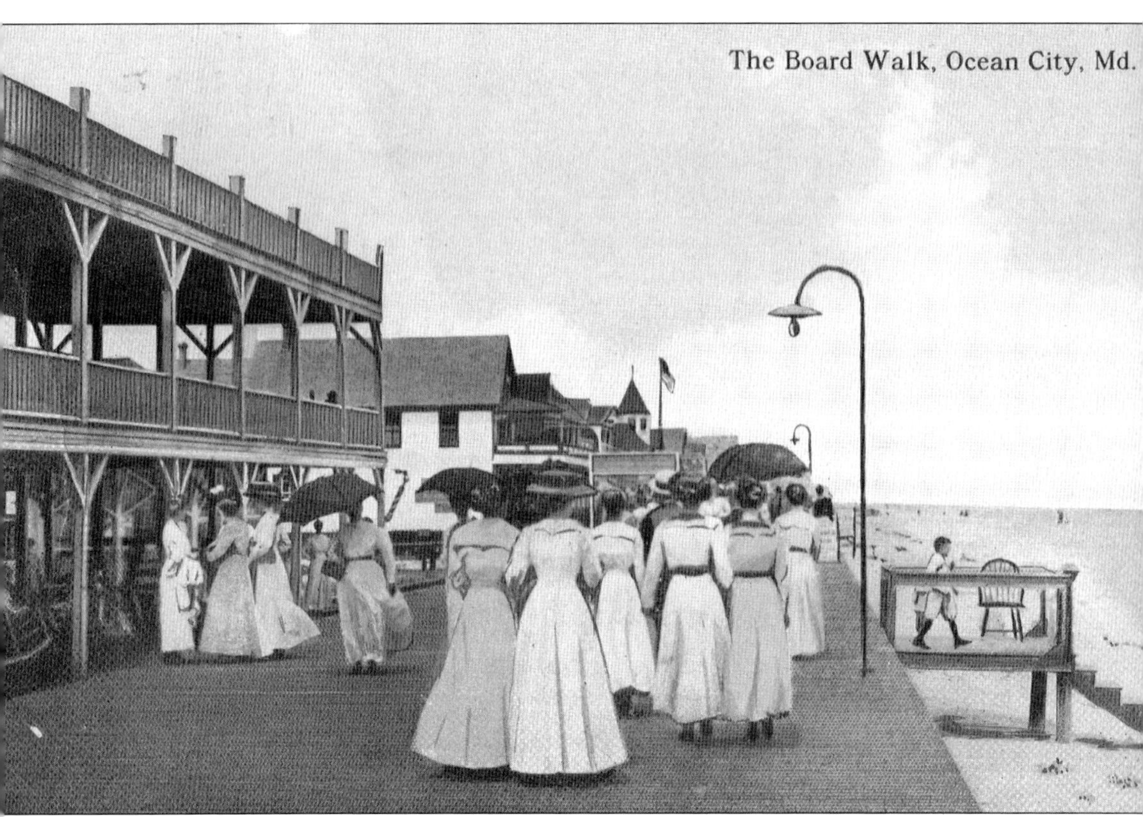

If it is nothing else, the history of the boardwalk is also a history of sartorial custom at the beach resort. This postcard, postmarked 1914, shows ladies in long dresses perambulating, some with umbrellas to shade fair complexions from the summer sun. Objective observers could graph a straight line of (in)decency that, as years increase, the amount of visible flesh on the boardwalk and beach also increases (see page 109).

Two

Boardwalk

Ocean City's historic boardwalk was an early wooden walkway intended to span the shifting sands and encroaching tides along the oceanfront of the new town. Although the term architecture is normally applied to residences, hotels, and commercial buildings in town, Ocean City's boardwalk is perhaps the town's best-known artifact of the built environment. Walkways and sidewalks of plank construction have been built in coastal, as well as inland, towns nationwide. In Atlanta, Georgia, for instance, Atlanta City Studio recently (2022) transformed a downtown city block into the Broad Street Pedestrian Plaza, known as the Broad Street Boardwalk whose linear plaza is flush with adjacent sidewalks to create a pedestrian-only space. The wood decking system mitigated topographical irregularities to provide even surfaces for perambulation and interaction with flanking businesses. It was a combination comparable to beachfront boardwalks, with their restaurants, tourist souvenir shops, and amusement venues overlooking the promenade, and hence, Atlanta city planners expropriated the name "boardwalk" albeit hundreds of miles from the sea.

Ocean City's boardwalk began, as did the use of the beach and surrounding waters, with a predevelopment phase. When Ocean City's earliest tourists arrived by train at the station platform (itself a short boardwalk), porters waited with wagons to roll luggage across the boards to the Atlantic Hotel, the first and largest of the town's early hotels. Baltimore Avenue was the town's main street, and board sidewalks, sometimes under porticos, served visitors who did not wish to walk across sand or mud to reach a hotel entry or place of business. Boardwalk-enriched side streets linked these planked sidewalks to the oceanfront promenade, often with planed ramps rising to the elevated "boardwalk."

Although the date is uncertain, several hotels first got together to construct sections of a makeshift boardwalk along the oceanfront of their premises. The perambulation byway became known as Atlantic Avenue, an address little recognized today; the emerging promenade is better known, as the Boardwalk. Although some records suggest the sections of the boardwalk were taken up at night to avoid high tide damage (or at the least were removed periodically, if not nightly, as a precaution against damage from approaching storms and hurricanes), it seems more likely (given two high tides per day), that the boards remained in place and were dismantled only seasonally, stored in lower crawl spaces during the winter, to be erected again the following spring for the summer season. In any case, as the town grew both north and south of the Atlantic Hotel, the oceanfront boardwalk grew in length and in substantiality, developing as a permanent wood promenade, soon to rival the renowned boardwalks at Atlantic City, New Jersey (5.5 miles, 1,870 feet), and Coney Island, New York (2.7 miles, 1923, 1925, 1941). Repeatedly repaired and enlarged, the Ocean City boardwalk extended from the inlet to Fifteenth Street, and after damage in the 1962 March storm, the rebuilt boardwalk was extended farther to Twenty-seventh Street and its present length of 2.45 miles.

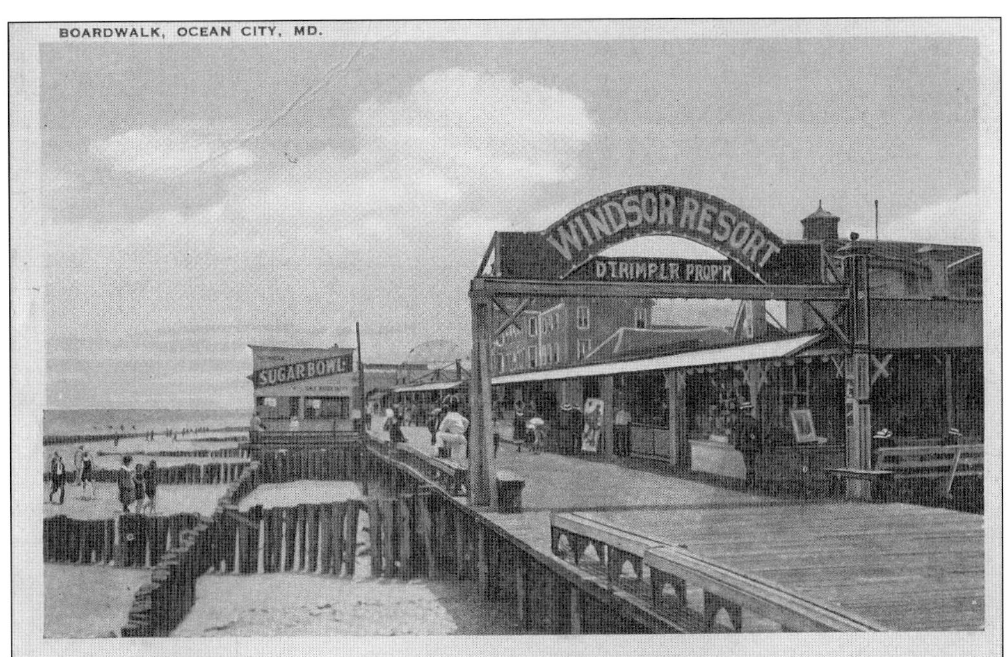

This Tichnor Brothers postcard view of the boardwalk south of South Division Street shows the entry to Daniel Trimper's Windsor Resort with its shops, amusements, and the saltwater taffy emporium Sugar Bowl, the progenitor of the contentious issue of allowing buildings east of the boardwalk. Visible are the amusement park's Ferris wheel and extensive pilings; note that some are supporting the raised boardwalk and others are extending as jetties into the ocean.

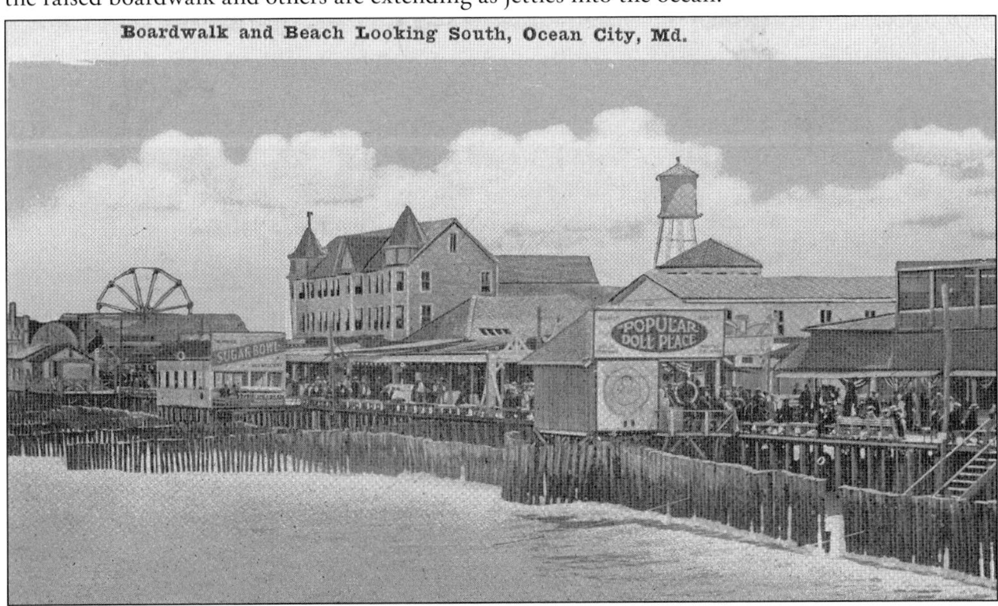

The two-turreted Windsor Hotel fronts the south boardwalk in what became known as the amusement section, the "south end" of the boardwalk still renowned today for its honky-tonk, its snack and souvenir shops, and its crowds of tourists frequenting "Trimper's Rides" (recently reclaiming its historic name Windsor Resort). Now three buildings appear east of the boardwalk, and (remarkably, considering the width of today's beach here), water extends to the boardwalk pilings.

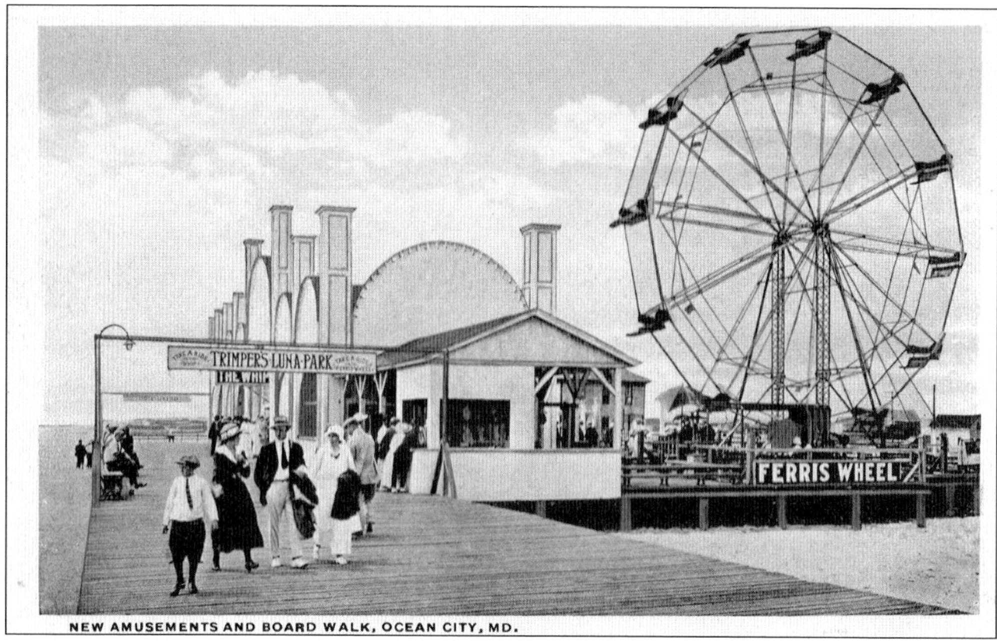

A 1916 postcard shows the south end of the boardwalk (ending about where it does today) with two overhead signs defining this block-length stretch of the boardwalk as Trimper's Luna Park. The amusement district, dominated by the Ferris wheel, was likely named for Luna Park that opened in Coney Island, New York, in 1903 (but was largely destroyed by fire in 1944). Fishing shanties occupied low land beyond the boardwalk's southern end.

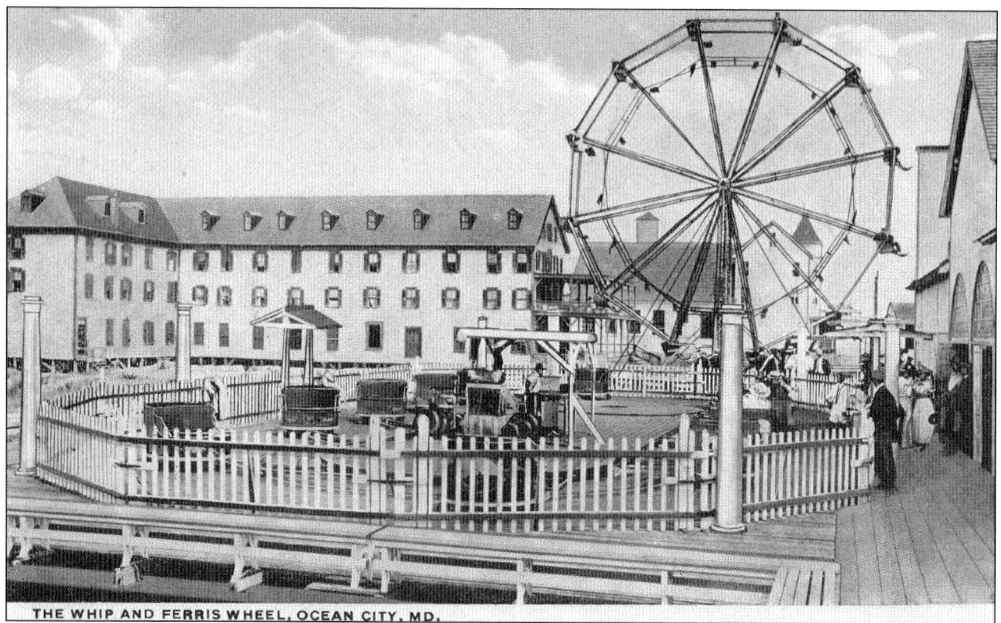

Postmarked 1921, this postcard shows the Ferris wheel next to another popular boardwalk ride, "the whip." Couples would sit on a bench affixed to a track that followed a rectangular route with rounded ends, around which the bench would "whip" (turn 180 degrees), forcing the couple, by centrifugal force, to snuggle closer.

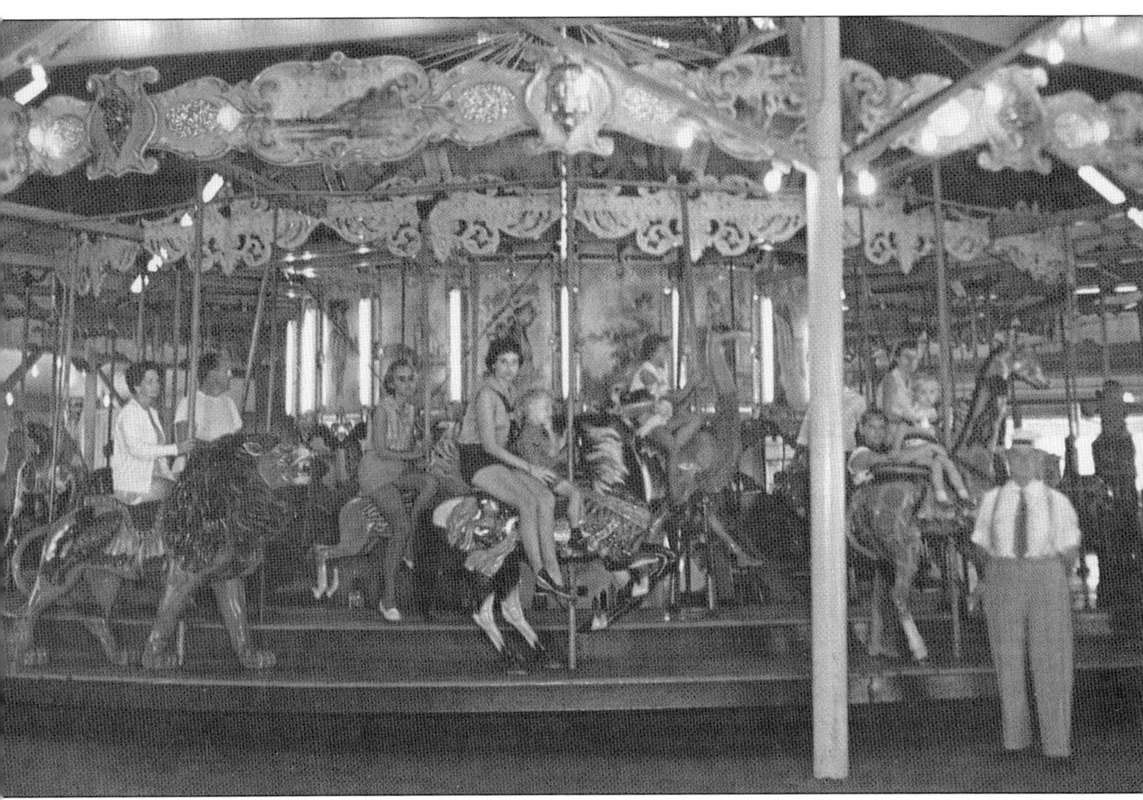

The highlight for the boardwalk perambulator remains Trimper's carousel, a menagerie-style all-wood merry-go-round. It was ordered in 1912 from the Herschell-Spillman Company of Upstate New York and is the oldest family-owned carousel in the country. The hand-carved and hand-painted animals, recently fully restored, include twelve jumping horses; eleven standing horses; two cats, dogs, frogs, giraffes, ostriches, roosters, mules, and zebras; and one camel, deer, dragon, goat, stork, lion, and tiger. Four chariots (either rocking or stationery) are also featured for couples. The carousel's calliope music enhances a stroll through the open sheltering frame tent of the original merry-go-round building, adding to the historic authenticity as one passes Trimper's still-operating 1920s W.F. Mangels Children's Carousel; Mangels Kiddie Whip; Mangels Kiddie Fire Engines; Mangels Kiddie Ferris Wheel; Duce Floyd & Baxter Big Dodgem Bumper Cars; and Bradley and King Kiddie Water Boats circling around a lighthouse over real water.

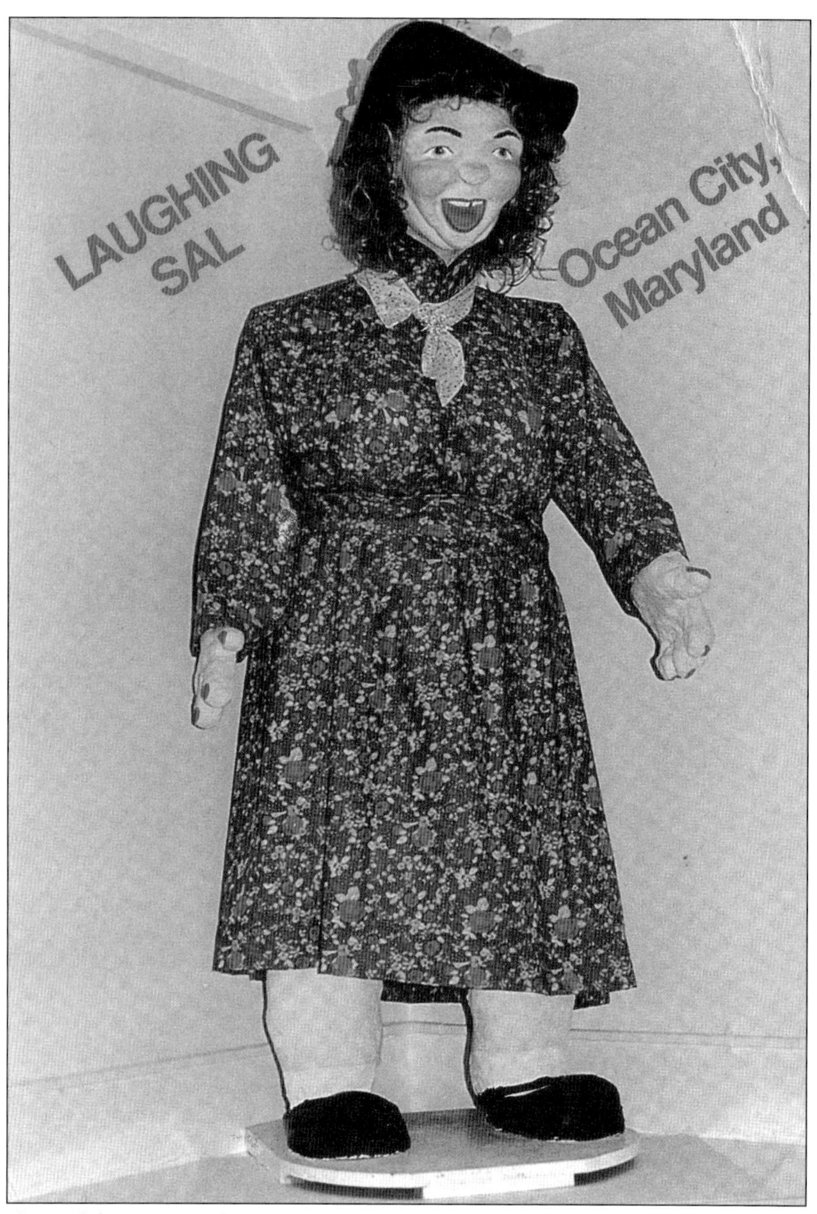

Laffing Sal stood for years at the entry to Jester's Fun House, located on Wicomico Street just off the boardwalk, and originally was operated in the late 1920s by Thomas Conway of Atlantic City. After four years, Lloyd Jester purchased the fun house and, in the early 1940s, paid about $300 to the Philadelphia Toboggan Company of Germantown for the over six-foot-tall robotic rag doll, perhaps the first animatronic of its kind and a concept of animated figures ultimately popular in carnivals and amusement parks worldwide, especially Disney's enterprises. Laffing Sal was dressed in a sartorially challenged bright floral dress, large Mary Jane shoes, and a floppy hat; she shook her head, waved her arms, and jerked her torso spasmodically, while an irritating but contagious laugh greeted fun house guests, at least until the 78 rpm recording ended, and the Jesters restarted the mechanical ballyhoo. In 1972, two years after the Jesters retired, the fun house was demolished (for Sportland arcade's expansion), and in 1980, Laffing Sal was donated to the Ocean City Life-Saving Museum and restored.

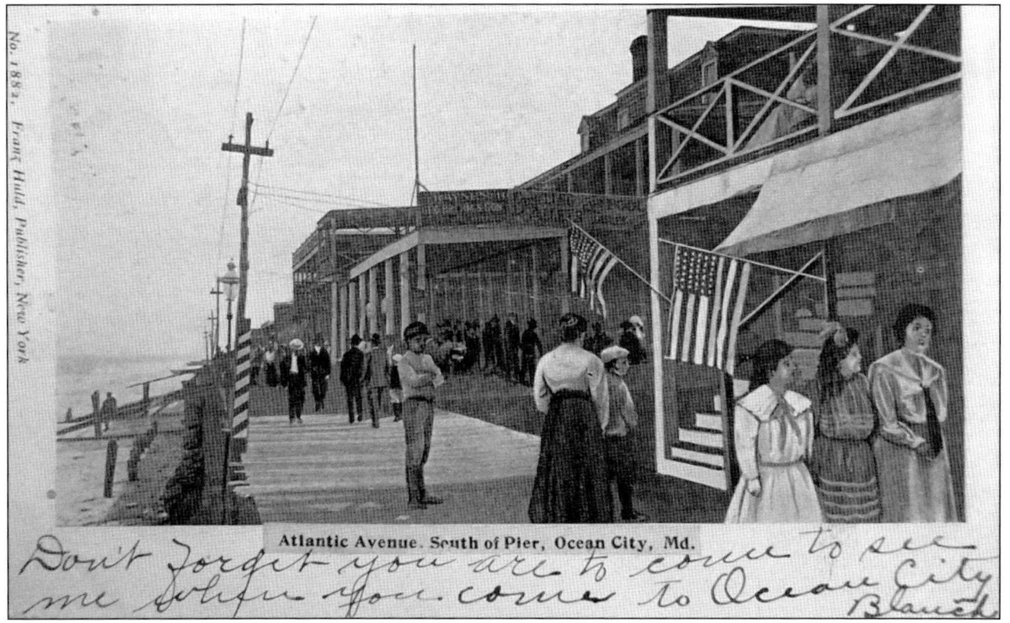

The south end of the boardwalk, between the pier and Windsor Resort, was fronted by early frame-built oceanfront hotels, including the Cambridge, Congress Hall, and Windsor Hotel (formerly Seabright Hotel) and farther north the Eastern Shore Hotel, Hotel de Cropper, and Raynes Hotel (on the site of the former Hotel Belvidere). In this 1906 Franz Huld postcard, signs indicate the following additional hotel amenities: bathhouses, bowling alleys, and pool (billiards) rooms.

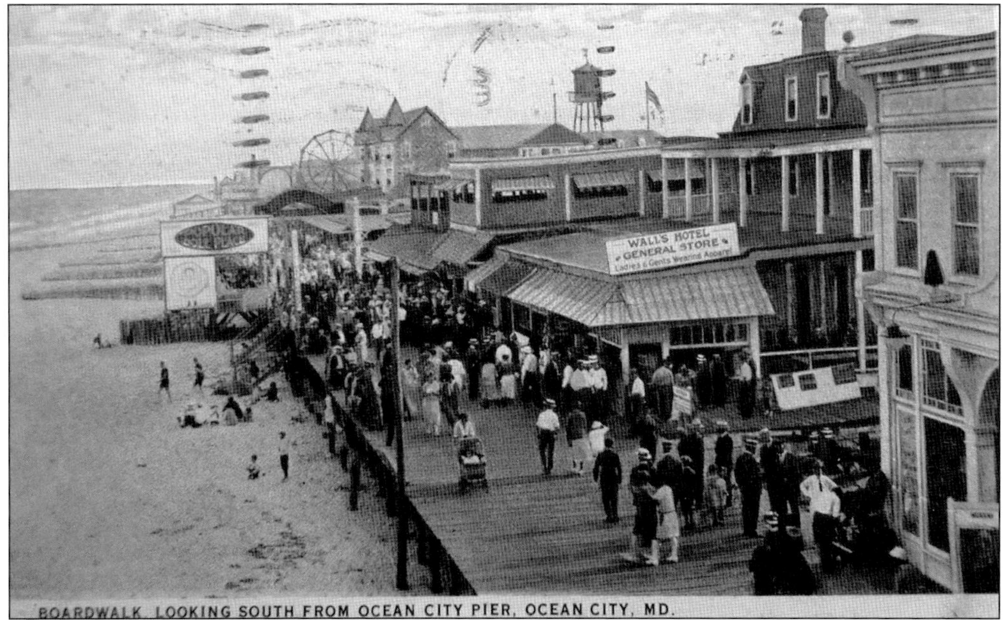

This 1939-postmarked postcard is likely an earlier view, but nonetheless illustrates a relatively unchanged boardwalk frontage south of the pier. Wall's Hotel is partially obscured by a general store offering "Ladies & Gents Wearing Apparel," a forecast of boardwalk bikini shops fronting or replacing hotel porches and hawking their goods at the very edge of the promenade. The light-colored building at the right edge of the view is the boardwalk Casino.

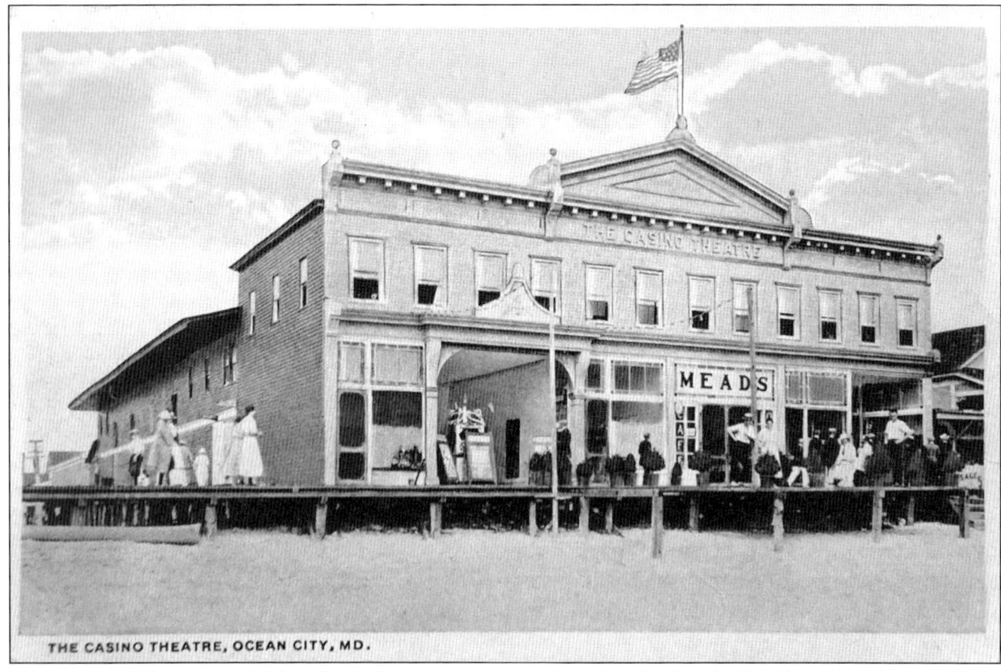

The Casino Theatre with Mead's Café, shown in this white-border Louis Kaufmann postcard (likely dating between 1915 and 1925), appears on the 1897 and 1904 Sanborn maps as containing a "casino" across the front, with bowling alley, bathhouses, and small stage behind. By 1911, the building was showing moving pictures, perhaps initially nickelodeon presentations, Vitagraph films, newsreels, and, after 1909, 35mm silent pictures. The Casino burned in the 1925 fire.

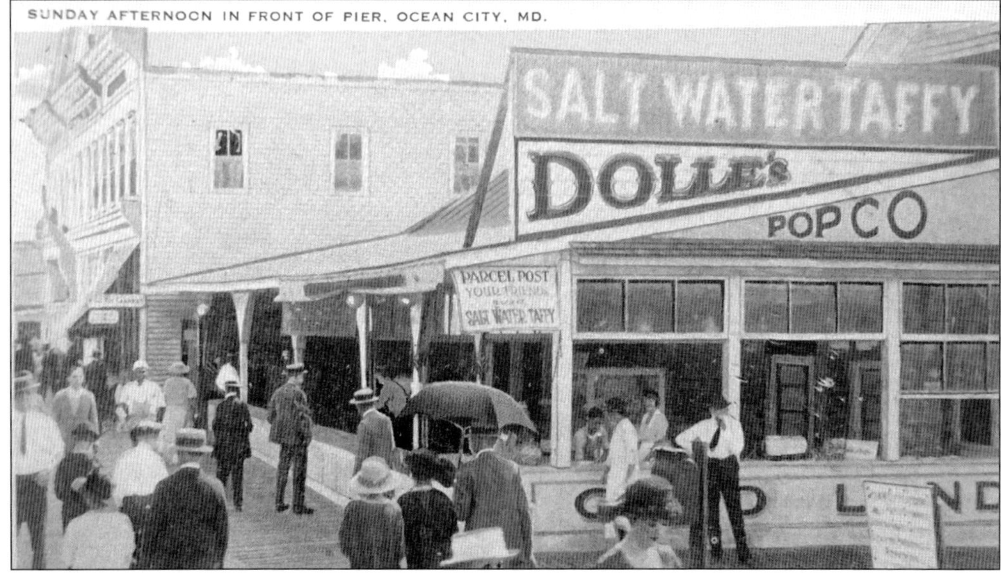

The Casino appears in the background of this Tichnor postcard view "Sunday Afternoon in Front of the Pier," featuring Dolle's Salt Water Taffy shop, established in 1910 on the boardwalk at Wicomico Street, opposite the entrance to the pier. Dolle's was lost in the 1925 fire, which consumed the two boardwalk blocks between Worcester and Somerset Streets, including the Atlantic Hotel. Both Dolle's and the hotel were immediately rebuilt.

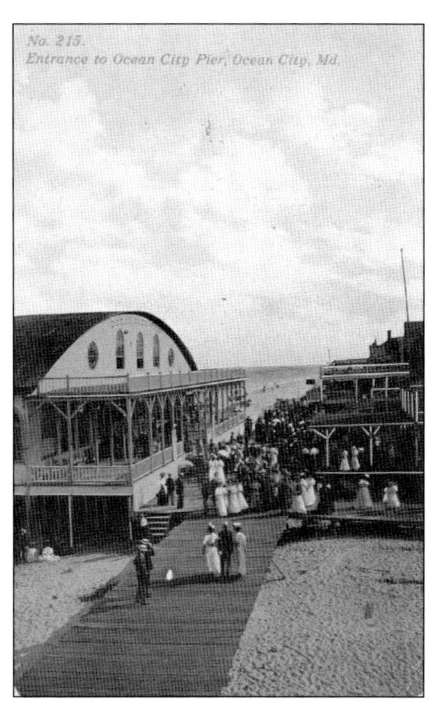

The postcard at right, postmarked 1911, provides an early view of the boardwalk at Wicomico Street showing the pier building with its raised full-width verandah and, opposite, the property where Rudolph Dolle operated his wood-carved carousel after 1906. In 1910, Dolle bought the corner property, by then a small stand selling ice cream and "honey coated corn." Below, a postcard, postmarked 1936, shows an enlarged Dolle's Candyland. Although the store sold candy, caramel popcorn, and fudge, saltwater taffy was the staple, and tourists lined up for decades to watch the taffy machine behind the counter pull and stretch the candy as it was produced on site. The enterprise grew, launched A&A Candy Company in 2000 (named for fourth-generation Dolles, Andrew and Anna), and opened new stores on 120th Street (2006), Sixty-seventh Street (2013), and West Ocean City (2018).

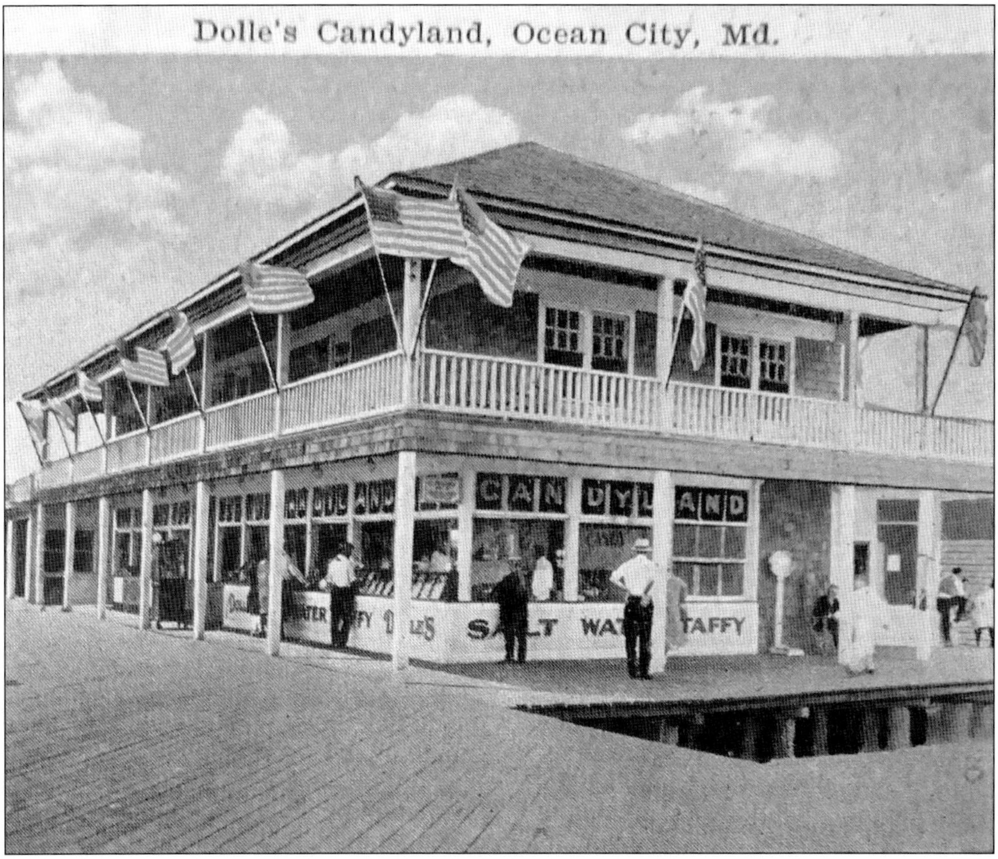

Dolle's Candyland, Ocean City, Md.

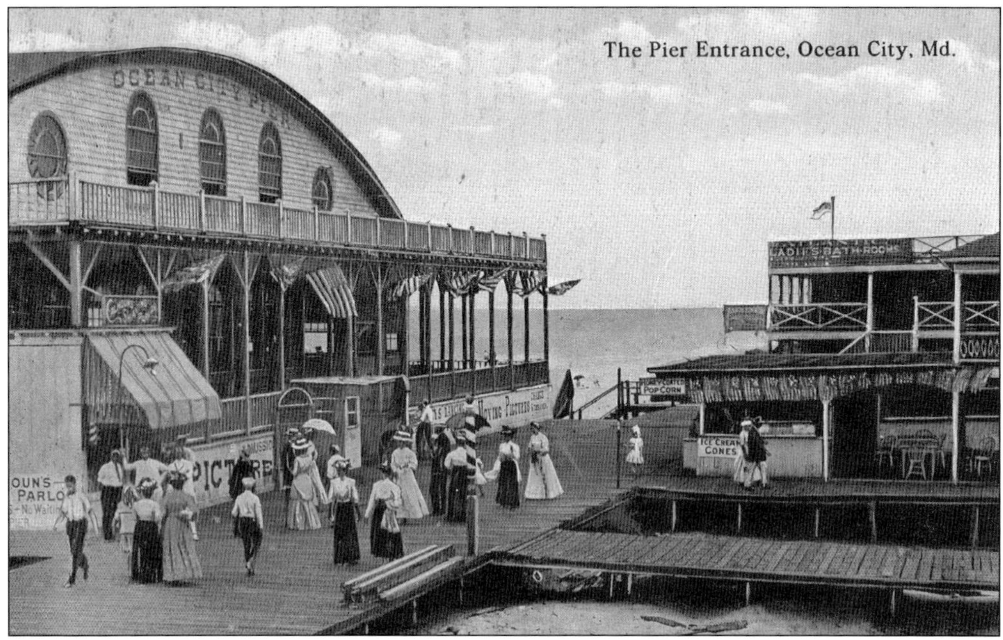

The Ocean City Pier Building (1907), also known as convention hall, offered a variety of entertainments, including dancing, moving pictures, and Calhoun's Shaving Parlor, pictured. Old-timers may well question whether Calhoun's proprietor was the same as, or related to, the owner of Calhoun's mid-century barbershop downtown, where, in the early 1950s, impressionable young boys were forcefully told to "Hold your damned head still!"

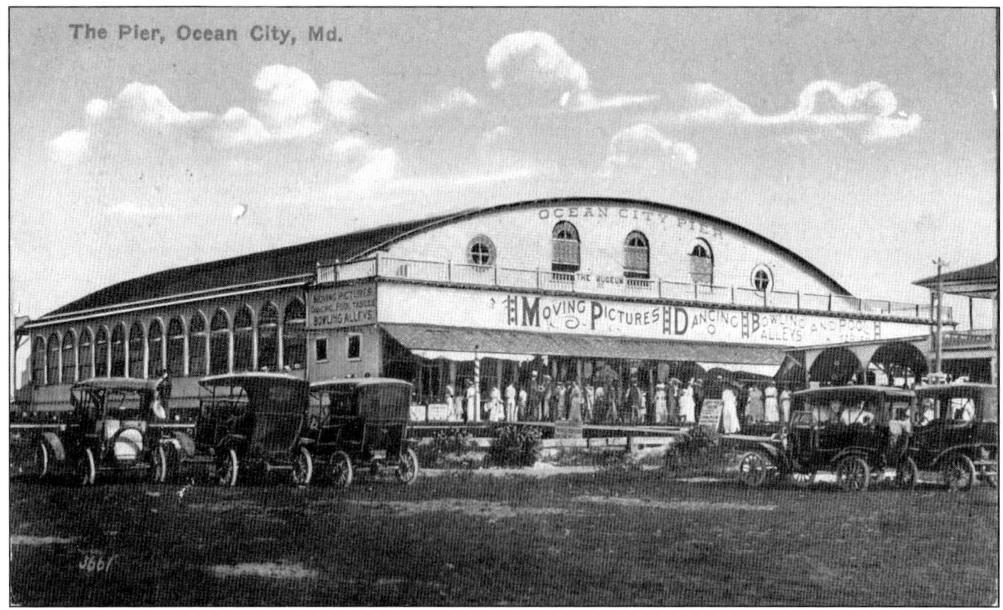

This Chessler Company postcard shows "the pier building" as it looked (judging from the parked Model Ts) around 1915. Featuring bowling alleys, moving picture theater, dance hall, and pool tables, the pier building was the town's social center. In 1918, the roof collapsed following a heavy snowstorm. Immediately repaired, the building completely burned in the 1925 fire. Rebuilt by 1929, its new classical form contained a second-story pier ballroom.

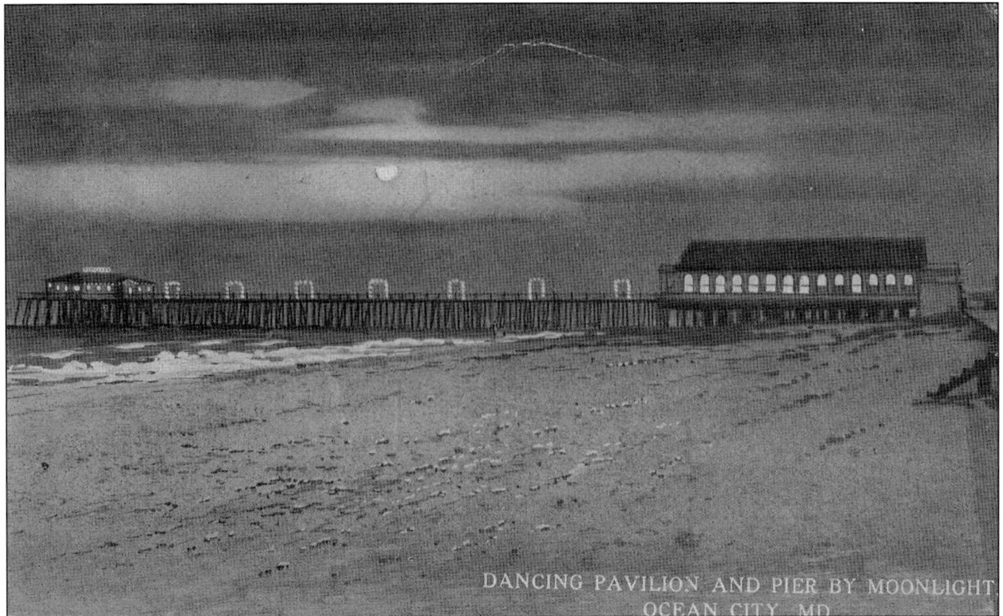

Local businessmen and community leaders financed the construction of the original pier with work beginning in 1904. The pier opened by the summer of 1907. A roller-skating rink occupied the small building at the end of the pier. This atmospheric postcard presents a romanticized view of the "Dancing Pavilion and Pier by Moonlight" and is undated. By the time of the card's 1926 postmark, the building had burned.

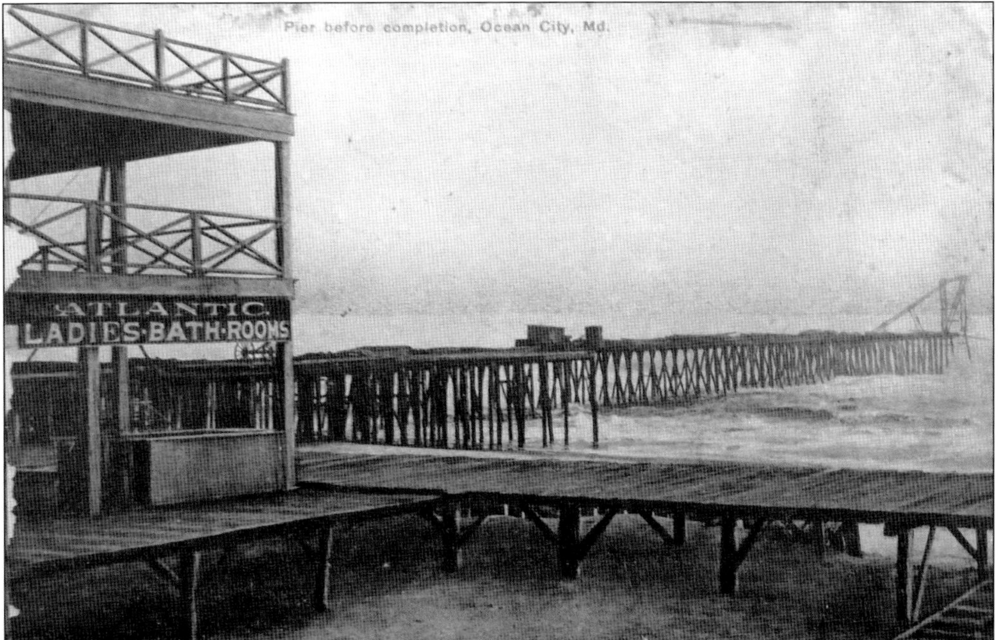

This postcard of the pier under construction shows the raised boardwalk with the surf just a few feet away. By the later 1930s, the inlet jetty would begin to build up sand to create a beach extending as far as the length of this pier. Today's Ferris wheel and Jenkins pier amusements stand on a later rebuilt pier whose fishing pier extension reaches another several hundred feet into the ocean.

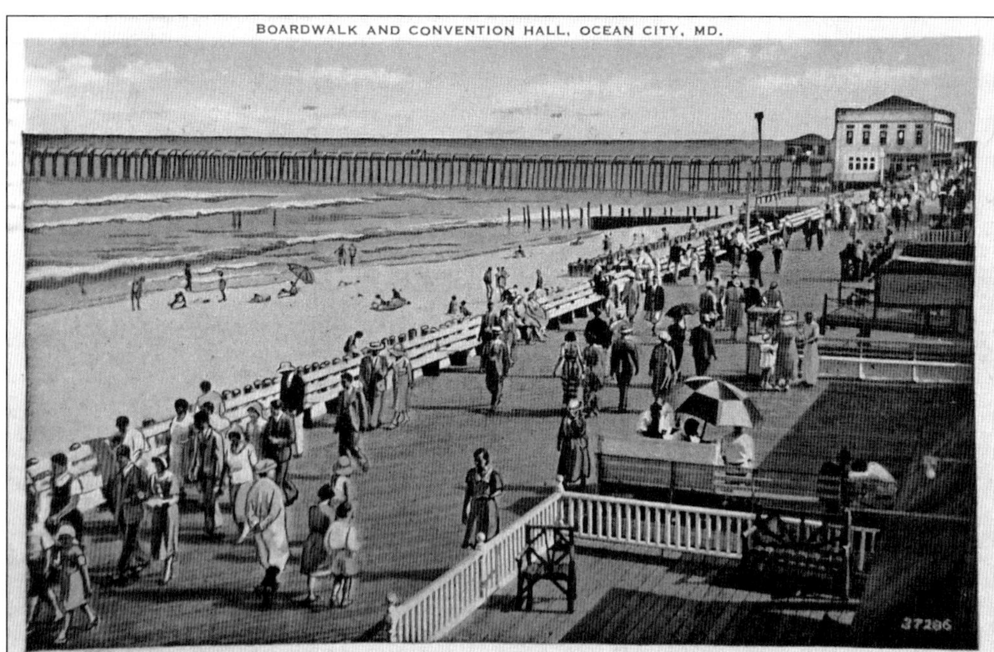

In this postcard postmarked 1938, the pier (viewed from the north) extends across a still narrow beach from the rebuilt convention hall/pier ballroom seaward. As previously noted, the 1925 great fire consumed the original convention hall building, two blocks of the boardwalk including Dolle's candy store, and the pier itself (see pages 50–52). Rebuilt, as shown here, the new pier reached seaward at a length greater than a football field.

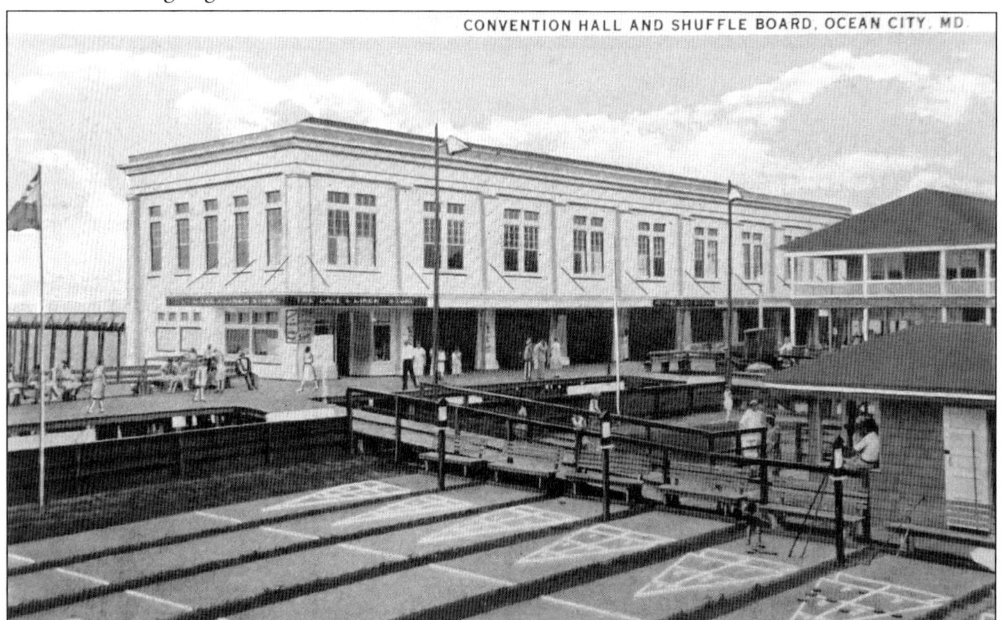

In this 1931 Curt Teich postcard of the rebuilt convention hall (pier building), what appears to be a 1931 Model AA Ford truck is visible at the end of Wicomico Street, a further indication of the date of the image. The Lace and Linen Store occupies a corner unit of the pier building's boardwalk frontage and in the foreground shuffleboard courts occupy the empty lot north of the Atlantic Hotel.

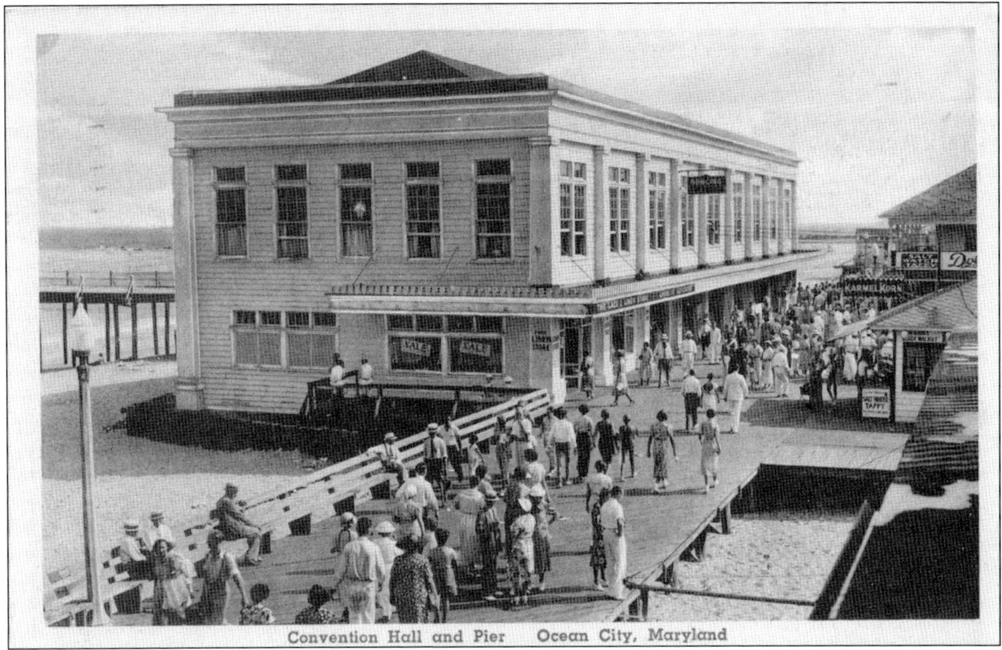

Convention Hall and Pier Ocean City, Maryland

In the postcard (above) postmarked 1939, the boardwalk at the pier building is crowded with strolling tourists. The pier ballroom (below), which occupied the entire second floor of the pier building, was at its height of popularity in the late 1930s through 1950s, offering dancing as a nightly entertainment with name bands normally featured on weekends. On August 22, 1938, for instance, Chick Webb and his orchestra, with Ella Fitzgerald, "played" the pier ballroom; tickets were $2.50 (advanced) and $3. Others said to have played Ocean City (either at the pier ballroom, Rick's Raft, or local night clubs) included Billie Holiday, Cab Calloway, Louis Armstrong, Woody Herman, George Shearing, Vaughn Monroe, and Duke Ellington.

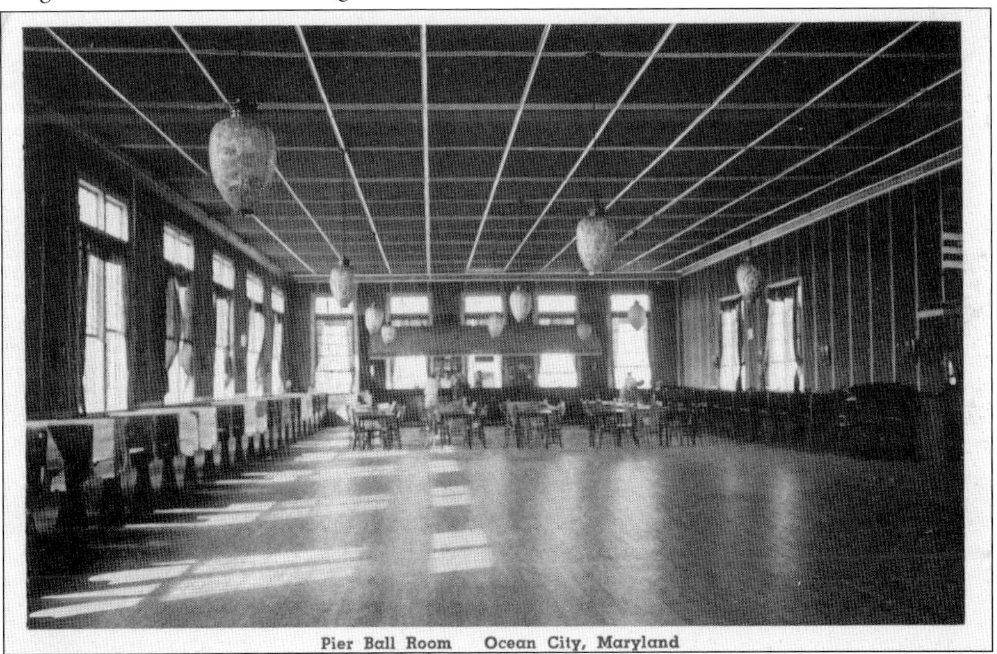

Pier Ball Room Ocean City, Maryland

-DANCING-

BY

ADMIRALS

DIRECTED BY

ANTHONY BOVE and Eleven Recording Artists.

Formerly from Patio Theatre, Brooklyn, N. Y., Also on Tour with Keith's Vaudeville Through the West and South.

PIER BALL ROOM, Ocean City, Maryland

SATURDAY, JUNE 6, 1931

Special Attraction, Novelty Singing and Dancing Trio.

SPECIAL PRICE: $2.00 Per Couple. Dancing 9:15 until 12:30

KELLY THOMPSON, Sponsor

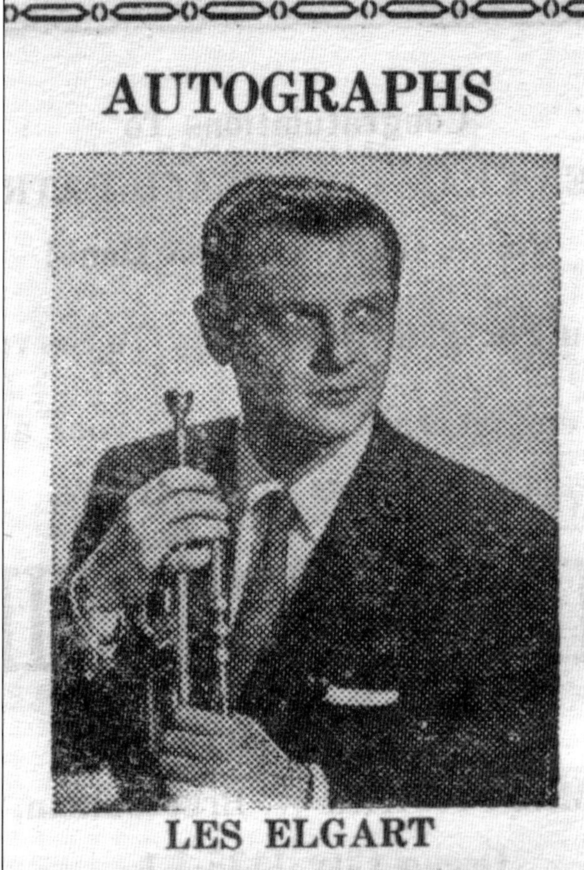

At the end of the summer season, a lifeguard benefit dance was held, usually at the pier ballroom, with Capt. Robert S. Craig bringing to the venue in the 1950s such bands as Les Elgart, Billy Butterfield, Claude Thornhill, Ralph Flanagan, and in the 1960s, local talent from Baltimore including the Admirals and the Lafayettes. The 1931 "Dancing by Admirals" ticket (above) was an earlier "Admirals" band; the Baltimore "Admirals," formed in 1958, came yearly to Ocean City venues for many years and remained popular because they could play everything from big band sound and jazz to contemporary ballads and doo wop. The pier ballroom finally closed in 1973. Today, the second floor of the pier building houses Ripley's Believe It or Not. (Both, courtesy of Robert S. Craig collection).

Captain Craig was particularly fond of the big band sound with lead trumpeters carrying the melody line. At home social events, he played recordings of Jackie Gleason's orchestra with Bobby Hackett's mellow mood music. Hackett had earlier played trumpet, cornet, and guitar with the bands of Glenn Miller and Benny Goodman in the 1930s and early 1940s. During the 1950s, he was featured soloist for Jackie Gleason's many mood music albums "for lovers only." Whether Craig tried to secure Gleason's orchestra for a lifeguard dance is not known, but Craig did travel around 1939 to Philadelphia to attend a "battle of the bands" dance with Tommy Dorsey's and Glenn Miller's bands alternating. Billy Butterfield's smooth trumpet and Ralph Flanagan's reprise of the Glenn Miller sound were brought to lifeguard benefit dances at the pier ballroom in 1957 and 1959, respectively. (Courtesy of Robert S. Craig collection.)

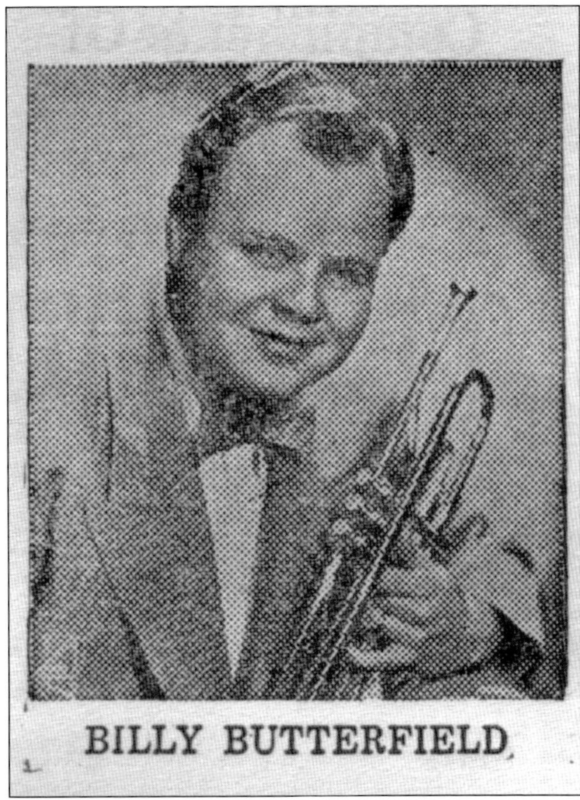

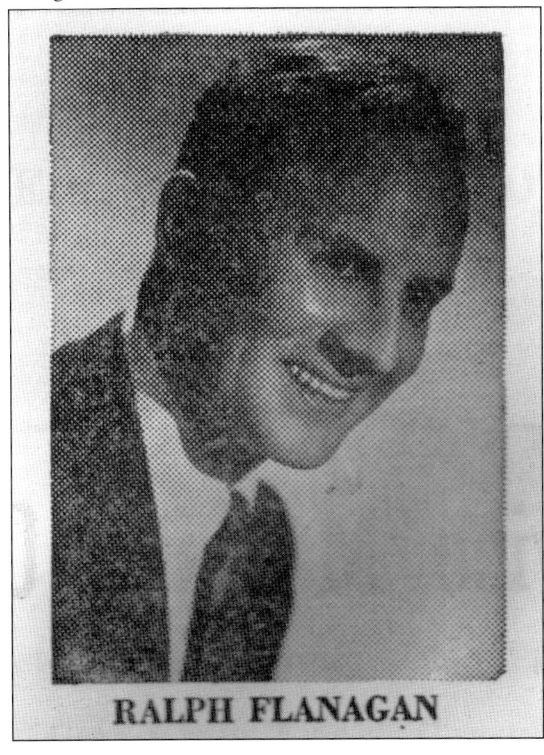

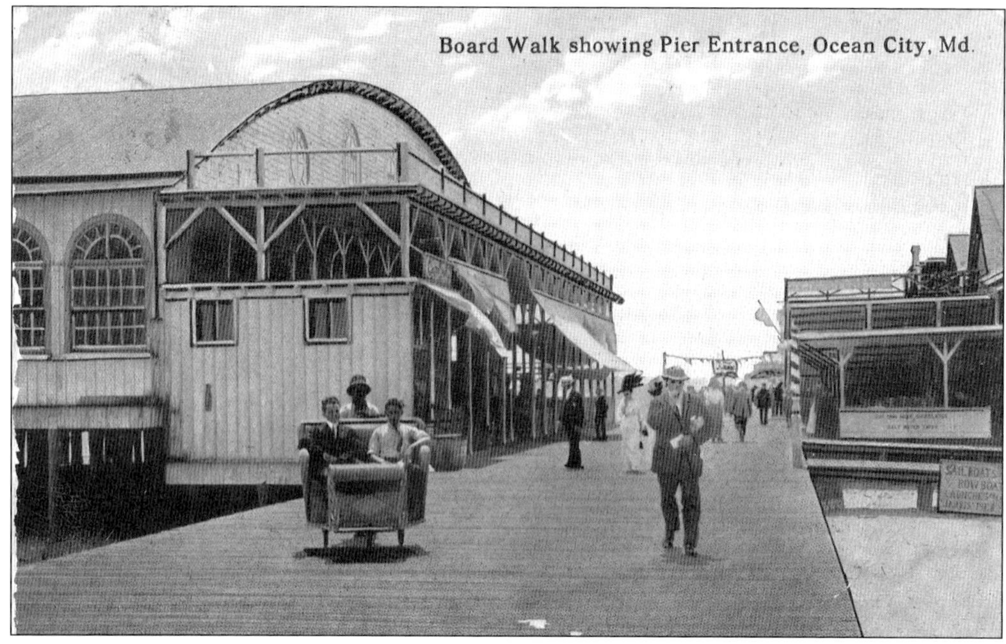

Roller chairs were a popular amusement on the boardwalk well before the recent era when hundreds of bicycles crowd the boardwalk in the early-morning hours. The roller chair was a wicker tricycle pushed from behind, often by a young boy hired out along with the roller chair. A 1913-postmarked view (above) of the "Board Walk showing Pier Entrance" features ladies with fashionable hats and gentlemen in coat and tie, with two young men being pushed in a wicker roller chair. Another smartly dressed group posing with two roller chairs is the subject of a postcard (below) postmarked 1916.

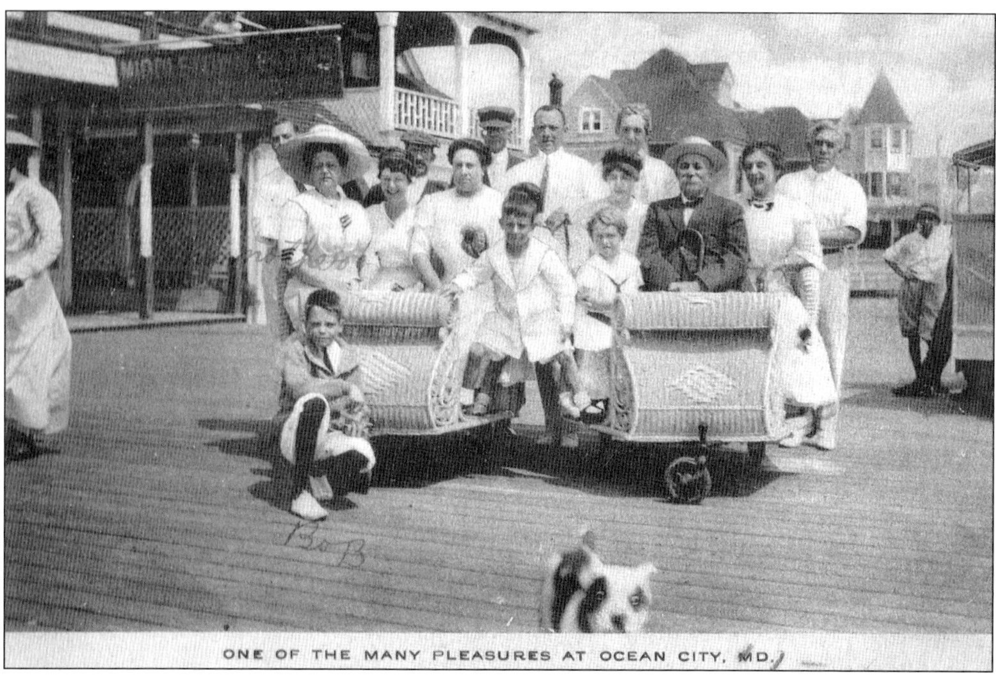

Two close-up photographs of wicker roller chairs provided souvenirs for the Beckman family (above) and the Townsends (below). Wicker was popular for cottage porch furniture and hotel lobby lounge furnishings. Dr. Frank Townsend Sr. operated the Washington Pharmacy on the boardwalk at Somerset Street where he introduced roller chairs to Ocean City in August 1912. A souvenir family picture, such as these, was available for an additional charge. The c. 1920 photograph (below) poses Frank Townsend Jr. and Jane Insley in a roller chair. Townsend's roller chair business ended with World War II.

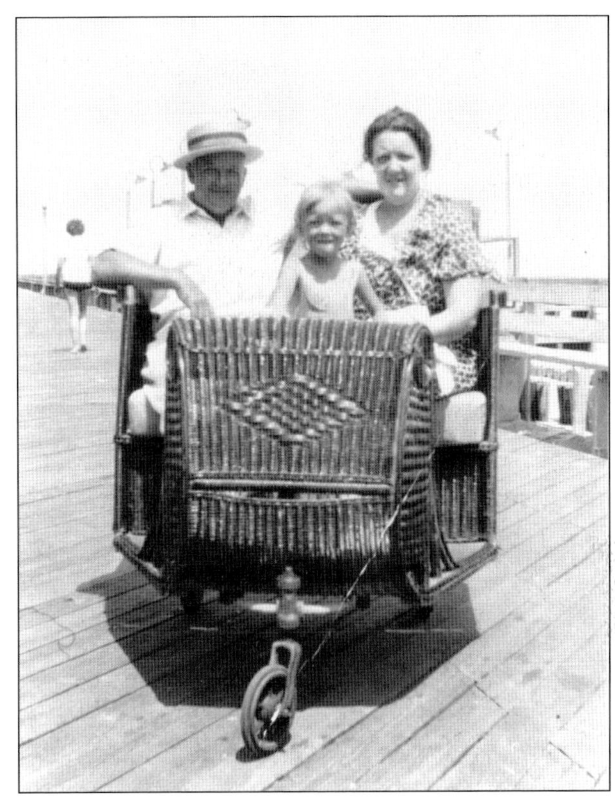

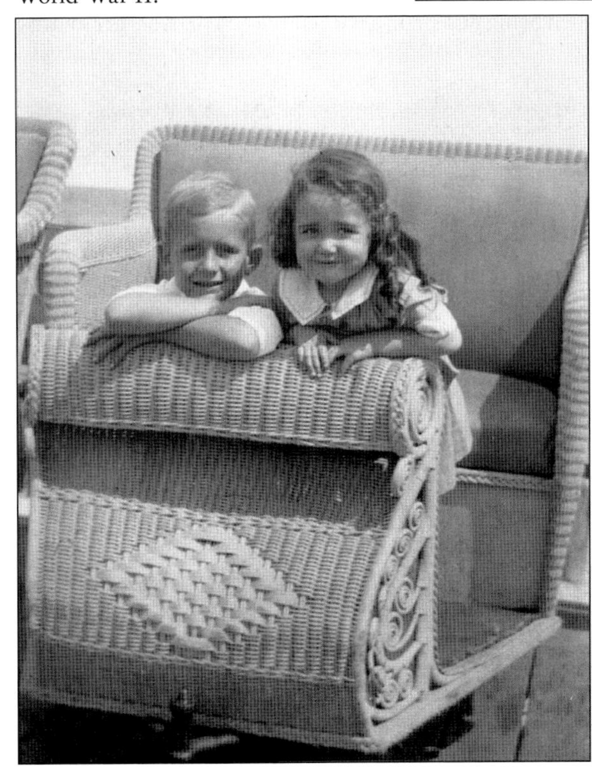

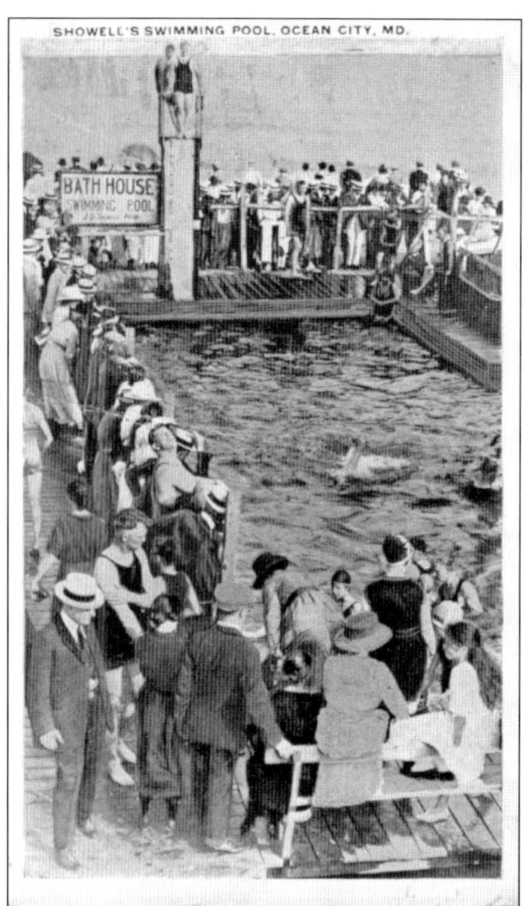

These Louis Kaufmann (above) and Tichnor Brothers (below) postcards show Showell's Swimming Pool surrounded by spectators watching swimmers and divers at Ocean City's first swimming pool. Located at the edge of the boardwalk between Carolina and North Division Streets, the site today is occupied by the building block containing Quiet Storm Surf Shop, formerly Edward's 5¢ & 10¢ (1934–?). At the end of the 19th century, the only boardwalk building in this block was the lifesaving station. By 1904, the Oceanic Hotel appears on Sanborn maps at the south corner of North Division Street. By 1921, the Sanborn map shows a swimming pool between the hotel and lifesaving station. Historian Bunk Mann dates the saltwater pool to 1917. Operated by John Dale Showell, the family business here grew to include a movie theater, bowling alley, restaurant, and bathhouse.

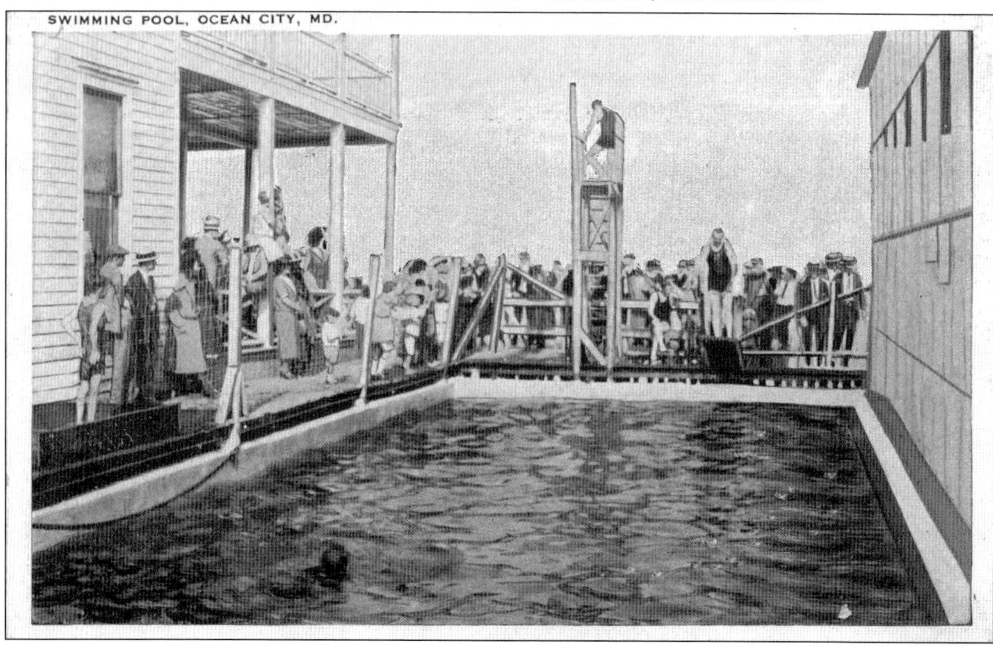

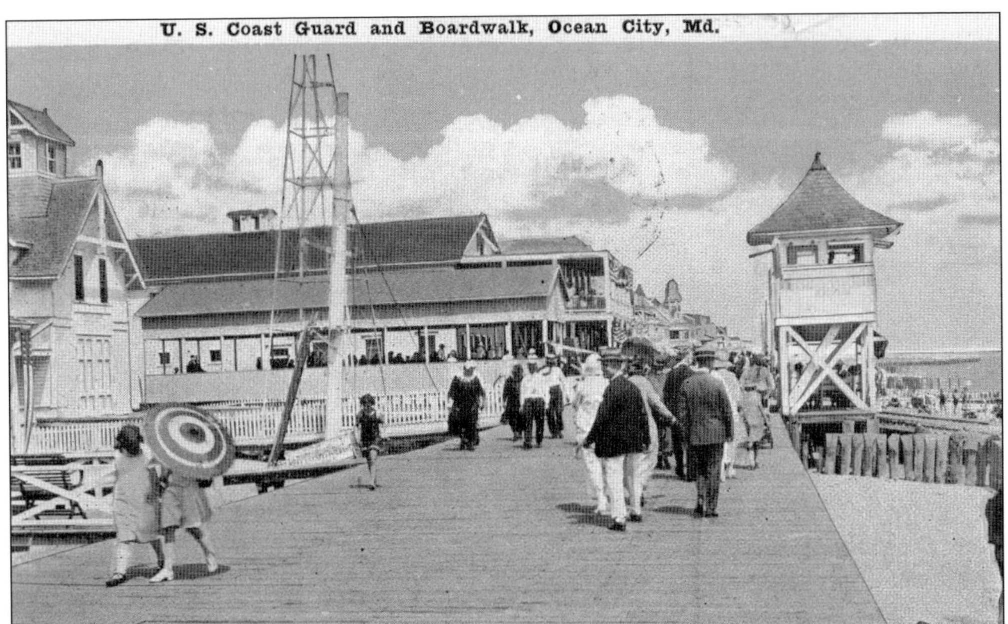

Postmarked 1929, the postcard above captioned "U.S. Coast Guard and Boardwalk . . ." looks north to the long gable-roofed Showell Building and the Oceanic Hotel with its two stories of oceanfront porches beyond. The Coast Guard (formerly US Life-Saving Service) station is at left with its picket-fenced forecourt, and across the boardwalk at right is the lookout tower, a distinctive structure of this section of boardwalk. Postmarked 1938, the postcard below identifies the Showell site as a fountain and a duckpin bowling alley (Ocean City's first), active before the days of automatic pinsetters (pinspotters). Gottfried "Fred" Schmidt invented the first mechanical pinsetter, taking out a patent in 1941. Showell's first hired pin boys to reset pins manually and then installed automatic pinsetters in 1960. Edward's 5¢ & 10¢ Store, built to the north, opened in 1937 (see page 70, below).

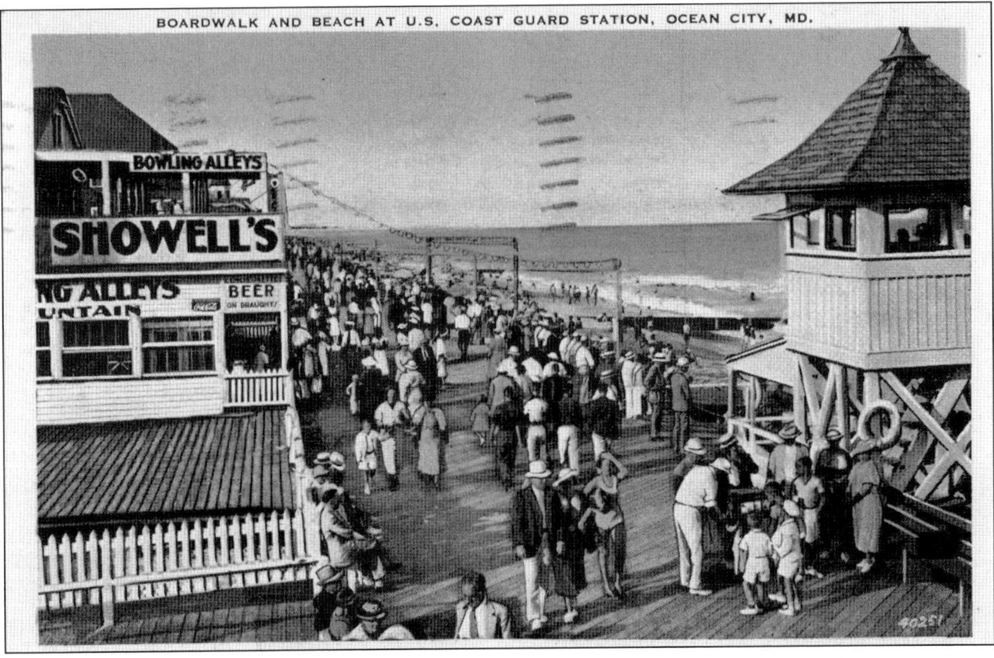

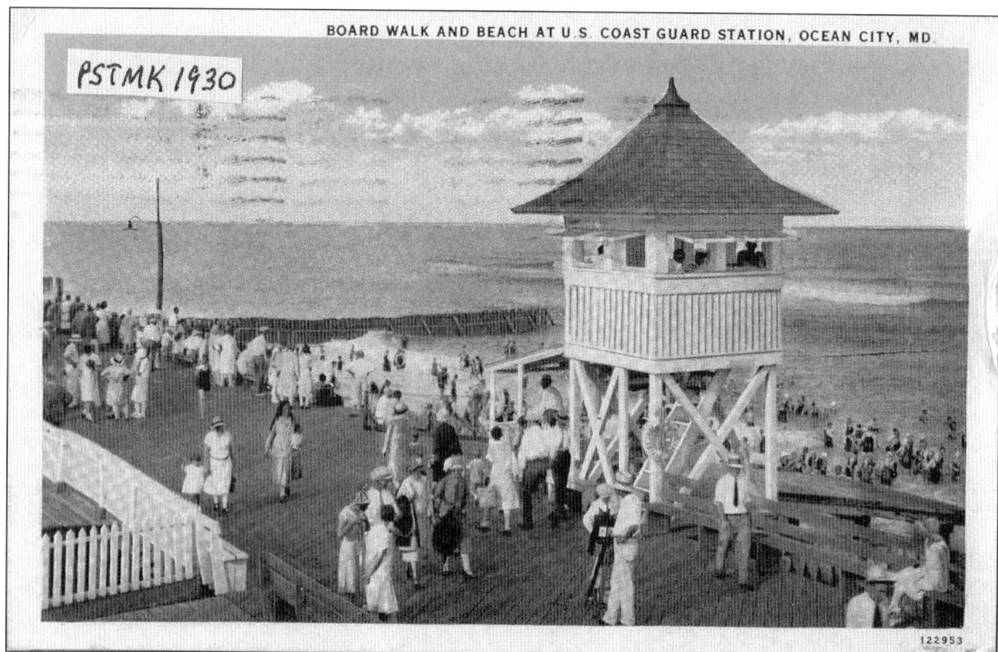

The postmark on this card is 1930, the year the Ocean City Beach Patrol (OCBP) was founded. The postcard shows a concentration of bathers in front of the Coast Guard tower and a jetty at the north side of the safe swimming area. Edward Lee Carey, OCBP's first captain, and John Laws were hired at the start of the summer with five other lifeguards by the end of the summer.

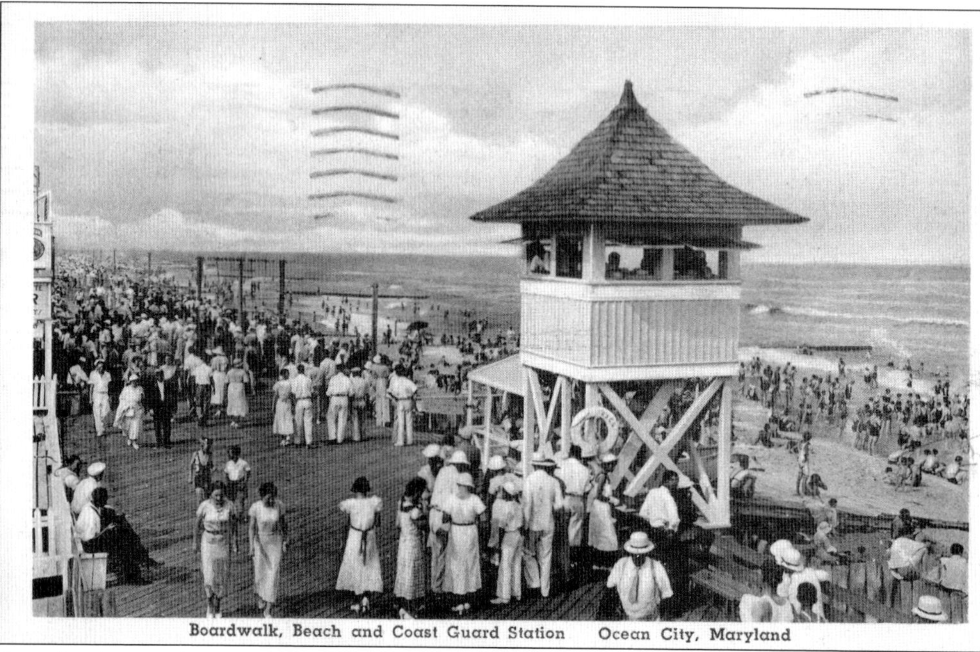

By 1940, the year this postcard was postmarked, the crowds on the boardwalk as well as the increased numbers of bathers extended the area of ocean overseen by the beach patrol to distances beyond what was readily visible from the Coast Guard tower. Lifeguards, "followed the crowds," and OCBP numbers steadily increased to 18 by 1941.

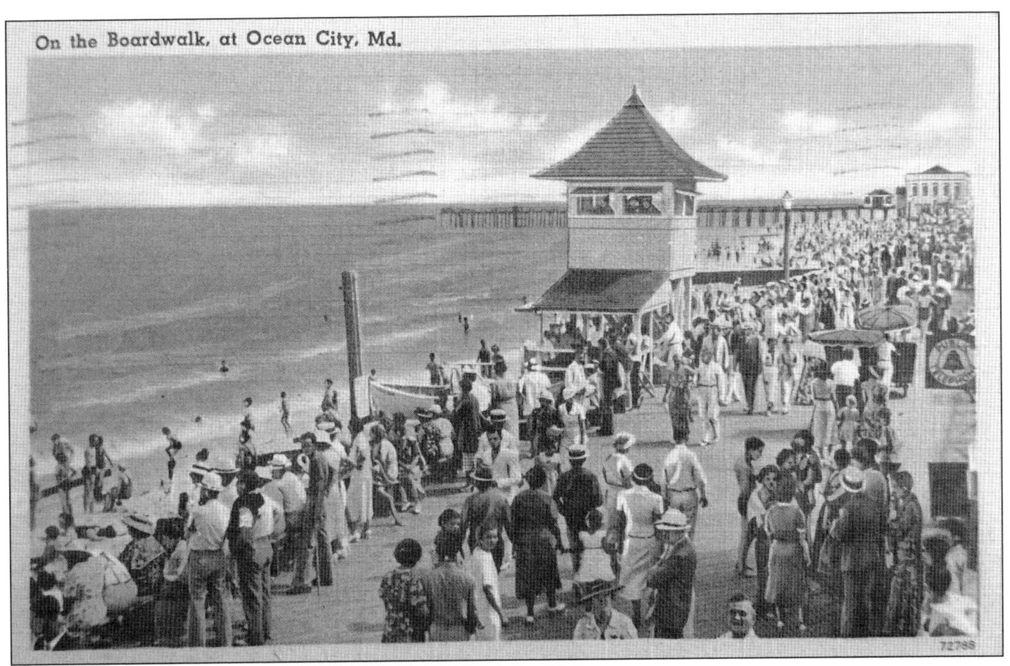

The boardwalk tower at the foot of Caroline Street was a boardwalk landmark for decades. Often the same photograph was published as a day view (above postmarked 1943) and colorized version (below postmarked 1942) to appear as a romantic moonlit night view, unreasonably showing the same swimmers at night in the same places with the same poses. Not only were the Coast Guardsmen and OCBP lifeguards off duty, but swimming in the ocean at night (especially after the 1975 movie *Jaws*) is universally considered less than prudent.

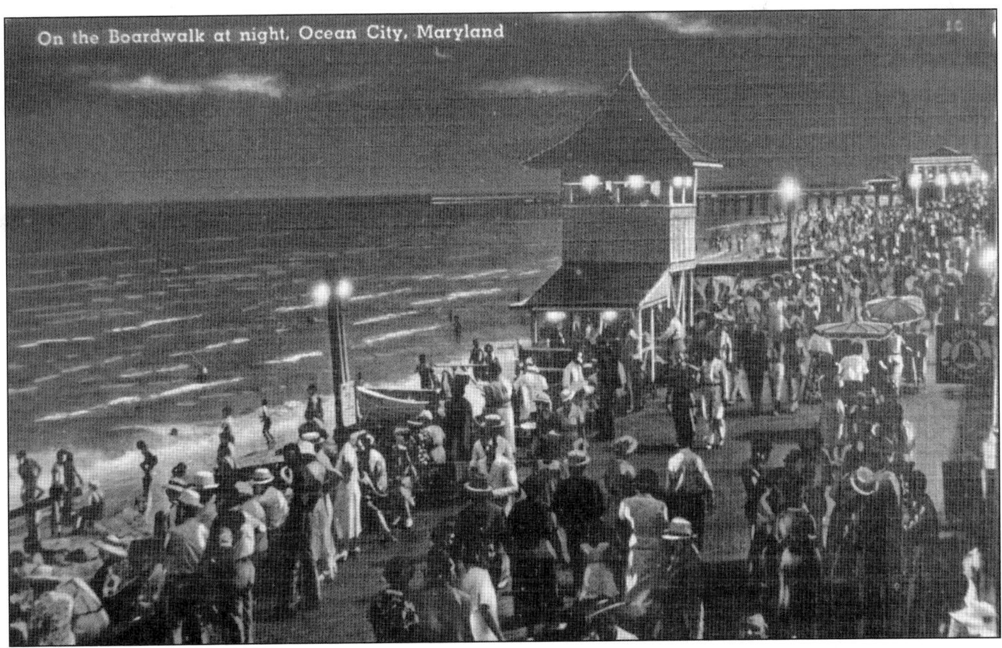

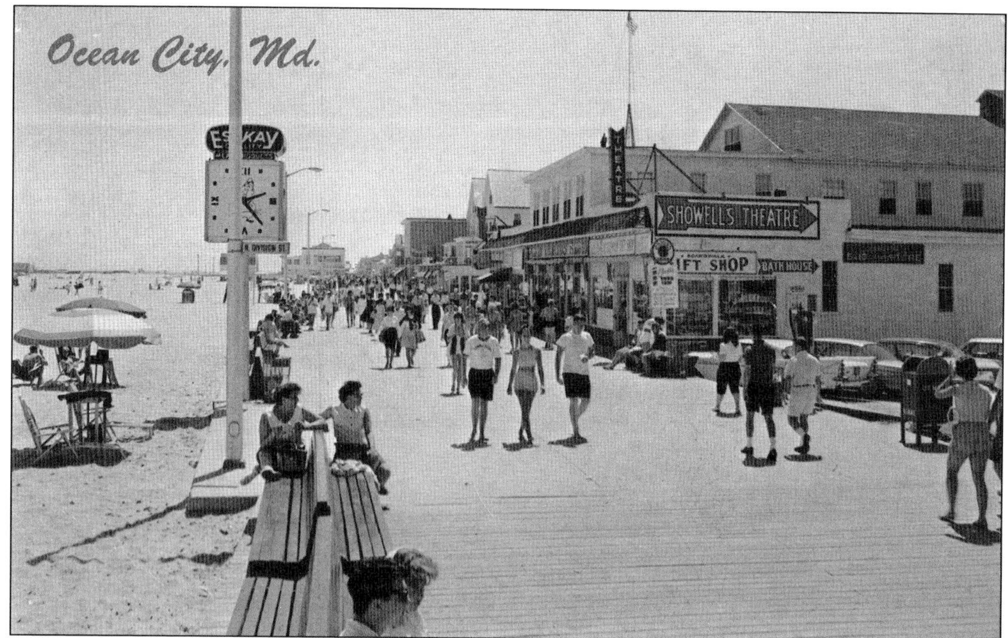

By the date of this Tichnor Brothers/Mardelva News postcard, postmarked 1953 (above), the Coast Guard tower had been removed from the boardwalk at the end of Caroline Street. In the foreground is one of several Eskay clocks erected along the boardwalk, and Edward's 5¢ & 10¢ store, which replaced the Oceanic Hotel and Showell's swimming pool, is behind the theater signs. Showell's Theatre on North Division Street open by 1936, closed briefly during World War II, opened again by 1945, and operated until 1978. Sometime before 1930, at the encouragement of fellow business owner and neighbor Frank Sacca, Dr. Frank Townsend erected a bandstand at the beach side of the boardwalk in front of his Washington Pharmacy on Somerset Street (below). Sacca conducted many of the concerts, and patrons then frequented Townsend's soda fountain for refreshments.

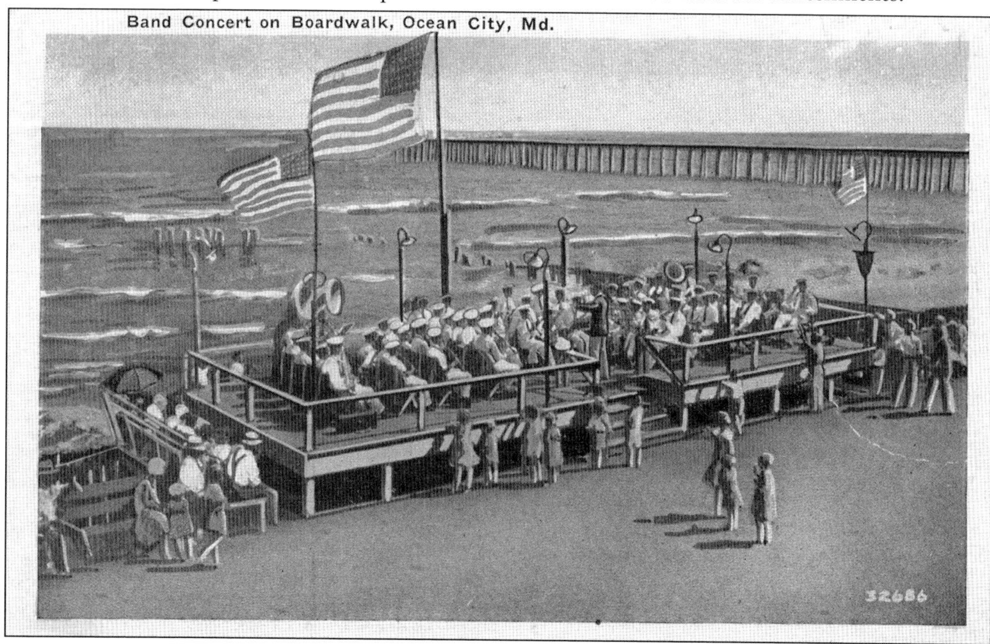

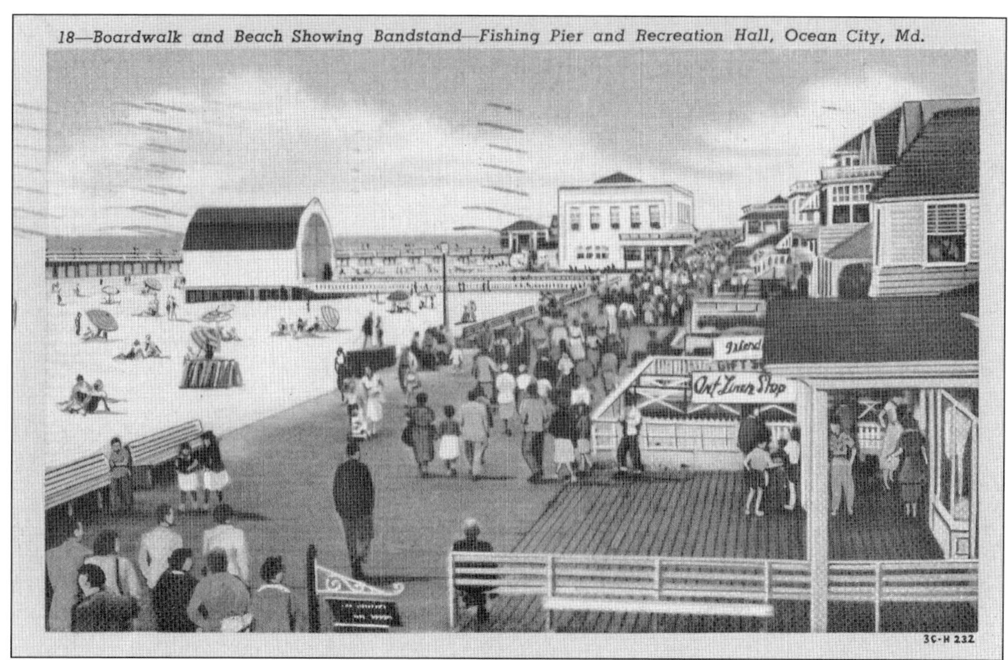

In 1949, the town built a bandshell and additional seating extending Sacca's orchestra venue eastward onto a wider beach, where sand had built up following the construction of the inlet rock pile jetty. Evening concerts continued until Sacca's death in 1955. Afterwards abandoned, the bandstand was not maintained, became derelict, and was finally demolished by the city in 1969. In 2014, free summer concerts and performances on the beach were reinstated by the mayor and city council at the Carolina Street Stage, located on the same site as the Sacca Bandshell (now east of the Carolina Street Comfort Station and near the popular Ocean City Firefighter's Memorial and Boardwalk Arch).

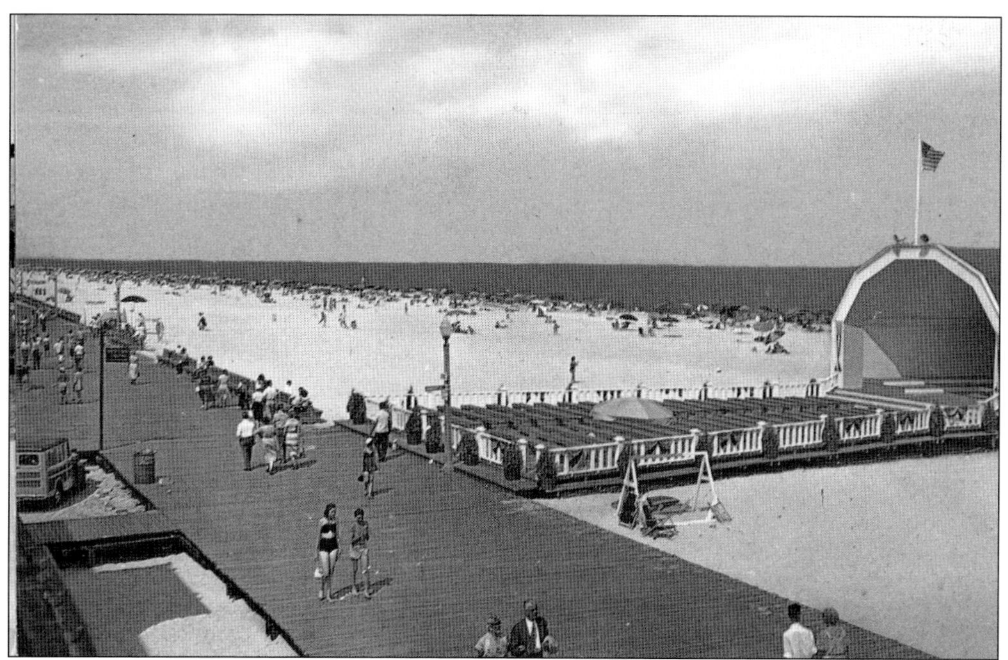

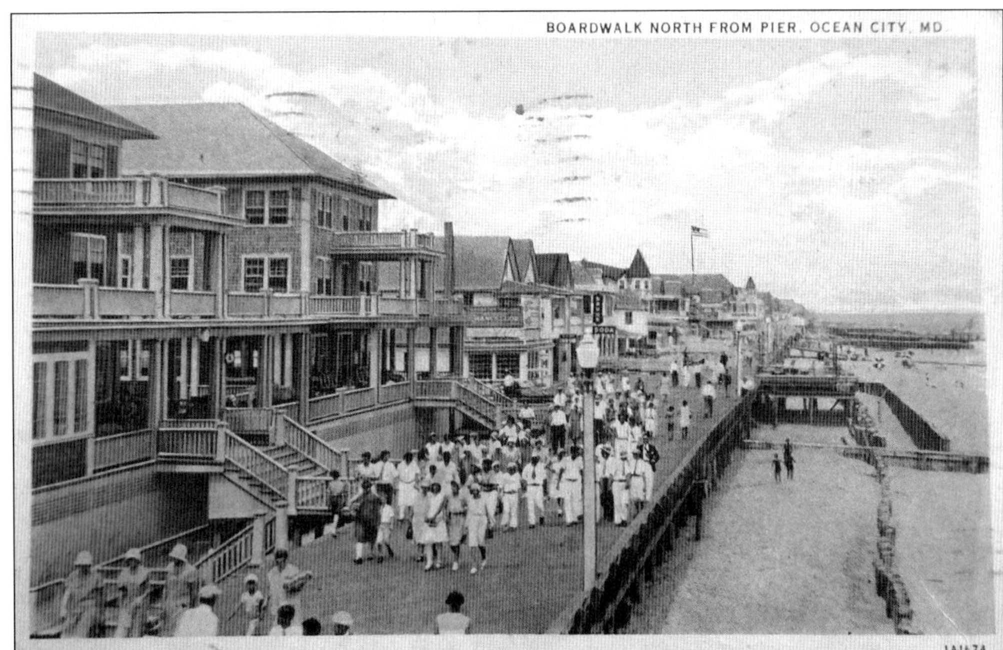

Prior to the mid-1930s, the boardwalk was raised on pilings some four to nine feet above the sand, overlooking a narrow strip of beach. At high tide, the surf often broke and rolled under the boardwalk encroaching on the setback hotels and cottages, which were also built on pilings. In order to protect the boardwalk (and buildings behind) against storm surf and erosive high tides, additional pilings were driven into the sand, forming a barrier about 15 to 20 feet out. Timber pilings also extended into the ocean as jetties and were intended to hold drifting coastal sand and to help build up the beach. The postcard below is postmarked 1935. By the 1940s, most of these timber jetties were buried under built-up sand. After the devastating 1962 storm, a concrete sea wall was constructed along the boardwalk with gates at each cross street beach access.

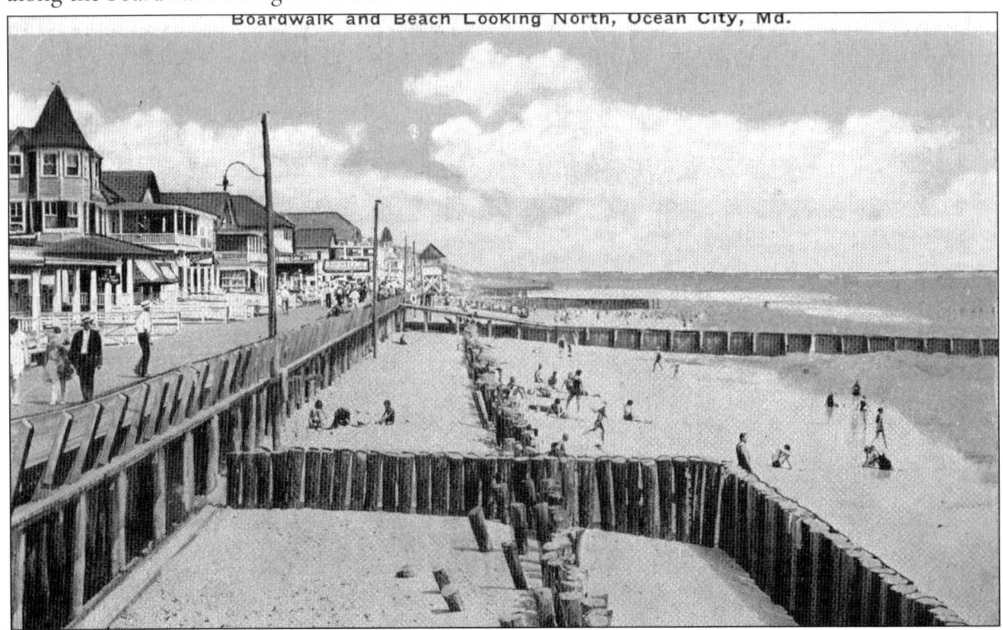

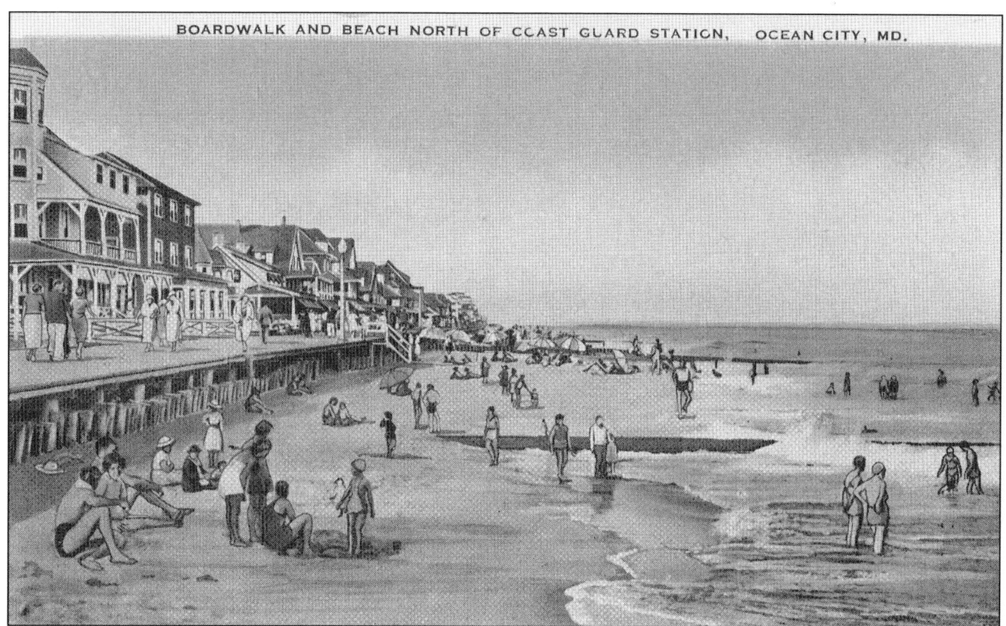

A late-1930s view (above) of the boardwalk and beach north of the Coast Guard station shows the raised boardwalk extending to the horizon line. Jetties mark every cross street, and stairs provide access periodically along the promenade. The 1946 aerial view (below), looking north from the inlet, shows the town's development and the boardwalk, which stops at Fifteenth Street. The photograph illustrates the effect of the inlet's rockpile jetty in widening the beach at the south end. The northernmost hotel in this view is the Commander on Fourteenth Street. Harrison Hall was built at the end of the boardwalk in 1951, and for years, it had a narrow beach reminiscent of pre-1930s town beaches farther south. By 1954, when the Sea Scape Motel (razed in 2016) opened in the next block, the boardwalk had been extended to Twenty-seventh Street.

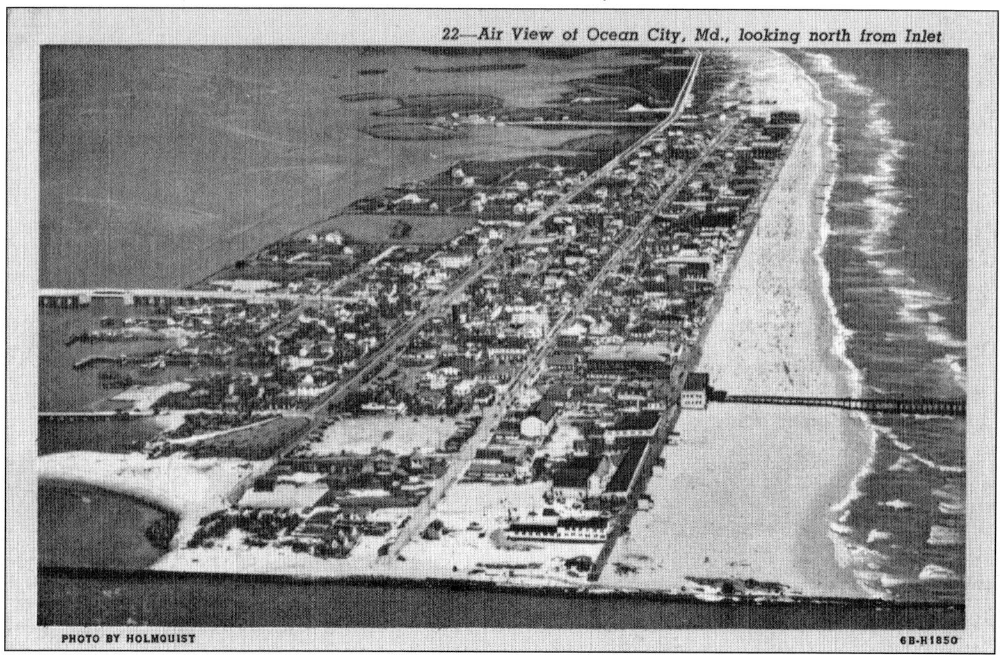

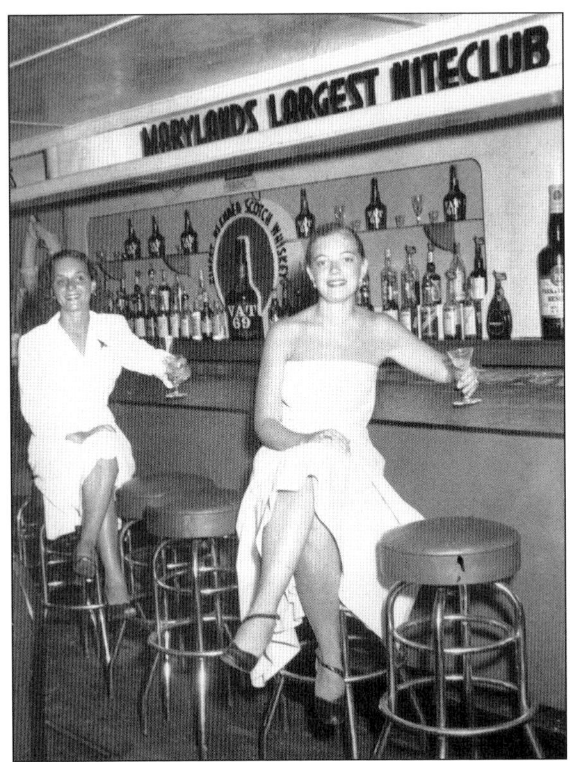

As the boardwalk extended northward, new venues for entertainment emerged including Jackson's Casino, the Blue Dahlia Lounge, and the Beach Club, all within a few yards of Ninth Street on the boardwalk. The nightclub scene here, especially popular during World War II, rivaled the pier ballroom, and music, dancing, and the bar scene continued to characterize Ninth Street into the 1960s. (Courtesy of Robert S. Craig collection.)

The Moderne graphics, three parallel "lines of speed," and the "Nautical Moderne" porthole opening at the entry to Jackson's Casino were all signs of contemporary streamlining, a phase of the Art Deco era made popular by industrial designers and the imagery of the 1939 New York World's Fair. Posters advertise the current attraction of the Johnny Bothwell Orchestra (see also page 69) with free admission and "never a cover." (Courtesy of Robert S. Craig collection.)

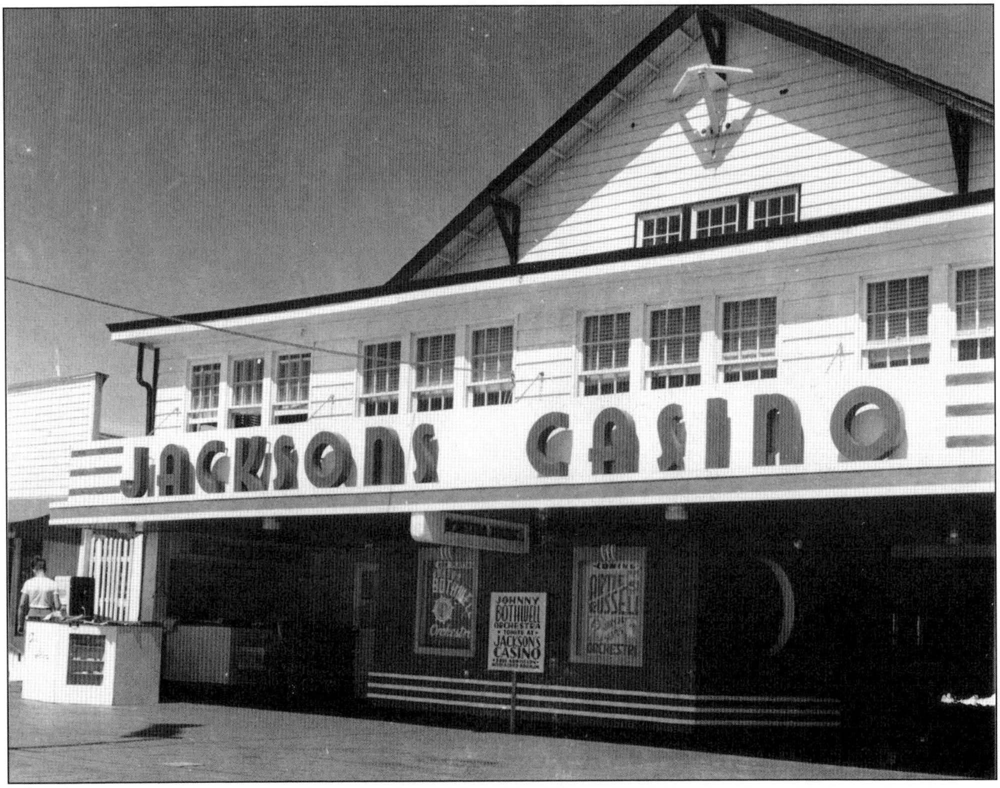

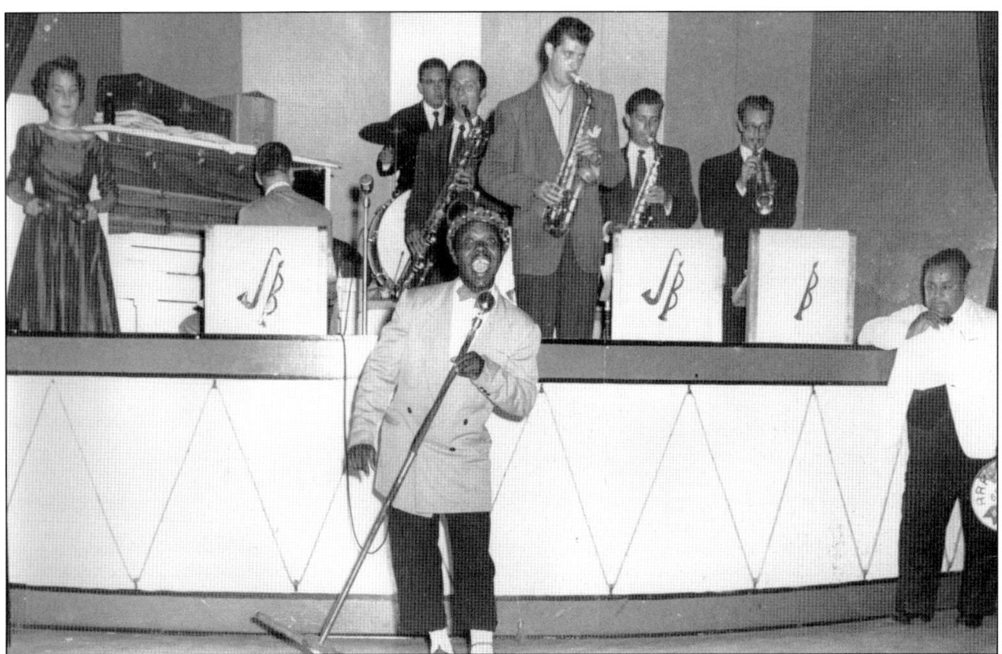

The 1940s was the era of gambling in Ocean City. Slot machines were in almost every hotel lobby, nightclub, restaurant, and bar; many existed to provide owners with additional revenue due to wartime rationing and price freezes on prepared restaurant food and beverages. Periodic raids on hotels resulted in the seizure of slot machines, and a July 1946 raid on Rick's Raft resulted in the apprehension of over 50 patrons; nonetheless, gambling persisted. Then, when Jack Sanford Jr. became Maryland State's attorney, he began his "clean-up campaign," and by the end of 1951, slots and other gambling activities were ended throughout Worcester County. Two years later, Jackson's Casino became Ocean Casino, and after damage from the 1962 March storm, it was replaced by a masonry arcade. These two photographs show a feature act at Jackson's Casino with Bothwell's orchestra behind. (Both, courtesy of Robert S. Craig collection.)

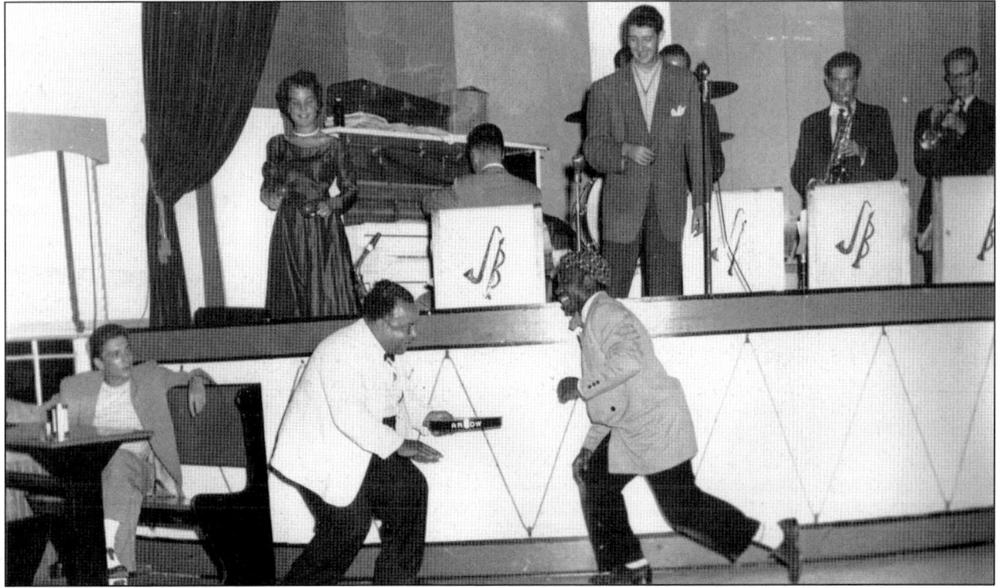

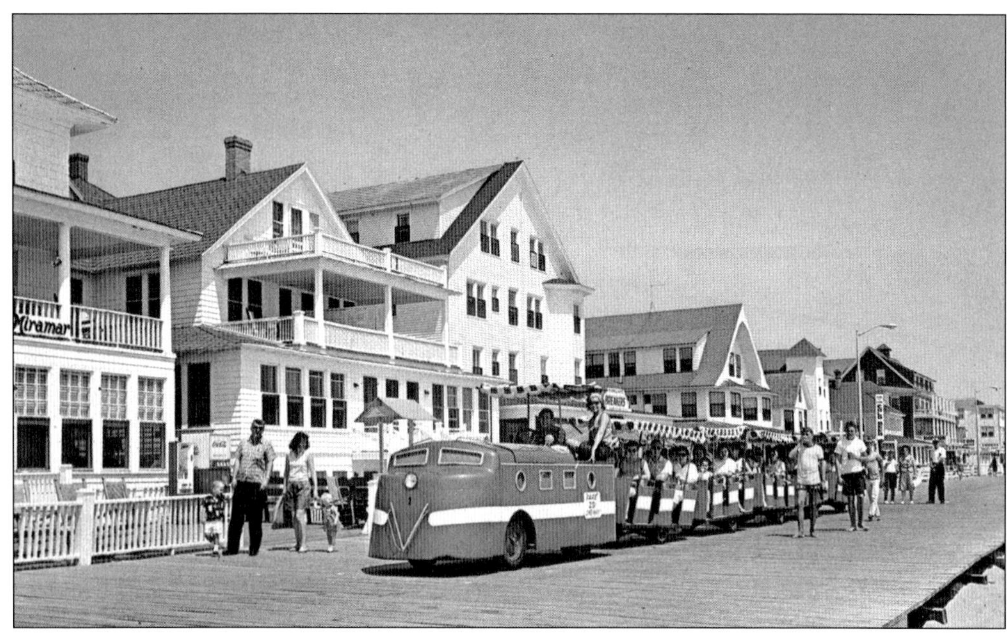

As the boardwalk lengthened, tourists sought some form of vehicular transportation between their north-end hotel or motel and the south-end amusement parks. An entrepreneur proposed operating a private boardwalk train with open passenger cars to haul visitors up and down the boardwalk. Town officials found the idea a potential source of town revenue, and since 1964, it has been the town that operates the profitable (now $4-per-one-way ride) boardwalk "tram" (although without tracks, it is not really a tram). Early styles for the engine/locomotive were streamlined; but soon, an ordinary jeep (see page 72) hauled less-stylish tethered truck platforms with benches and canopy (akin to parking-lot-to-entrance-gate transport at such venues as Six Flags or Disney). After walking miles to and among "the rides," weary tourists are glad for any ride back to their hotel or condo.

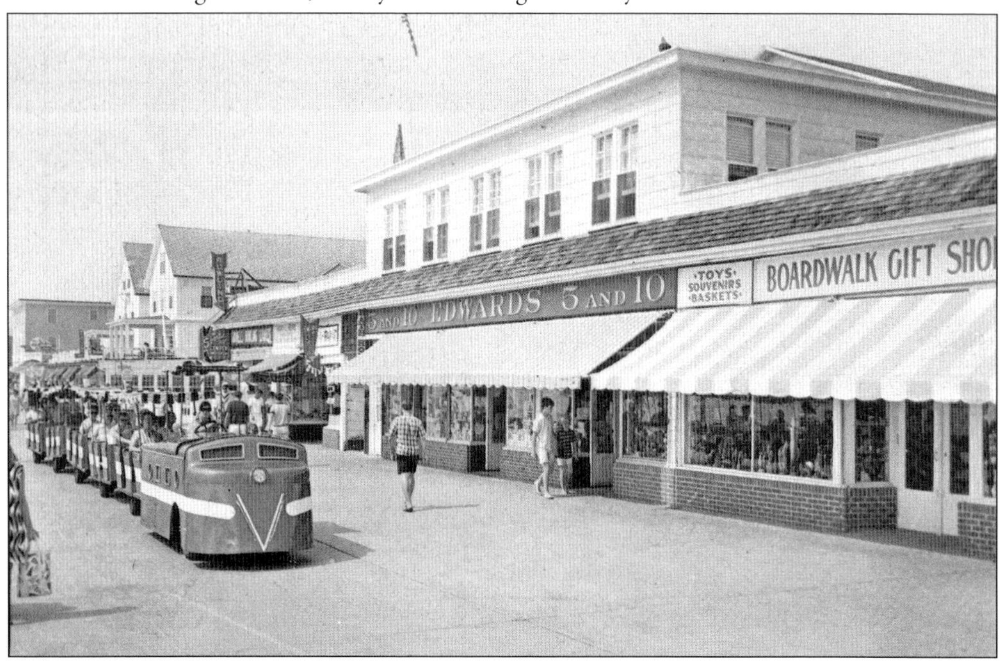

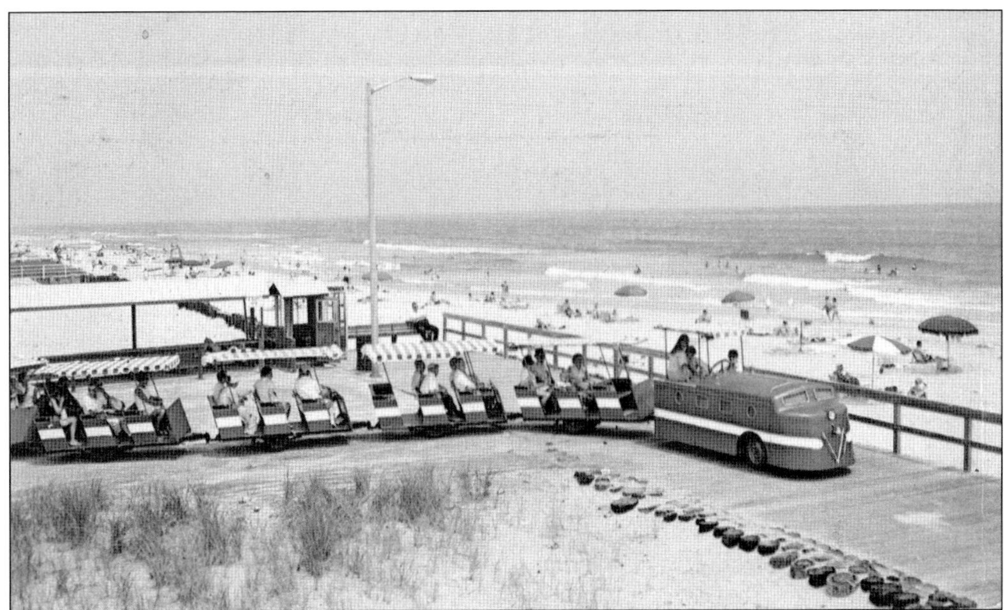

Although the wood boardwalk was structured to sustain the weight of vehicles (recognizing that fire trucks need boardwalk access to fight fires at oceanfront hotels or souvenir shops), proposals for a concrete boardwalk occasionally arise. Particularly heavy usage from larger crowds in the "amusements" (south) section of the boardwalk, prompted city officials to replace some sections of the south boardwalk with concrete. It was not a well-received gesture, so it was subsequently replaced by wood. Trams now leave the inlet tram station traveling along the inlet parking lot, turn east around part of the pier rides and across the pier, returning back to the boardwalk where a concrete tramway was installed along the beach side of the boardwalk between the pier and Fourth Street. North of Fourth to Twenty-seventh Street, the tram shares the wood boardwalk with pedestrians.

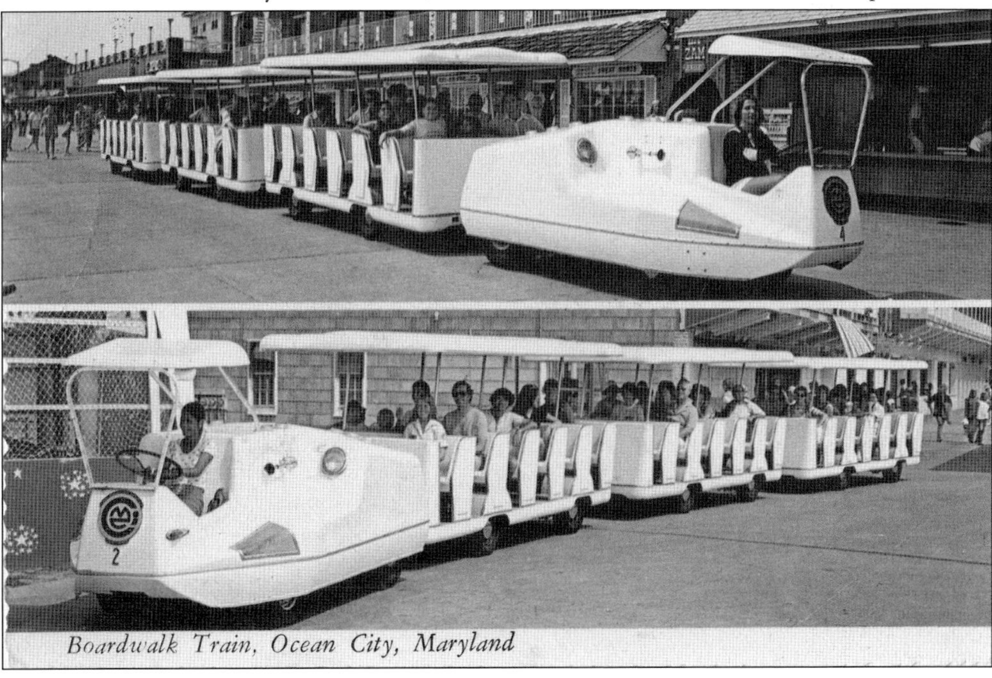

Boardwalk Train, Ocean City, Maryland

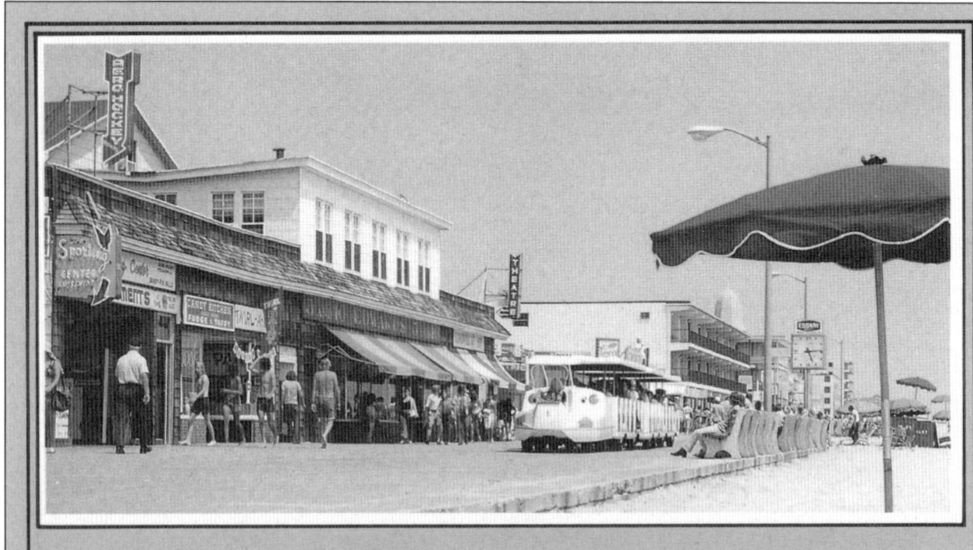

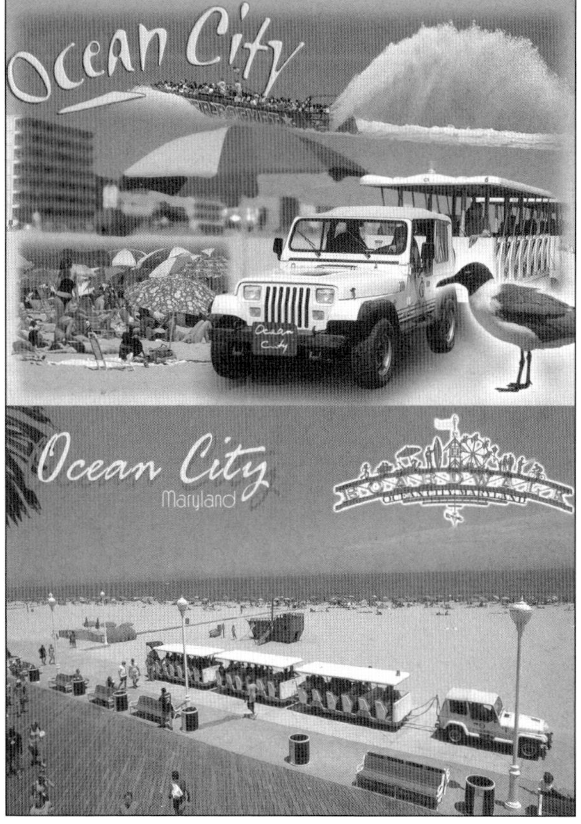

The traditional wood boardwalk, whose yellow pine decking's life expectancy is 10 years, takes additional beating from annual "Cruisin'" [classic car] boardwalk parades, as well as from the summerlong boardwalk tram traffic in which jeeps pull three carriages, each tram load carrying some 70 passengers. In 2010–2011, and again in 2021–2022, a complete redecking of the boardwalk was undertaken. The 2010 project raised the issue of possibly forming a center lane in concrete (either plain or stamped to simulate wood) for the entire length of the boardwalk in order to accommodate vehicular traffic. Although citizen objections prompted city council to reject concrete surfaces, a concrete substructure was approved for below-deck support posts long-needing replacement. The most recent 2021–2022 resurfacing remained all wood, with geometric wood patterns marking cross streets, and angle boards forming herringbone patterns throughout the boardwalk's length.

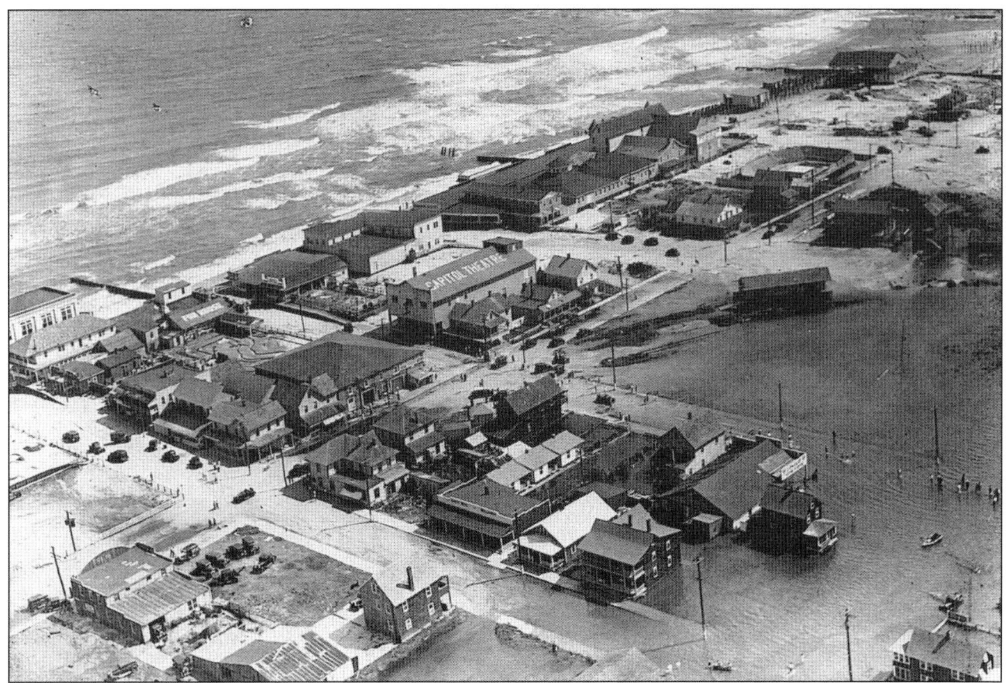

Storms have wreaked havoc on the boardwalk on more than one occasion. The August 1933 storm that cut through the inlet flooded large portions of Ocean City. The bottom-right corner of the above image shows bay water overflowing onto Wicomico and Worcester Streets. The angled building overlooking the flood waters is the railroad terminal. At the top of the image are pilings of the destroyed boardwalk at Windsor Resort.

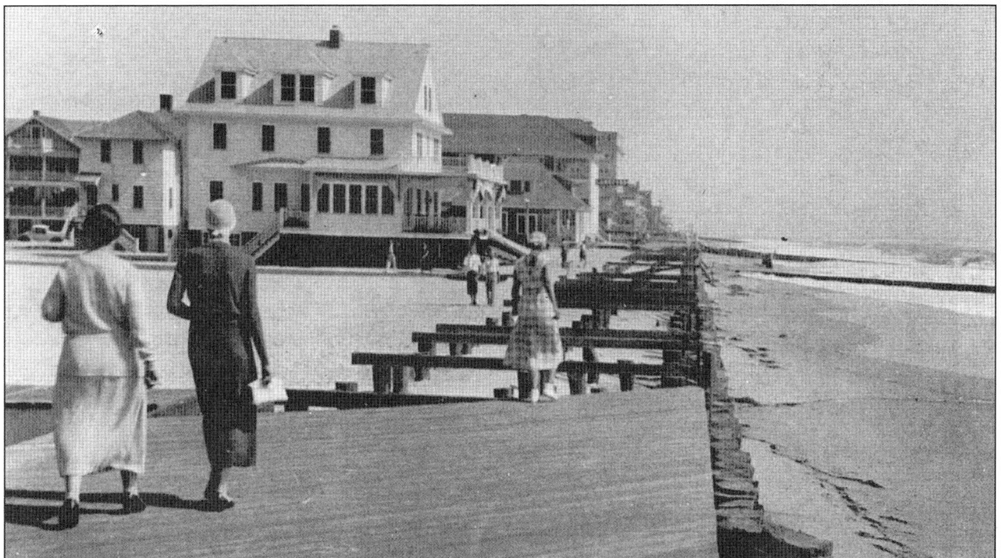

1933 storm surf detached the boardwalk's surface planks in large sections throughout its length, leaving only the sub-framing, support posts, and pilings along the east edge. The foreground boards are intact in front of the Majestic Hotel. The Chew House on the corner of Surf Avenue is prominent (the 1945 residence beyond [today containing Malibus] was not yet built). Beyond the (now razed) hipped-roof cottage is the columned Lankford Hotel.

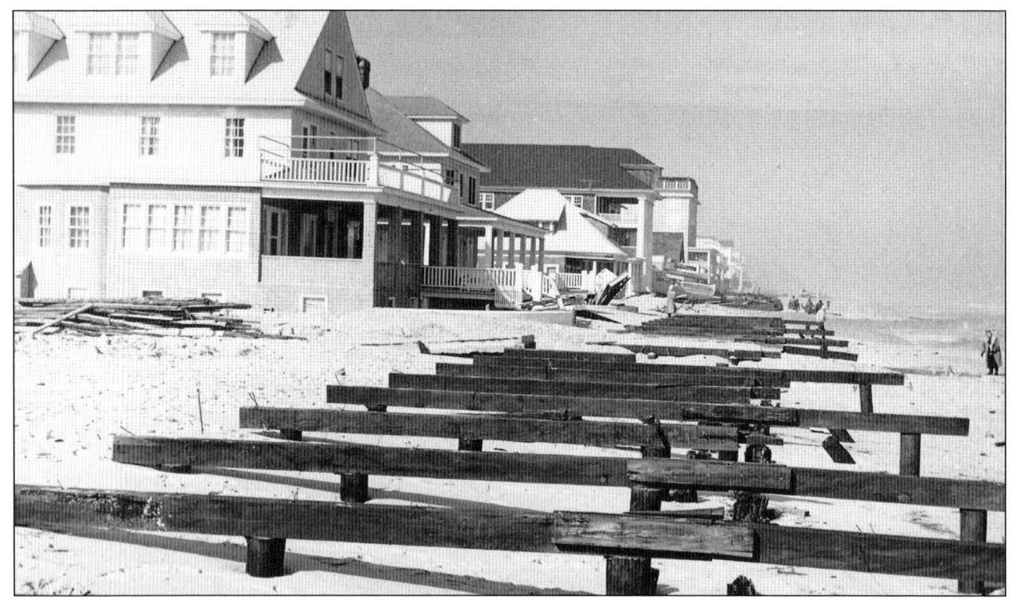

In the same view as the below image on page 73, the boardwalk at Surf Avenue is again ripped apart by the "Ash Wednesday" March 1962 northeaster, the worst storm to hit Ocean City in three decades. The row of buildings in the view above includes the pre-1929 Chew House; the 1945 residence, which would house Malibu's Surf Shop two decades later; a cottage, which was later raised for the expansion of the Lankford Hotel; the columned 1924 Lankford; the gabled Ocean Casino (formerly Jackson's; see pages 68-69); and the 1931 George Washington Hotel. A closer view of boardwalk damage at the latter two sites is below. At the far right of this image, sand is piled up blocking view of additional boardwalk damage farther north. Everywhere storm surf pushed beach sand into the lower levels of hotels and onto back streets.

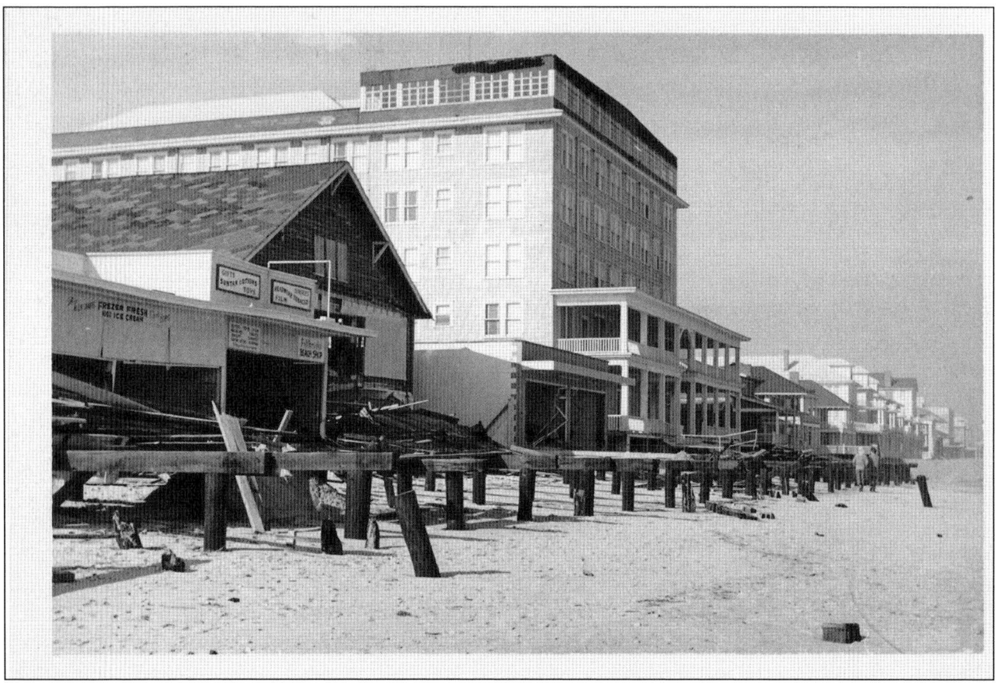

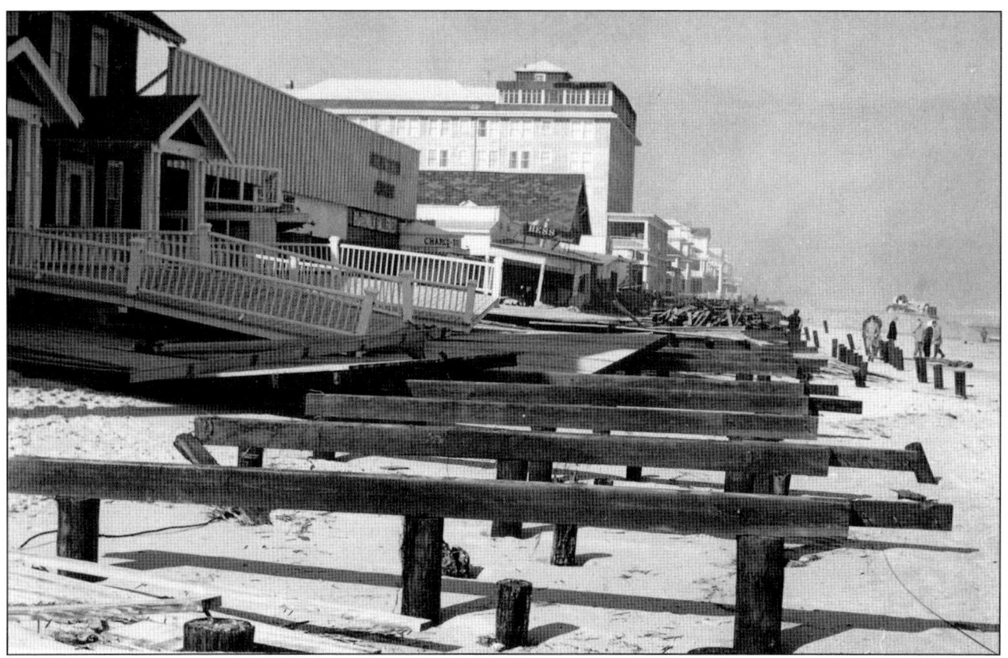

High waves pushed a large section of the boardwalk decking under the entry porches at Ayresbilt and filled the undercroft of the Lankford Hotel with sand. Just days earlier, Betty and Warren Frame had acquired both buildings, the hotel built 38 years earlier by Betty's aunt Mary Quillen. Betty's mother, Elizabeth Ayres (later Swindler), operated the town's prominent rental real estate business, Ayres Realty, from offices within the Ayresbilt apartments.

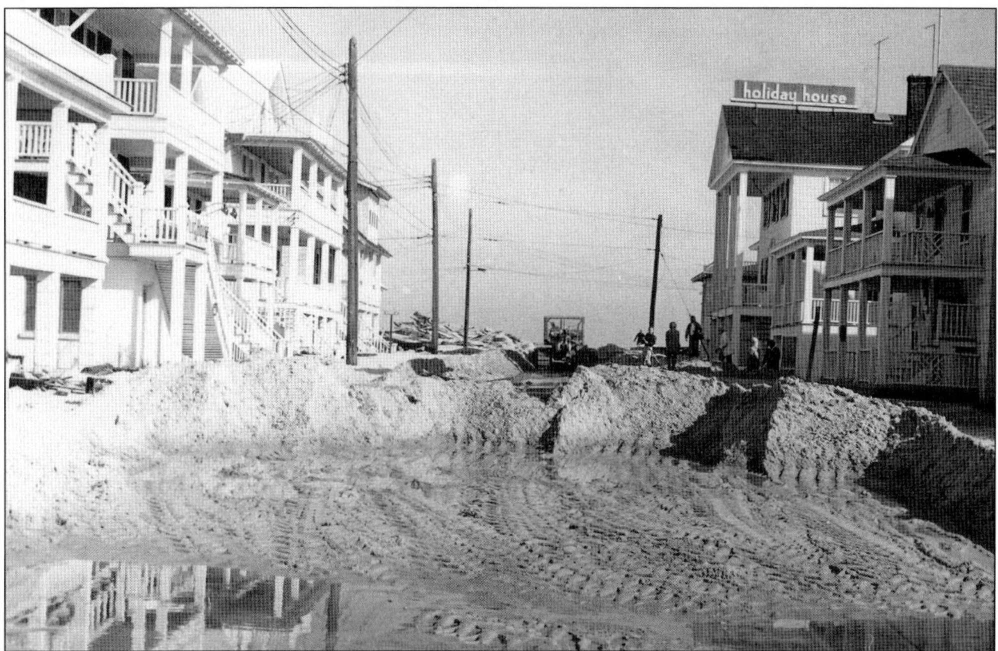

Around the corner from the Lankford and Ayresbilt, sand is being removed from Eighth Street, which (like cross streets throughout town) was covered in beach sand pushed across the island by storm surf. Debris from the damaged boardwalk and building fronts is visible piled high at the end of the street.

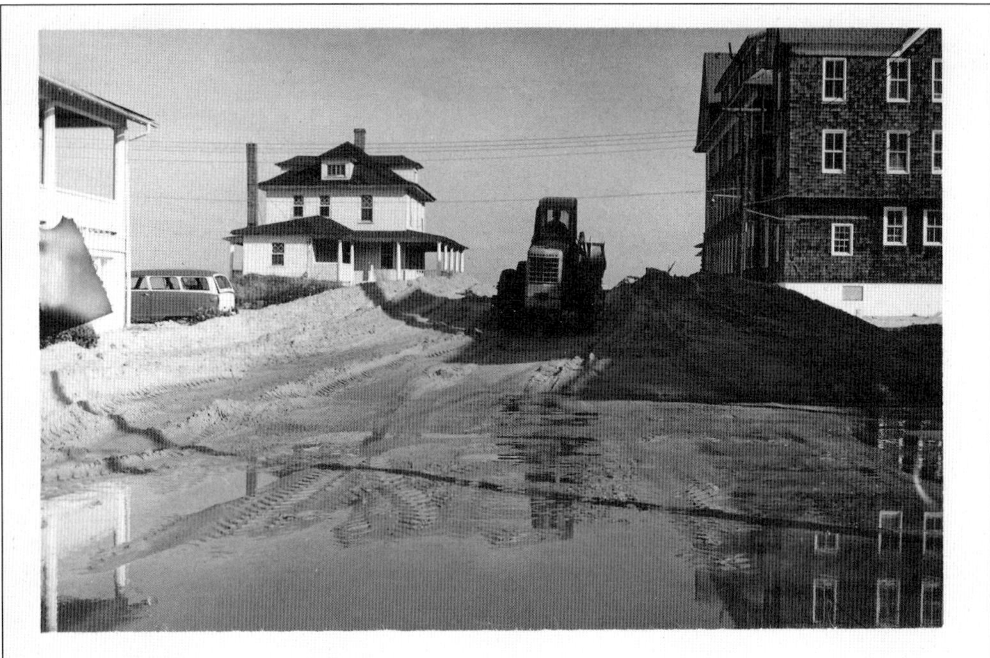

Views of Fourth Street and the boardwalk in front of the Shoreham Hotel, four blocks south of the Lankford, show similar damage and clean-up effort. Even the wide beach in front of the Atlantic Hotel downtown shifted to cover the boardwalk and blow into the hotel. It has been said of the 1962 storm that had the northeast wind not changed by the next high tide, much of the barrier island and its resort buildings would have been washed away. When Hurricane Gloria swept past Ocean City in 1985, the boardwalk was damaged again. Citizens continue to support rebuilding in traditional timber, recognizing the iconic structure as one of the town's most important tourist attraction.

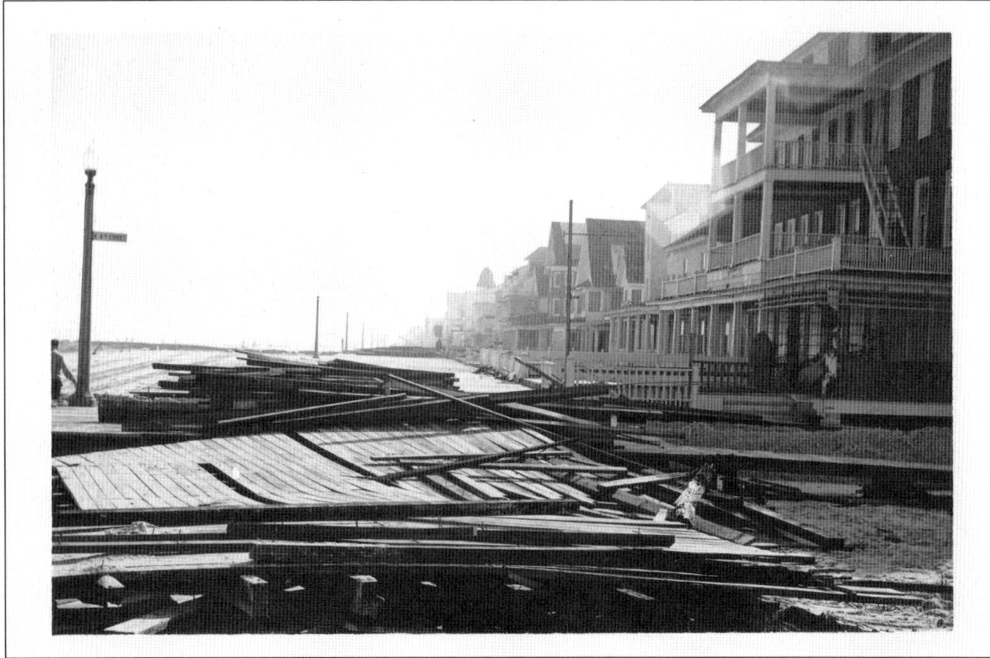

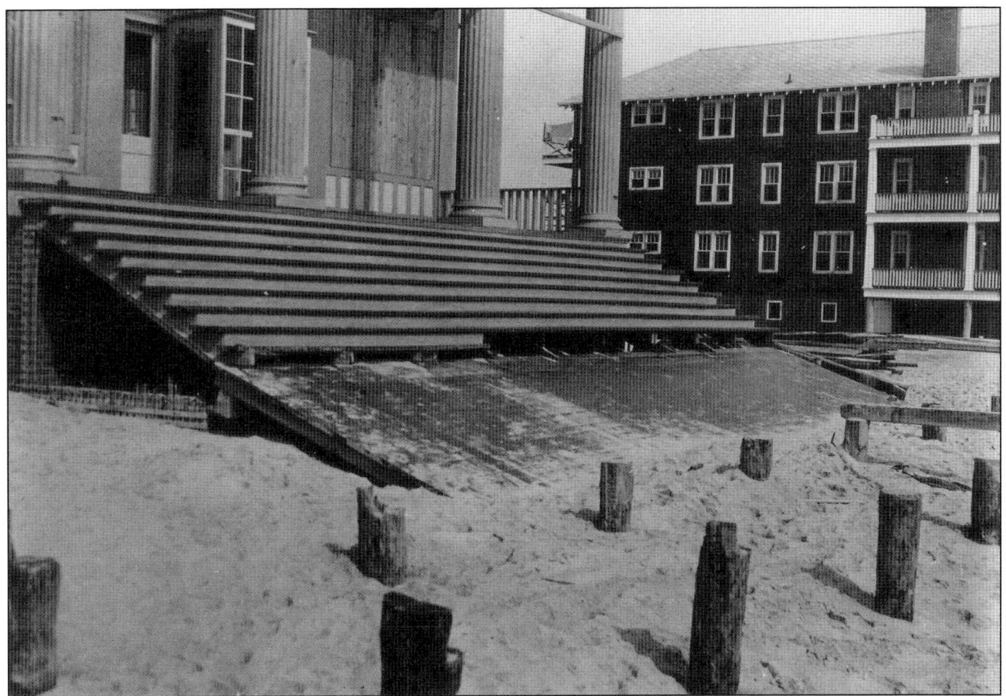

Boardwalk damage in 1962 in front of the Stephen Decatur Hotel on the boardwalk at Twelfth Street shows the platform connecting the hotel's porch stairs to the boardwalk has collapsed and the boardwalk's timber structural framing and surface boards are missing, leaving only the support posts. The postcard below, manufactured in 1940 but postmarked in 1963, appears to be mailed to show what the scene used to look like, inasmuch as the intact boardwalk was destroyed in the March storm the previous year. On the other hand, demands of seasonal businesses encouraged the boardwalk's rapid rebuilding.

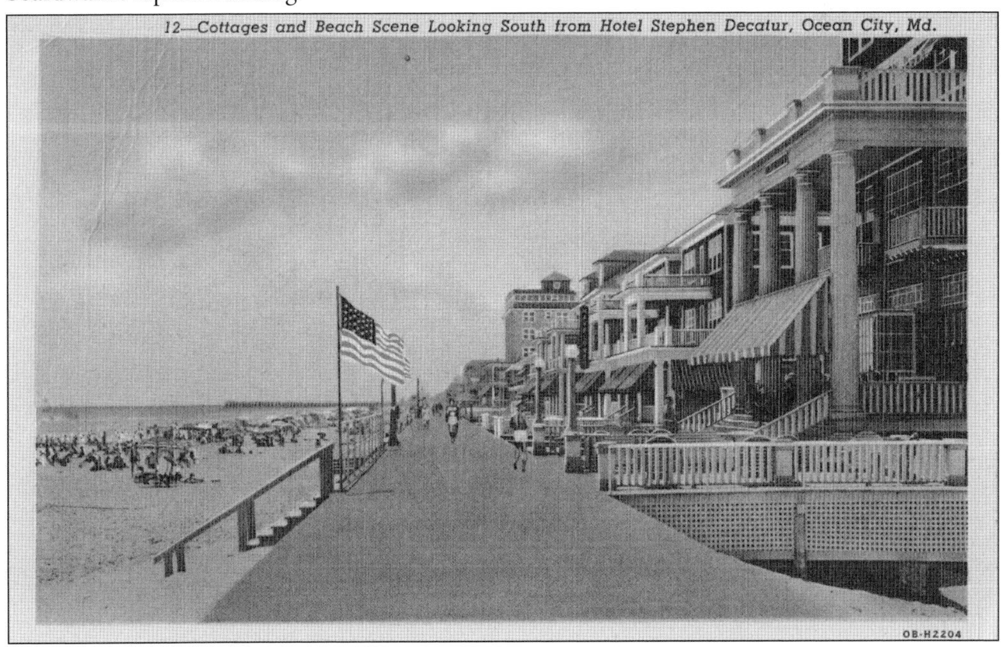

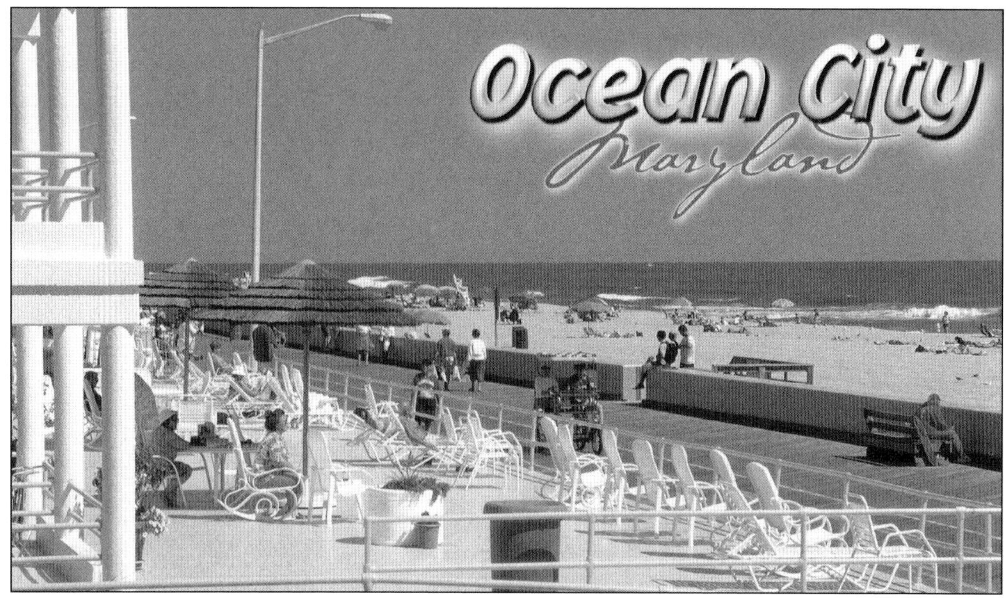

Despite its periodic destruction, rebuilding, and regular repair demands, the boardwalk remains Ocean City's well-established and popular promenade. It has always been a recognized locale for people watching. The hotel observation porch tradition continued in the open forecourt at the 1956 Santa Maria Motel (above). Proper dress on the boardwalk was expected throughout past decades (see page 42); although today, any degree of dress or undress appears to be tolerated. Periodically, city ordinances set standards, requiring (during the 1950s and 1960s, for instance) that even men wear shirts covering upper torso whenever west of the public beach (that is on the boardwalk or on public streets). The two lads in bathing trunks (and socks and shoes) stepping onto the boardwalk bare chested in the 1953 postcard below would be breaking the law during the decades when this ordinance was in effect.

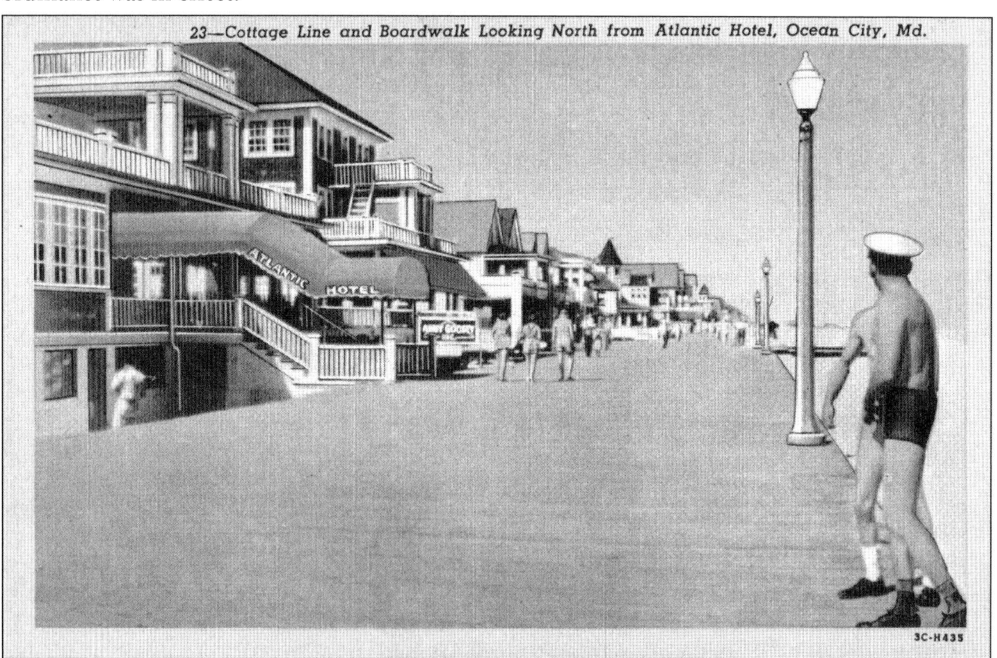

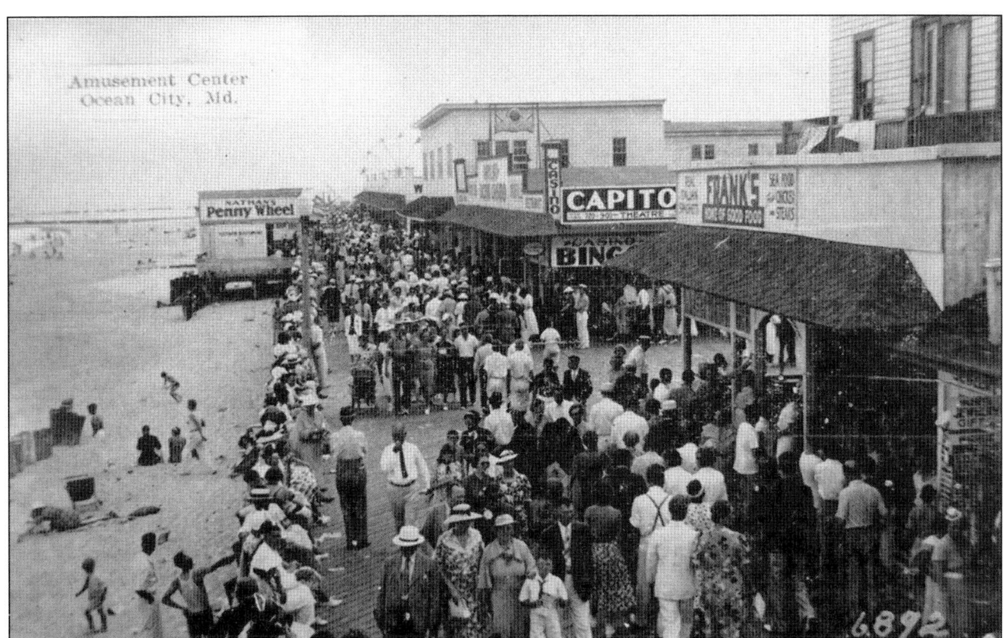

From the earliest era when hundreds of visitors crowded the amusement end of the boardwalk (above) to countless Fourth of July weekends during subsequent years (the detail below is from a postcard postmarked July 1926), when the boardwalk was mobbed with ladies in long dresses, gentlemen in coats and ties, and both wearing fashionable hats, the boardwalk was full of vacationers looking out to the bathers and ocean scenery, chatting in groups, or merely "strolling the boards." This was the place to be, and town businessmen continued to support the costs of installing protective pilings, maintaining the boardwalk, building connecting walkways, and rebuilding any of this timber hardscape after storms. Hotels and summer cottages filled every available lot along the promenade, and then, they were converted to retail use for beach clothing stores, souvenir shops, restaurants, bars, and lately, tattoo and piercing emporiums.

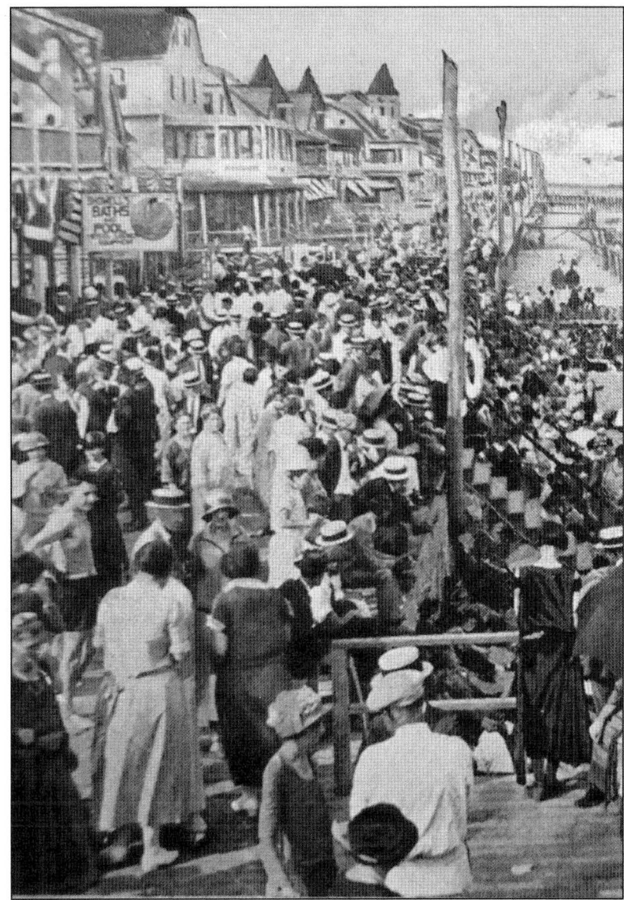

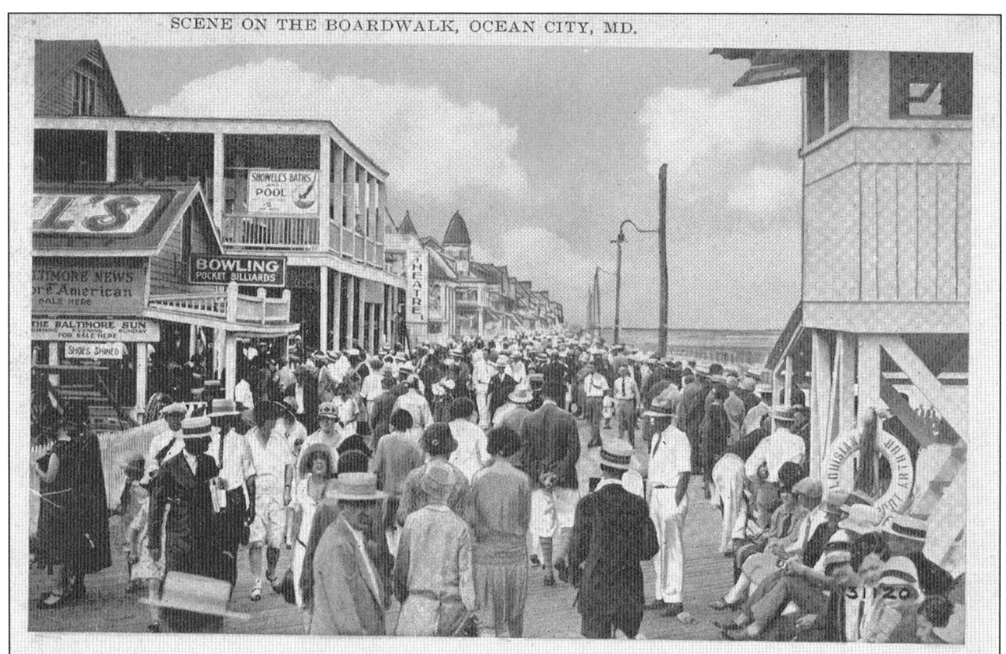

The postcard above, postmarked 1929, shows the boardwalk north of the original town plat, which is north of the Coast Guard station looking toward Showell's Theatre sign at North Division Street. The sharp linear perspective of the image focuses the view on the unending crowds extending to vanishing point. Bicycle rental and boardwalk bicycle rides (below) have become popular in recent years. Due to crowds of boardwalk-strolling tourists, bicycle riding on the boardwalk was allowed daily only before 10:00 a.m. During the 1950s, the only man allowed to bicycle on the boardwalk after 10:00 a.m. was Robert S. Craig, captain of the beach patrol, who pedaled his "official" beach patrol bike the length of the boardwalk to check on his lifeguards. With their eyes watching the ocean, his charges never knew when the captain was monitoring them from the boardwalk behind.

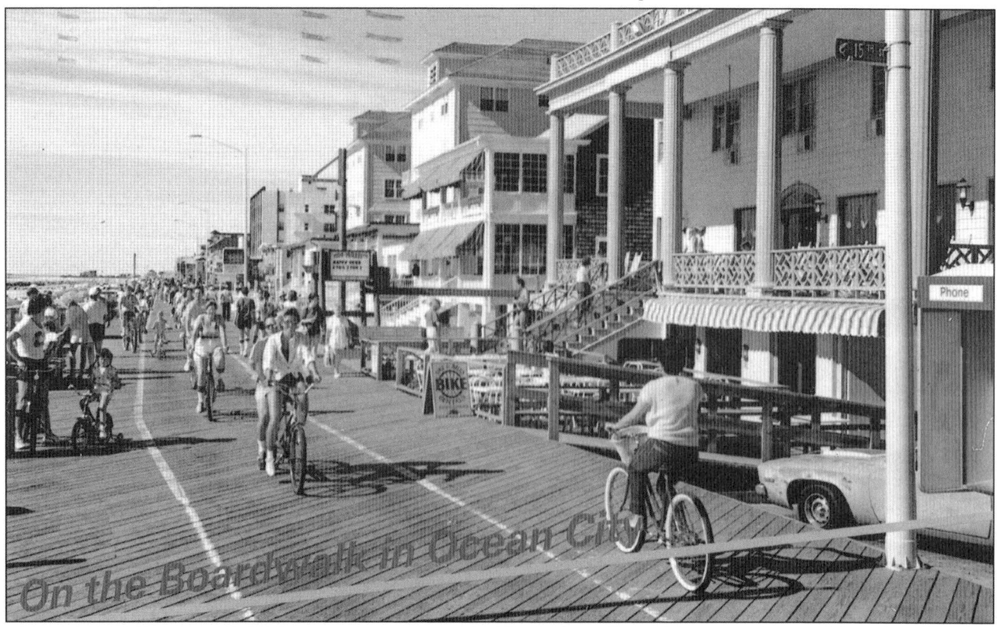

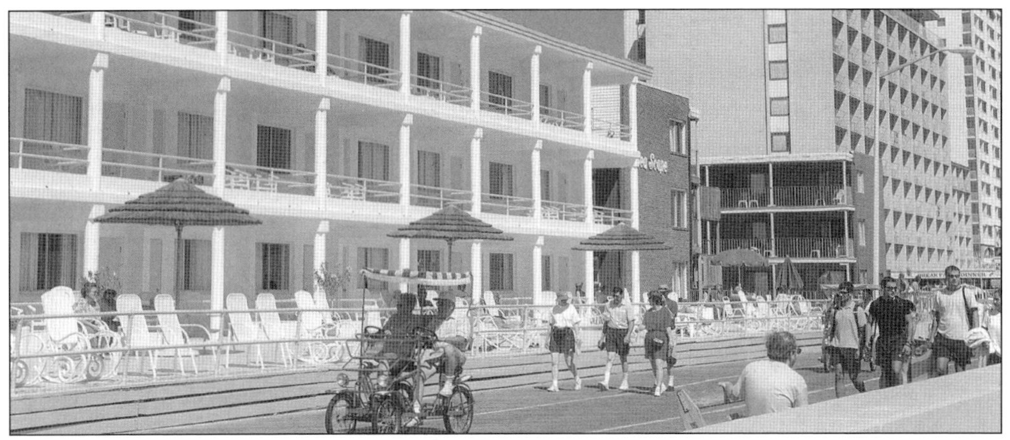

Boardwalk bicycling took many forms and attracted all ages. For the sedate cyclist, the two-seated surrey bike (shown above in a postcard image by Kevin N. Moore) was more popular than the tandem "bicycle built for two," in which a second seat was behind the main pedaler. Moreover, family quadricycles with two benches, which allowed for four riders, were also available to rent. Red-and-white-striped waterproof canvas tops were traditional. R.C. Pulling's postcard (below) shows the early morning boardwalk (from a later decade but the same view as page 77 below) and features five surrey bikes, including family surreys for four, and lone riders on traditional bicycles, but few pedestrians. During these pre-10:00 a.m. hours, the boardwalk is the domain of cyclists and pedestrians must beware and remain watchful of teenaged bike-trick performers and speed racers worthy of the Tour de France.

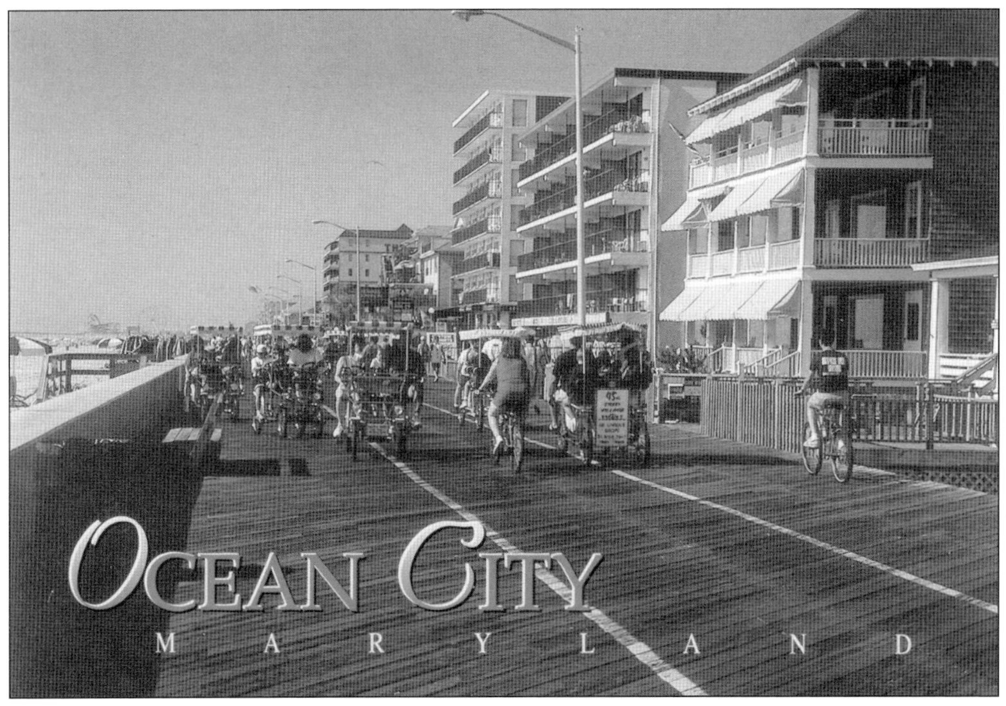

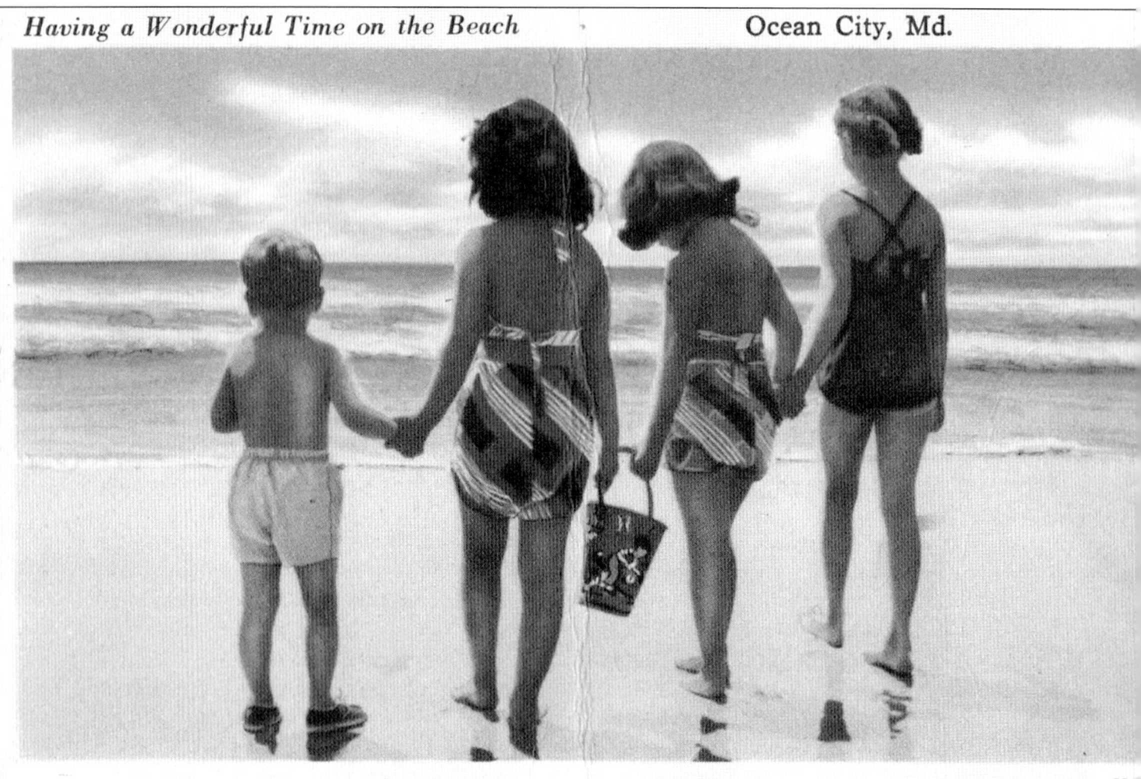

The beach is especially for children. A child with a sand bucket and shovel, a calm sea at low tide, a sun-filled summer day, and vacation time—what could be better? Ocean City has prided itself as a family resort, with an enviable water safety record that is the pride of its almost century-old Ocean City Beach Patrol. Tourists flock here for many reasons—the boardwalk, the amusement parks, sailing, clamming, or fishing on the bay—but the chief attraction is the beach itself. Over the years, thousands of young children making castles in the sand, think so. It is the beach that draws people to Ocean City.

Three

Beach

The Ocean City beach has been shaped by changing conditions over the centuries that have built up barrier islands along the Atlantic coast, then altered the coastline by storm, human habitation, and architectural and urban development, and finally reshaped the coastline and beaches by efforts of reclamation and beach replenishment. When "The Ladies' Resort to the Ocean" began to emerge around the Atlantic Hotel after 1875, the beach was a narrow strip with a barrier of pilings and few jetties to trap sand and to minimize erosion while protecting the coastal edges and oceanfront architecture from tides, currents, and storm surges.

A historic alteration of the beachfront occurred in August 1933 when a storm battered the island from both sides, crashing tidal surges across the narrow beach and into the town from the east and pouring such downpours of rain over four days into the Sinepuxent Bay west of the island to fill the bay to overflowing. Baywater found an outlet in the lowlands of the fishing village south of Windsor Resort, and the 1933 storm cut a 50-foot-wide, 8-foot-deep inlet from bay to ocean, flooding the lowlands south of South Second Street and destroying the few fishing shanties, shacks, and cottages in its way. The fishing camps were literally erased from the landscape by the storm, separating the south end of town from what is now known as Assateague Island.

In order to stabilize and preserve the inlet, the federal government and the State of Maryland partnered in the building of two stone jetties, one on each side of the cut. Since dredged to 10 feet or more in depth, the inlet provided a highly desirable ocean access to the coastal bays, where docks and harbors soon developed. On the beachfront, coastal sand that drifted south as part of the natural process of the migratory barrier island began filling in behind the new stone jetty at the south end of Ocean City, widening the white, sandy beach.

When Hurricane Gloria (1985) eroded the beach, tore up the boardwalk, and moved tons of sand onto the town's streets, the Atlantic Coast of Maryland Shoreline (a.k.a. Storm) Protection Project, coordinated with the Army Corps of Engineers, introduced a program of beach replenishment and maintenance, which included (beyond the north end of the boardwalk) the dunes, dunes crossovers, dune planting, and fencing. Dredging operations would be repeated approximately every four years with an estimated average of 700,000 cubic yards of sand to be moved from the Weaver Shoal, which is located more than three miles from the coast of Ocean City on the Outer Continental Shelf. The first phase, completed in 1988, pumped 2.3 million cubic yards of sand along the beach berm between Third and 146th Street. In the second phase, completed in 1992, the beach berm was expanded, and 3.6 million cubic yards of sand were dredged to construct a 6.9-mile-long dune from Twenty-seventh Street (end of the boardwalk) to 146th Street, while along the boardwalk itself, north of Fourth Street, a 1.5-mile, steel-and-concrete seawall was constructed.

Then, in 1994, the State of Maryland, Worcester County, and Ocean City in partnership with the Army Corps of Engineers accepted responsibility for future maintenance of the completed Atlantic Coast of Maryland Shoreline/Storm Protection Project, in both phases, including periodic beach replenishment, maintenance of dunes, dunes crossings, planting, and fencing, as well as the seawall. Today, a long, wide, flat beach berm is maintained to seven feet above mean high tide, backstopped by the concrete-and-steel bulkhead along the boardwalk, and by the sand dunes north of the boardwalk extending to the Maryland-Delaware state line.

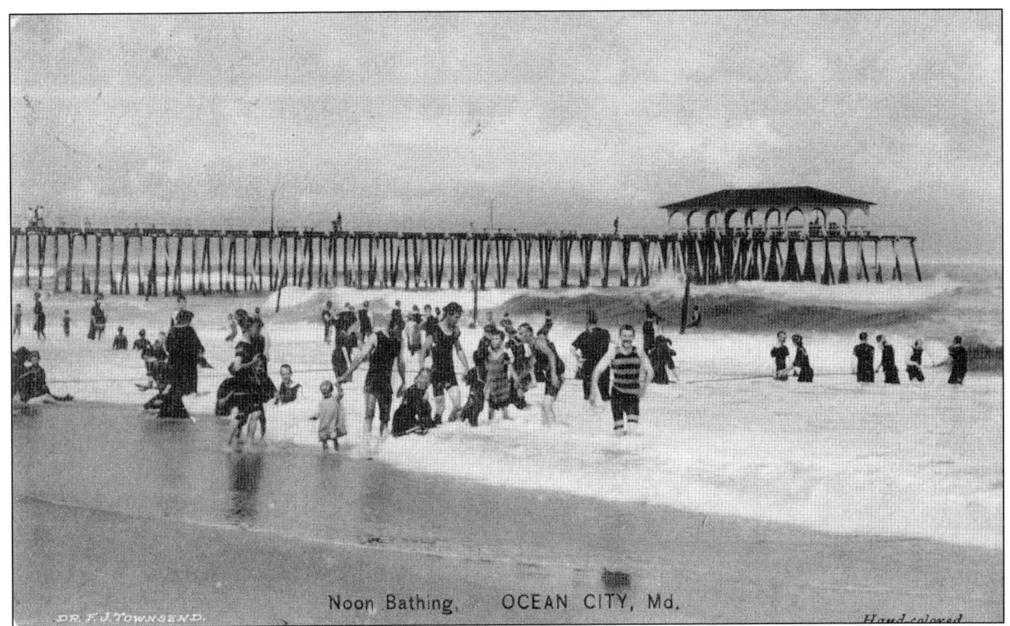

An early view of "noon bathing" just south of the pier shows bathers holding a safety rope, one of several that have been strung from the boardwalk pilings to posts along the shore break. Vacationers who cannot swim or who lack confidence in the water can still engage in "fanny dipping" while clinging to the safety rope. At the right edge of this hand-colored Frank Townsend postcard view (above), postmarked 1909, are several bathers, holding the rope and edging toward the breaking surf. In the c. 1926 white-border view of a calmer sea at low tide (below), the rope is visible from the vantage point of the pier, stretching from the boardwalk to a post just beyond the photograph's left edge. In this pre-inlet view of the very narrow south beach, there is almost no dry sand for sunbathing.

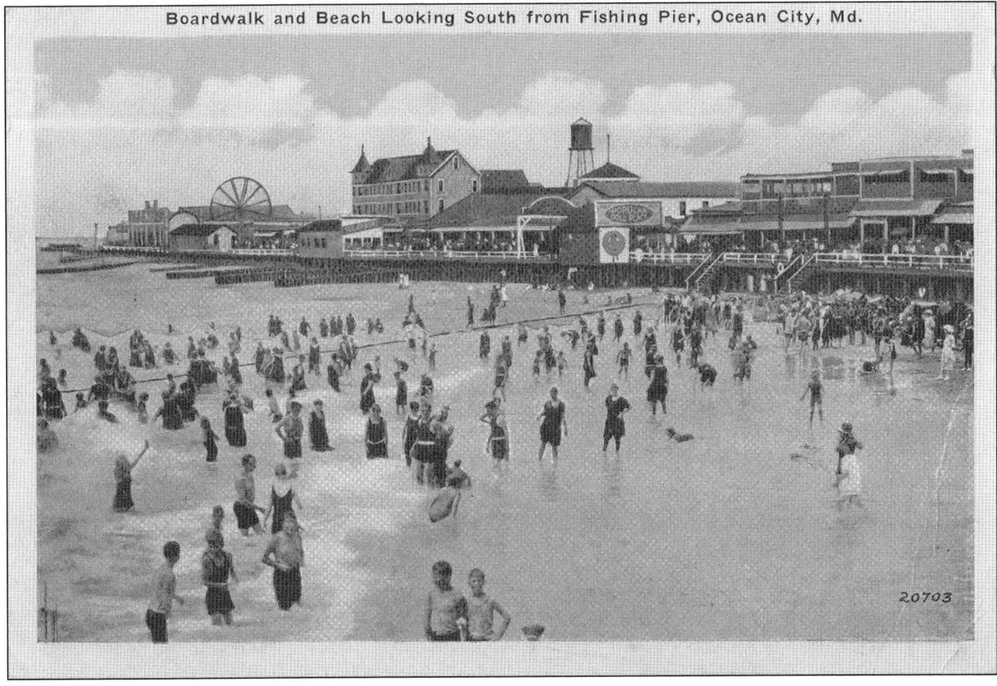

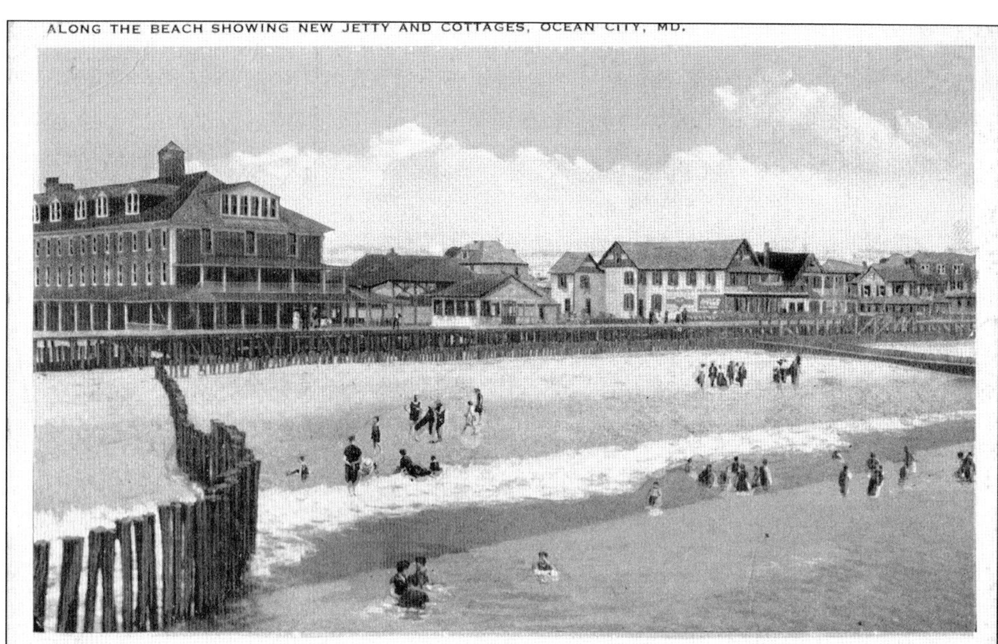

During the 1920s, the beach was narrow and at a level several feet below the boardwalk. Pilings (posts hammered deep into the sand) were aligned as a barrier to prevent high tides and storm surf pushing debris and tons of sand through the boardwalk substructure and into the undercroft of oceanfront hotels and cottages. This postcard shows the Atlantic Hotel and a new jetty intended to build up its beach.

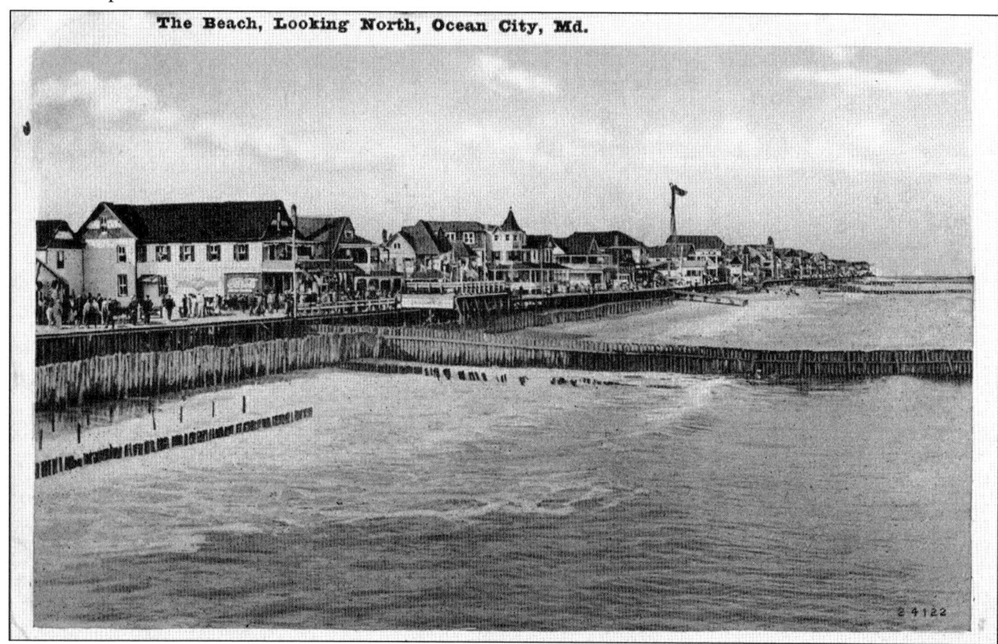

Looking farther north along this narrow beachfront, pilings, jetties, and a high boardwalk characterize the years before the August 1933 storm that formed the inlet. With the new rock jetty at the inlet, serving as a dam against which the beach to its north built up and grew wider, these pilings and jetties were eventually buried beneath the sand as the beach sand rose to the height of the boardwalk.

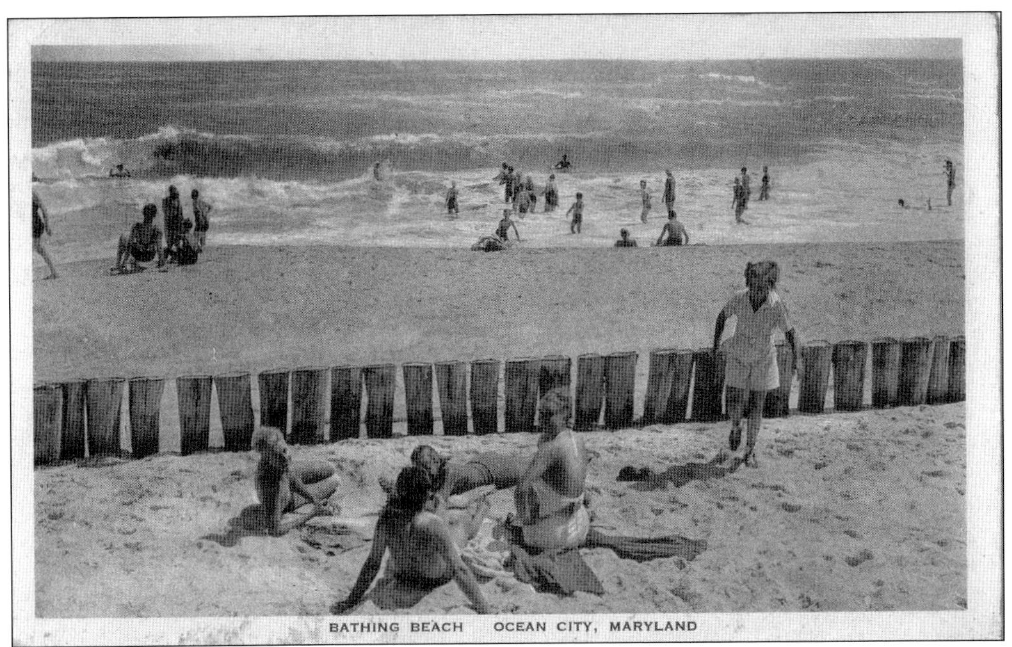

In the 1936-postmarked card (above) and the 1939-postmarked card (below), pilings are still visible but exposure is less, and more beach sand has been built up. The exposed jetties remain dominant features along the late-1930s through 1950s oceanfront, trapping and building up more and more sand. But just as the jetties' west ends are invisible (below), buried in the sand (the buried jetties actually stretch back to beyond the boardwalk), so by the 1960s, the entire jetty would be below built-up sand levels. Both pilings and jetties in the postcard view south, below, had entirely disappeared within 40 years of the forming of the inlet and construction of the massive rock jetty at its edge.

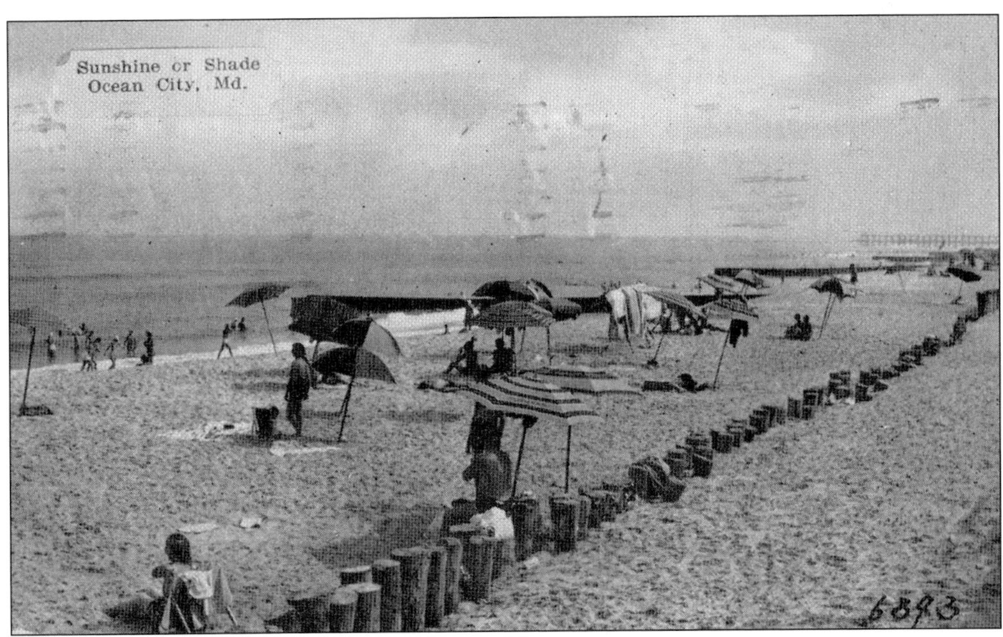

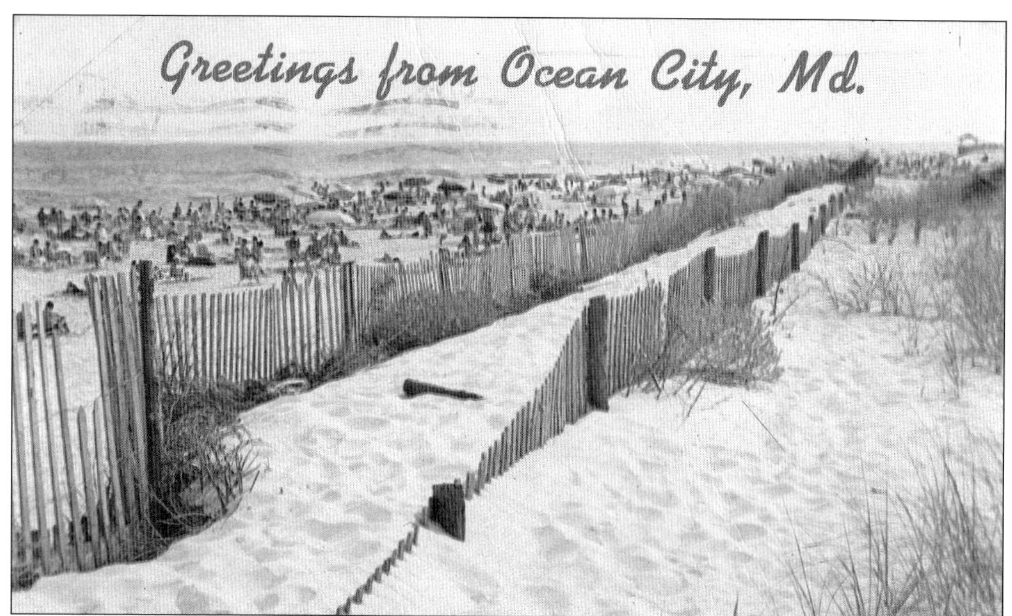

The preservation of the threatened dune line north of the boardwalk maintained a more natural setting at the northern beaches, as seen in this Tichnor Brothers card postmarked 1974. Dune fencing, natural seagrass serving to hold the dune sand in place became a backdrop for the bathing beach at the north end of the barrier island, with dune crossings regulated and a general respect for the naturel environment well established. What was a favorite locale for surfing and beach parties in the 1960s, became Condo Row by the end of the 1970s. Again, to encourage increased areas for beach use, huge rock jetties were built along the north beach. The view below of Condo Row is by Kevin N. Moore for Marketplace Publications.

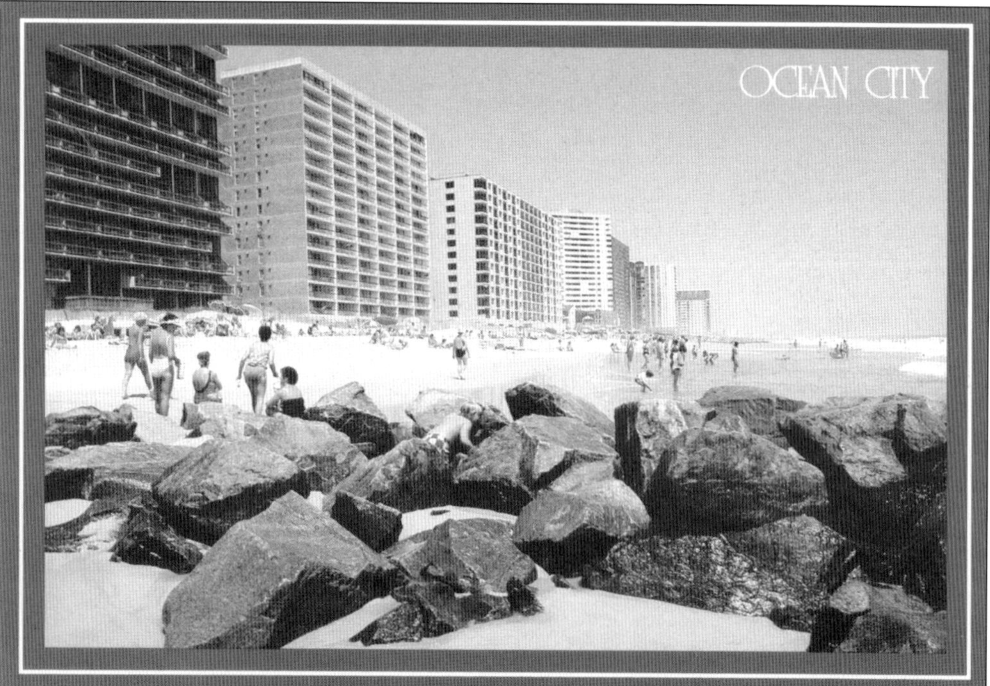

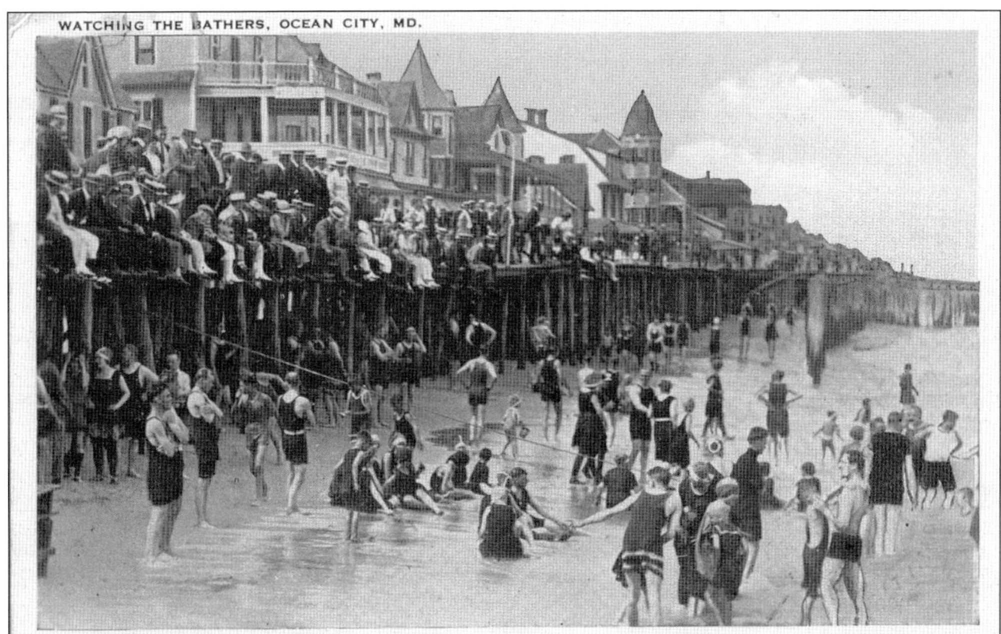

In "Watching the Bathers," a postcard postmarked 1929, the dramatic difference in level between the narrow beach and ocean and the high boardwalk provided a platform from which boardwalk pedestrians could become spectators, observing the heartier "fanny dippers" below. Note the safety line, one end tied to a boardwalk pier and the other tied to a pole near the breaking waves. Non-swimmers ventured into the surf holding this line.

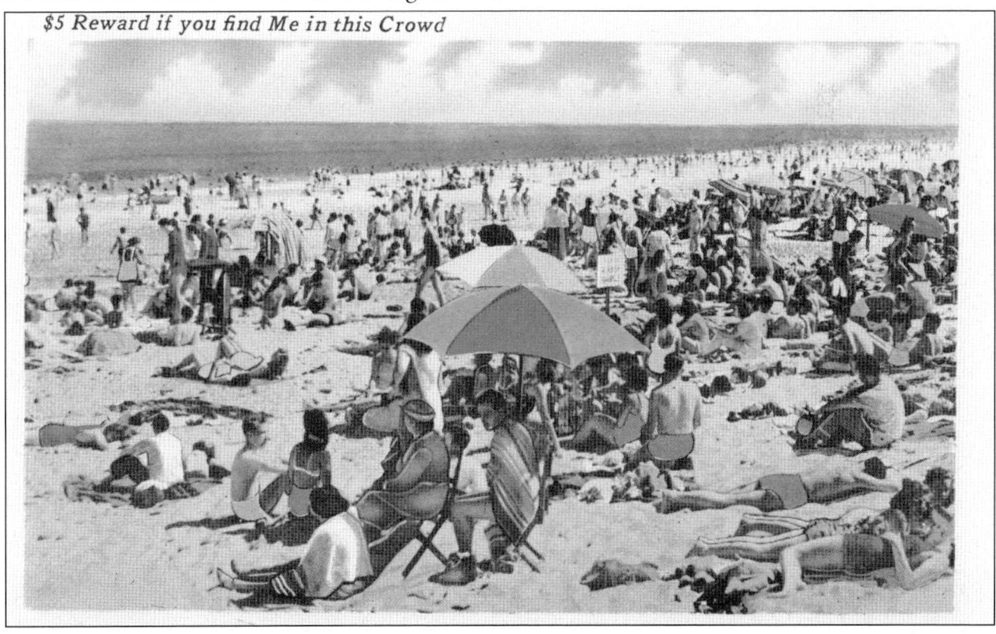

Here is another view of the crowded beach after the inlet jetty built up wider acreage of sand; it features large numbers of sun worshippers and bathers in the calm waters at low tide. The whimsical caption offers "$5 Reward if you can find Me in the Crowd," a challenge affixed to other postcard views during the period.

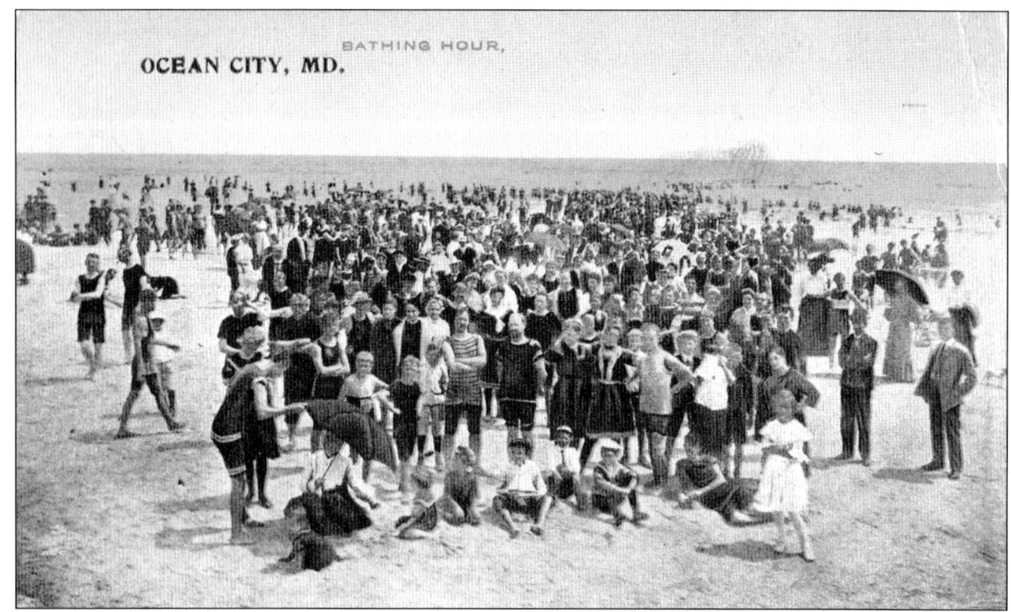

This early photograph, published by the Postal Card Distributing Co. of Atlantic City, New Jersey, has no identifying feature to specify the location along the Atlantic coast's beaches and was probably used in more than one market. Affixing the title "Bathing Hour," the publisher then stamped "Ocean City, MD," (not even aligned) below, suggesting the same scene was likely sold and relabeled anywhere from New Jersey shores to Miami.

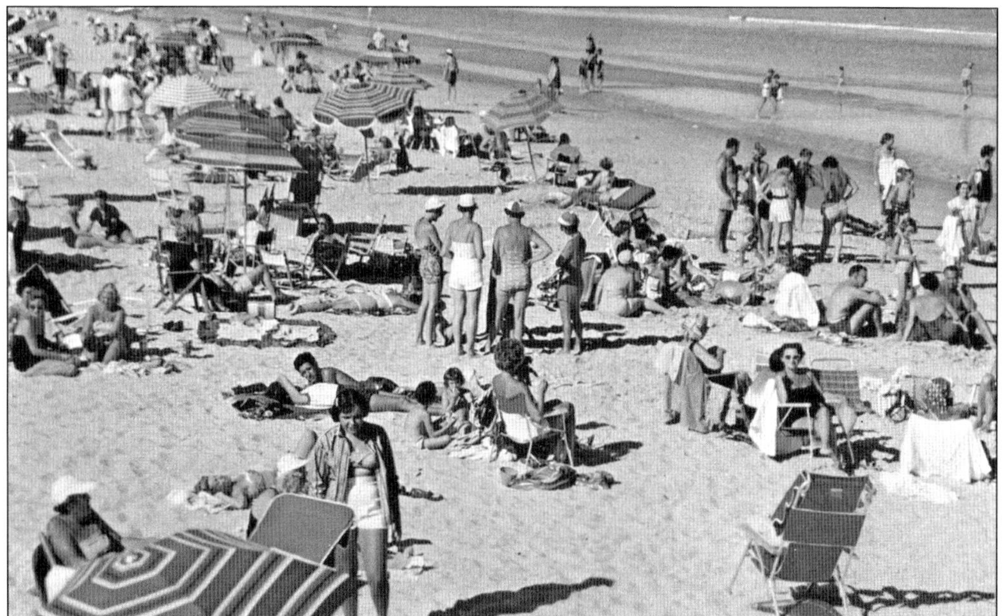
This beach scene postmarked 1958 is a typical depiction of family groups establishing their own personal beachhead on a crowded beach. Like standard bearers of old, they sink an umbrella into the sand, gather their beach equipment in and around its shadow circle, and stretch out on beach towels claiming their own turf. Swimmers walk through this maze of sand passages and reclining bodies in order to reach the ocean.

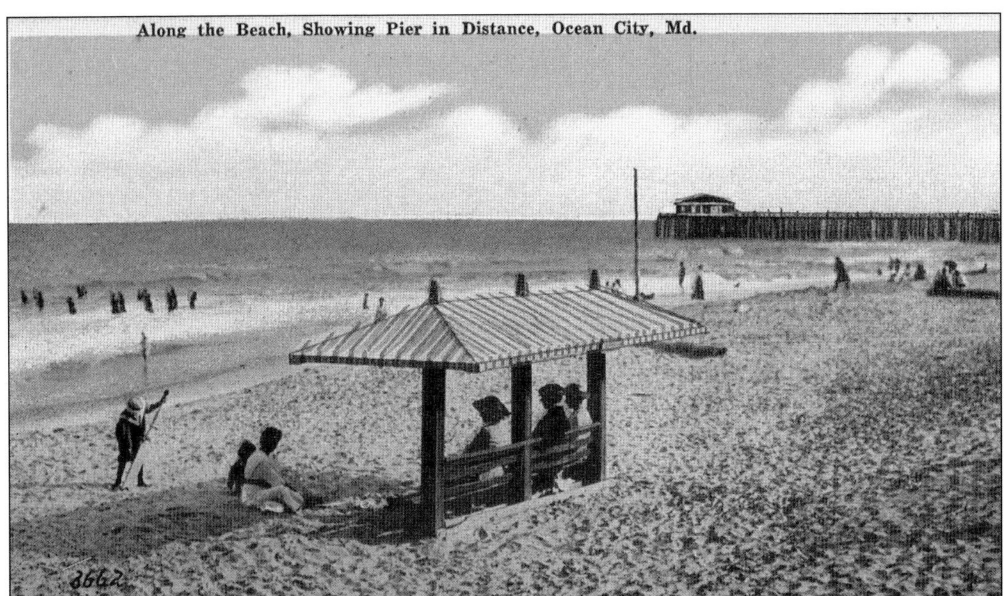

Throughout the early decades of Ocean City's development, hotels provided amenities for their guests beyond the hotel premises. Wood benches were erected along the boardwalk, a practice revived recently in the memorial benches the town sponsors. This postcard shows a wood bench with sheltering canopy (on the beach itself), more permanently planted than today's portable beach chairs, and appearing here like a bus stop, likely built by the Atlantic Hotel.

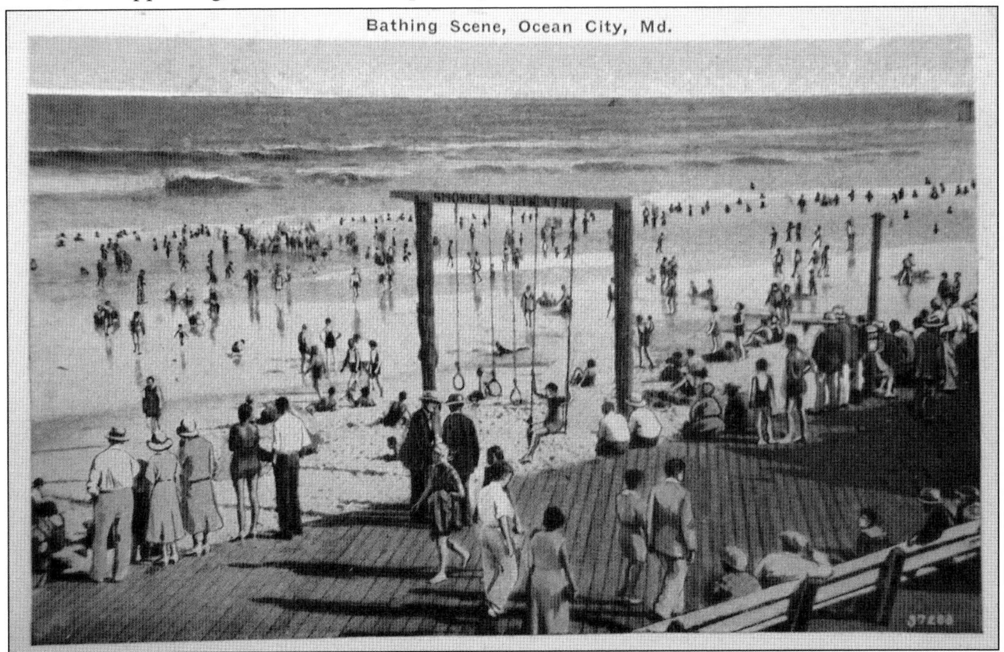

The Showell's compound (bathhouse, bowling alley, and theater) sponsored this swing and ring gymnastic set, erected on the narrow beach at North Division Street. The US Life-Saving Service, also known as the Coast Guard, station was located adjacent to Showell's, so the concentration of beachgoers and swimmers is evidenced here in the days before the 1930 establishment of the Ocean City Beach Patrol.

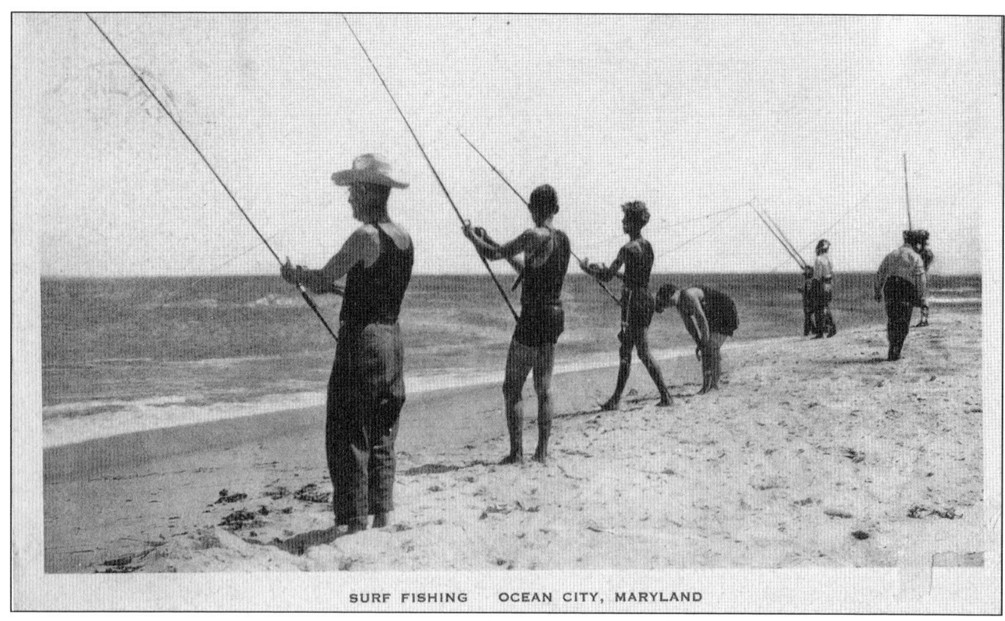

A recreational activity, which is generally prohibited on today's beach at the height of the summer, is illustrated in this postcard postmarked 1925—surf fishing. As beach usage increased at the southern end of town, northern beaches fronting the undeveloped dunes were frequent scenes of surf casters. The unwelcomed experience of parents and lifeguards trying to comfort a small child with a fish hook in his/her foot encouraged a summertime surfcasting ban.

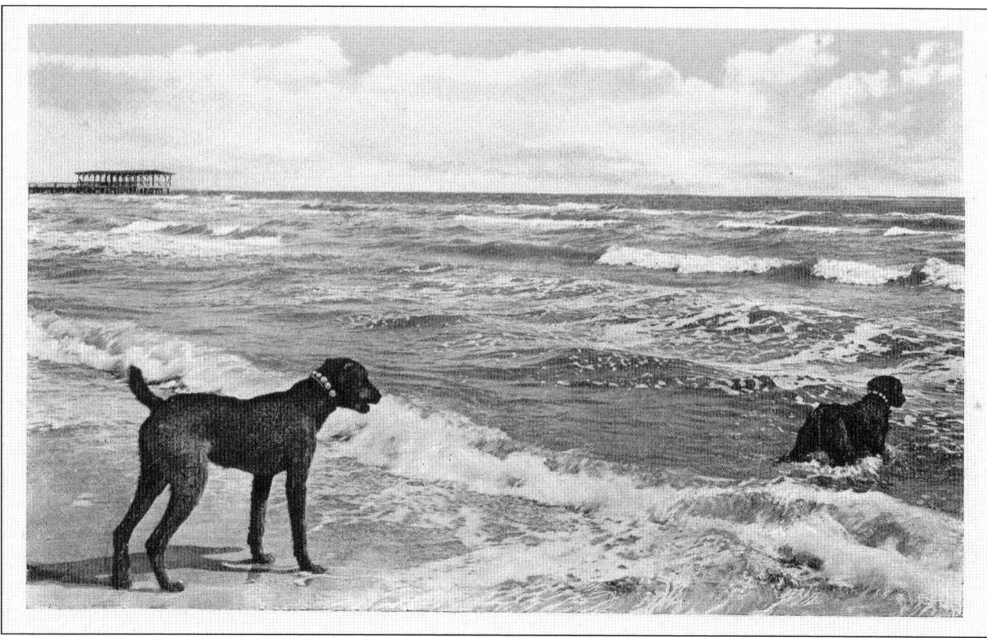

Dogs and other pets are also prohibited from the beach during the summer season by reason of what they leave behind. This idyllic Louis Kaufmann view of two dogs entering the surf appeals to dog lovers everywhere, but between May 1 and September 30, pets are banned from the town's boardwalk and beach. Year round, pets are allowed in the Assateague National Seashore Park but not on state park beaches.

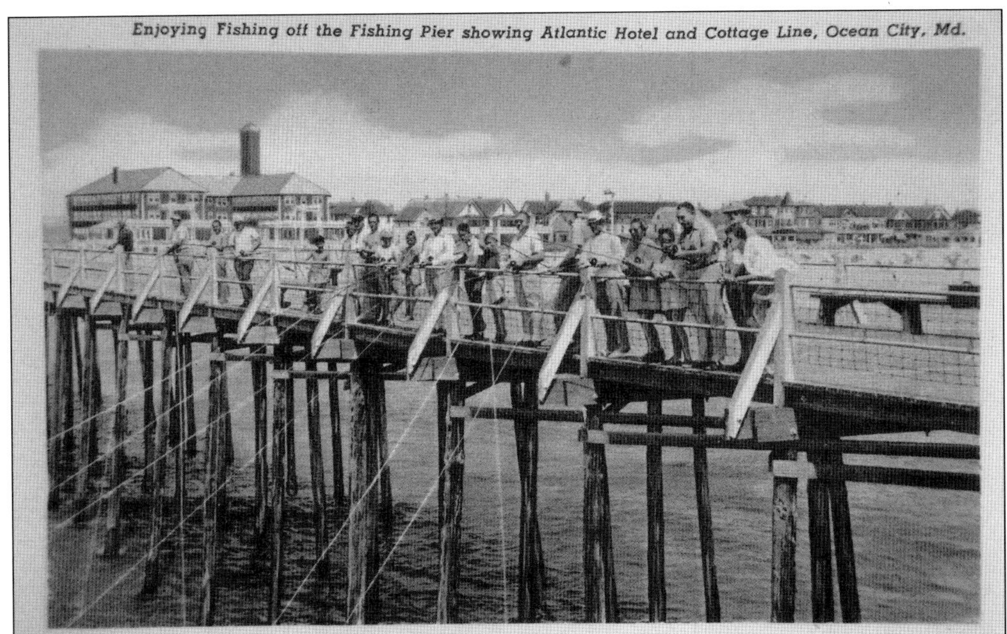

Fishing from the fishing pier remains a popular pastime, and in today's era of over-taxation and license requirements, it is an added benefit that no fishing license is required to fish on the ocean pier. Fish being caught include striped bass, bluefish, croaker, sand perch, sea trout, ling cod, kingfish, spot, and occasionally sand sharks—also skates and rays, blue crabs, spider crabs, and horseshoe crabs.

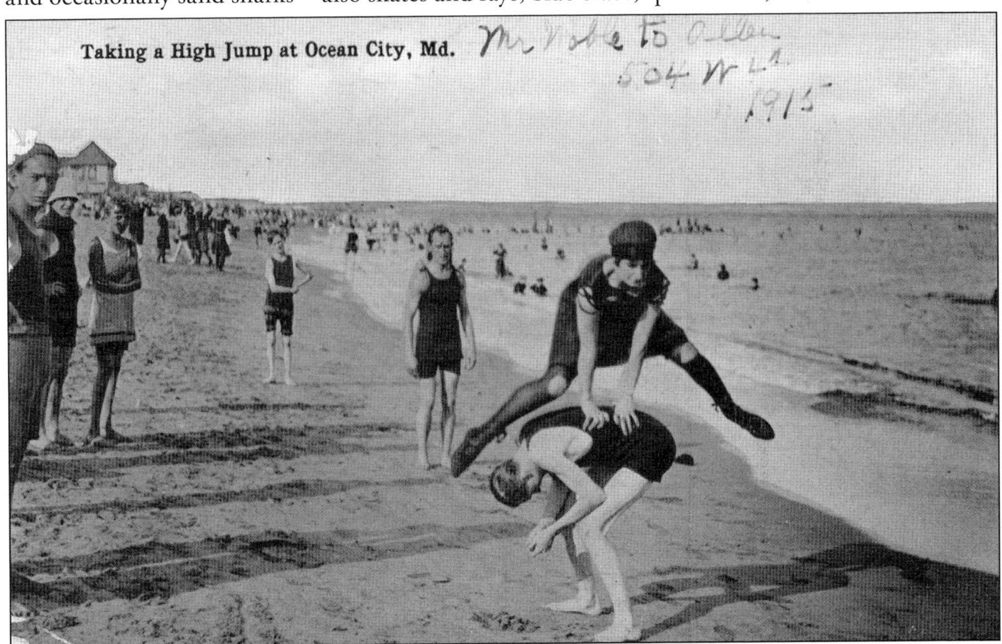

Because the beaches and surf are frequently crowded, organized sports such as football, soccer, lacrosse, and similar recreation (that would kick sand onto nearby tourists or threaten collisions with nonparticipants) are prohibited both on the beach and in the ocean. Recently, beach volleyball nets have been set up in the open beach near the boardwalk. In this postcard marked 1915, an improvised "high jump" attracts interest along the shore.

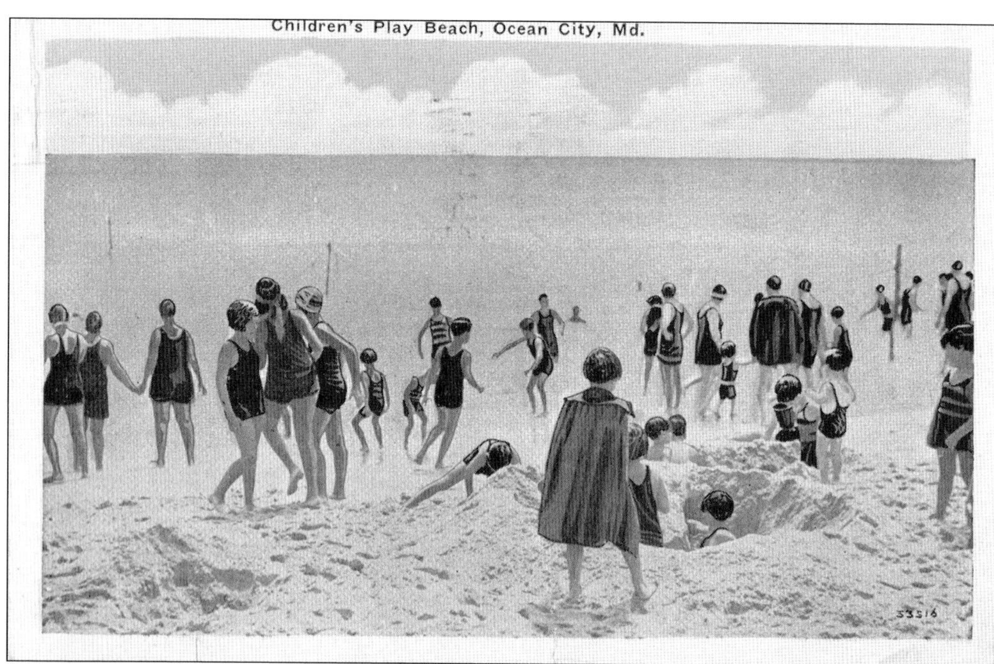

Children are the great improvisers when it comes to play. Digging holes in the sand is a common summertime pastime; however, they can potentially be dangerous when holes get too deep and unstable dry sand walls collapse. Although not always monitored by parents, burying someone (lying flat) up to the neck in sand is mostly safe.

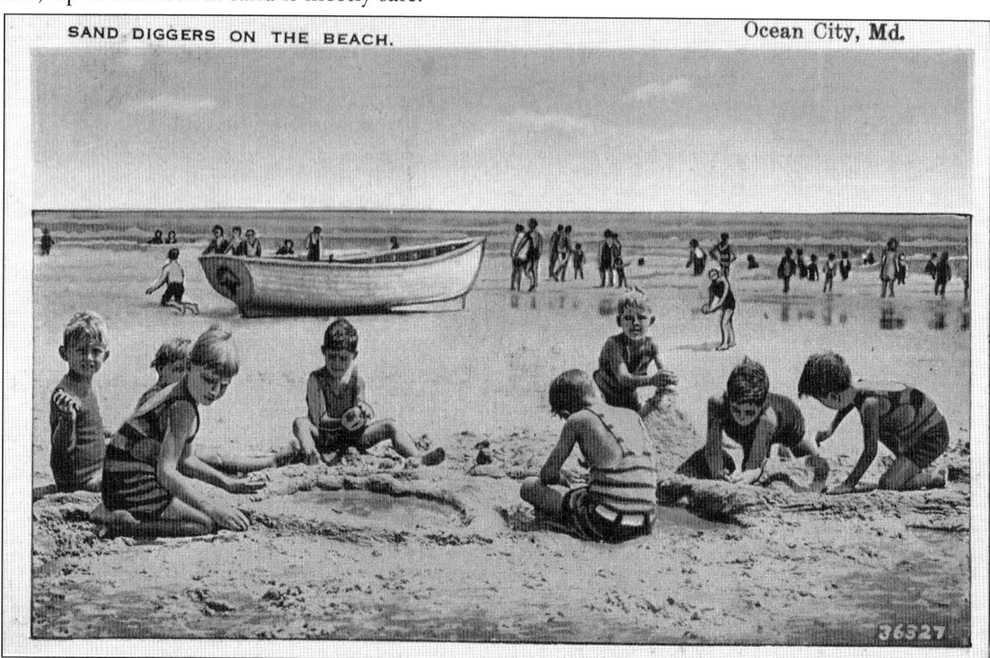

In this postcard sent in 1936, boys engage in the age-old pastime along the ocean shore, which is building forts in the sand. Sandcastles call for ramparts; moats; bridges, which were likely to collapse immediately; and mottes topped by drips of watery sand to create Antoni Gaudí–esque pinnacles and turrets worthy of the Sagrada Família in Barcelona. Some of these boys might become architects.

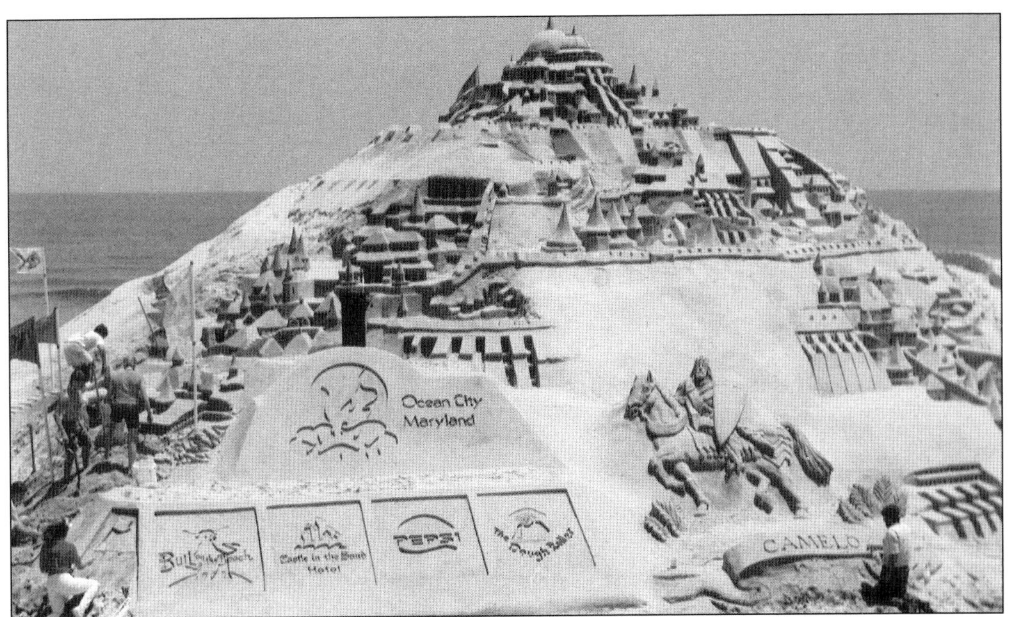

The largest sandcastle in Ocean City's history was Adam Showell's elaborate pile built in June 1989 to a height of 30 feet and estimated to have moved and shaped 7,777 tons of sand. Falling just inches short of the largest sandcastle, at the time, according to *The Guinness Book of World Records*, Showell's sand fortress lent publicity to his family's Ocean City hotel, Castle in the Sand, which opened in 1960.

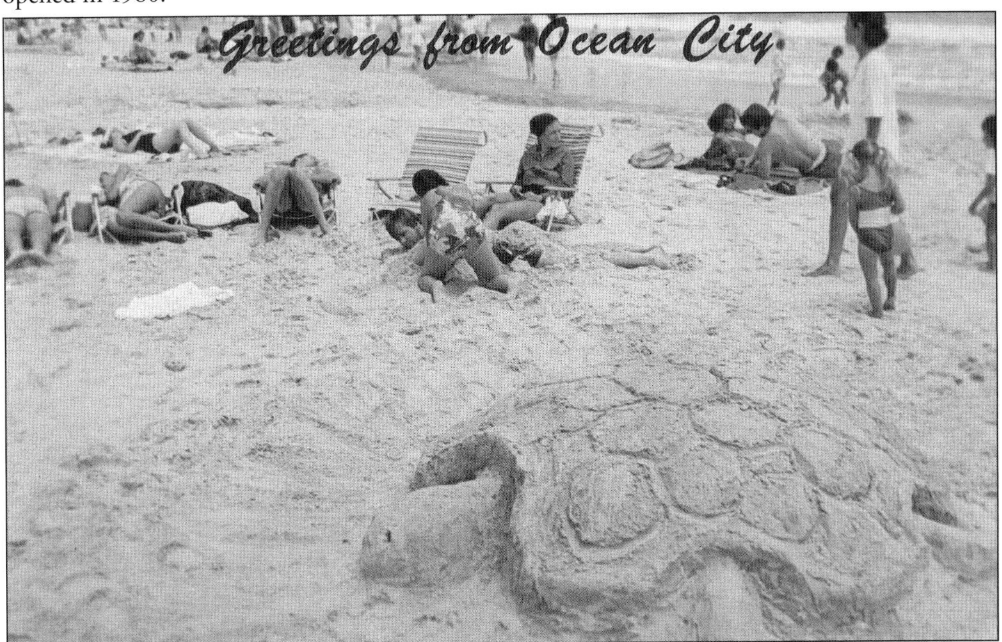

Most sand modeling takes the form of moats and castle walls, but occasionally, a sculpture, such as this turtle, is shaped out of beach sand and stands isolated until some mischievous child, lacking art appreciation, stomps it back to the natural beachscape. This postcard, distributed by Joseph Brigantine of New Jersey, also shows another beach pastime in the background—a child burying her prone father in the sand.

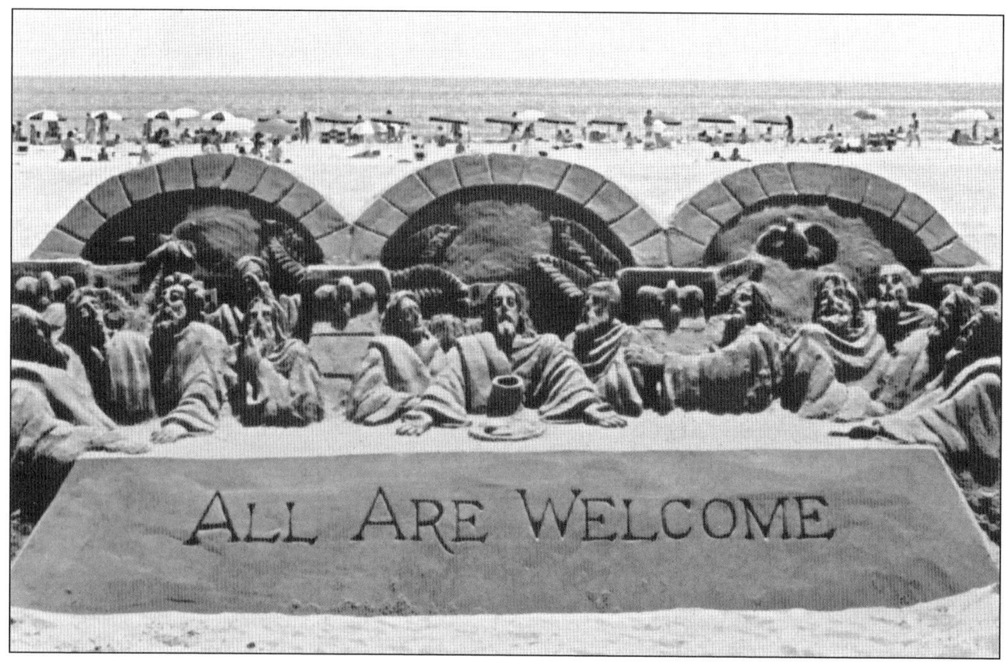

The most remarkable sand sculptures over the decades have unquestionably been those of artist Randy Hoffman whose remarkable creations in sand, sculpted since 1981, are located on the beach at the boardwalk's edge in front of the Plim Plaza Hotel on North Second Street. Hoffman's work is part of the worship and ministry outreach group at Son'Spot, a local Christian Fellowship Center. Each sculpture requires an entire day of work and lasts about a month. Hoffman utilizes water, a plastic knife, and biodegradable glue to create a surface crust over the sculptures as a protection from wind and rain. His Last Supper renditions are astonishing displays of artistic control in this shifting medium. He includes various inscriptions with his sculptures such as the following: "All are Welcome," "You will Seek Me and Find Me . . ." and "Wise Men Still Seek Him." (Below, photograph by Robert M. Craig.)

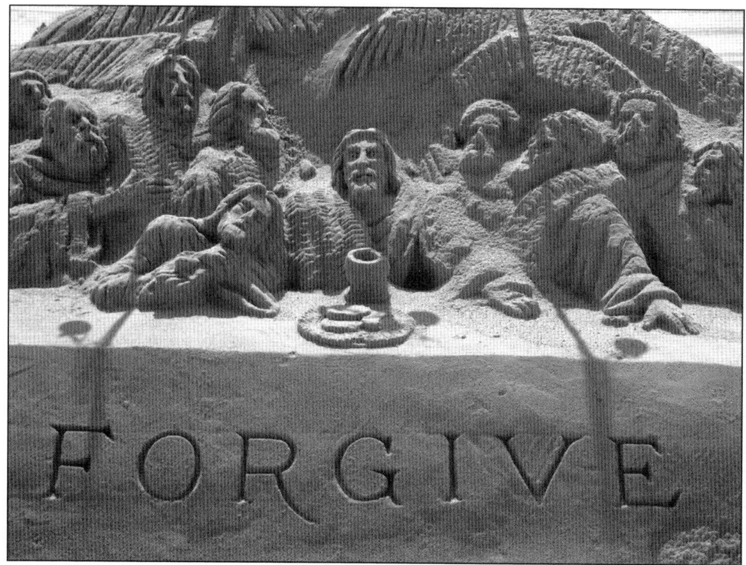

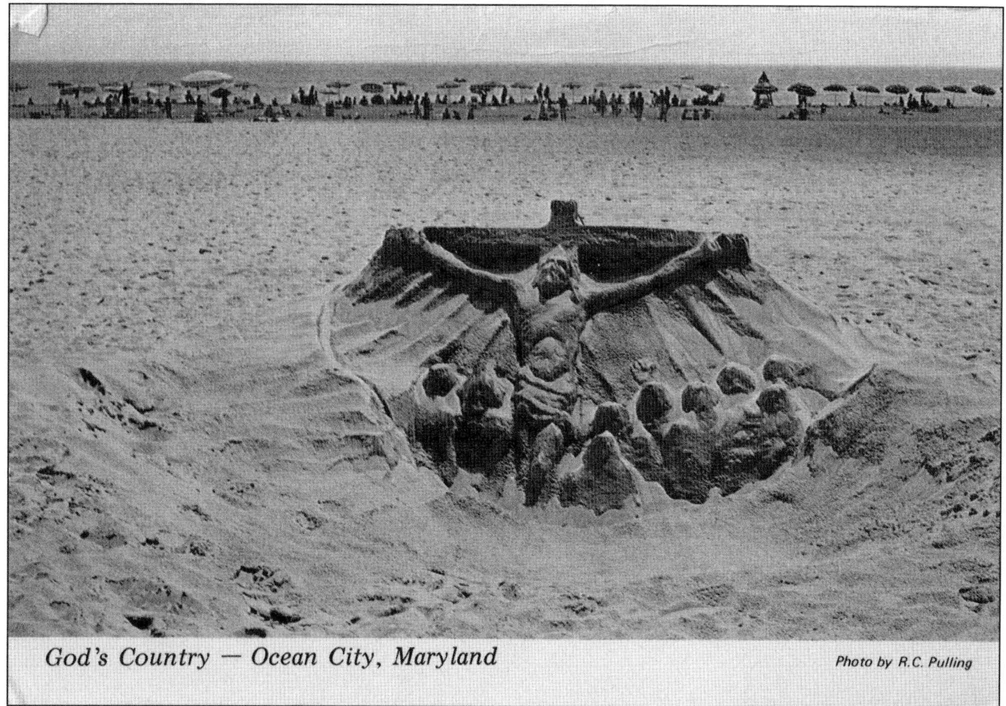

Photographer R.C. Pulling recorded an early Hoffman calvary sculpture in this postcard captioned "God's Country." The small scale of the sand sculpture is more typical of what Hoffman would position as a side image in a triptych whose centerpiece was of increased complexity in later years. Here, the image appears to rise miraculously out of the coastal sand; it is a spiritual expression in natural materials.

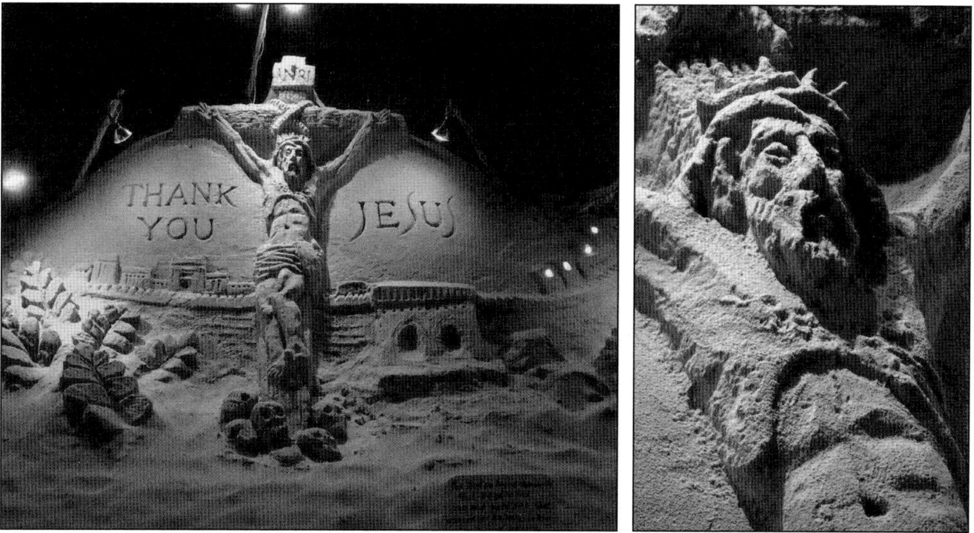

Night lighting enhances the tour de force of artistic expression of this unusual medium. Hoffman frequently captions his crucifixion scenes "Thank you Jesus," conveying the subliminal message that Jesus died for us and that salvation prompts this expression of gratitude. The realism of the figure is remarkable and belies the transient nature of sand, seemingly here untouched by coastal wind and rain. (Photographs by Robert M. Craig.)

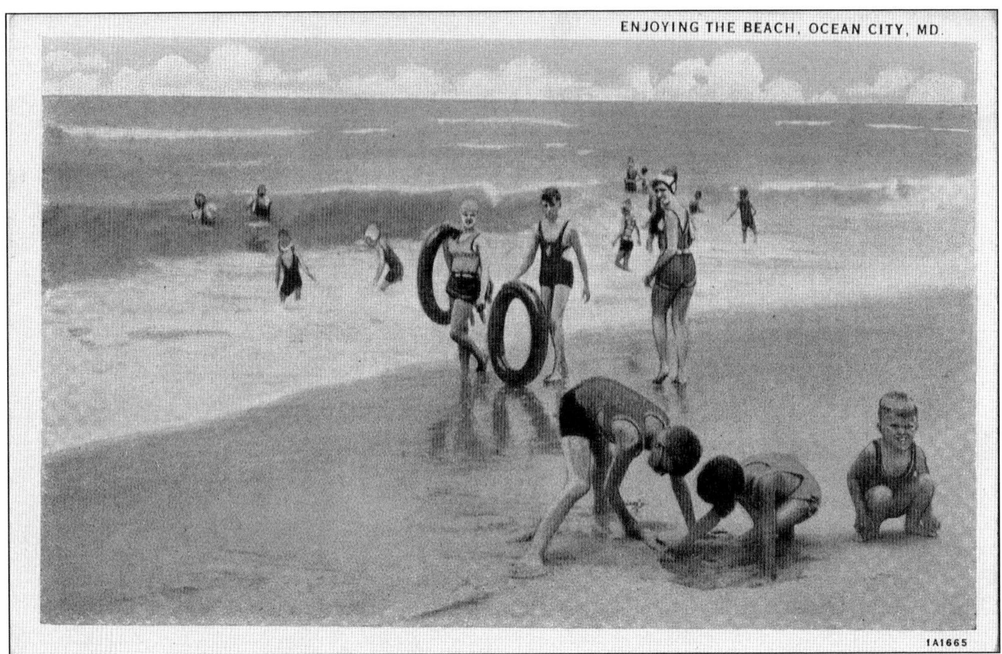

The boys in this 1931 "Enjoying the Beach" postcard (above) are engaged in the same activity— digging for sand crabs—as the children (below) in the c. 1960s card, photographed by Fred Brueckmann. No bigger than a thumb, the sand crab moves only backwards to burrow itself in the shifting sand. Its gray shell offers camouflage in gray wet sand, and it has no claws, so children scoop them up and put them in beach pails for closer observation, hopefully returning them to the beach sand when their play ends. The inner tubes visible in the above image remain a popular floatation device even today; although these likely came off a Model T Ford. Canvas surf mats, boogie boards, and other recreational beach equipment are much in evidence in later decades.

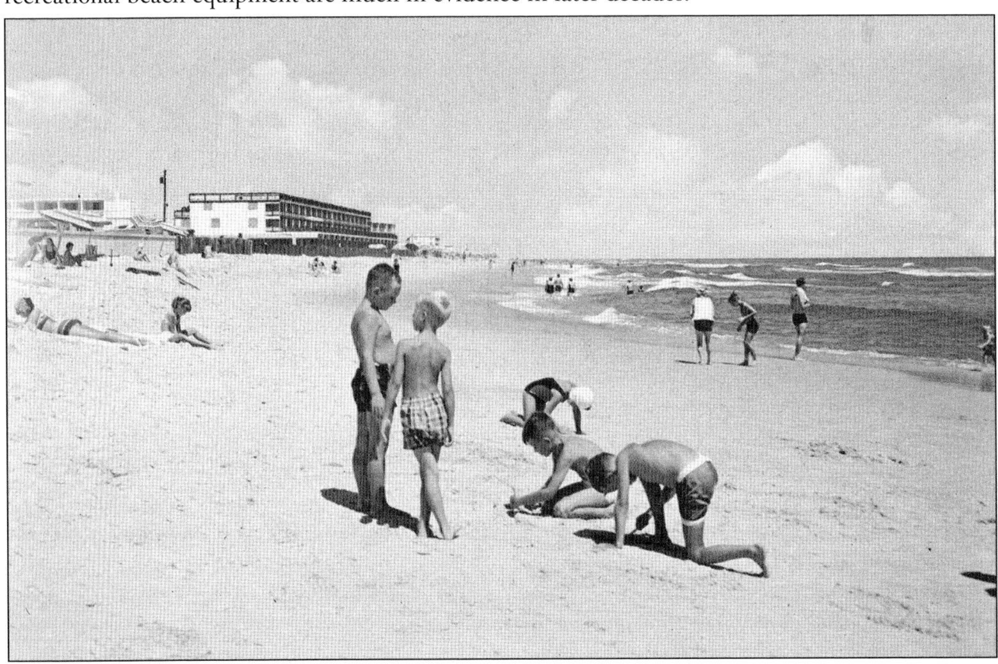

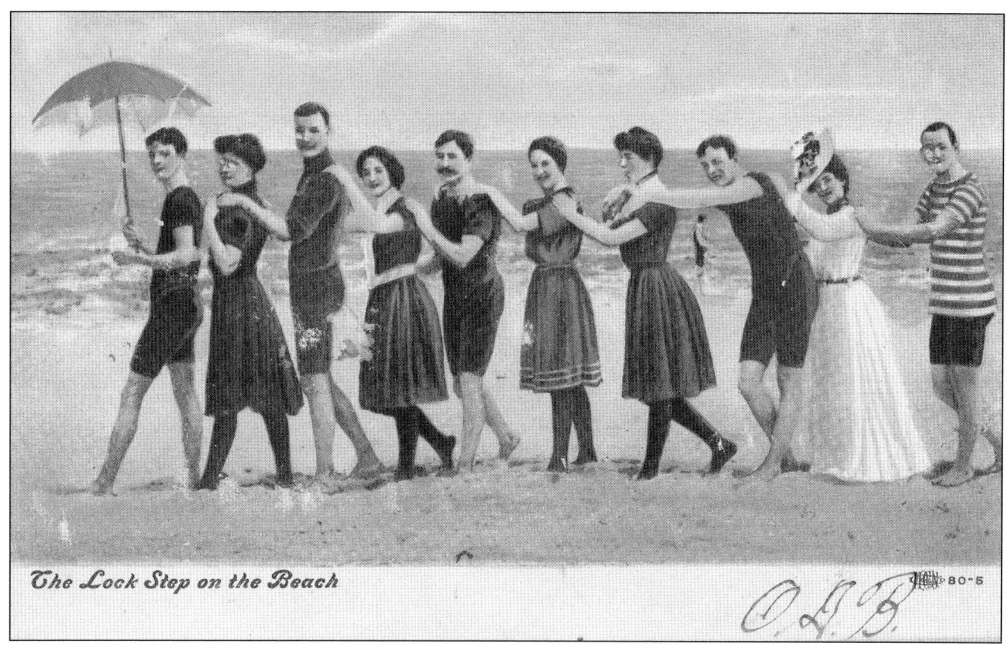

"The Lock Step on the Beach" was postmarked 1907 and offers a posed display of beachwear during the Edwardian era. The white "seaside walking dress," might appear on ladies walking the beach or boardwalk, but the other female "bathing costumes," with skirts down to, or below, the knees, were the customary attire for on the beach or in the water. Sailor-inspired stripes were popular for girls' hems or boys' shirts.

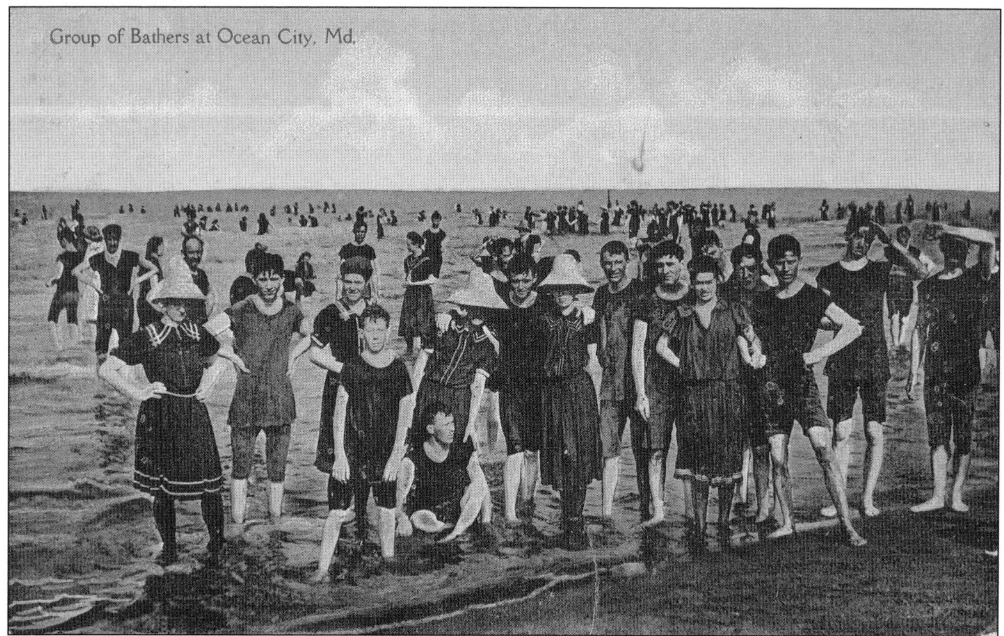

This motley group of pre–World War I bathers includes three girls wearing broad-brimmed Coolie sun hats. However, what is most striking is the drowned-rat appearance and soaking-wet bathing dresses, often made of flannel. As Capt. Robert S. Craig, who joined the town's lifeguards in 1935, later observed, "those old woolen bathing suits would drag you under like a sinking ocean liner."

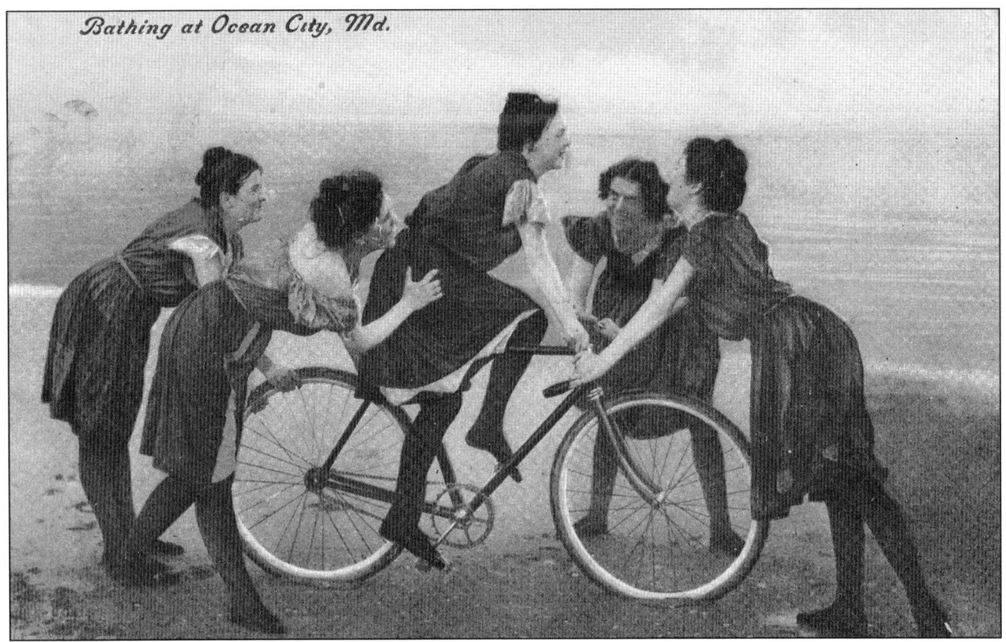

This unusual publicity photograph, captioned "Bathing at Ocean City, Md.," poses women in bathing costumes on and around a bicycle, a recreational craze that the *Atlantic* magazine declared "meant fashion freedom and transportation independence" for women. Susan B. Anthony and Elizabeth Cady Stanton agreed that the "woman is riding to suffrage on the bicycle." (Adrienne LaFrance "How the Bicycle Paved the Way for Women's Rights." *Atlantic*, June 16, 2014).

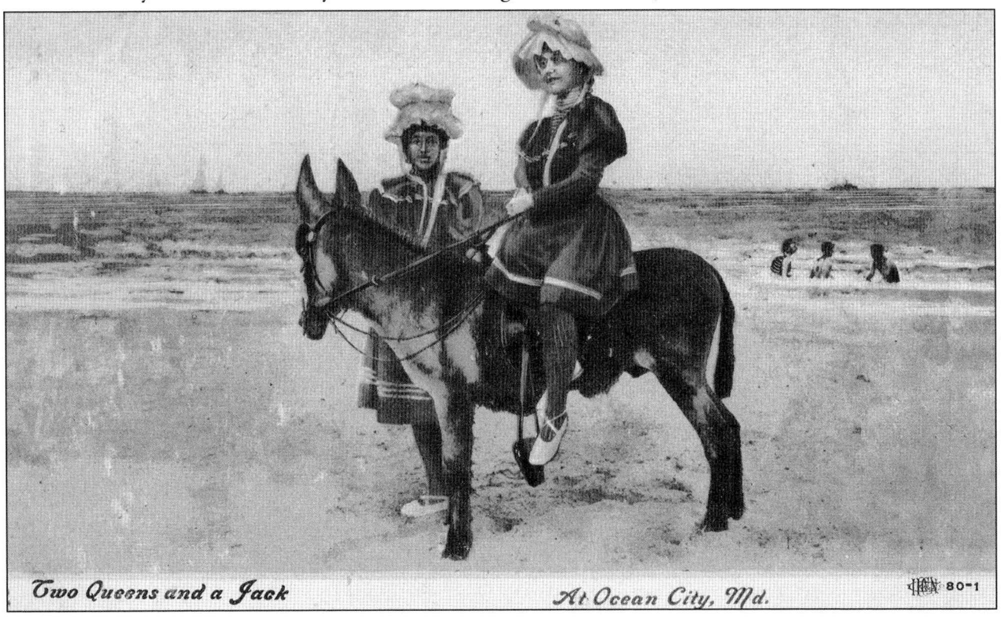

Other women were depicted riding the beach on a jackass. This novelty postcard, captioned "Two Queens and a Jack" and postmarked 1907, was published by the Postal Card Distributing Co. of Atlantic City, New Jersey. It features two females, wearing stylish bonnets and fashionable bathing costumes, whose puff-shoulder sleeves would deflate when wet and promote a less than au currant demeanor (see page 99, bottom.)

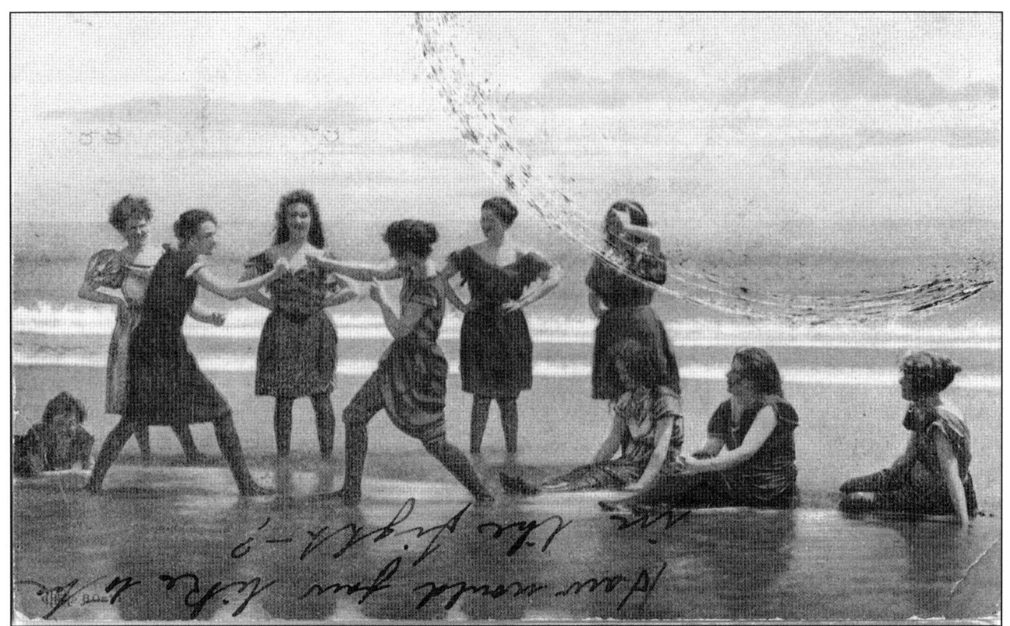

Another posed photograph, published by the Postal Card Distributing Co. and postmarked 1908 shows, four wet and four dry observers watching a staged bout of female fisticuffs. Skirts are full and knee length, and one bather displays fashionably puffed shoulders destined to weigh her down farther in the surf. The revealed shoulders on other onlookers are minimally risqué. The correspondent writes, "How would you like to be in the fight?"

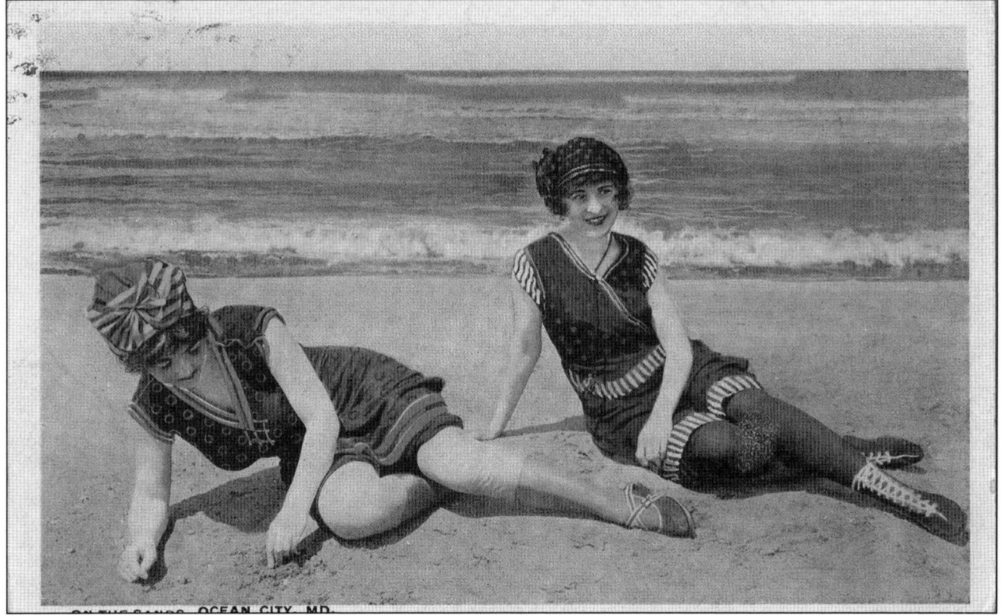

A "White Border Period" card, postmarked 1917, illustrates that women often wore shoes on the beach and not infrequently in the water to avoid stepping barefooted on sharp shells or crabs. Here, two young ladies are fashionably dressed in skirted bathing dresses both with covered shoulders but one with plunging neckline. Tight-fitting undergarments normally extend to calf to cover knees, while one of the girls wears full-length stockings.

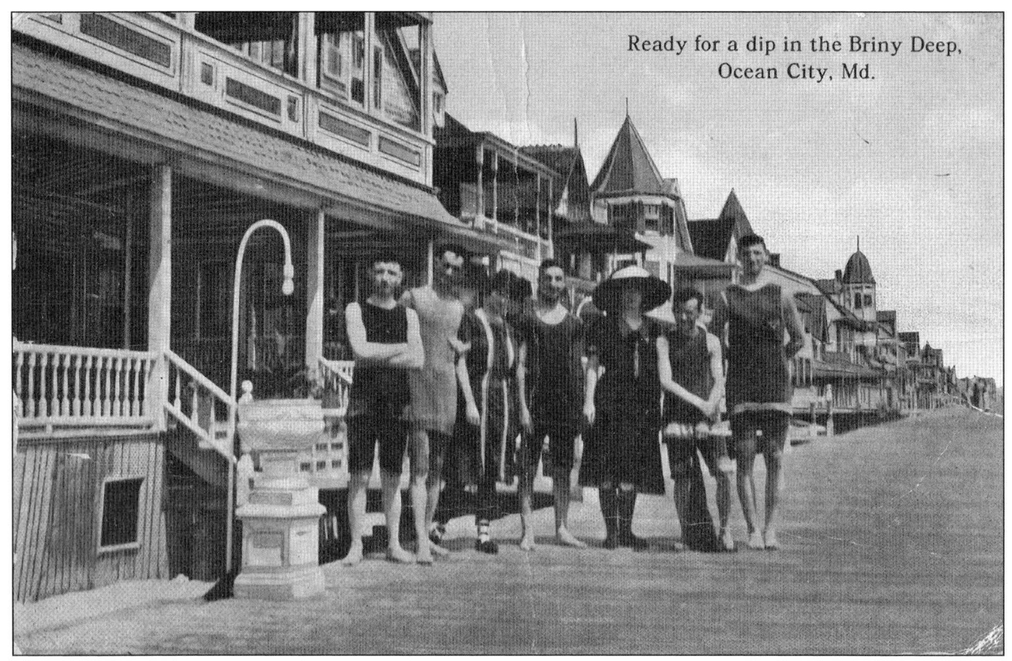

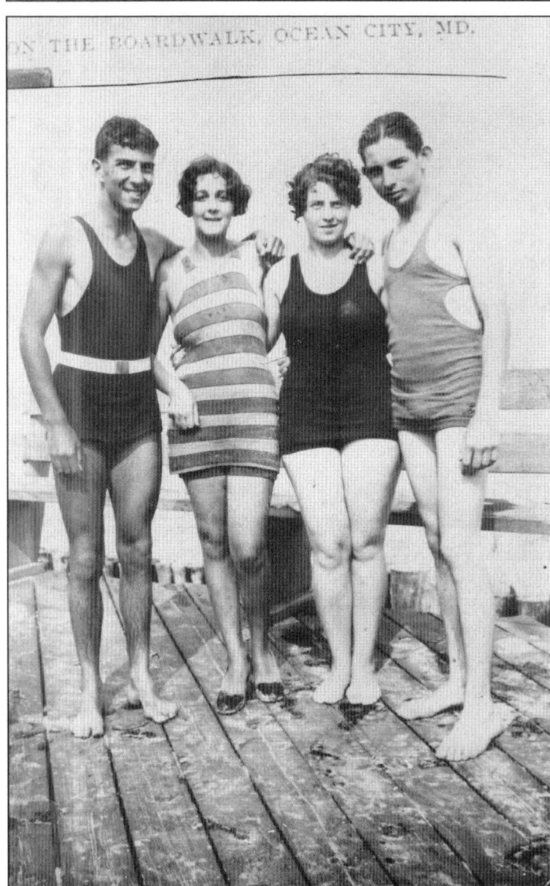

Men's swimming attire is on display in this postcard, captioned "Ready for a Dip in the Briny Deep, Ocean City, MD." Some men's bathing trunks extended to the knee, while others rose higher, but shirts typically hung to below the hip and were usually mid-thigh length. The upper body was covered by T-shirts with or without sleeves.

The styles of bathing suits worn by this foursome in a postcard from the Thelma Davis Collection suggests a 1920s date. One man wears a popular black suit with a white belt, and the other is in a pale-colored suit—both are wearing tank tops. While all four bathing suits are body-clinging, one woman's swimwear hangs lower, since the allowable length of bare skin above the knees was regulated on some beaches; the other woman's style looks forward to later one-piece bathing suits popularized by Esther Williams in the 1940s and 1950s.

A 1907 postcard shows children's beachwear during the period The little boy need not cover either upper or lower body above his striped trunks, while the little girl covers herself from shoulder to knee. The fanciful landscape is the sort depicted on carnival boards in which the children stick their heads through a hole for a photograph or simply pose thus to amuse family or onlookers.

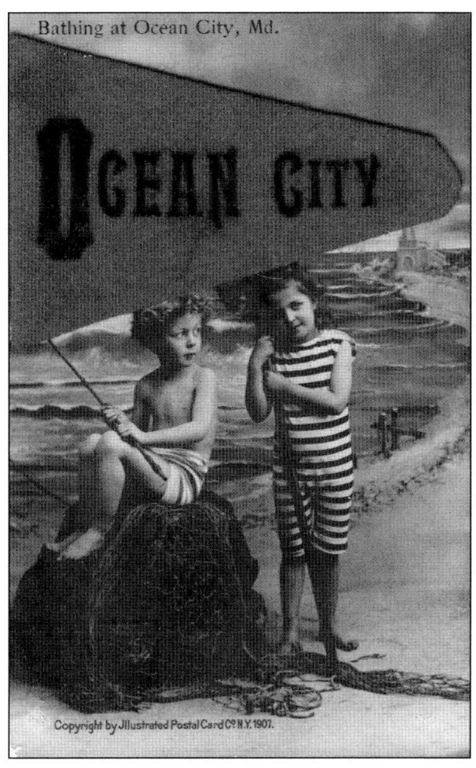

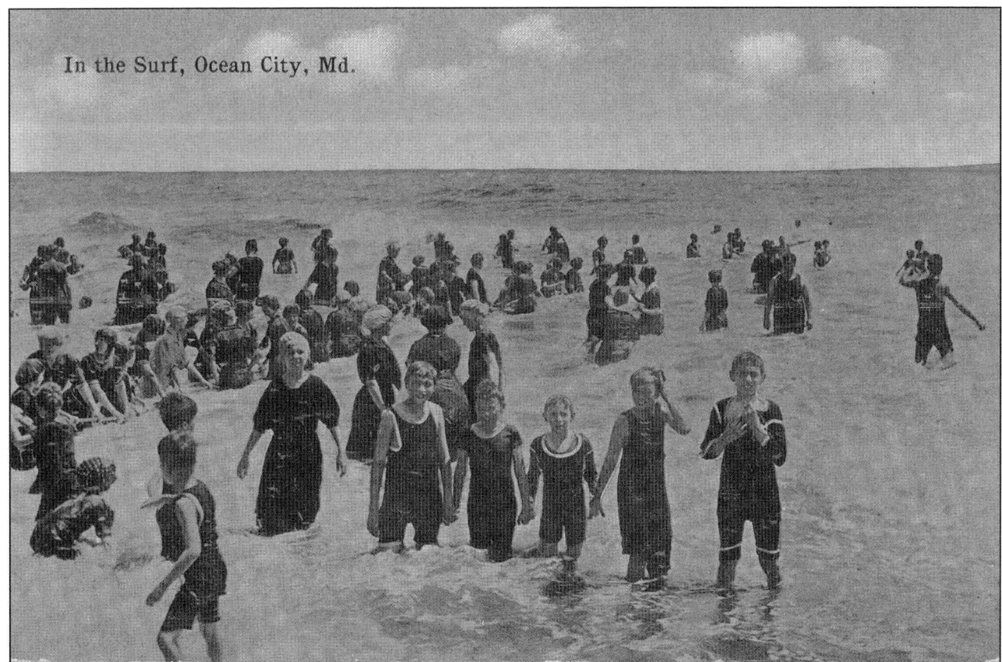

The swimming attire of the young boys lined up "in the surf" in the foreground of this card, postmarked 1922, shows the continued popularity of everything from sailor stripes to tank tops over knee-length bathing suits. Note the crowded line of bathers holding on to the safety rope in the background (see page 85).

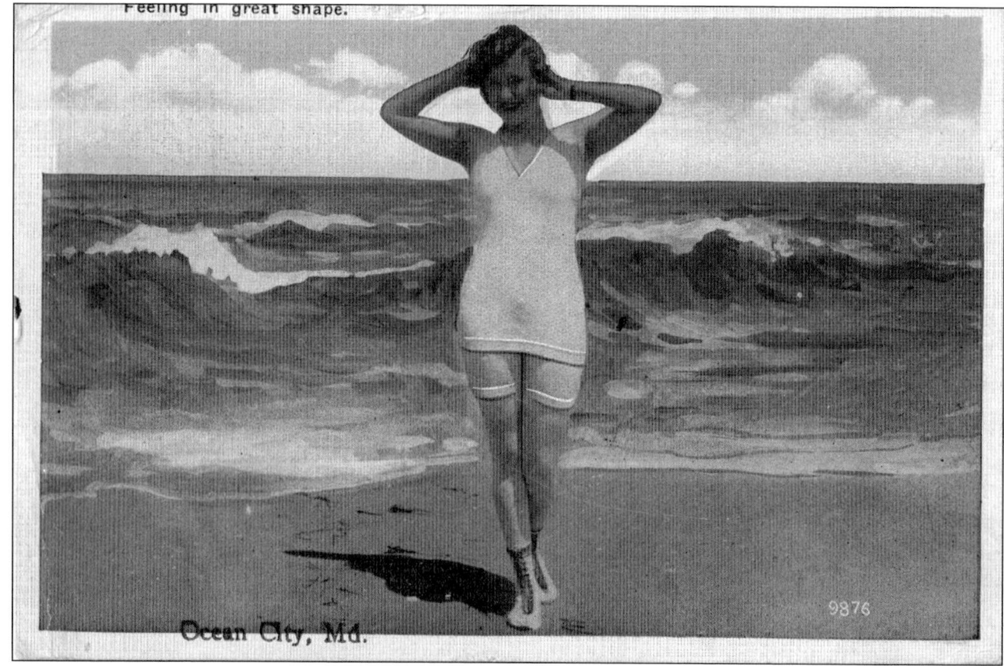

"Feeling in great shape," this bathing beauty of the early 1920s wears a more body-clinging bathing suit with under-leggings covering her upper legs to mid-thigh and with beach shoes as also seen on page 101 (below image). The bathing attire looks forward to one-piece swim suits for women that appeared more universally in later decades.

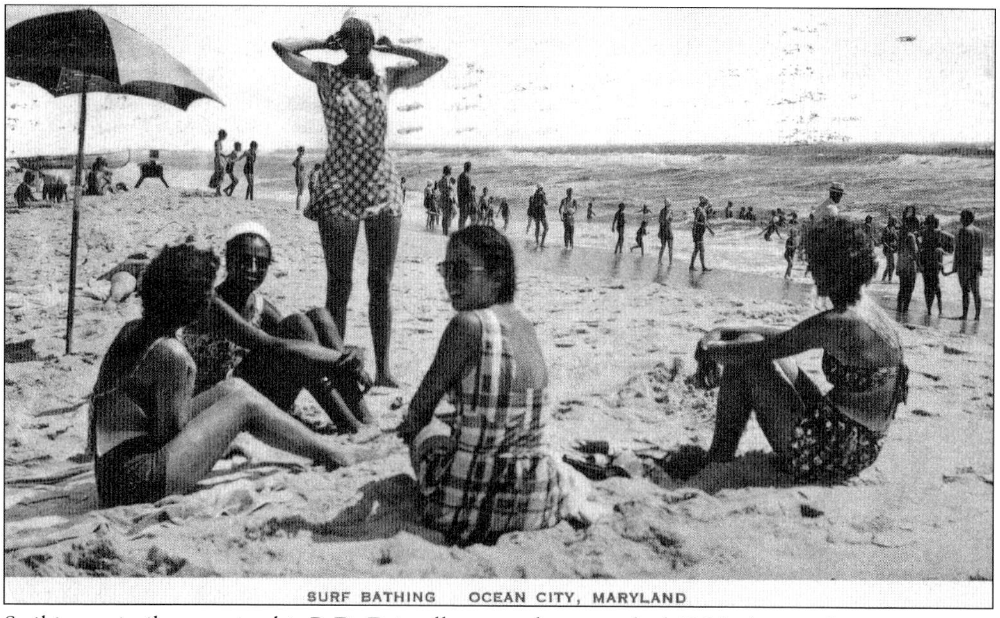

Striking a similar pose in this R.D. Driscoll postcard postmarked 1934, the standing woman in a patterned one-piece swimsuit adjusts her bathing cap, part of the ocean attire of the period. High-waisted two-piece suits, featured in the 1935 Miss America swimsuit competition, were also popular in the 1930s and 1940s. When the Atlantic City pageant began in 1921, contestants wore skirted "bathing costumes" much like those on page 101.

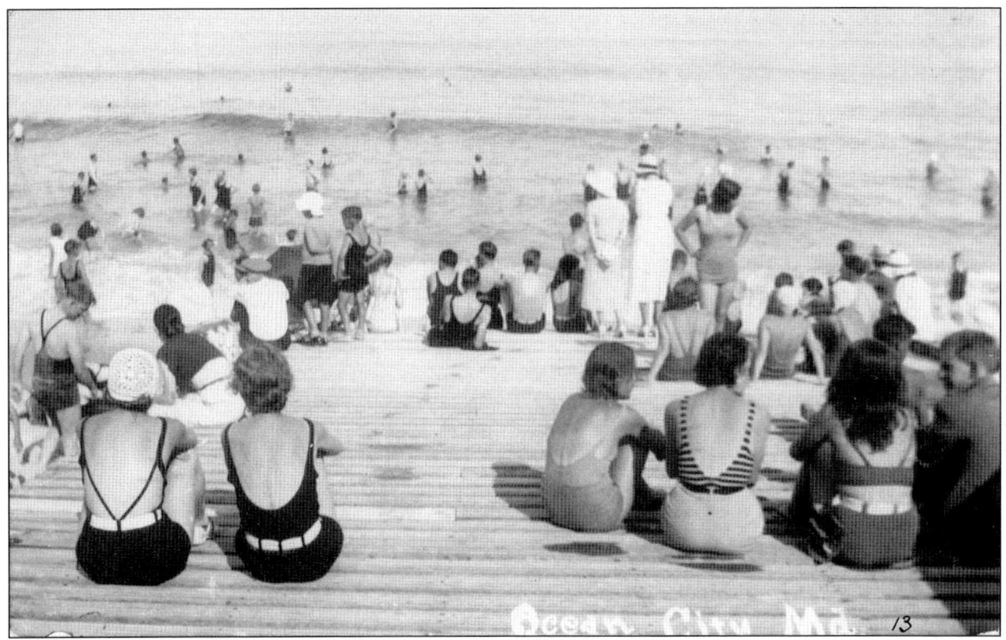

Postmarked 1936, this postcard shows a group of bathers sitting on a boardwalk ramp that leads to a narrow beach, likely in front of the Coast Guard station on Caroline Street. They are watching bathers in a calm sea. Men wear bathing suits with tank tops, while women appear in one-piece suits, which are low cut in the back and expose their shoulders. At right is a high-waisted two-piece suit.

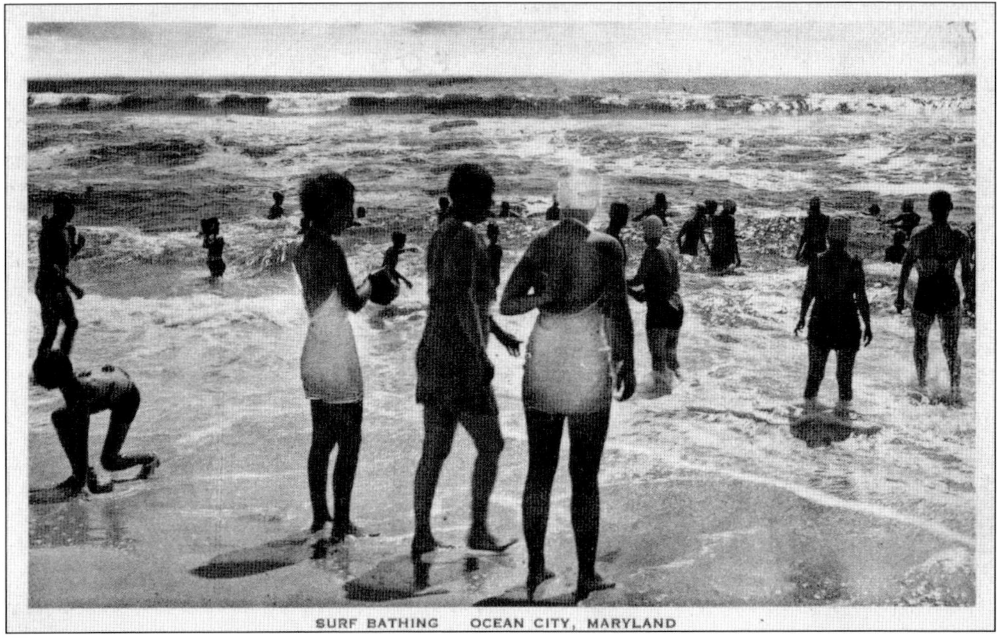

This contemporary "surf bathing" postcard shows women wearing one-piece suits and latex or silicone bathing caps, the latter appearing in the 1920s. The image of the tight-fitting cap accorded with head-hugging cloche hats of the day. After rubber was diverted for military use during World War II, bathing caps made a comeback due to the popularity of Esther Williams movies in the 1940s and 1950s, featuring stylish one-piece suits and floral caps.

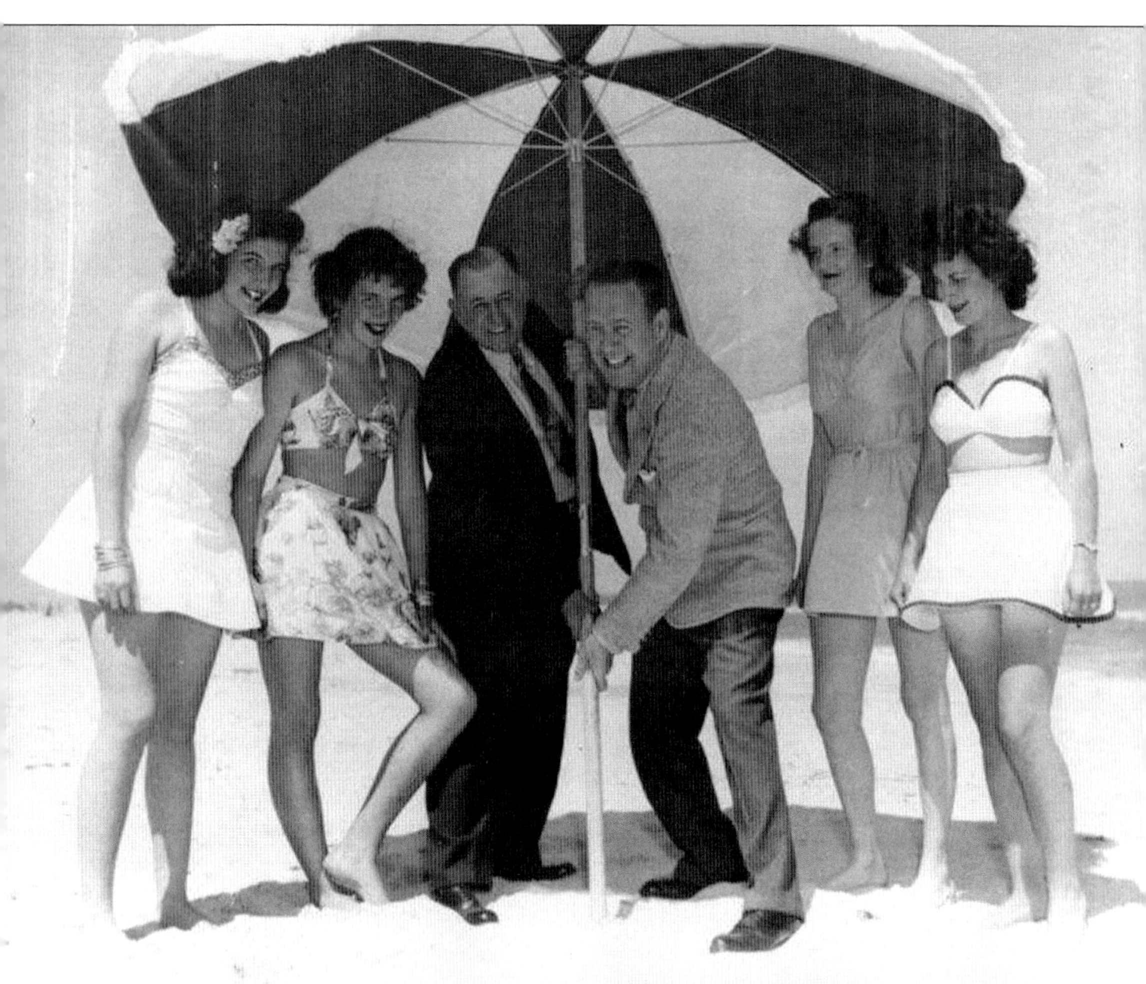

A postwar publicity photograph shows Ocean City mayor Daniel Trimper Jr. and Maryland governor Herbert R. O'Connor securing the "first umbrella" in the sand for the 1946 summer season. Trimper was town mayor from 1944 to 1959. Flanking the men, from left to right and wearing the fashionable skirted one-piece and high-waisted two-piece swimsuits of the day, are Suzanne Mason (later Chatham) and Mary Lou Mason (later Brueckmann) (the author's aunts, the latter aged 15) and on the right side, Betsy Jane Dennis and Esther Simpson. In 2019, Mayor Rick Meehan and Gov. Larry Hogan recreated the ceremonial umbrella planting posing with members of the Ocean City Beach Patrol. Two years later, they posed again with members of the town's police force. As Disney might observe, the subject should return to its original casting: Beauty and the Beach. (Author's collection.)

1950s one-piece swimsuits fill the foreground of this postcard postmarked 1956. Shoulders, arms, and legs are fully exposed, so it is no wonder that such suntan lotions as Coppertone and Sea and Ski appeared during the decade as suntans replaced white skin as favored indicators of summer beauty. "Don't be a paleface," Coppertone advertisements advised, and the company wisely provided free Coppertone to town lifeguards during the period.

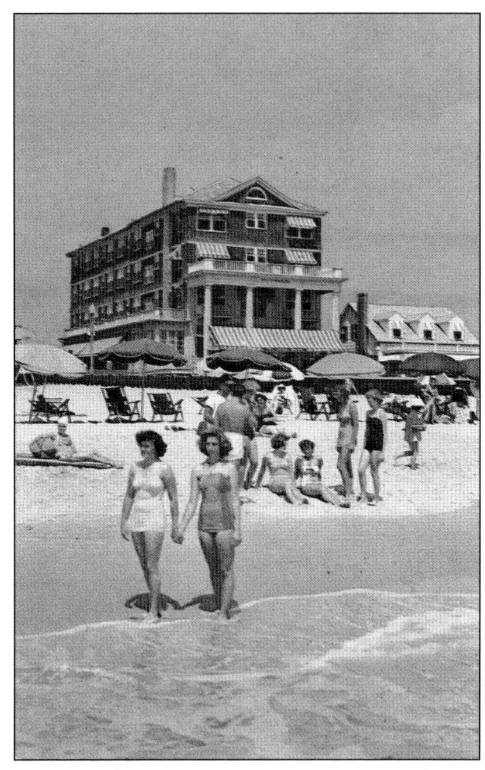

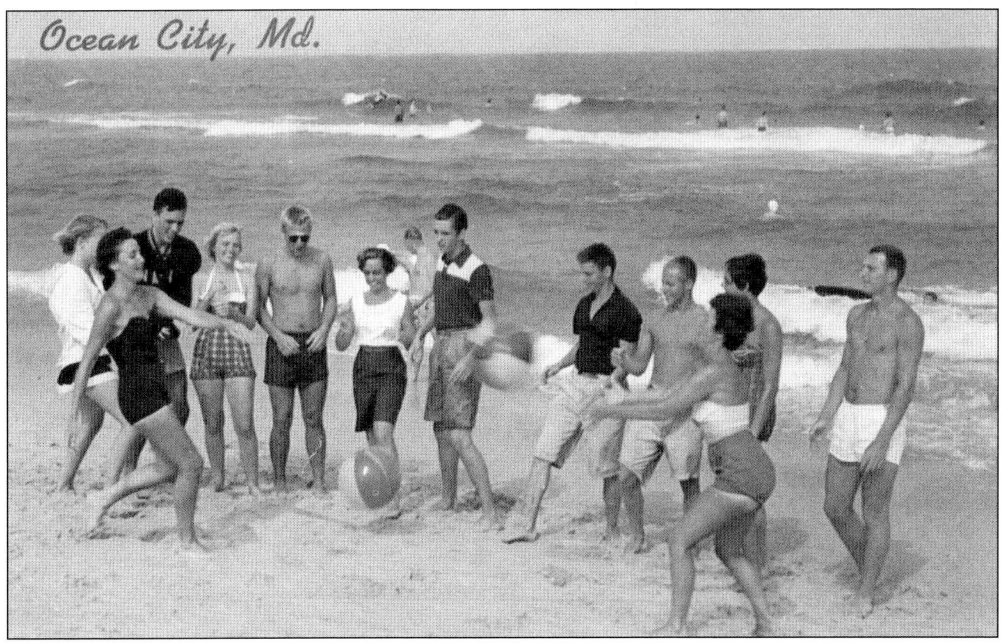

Here, a group of people watch two young ladies toss beach balls. Note a full array of beach attire in this Tichnor Brothers postcard. Some wear fashionable Bermuda shorts, while others are in swim attire, but everyone has a well-toned summer tan. Nobody seems to notice that the swimmer behind the rightmost spectator is off his surf mat and may be struggling in white water trying to return to ashore.

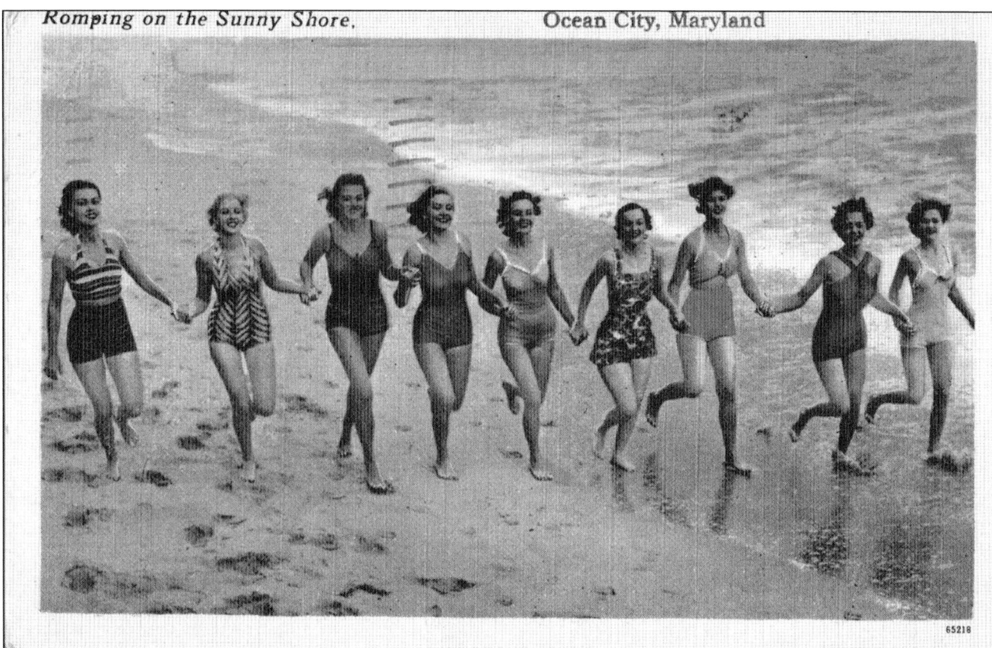

This "Romping on the Sunny Shore" postcard is another generic photograph that could have been taken anywhere, and in fact, it was stamped with more than one location identification as it was sold from postcard racks up and down the Atlantic coast. Postmarked 1959, the card depicts a row of "beathing beauties," running hand in hand and sporting the then latest fashions in swimsuits.

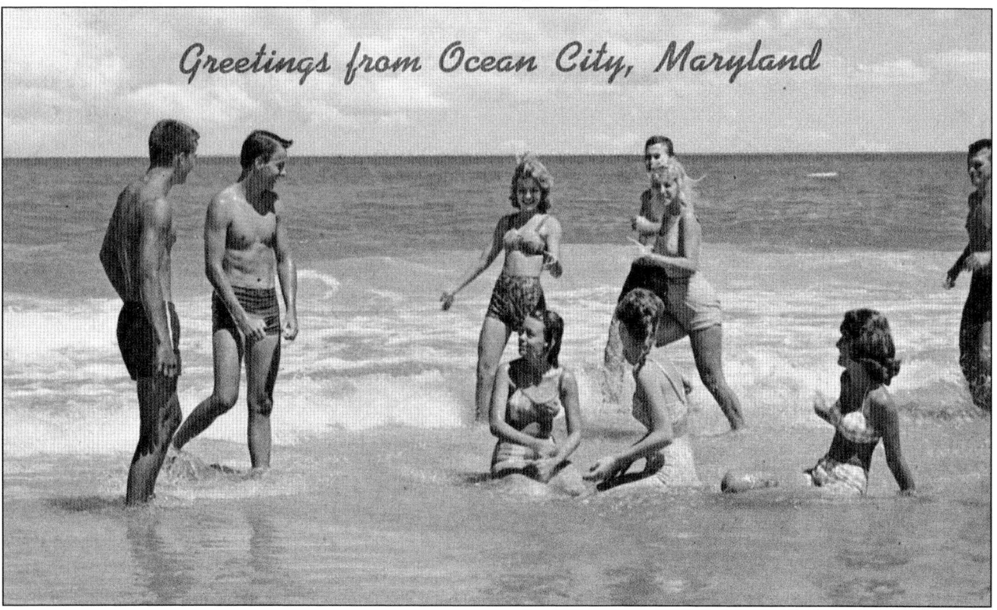

This 1960s scene features teenagers wearing swimsuits popularized in Gidget beach and surfer movies as well as in films starring Frankie Avalon and Annette Funicello. It was a California look, accompanied by the California sound of the Beach Boys and the Ventures (albeit the latter formed in Tacoma, Washington); imported California surfer culture took hold along the Atlantic coast's beaches (see pages 124 and 125).

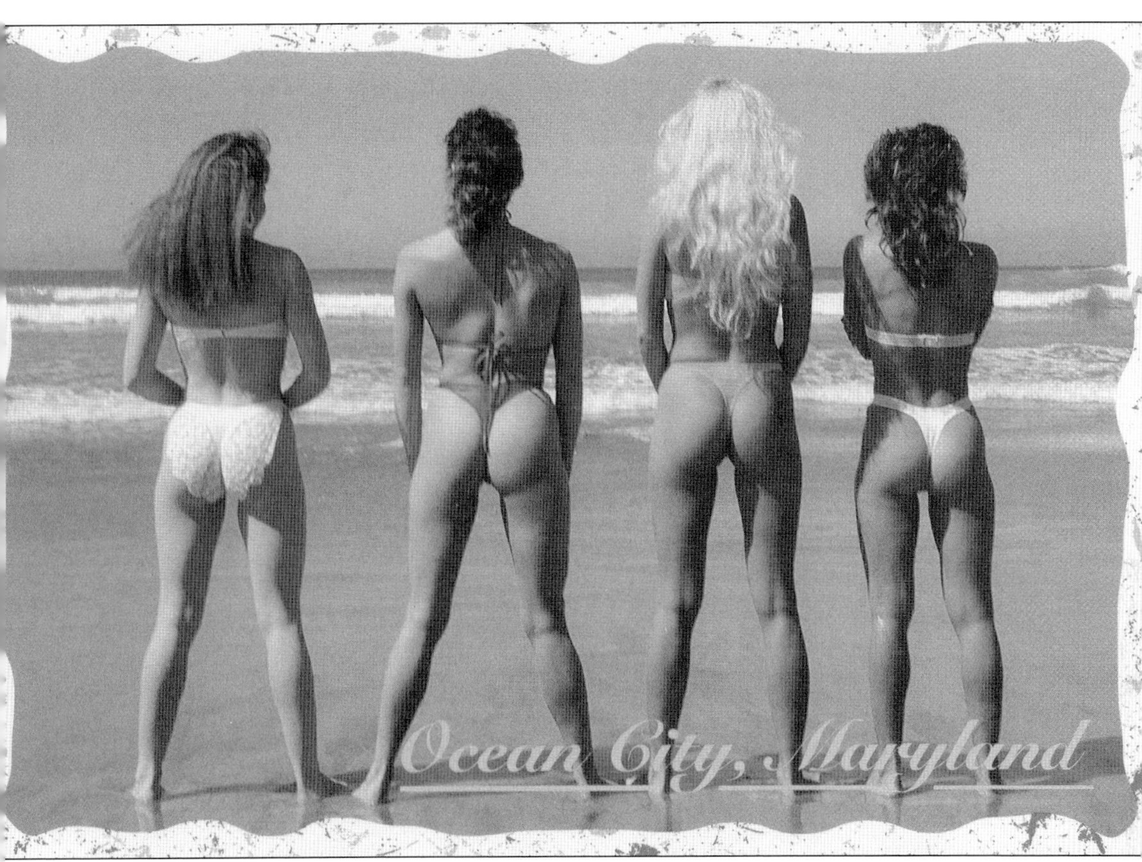

This postcard postmarked 1998 marks the end (pun intended) of the bathing attire section of this chapter on the Ocean City beach; there is no further minimalization of garb that can take place short of a nude beach. Then, in August 2016, Chelsea Eline announced that she intended to sunbathe topless on the Ocean City beach. Mayor Rick Meehan immediately declared Ocean City was not, and would never be, a topless beach. In June, an emergency ordinance was passed, aimed at preserving the "family-oriented character" of the town and its beaches, prohibiting topless women. Eline sued, a federal appeals court upheld Ocean City's ordnance, and so the topless advocate appealed to the Supreme Court of the United States (SCOTUS). In February 2022, SCOTUS refused to hear the case, so for now, public nudity remains banned, except for an apparent backsliding in the case of thongs.

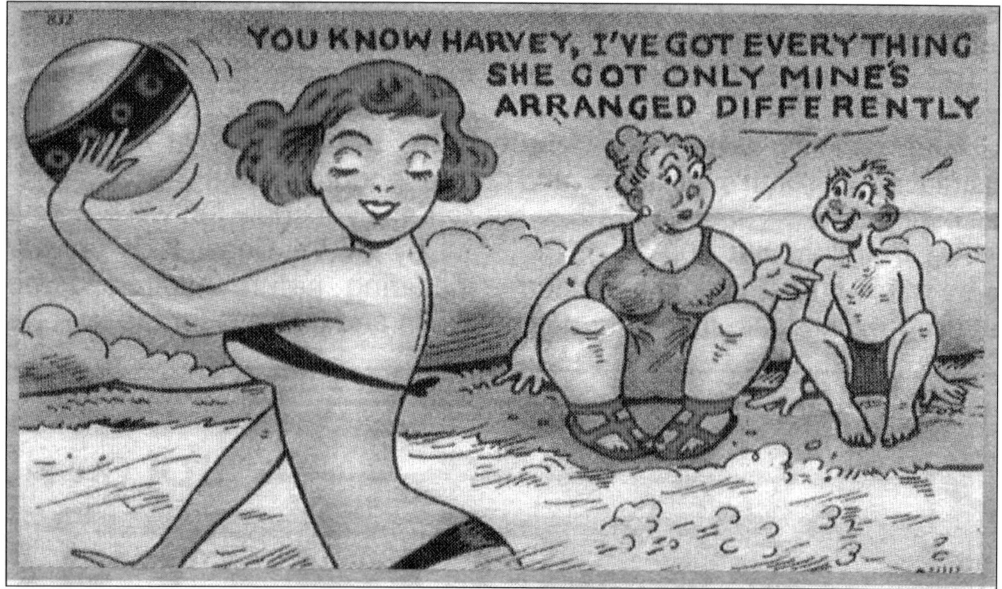

The cheesecake display of the previous postcard offers a transition to the popular novelty postcards featuring beach subjects in either cartoon or photographic form. The caption, "You Know Harvey, I've Got Everything She Got Only Mine's Arranged Differently" is classic. Throughout the decades, vacationers mailed novelty postcards ranging from "fish stories" of unlikely oversized catches to encounters with curvaceous beauties in scanty bikinis, caricaturized as everyman's dream. (Courtesy of *The Dispatch*.)

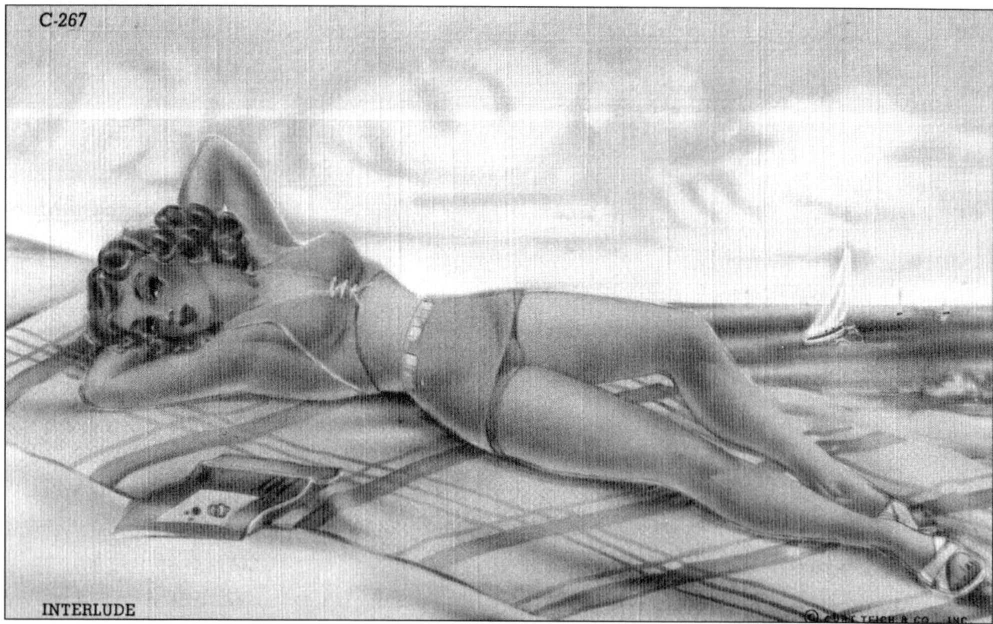

The Curt Teich Co. joined the cheesecake tradition in this classic pose recalling Francisco de Goya's *The Naked Maja*. Here, a bathing beauty stretches out on a beach blanket, her paperback book cast aside, as she looks directly and seductively into the camera. Titled "Interlude," the card is likely from the late 1930s or 1940s, based on the brief skirted "bottom" and swimsuit still covering the navel (consistent with Hollywood's Hays Code).

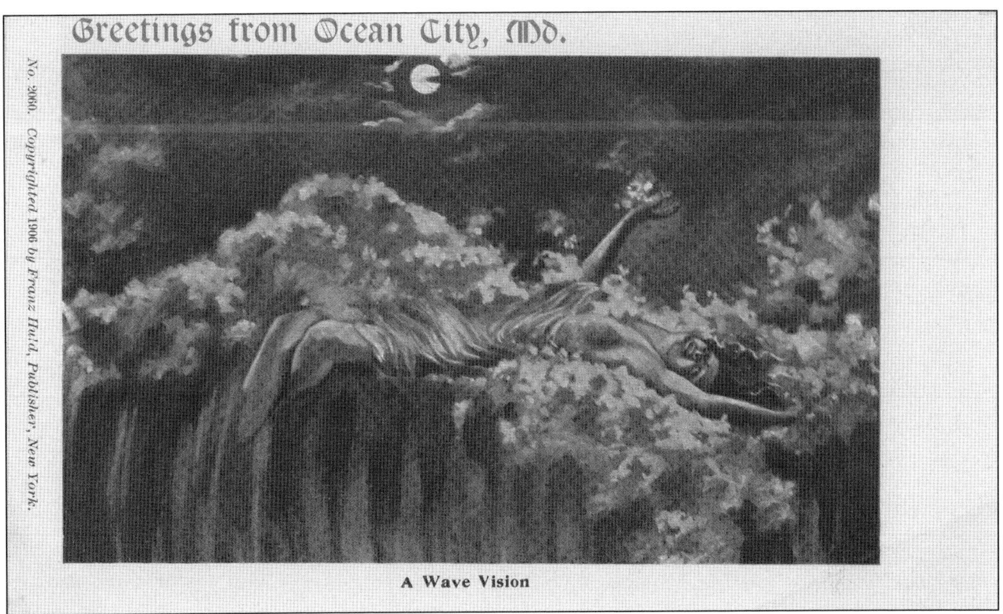

A projected eroticism goes back to the earliest postcards as this 1906 image made for the Ocean City market by Franz Huld Publisher in New York suggests. Captioned "A Wave Vision," it looks forward to Hollywood scenes of Marilyn Monroe in a bubble bath, as well as to numerous "mood" images (sans sea goddess) depicting the ocean in the moonlight (see pages 20, 24, and 27).

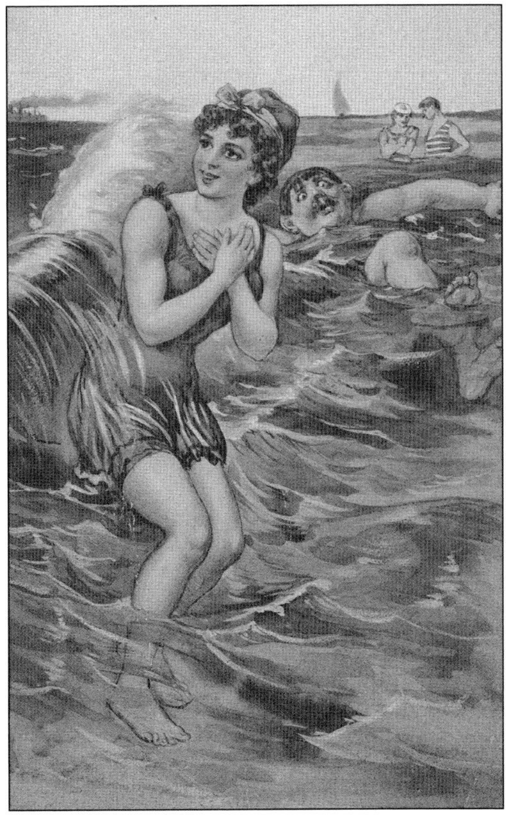

This novelty card artist played on the fact that certain fabrics, when saturated with water, not only cling to the body but become almost invisible, lending a view of the female nude body that has not gone unnoticed by the less than svelte and bug-eyed male swimmer frolicking in the surf behind.

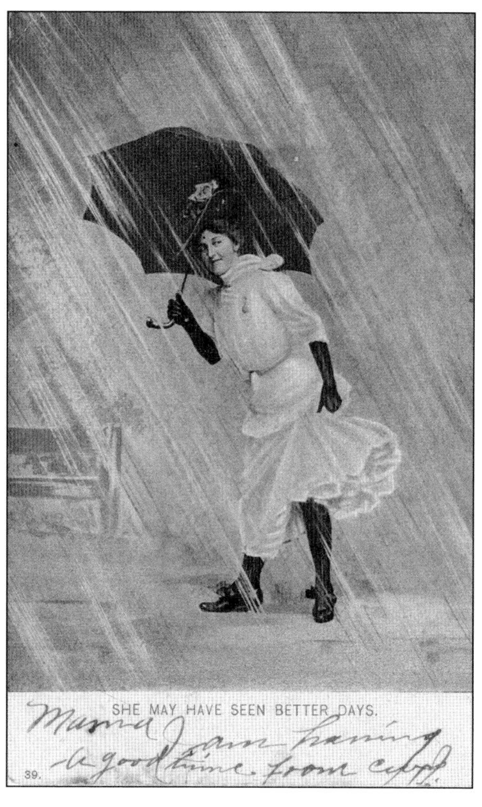

These two early-century novelty cards, postmarked 1907 (above) and 1908 (below), display the fashionable beachwear of the first decade in scenes intended to add humor to the holiday greeting. A stylish lady, with modish hat, windswept flowing dress, long sleeved gloves, long black stockings, and shoes with bows, leans into the wind as the rain pours down on her perambulation. The postcard suggests that "she may have seen better days," but the sender writes, "I am having a good time." Wearing colorfully patterned bathing costumes not unlike the beach dress, and irrespective of hair ribbons and hat, two girls with waists cinched to the point of breathlessness wade into the surf seemingly unaware of the wave building up behind them.

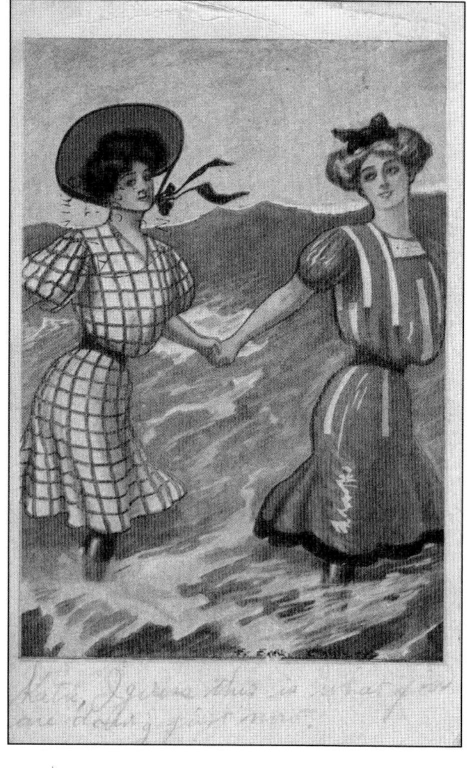

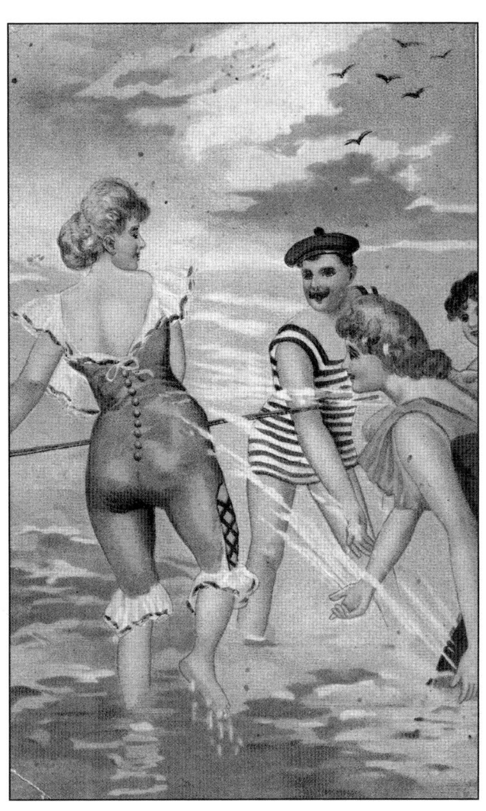

The girl on the left, with a hairdo right out of the Gibson Girl tradition, is being splashed by her fellow beachgoers. The frills at the shoulders and knees contrast with the figure-revealing wet fabric clinging to her body. In the second 1912 novelty card, captioned "The Douche," three girls in their bathing finery surround a lad in a striped bathing shirt. The females are sending sprays of water in all directions, conveying, perhaps, a playful revenge against the handsome and equally mischievous male. The ocean is as calm as a lake, allowing puff shoulders, hairdos, and demeanor in general to remain unruffled.

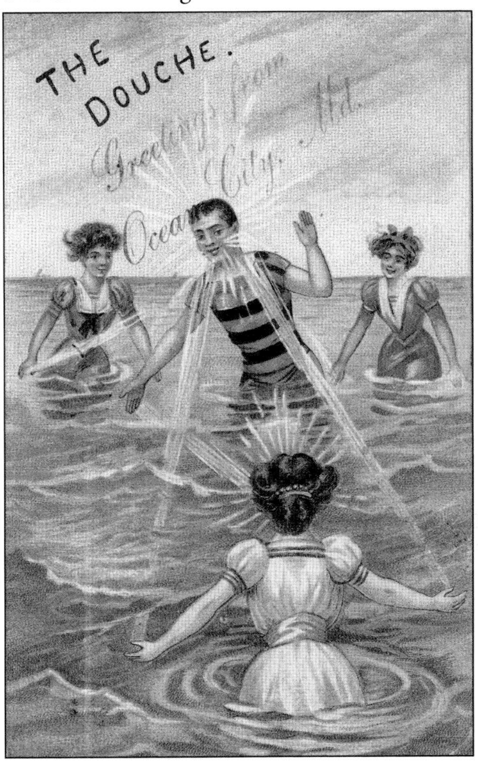

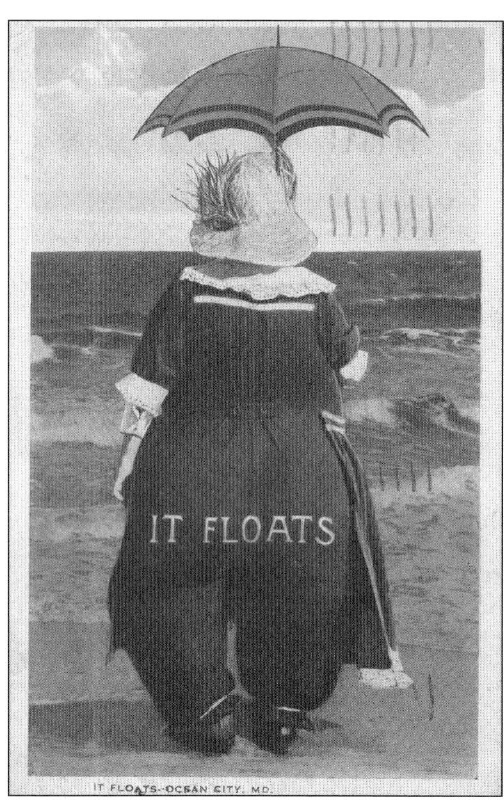

The "anatomically challenged" bather looking out to sea is the butt of a novelty card joke when the message "it floats" is pasted across the woman's derrière. She stands, back to the viewer, staring out to sea; her straw hat is torn and disheveled in two places as though to suggest she had borrowed it from a donkey. The card is postmarked 1939. In a similar view, the pronounced backside of a lady is ironically front and center as she (and it) block the view of the water and amusement park building beyond. Her shoes with crisscross ankle straps, tied bows at the knees and shoulders, and broad-horizontal stripes on the lower garment convey an almost comic demeanor even from the rear.

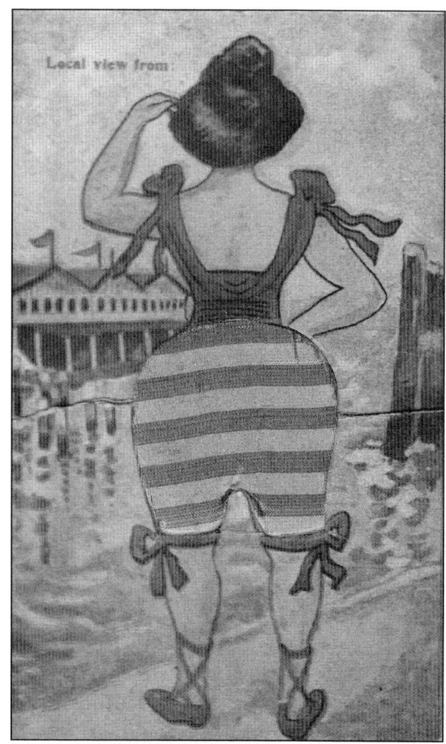

Curt Teich's postcard of a "Saucy Sailorette" could be as early as 1905. Stamped at the top "Ocean City, MD," the sailorette could be prowling along most any beachfront. The plank pilings, sand pail, model sailboat, and ring buoy are emblematic paraphernalia added to the painted scene much as historical portrait settings during past centuries were furnished with symbolic objects.

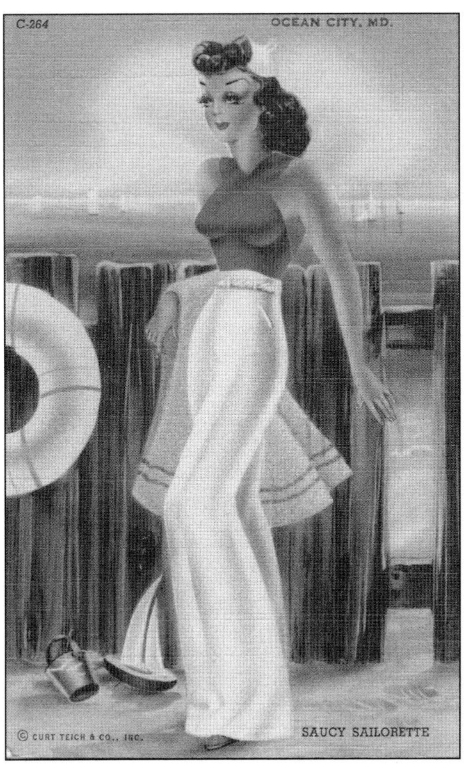

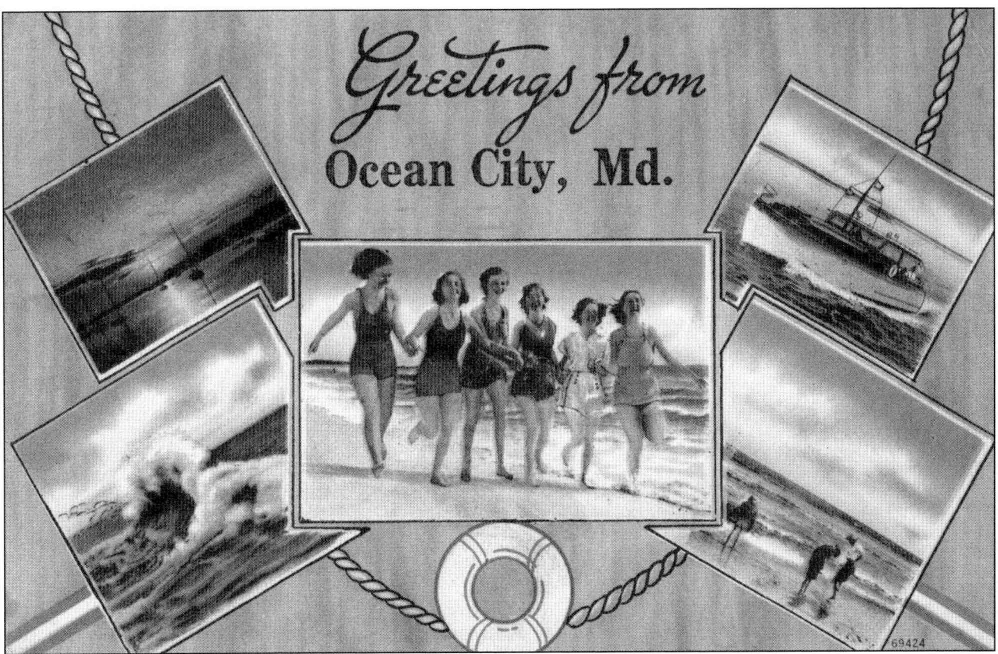

Novelty cards also included, for those purchasers who cannot make up their minds, multiple views from other postcards here providing a mixture of beachcombers, sailboats on the bay (see Chapter 4), crashing ocean waves, charter fishing boats, and, at center in this card, six bathing beauties running along the shore. The background rope and ring buoy add to the nautical themes at the summer resort.

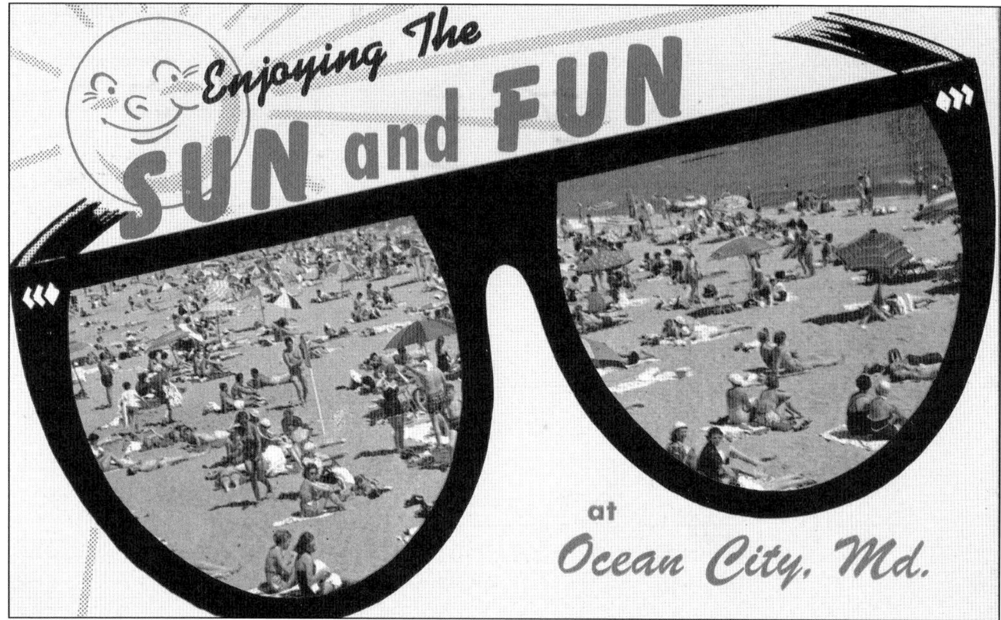

Stencil cards were published in a variety of forms. In this Tichnor Brothers 1964-postmarked card, sunglasses frame beach scenes. The postcard template includes a written message with stencil surround disclosing one or multiple scenes beyond. On page 2 is an example of the most common type in which the name of the town is spelled out in large letters, each providing a frame for a scene from another postcard.

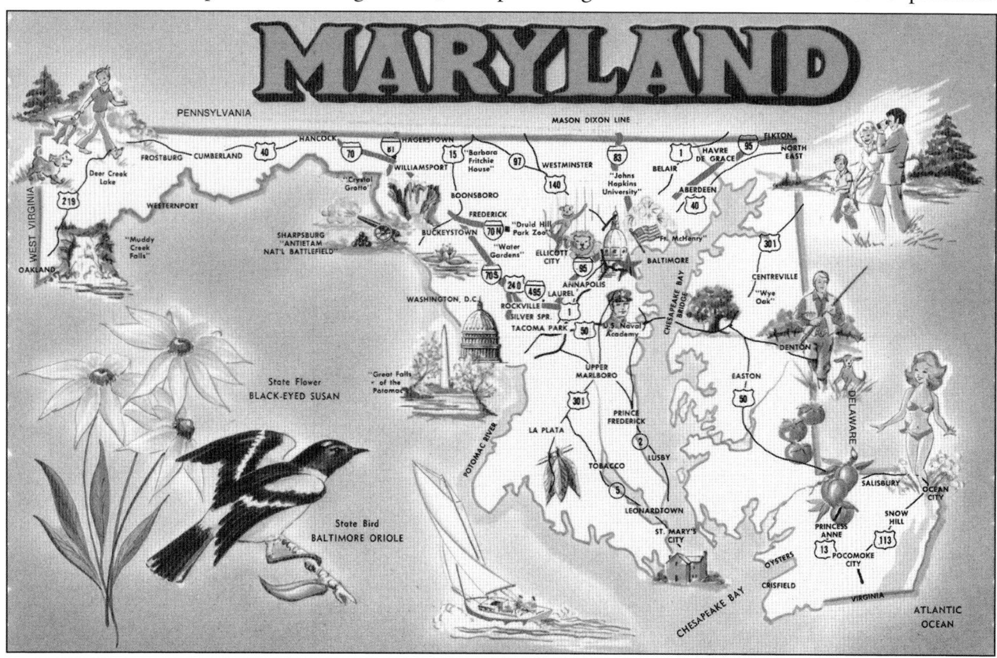

Also popular were postcard maps of Maryland whose towns are highlighted by identifying images like those of buildings; landscape scenes, such as Crystal Grotto and Muddy Creek Falls; battlefields, such as Antietam and Fort McHenry; people, such as duck hunters, Chesapeake Bay sailors, or (in the case of Ocean City) a bikini-clad sunbather. The card, postmarked 1979, identifies the black-eyed Susan as the state flower and the Baltimore oriole as the state bird.

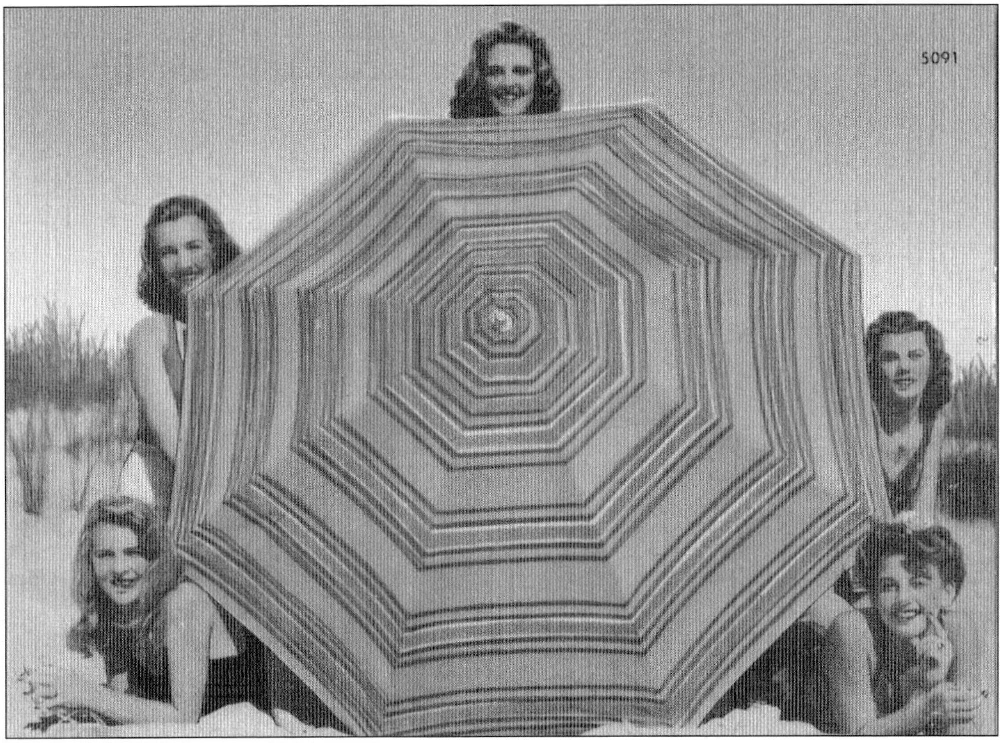

The beach provided two of the most sought after summer jobs for teenagers and young adults, which were operating "beachboy" stands and lifeguarding, both considered girl magnets. A 1945 postcard view (above) is filled with the eye-catching pattern of a striped umbrella behind which five bathing beauties look out at the cameraman. The image was shot in the northern dunes, but the engaging scene of a beach umbrella rental stand, operated by a suntanned beachboy and usually populated by multiple teenaged girls doting on the "hunk" manager, was repeated at every hotel front and roadhead along the beachfront. Below is a detail of a postcard photograph by Kevin N. Moore showing an S&H Beach Service stand (storage box, body boards, beach chairs, and umbrellas for rent). Under the umbrella, the beachboy enjoys his summertime "life of Riley."

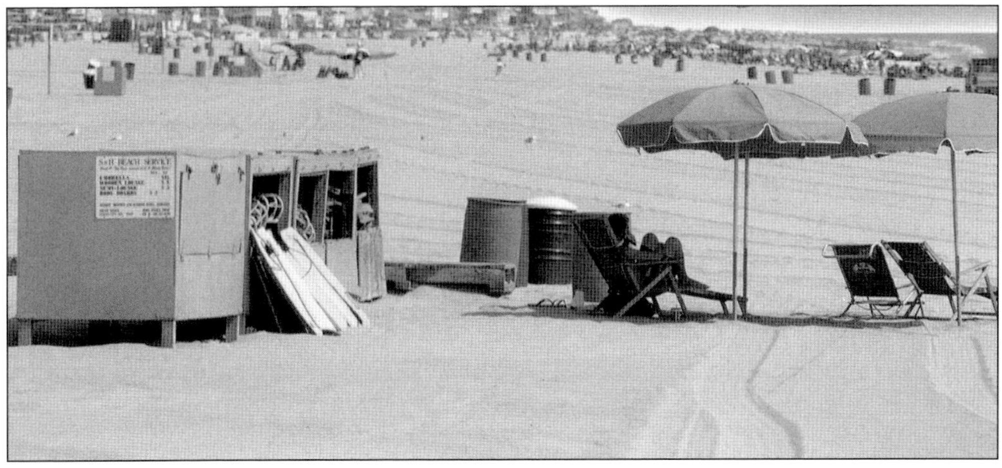

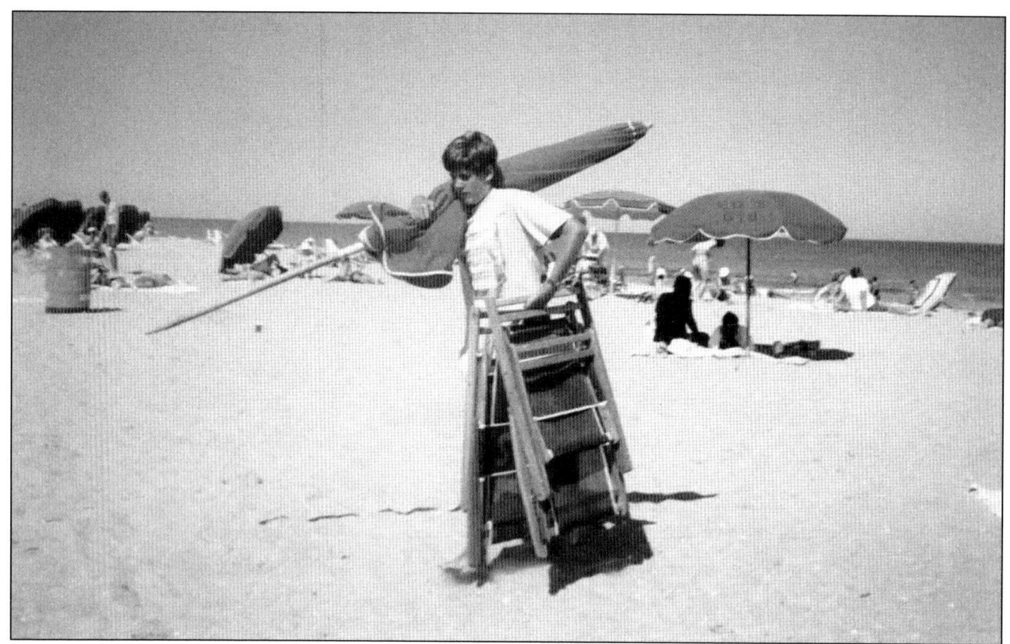

The job of the beachboy was to set up rented beach chairs and umbrellas close to the ocean and to retrieve them at day's end. In the photograph above, Christopher Kyle Craig (the author's son) hauls back to his beach stand a typical family's daily rental of an umbrella and two chairs. With wood pole and wood frames, these substantial furnishings were more durable for beach conditions but were heavy to haul across yards of sand. The daily setup and retrieval involved dozens of umbrellas (see pages 118 and 119), challenging the beachboy to pile 10 more or less umbrellas on his shoulder at once to save trips. Walking across dry sand with a stack of wood, wire, and canvas umbrellas builds up calf muscles, and four chairs on each arm tones the biceps! All to impress the girls. (Above, author's collection.)

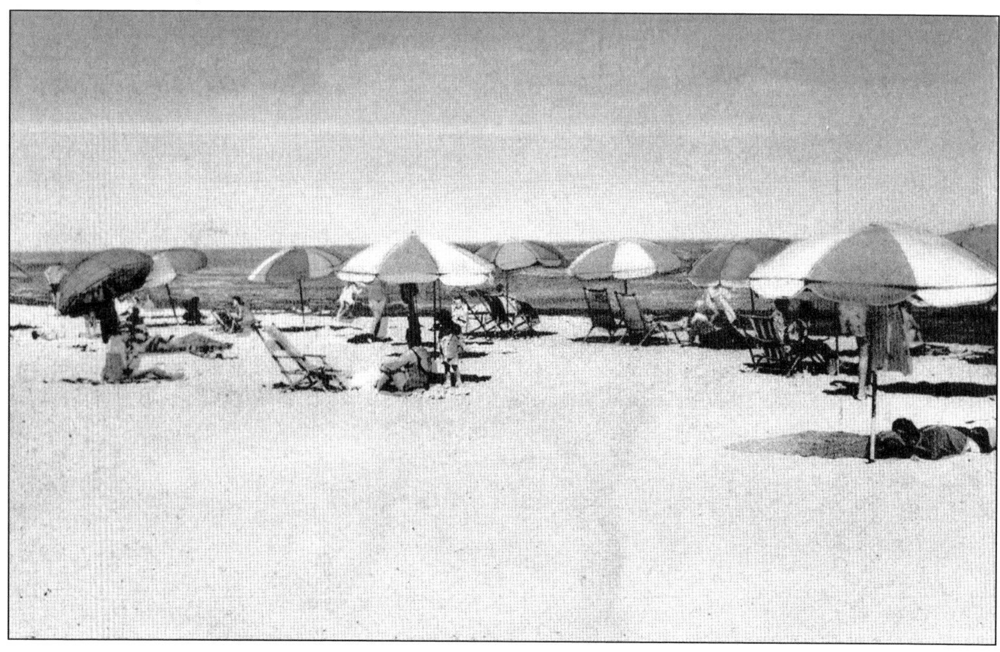

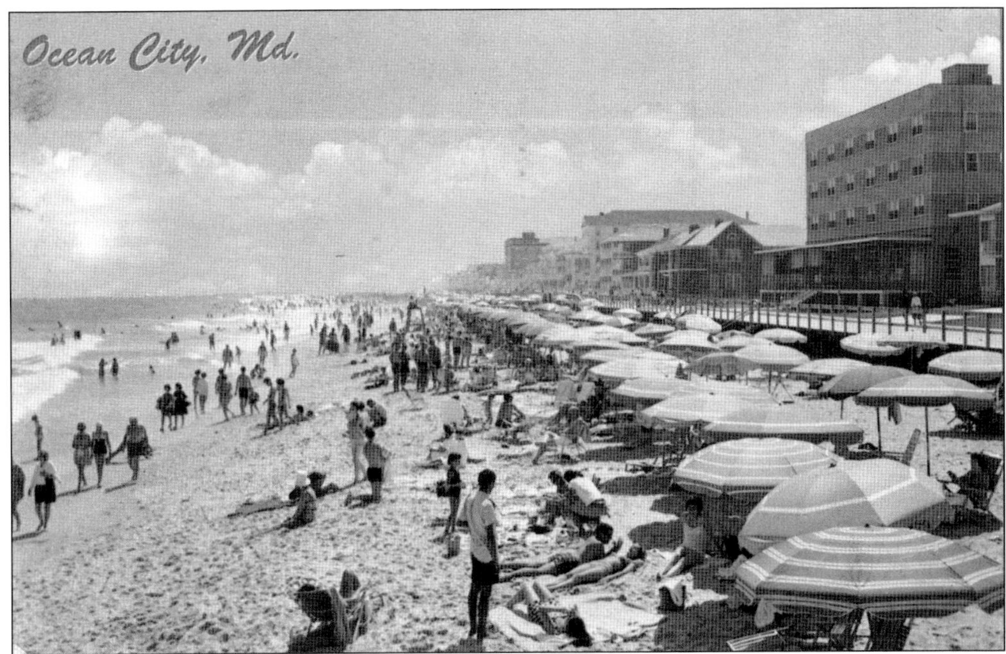

The "front line" of weekly rented umbrellas was established as a neat row between lifeguard stands. At 10:00 a.m., the lifeguard dragged the wooden lifeguard stand just forward of the umbrella line in order to maintain his line of site. Behind this line throughout the day, umbrellas filled every available space near the water; sometimes, individuals tried to set up in front of the front line not knowing they were blocking the lifeguard's view of the surf. However, the unobstructed path created at the water's edge remained open for walking barefoot, beachcombing, and building sandcastles. The Tichnor postcard above, postmarked 1965, shows the front line at Fourteenth Street looking south. The postcard below, postmarked 1967, was photographed by Robert S. Craig, captain of the lifeguards.

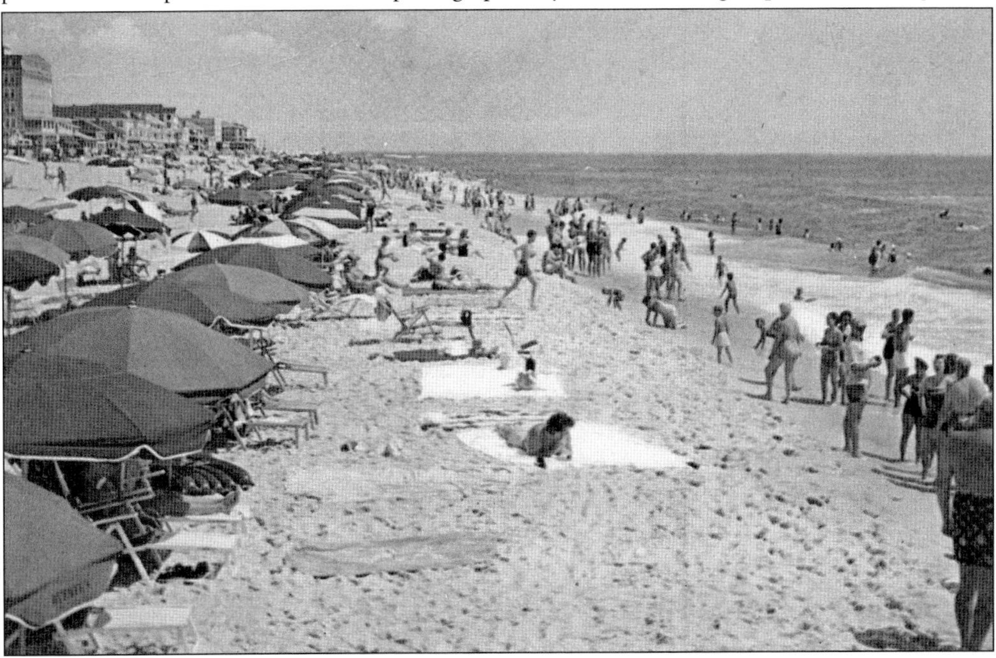

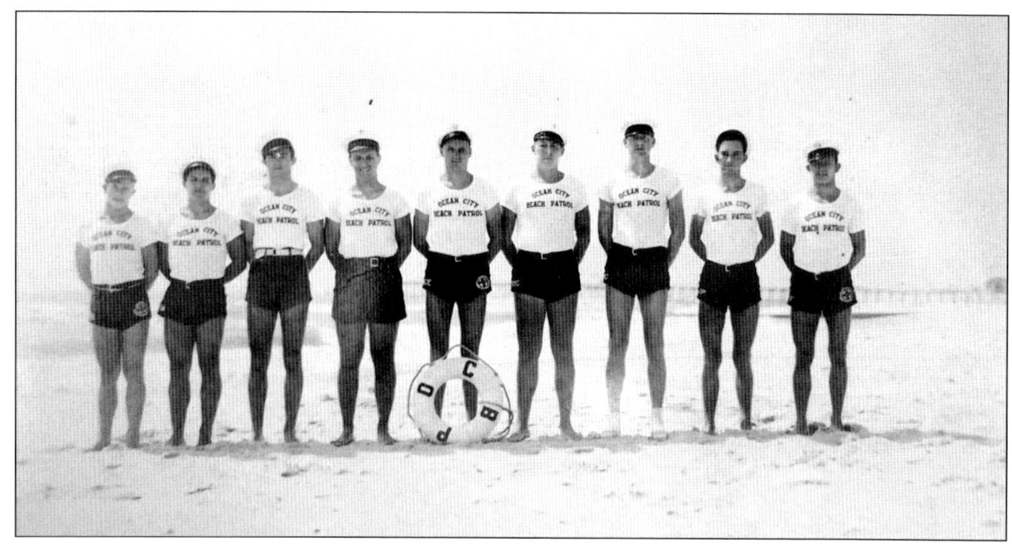

Lifeguarding at Ocean City officially began in 1930 when Ocean City Beach Patrol was established. "Following the crowds" when swimmers ventured beyond the "safe" beach in front of the Coast Guard station, two lifeguards were employed at the start of that summer, and five more were hired by summer's end. Robert S. Craig became a lifeguard at age 16 in 1935 and is seen above (fourth from right) in the 1938 patrol photograph. He was named captain in 1946 and remained in charge until his retirement in 1987, by which time the patrol had grown to over 150 members (below). Craig's 52 years of service is rivaled only by the current captain, Butch Arbin, who celebrated his 50th year in 2022. Each summer, a group photograph documents the patrol. (See Arcadia's *Maryland's Ocean City Beach Patrol.*)

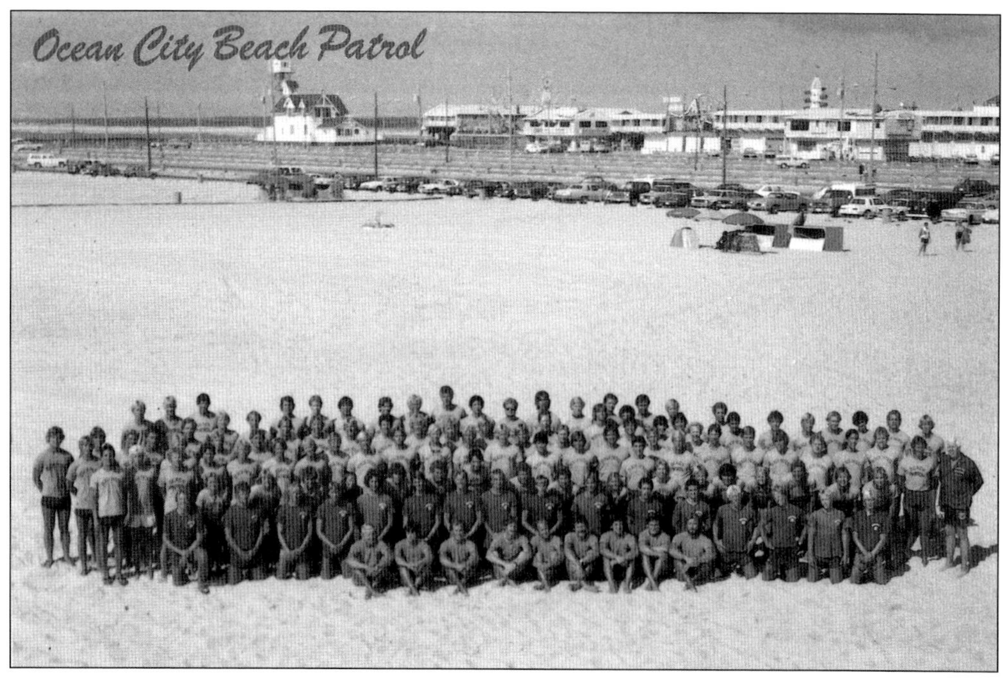

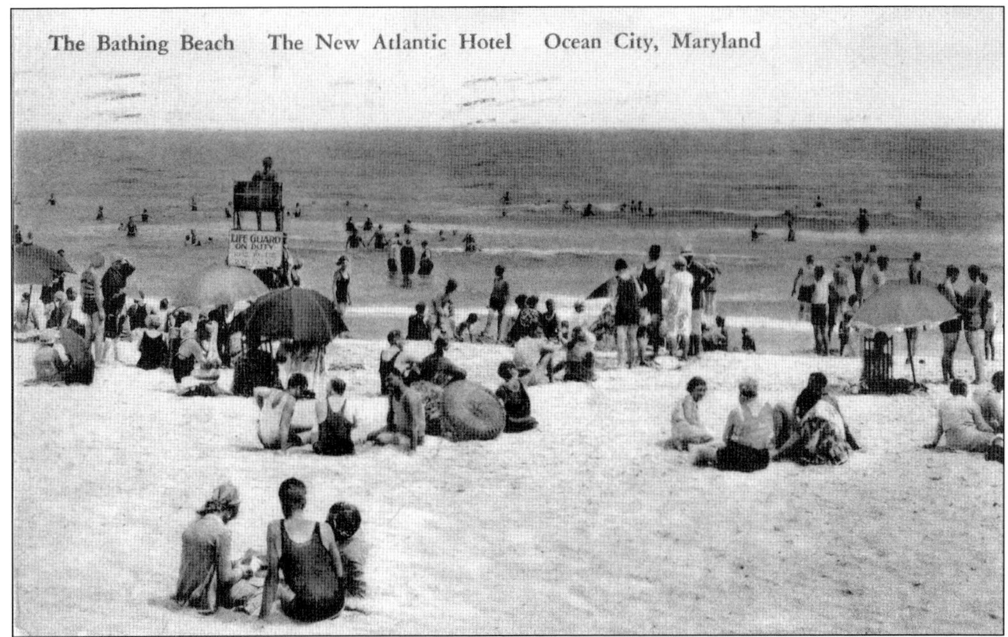

This card, postmarked 1936, shows a lifeguard on duty in front of the New Atlantic Hotel and documents that the simple wooden lifeguard stand with signposted hours (and later beach rules) was a beach landmark from the earliest years of the Ocean City Beach Patrol (OCBP). The top was a flat platform, so a portable beach chair had to be balanced for the duration of the eight-hour day.

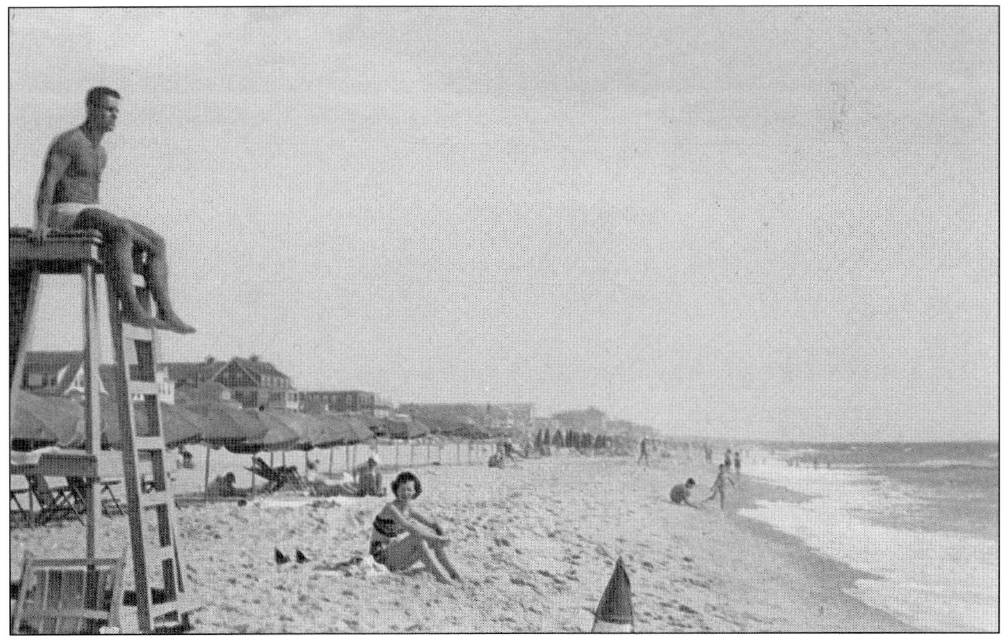

The same raised flat platform with ladder remained in use in the 1950s when this 1953 photograph, looking north, was taken of the lifeguard on Second Street. Note the torpedo buoy positioned in the sand in front of the lifeguard stand; it is a rescue device introduced in 1947 and still used in a revised style today. Also note the even front line of umbrellas behind the guard stand.

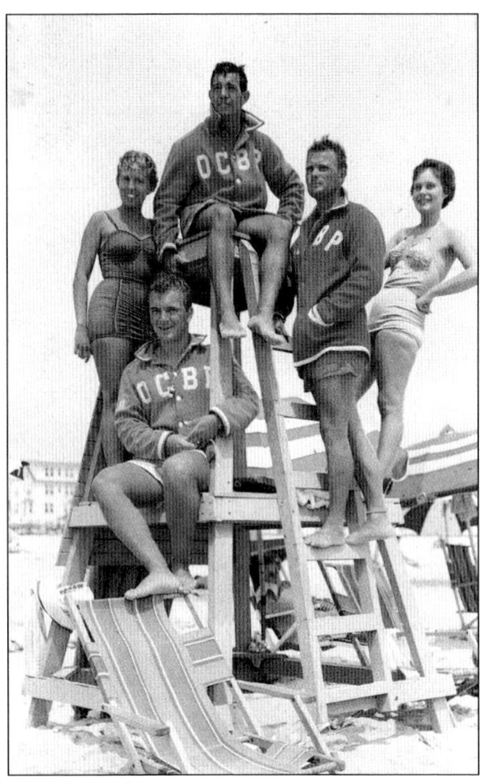

Also from 1953 is this publicity photograph of three lifeguards with two girls (not on the patrol, since the first female hire was in 1978). The lifeguards appear in officially issued uniform jackets but not yet uniform bathing suits. Blue tank suits and white T-shirts would become the uniform OCBP attire during the 1960s and red suits, jackets, and sweats from the 1980s on, with officers in different colors.

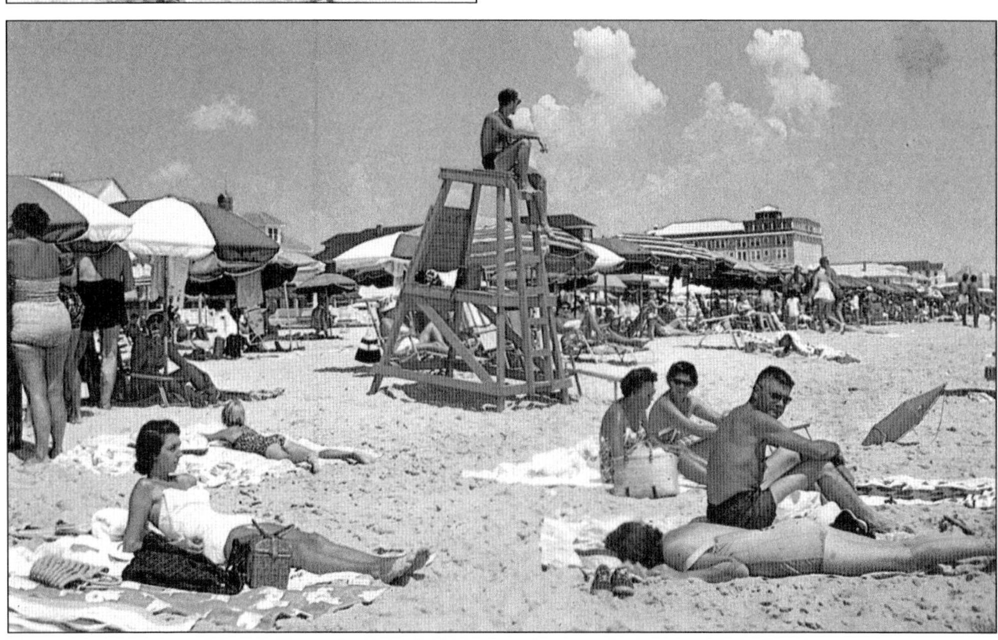

Capt. Robert S. Craig, a semiprofessional photographer, took group and individual photographs of members of the beach patrol, providing a historical documentation of the organization as well as mementos for individual lifeguards. This (likely late-1950s/early-1960s) postcard by Craig shows the lifeguard on Seventh Street with a background view of the Tenth Street George Washington Hotel in the distance.

Also likely from the 1960s is this beach scene (above) with a lifeguard sending semaphore from atop his stand. Semaphore (signaling by flags) was also introduced to the patrol by Captain Craig (in 1952) and has served ever since, especially when used to reunite lost children with their parents. Based on a description from a lifeguard, a "lost" message is flagged up and down the beach, and when a child is found, a "found" message speeds from stand to stand until it reaches the lifeguard reporting the lost boy or girl. "Your lost child is at the lifeguard stand on Fourth Street" is a welcome message to a distressed parent. Air-filled canvas surf mats, visible in the center of the above photograph, were rented by the hour from the beachboys. OCBP crew competitions (below) have been popular public events to display lifeguard skills.

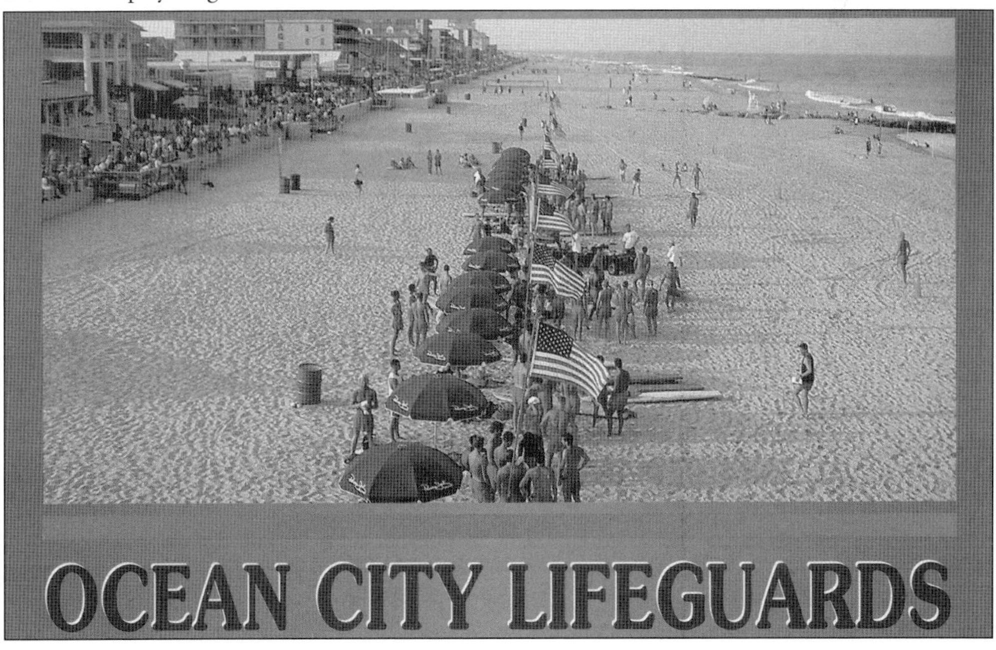

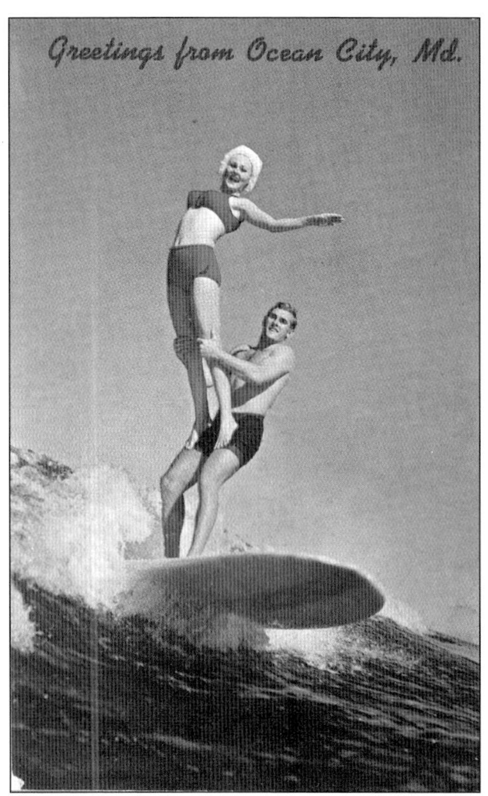

Although Ned France, the erstwhile magician, eccentric entrepreneur, and proprietor of Berlin, Maryland's unique and most bizarre general store, has claimed to be Ocean City's first surfer, another local celebrity George Feehley (one-time lifeguard and later city councilman) was photographed with Geri Chaski in 1969 tandem surfboarding. This Lusterchrome (trademark of Tichnor Brothers) postcard of another pair of tandem surfers was, in any case, an unusual scene for Ocean City.

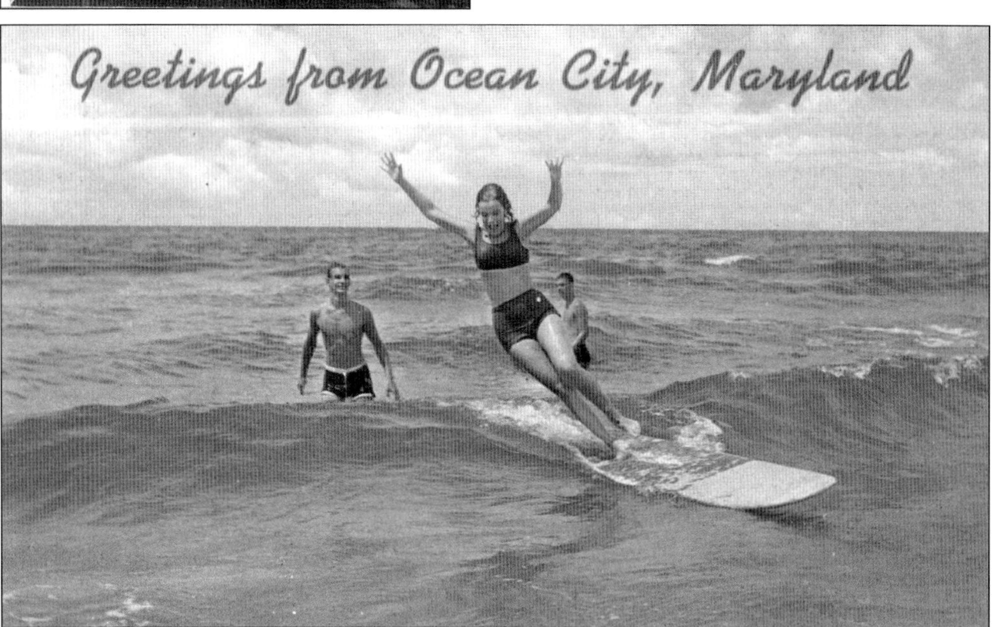

More typical was the impending wipe out on a small wave in this Tichnor Brothers postcard. Surfers appeared in the early 1960s on beaches outside city limits, but the real surge of interest in surfing followed the showing of Bruce Brown's documentary film *The Endless Summer* (1966). The town's first surf shop, the Eastern Surfer, opened in 1964 in the basement of the Sandy Hill Motel on Eighteenth Street (razed).

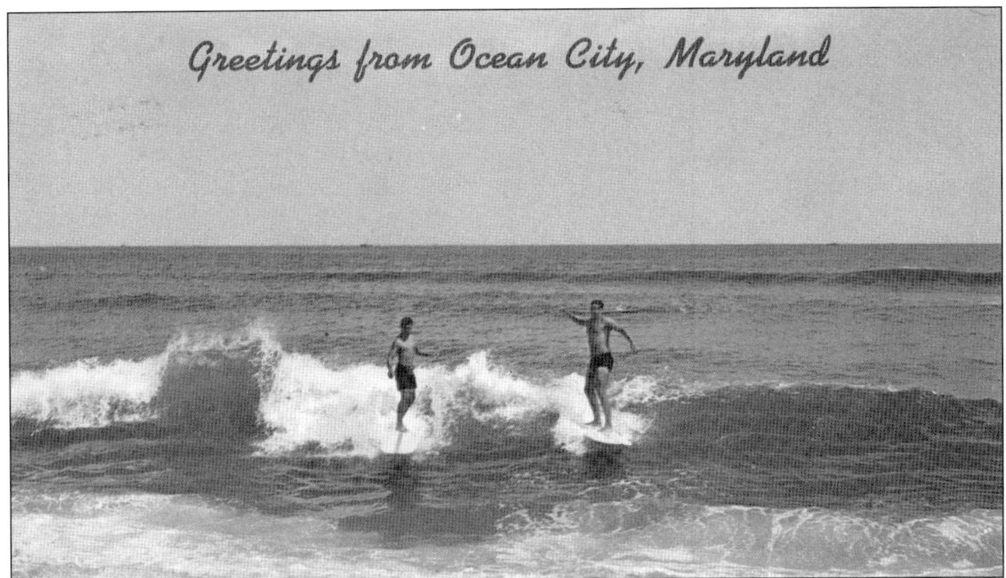

This card was postmarked 1968, two years after the theater release of *The Endless Summer*; it had been shown in private screenings across the country in 1964–1965. The film followed two surfers on a worldwide tour in search of the perfect wave. The film netted $20 million worldwide and started a craze for surfing that has little abated, including in Ocean City where waves are seldom (or never) too big to ride.

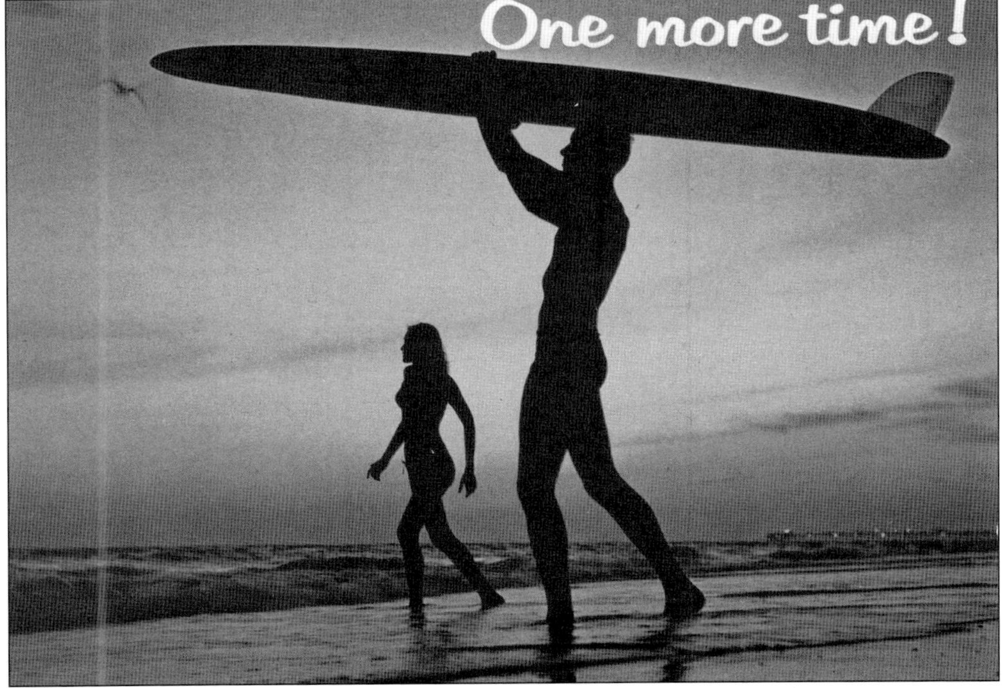

"One more time!" features a surfer and his girlfriend silhouetted against a sunset sky heading for the water and "one last wave." A full moon surf, with a west wind to build up a smooth and high break, make ideal conditions. Hours when the surf is "not up" may be spent at Ocean City's iconic surf shops, including the Endless Summer (1983), Malibu's (1986), or Ron Jon (2013).

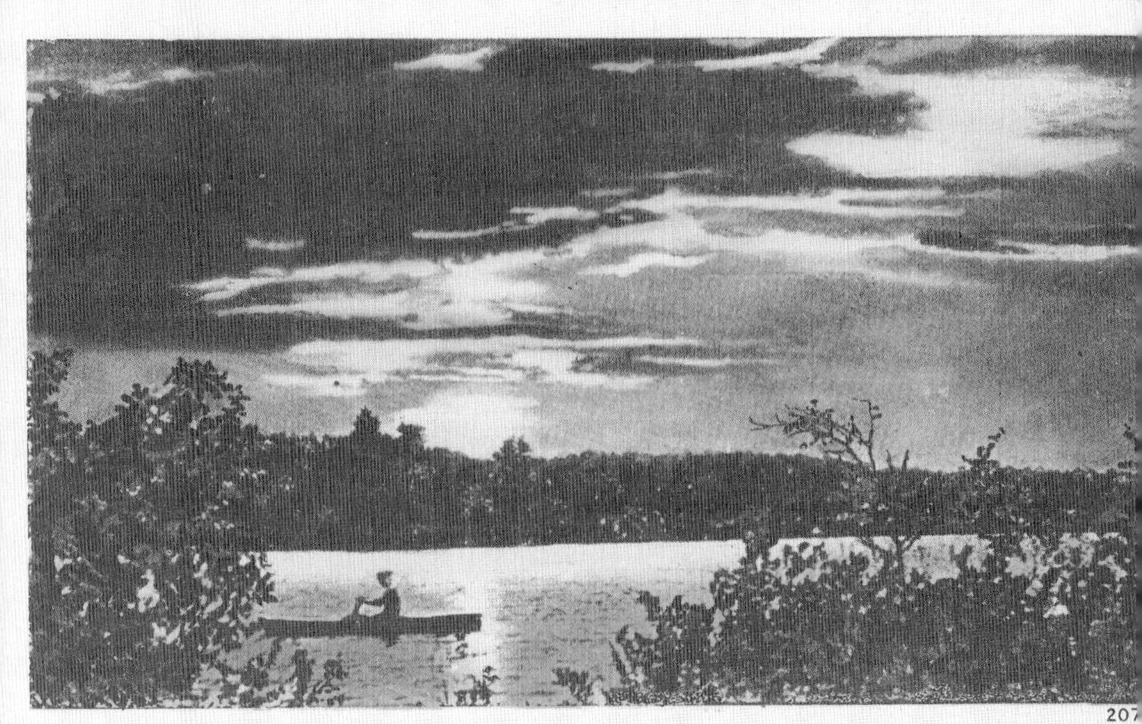

"Along the Sinepuxent Bay, Ocean City, MD." is a romantic moonlit or sunset postcard of a lone boater photographed on the calm bay, postmarked 1946 but likely published a decade earlier. The Prussian blue and gray sky is accented with pink, white, and yellow clouds reflected on the mirrored surface of the bay below. Green island foliage frames the view across to the mainland beyond.

Four

Bay

The bays and tidewater coves and marshes west of the barrier island (Assateague Island into Virginia, Ocean City, and Fenwick Island in Delaware) are known by the following names: Chincoteague Bay (north of Wallop's Island, Virginia), Sinepuxent Bay and Newport Bay (north of South Point, Maryland, to downtown/midtown Ocean City), Isle of Wight Bay and Assawoman Bay (west of Ocean City, Maryland), and Little Assawoman Bay (Delaware). Storms have periodically cut inlets across the island joining west-side bays to the Atlantic Ocean, most notably the permanent Indian River Inlet in Delaware and the more recent 1933 Ocean City inlet in Maryland. Sinepuxent Bay extended along the backside (west) of the barrier island, which, before the 1933 inlet broke through, was continuous from Assateague Island northward to Isle of Wight Bay at Ocean City. The 1933 August storm, a hurricane before hurricanes started to be named (1953), poured so much rain into Sinepuxent Bay that it literally overflowed, cutting the Ocean City inlet through to the ocean.

The force of the storm and the extent of flooding nearly destroyed the town, but in many ways, it also was a blessing. The inlet provided ocean access to the bay, and with a safe harbor bayside, fishermen no longer had to beach their boats overnight among the sand dunes and above high tide lines (see pages 31 and 40). Bayside bulkheads were constructed, and commercial and recreational fishing expanded with a mainland harbor and both commercial and recreational docks developed in West Ocean City. In 1942, a new and permanent US Route 213 bascule bridge (drawbridge) opened crossing the bay. Six years later, in 1948, the road nomenclature changed to US Route 50 with signage today identifying Sacramento as the western terminus of the 3,073-mile-long national road.

In the years that followed, "Sinepuxent" Bay (also known as "Synepuxent" Bay) appeared on postcards, which were likely scenes of what today is Isle of Wight Bay west of Ocean City. The protected bays became the sites of recreational activities from fishing and clamming to jet skiing, motorboating, and sightseeing on a "pirate" boat. Charter boats for deep-sea fishing and private yachts and recreational boats established docks along bayside harbors both downtown and at the Ship Café docks (now Harbour Island).

In 1939, Pres. Franklin D. Roosevelt was part of a marlin fishing party out of the six-year-old Ocean City inlet, and afterwards, he bestowed on the town the following title: "The White Marlin Capital of the World." (The blue marlin world capital title is claimed by the Kona coast on the Big Island, Hawaii, by Los Cabos in Mexico, and by Cape Verde, a Portuguese archipelago in the

Atlantic off Western Africa.) Ocean City's white marlin capital claim is sustained by the annual White Marlin Open Tournament in August, which has been held yearly since 1974. It is billed as the largest billfish tournament in the world in terms of participation and payout. In 2022, angler Jeremy Duffie on the boat *Billfisher* landed a 77.5-pound white marlin to win the largest prize ever paid out in a fishing tournament—$4,536,926. The previous year, winning the Mid-Atlantic Tournament, the same boat landed a 1,135-pound blue marlin breaking a Maryland State Record. In 2023, the White Marlin Tournament will celebrate its 50th anniversary.

Much like the boardwalk and beach, the bay became the subject for numerous postcards recording its natural settings, its views of the town's skyline from the west, and its bridges, docks, and harbors, enticing postcard recipients to come to Ocean City to fish, sail, and enjoy other water recreation.

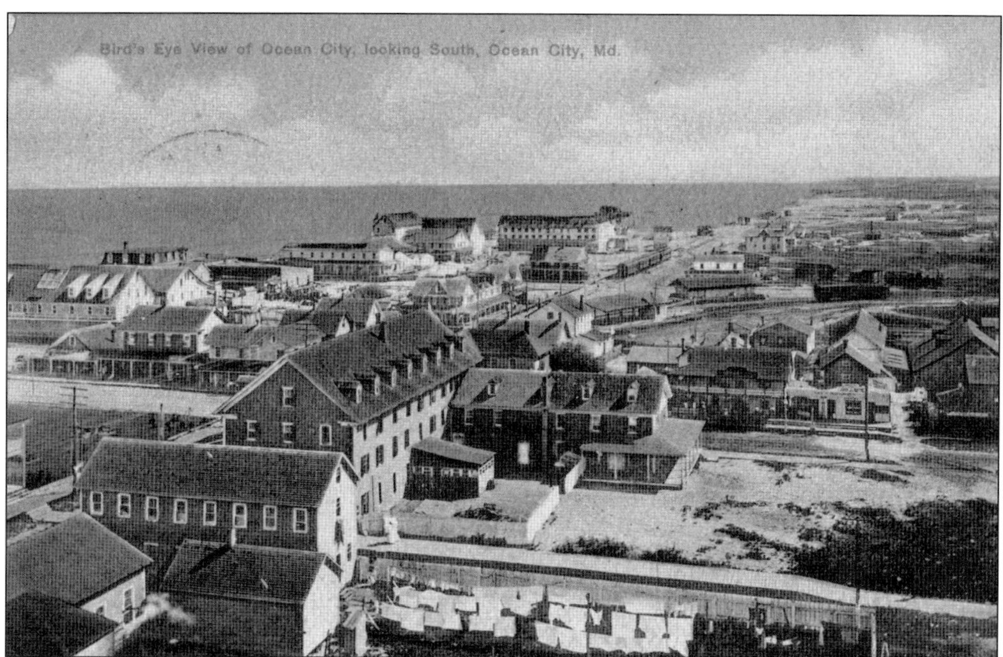

In this aerial view of Ocean City postmarked 1908, numerous details serve to document the history of the town. Entering the view from the right is the rail line with a dark railcar just west of the rail station sited on the curve. The rail line extended both north and south along Baltimore Avenue. Four railcars are visible near South First Street (top center). Note there is no inlet. While there are a few buildings south of the rail line, the barrier island continues to the horizon, land-connected to what is today Assateague Island beyond the future inlet. The c. 1910 Louis Kaufmann postcard below features the railroad station. The Baltimore, Chesapeake & Atlantic Railroad (nicknamed Black Cinders & Ashes) was chartered in 1886 and ran from the Chesapeake Bay steamship port of Claiborne, Maryland, to Ocean City.

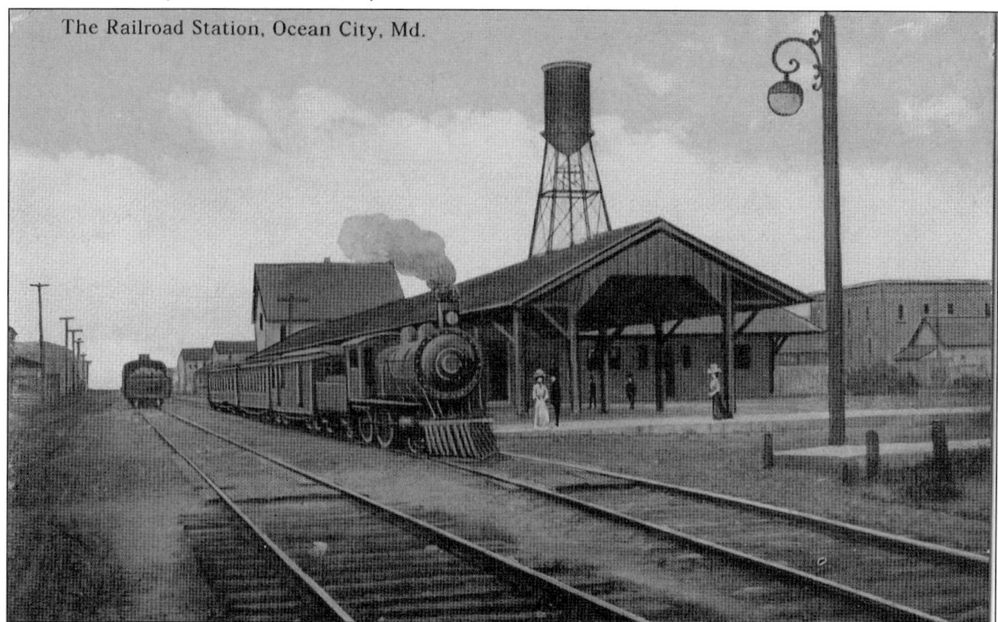

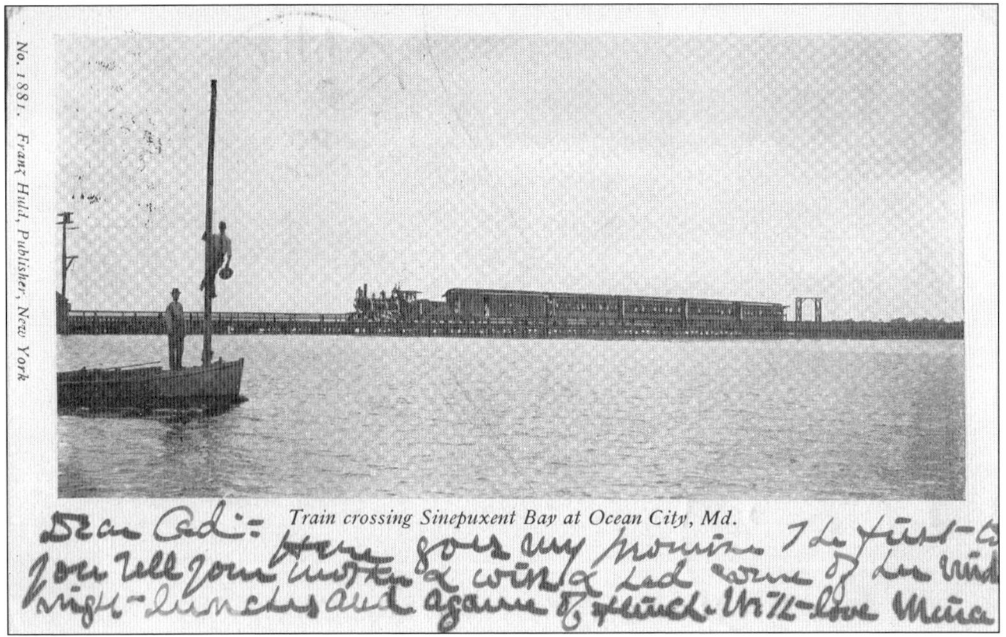

Franz Huld published this early view of a "Train crossing Sinepuxent Bay at Ocean City, Md." (above). Postmarked 1907, the card illustrates a postal regulation of the time; the sender's message could only be squeezed on the picture side of the card since the reverse side was limited to the recipient's address. Between 1876 and 1933, the narrow wood trestle bridge with a center pivot section brought passengers to town at South Division Street turning north along Baltimore Avenue to an early station at the Atlantic Hotel; a larger station was built in 1903 on South Division Street. The Louis Kaufmann postcard below, of about the same date as the Huld card, romanticizes the scene as a moonlit evening with light reflected off the calm bay and puff clouds, likely hand painted, over the photograph.

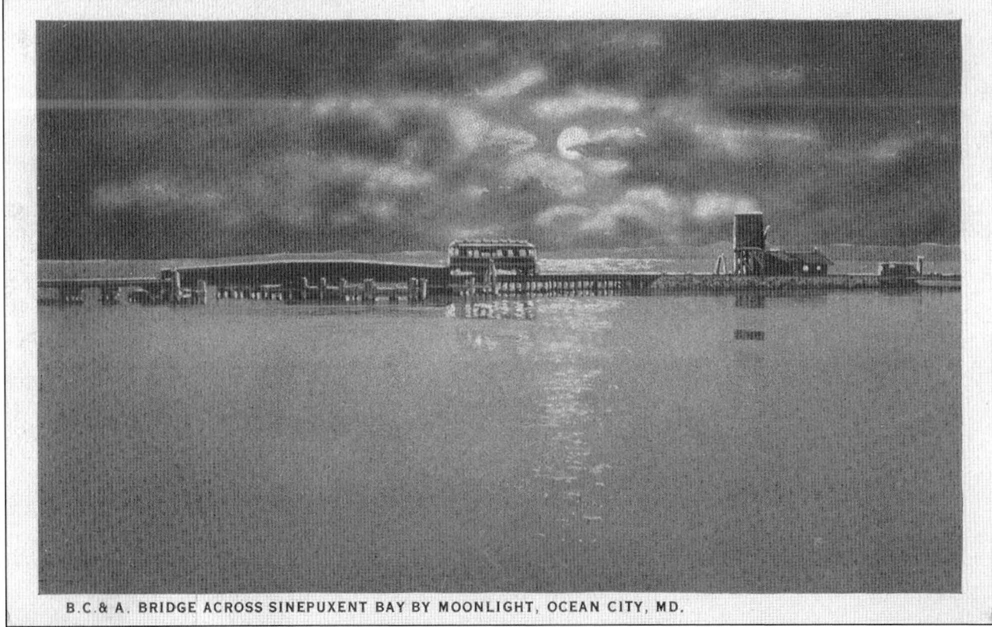

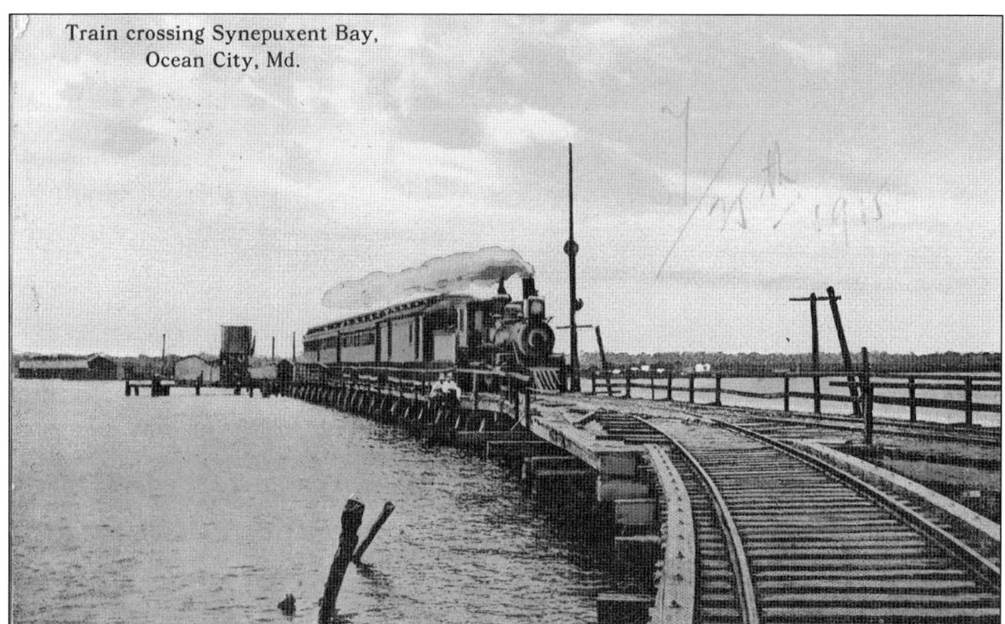

The sender has scratched the date July 25, 1915, over the image on this postcard captioned "Train crossing Synepuxent [*sic*] Bay, Ocean City, Md." With a single track across the bridge, a split track at the town end served the train's arrival and departure without the need for a railway turntable. The final leg of the trip, from Salisbury to Ocean City, was originally via the Wicomico & Pocomoke Railroad.

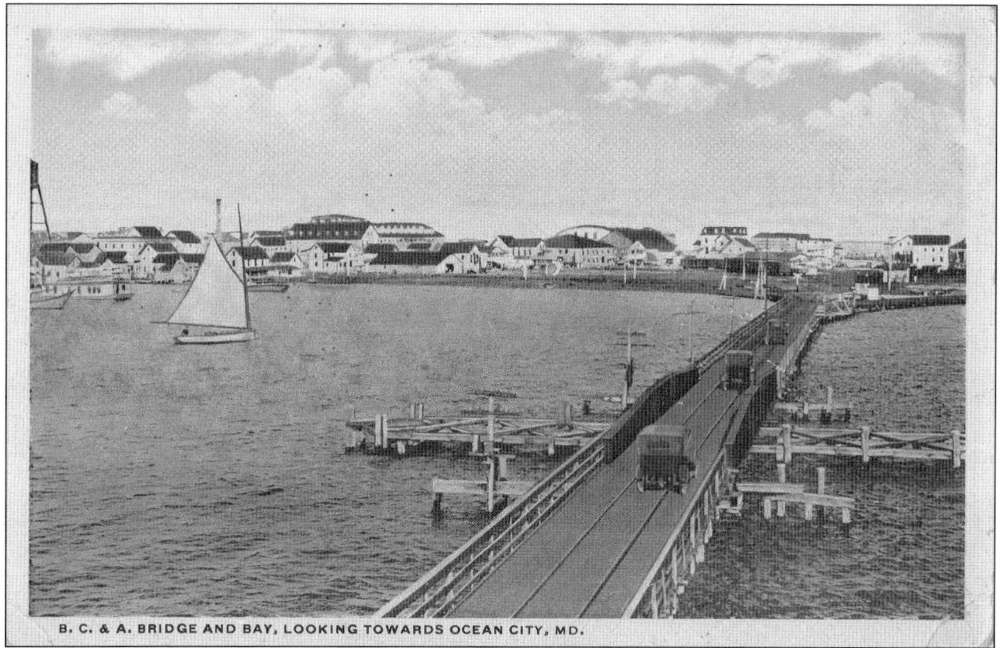

Since 1908, Henry Ford sold Model T automobiles to Americans who were increasingly interested in taking road trips. By 1917, almost five million cars were registered in the United States. As shown in this postcard view (postmarked 1917 but of an earlier photograph), planks were laid over the railroad bridge to accommodate automobilists who paid a 5¢ toll to drive across the railroad bridge. In 1916, a two-lane state road bridge opened adjacent.

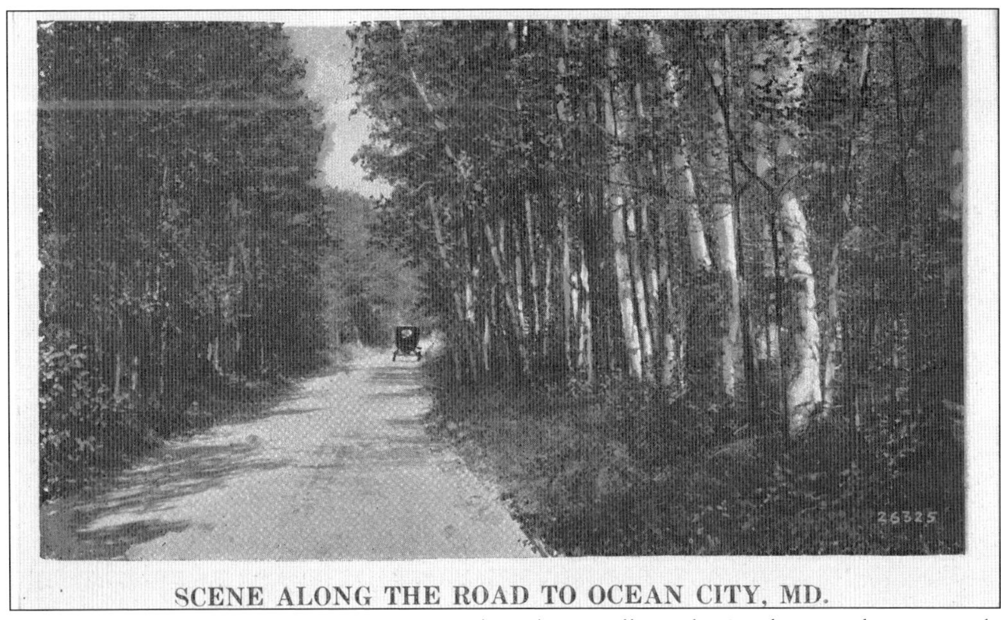

Eastern Shore roads, as was the case nationwide and especially in the South, were almost entirely unpaved, cutting narrow dirt paths through woodlands where rain brought impassable mud and where rural isolation added to the problems of mechanical breakdowns. Postcard publishers, however, romanticized road trips with such postcards as this "Scene Along the Road to Ocean City, MD" with its jaunty Model T in the distance.

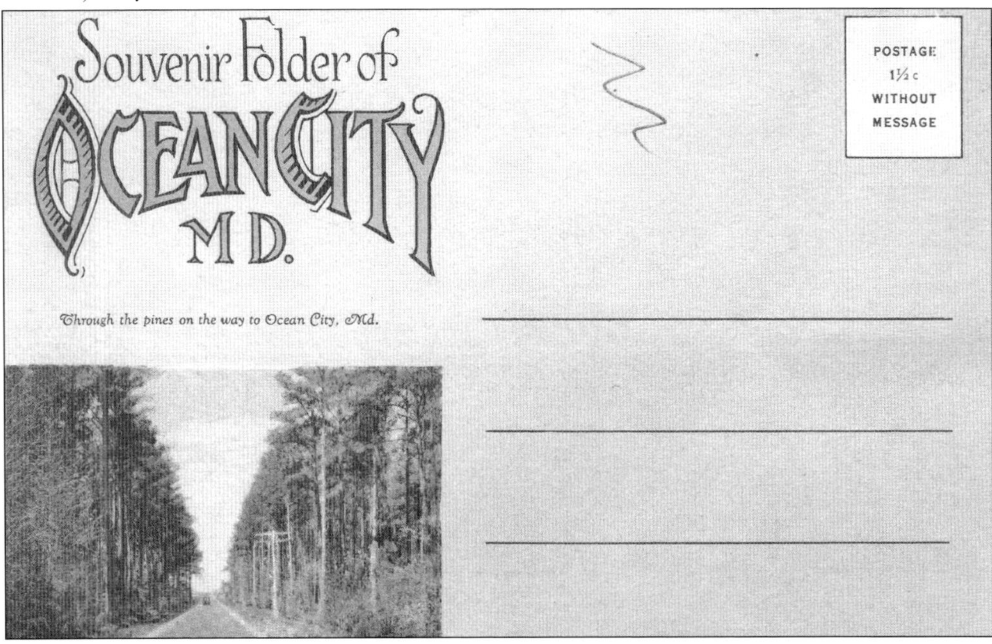

A souvenir folder with a view "Through the pines on the way to Ocean City, Md." features a landscape not unlike sections of the uncommercialized Route 50 west of town as the road passes today between Berlin and Salisbury. Motorists arriving on the west bank of the Sinepuxent Bay still had to cross the waterway where, until 1916, there was only a railroad bridge for the Baltimore, Chesapeake & Atlantic.

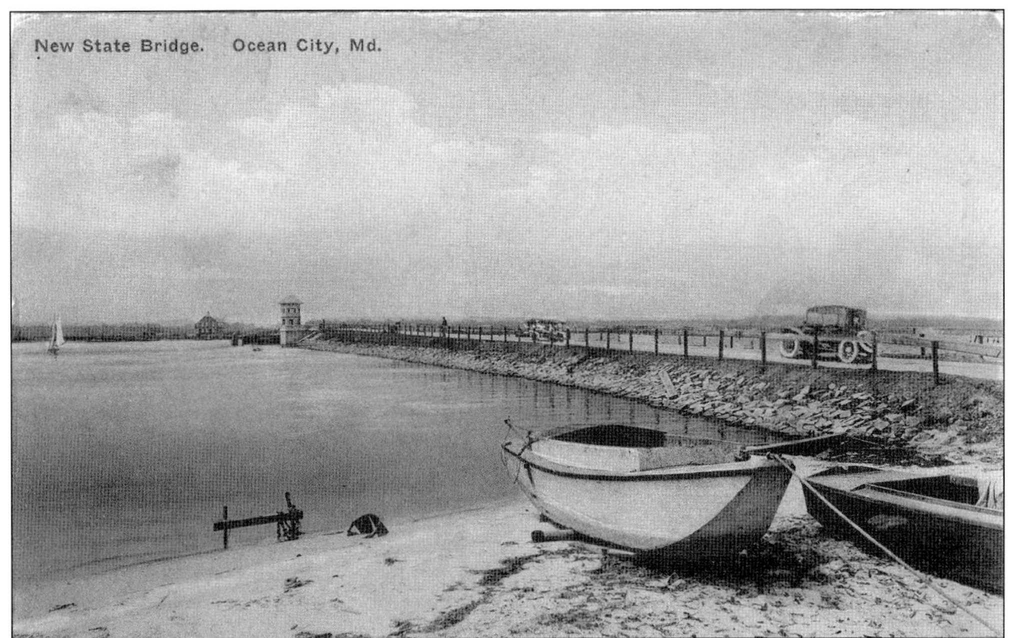

The new state road, which opened in 1916, is shown with its two-way traffic in a picturesque Albertype postcard, postmarked 1919. The tower marks the bay channel and bridge opening. The bridge was built alongside and just north of the railroad bridge, entering Ocean City at Worcester Street, a block north of the South Division Street rail line.

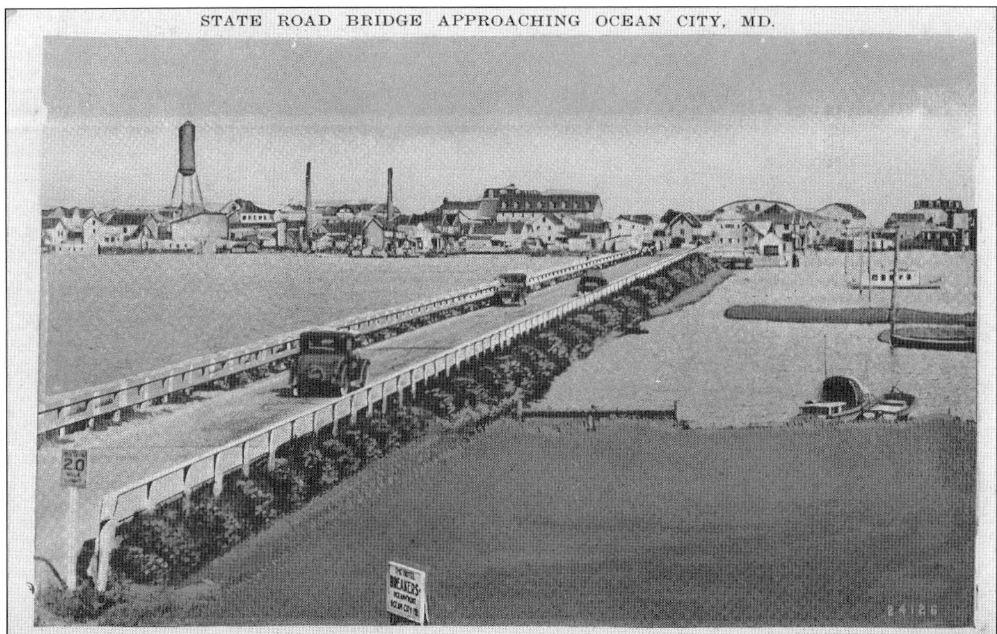

This 1929-postmarked card shows the state road bridge approaching Ocean City. The curved roof on the skyline (at Wicomico Street on the Boardwalk) is the convention hall. To the left, the tall buildings on the horizon are the mansard-roofed Atlantic Hotel rising above the broad Seaside Hotel. All three buildings were burned in the 1925 fire, with the Seaside never rebuilt, so the photograph is pre-1925.

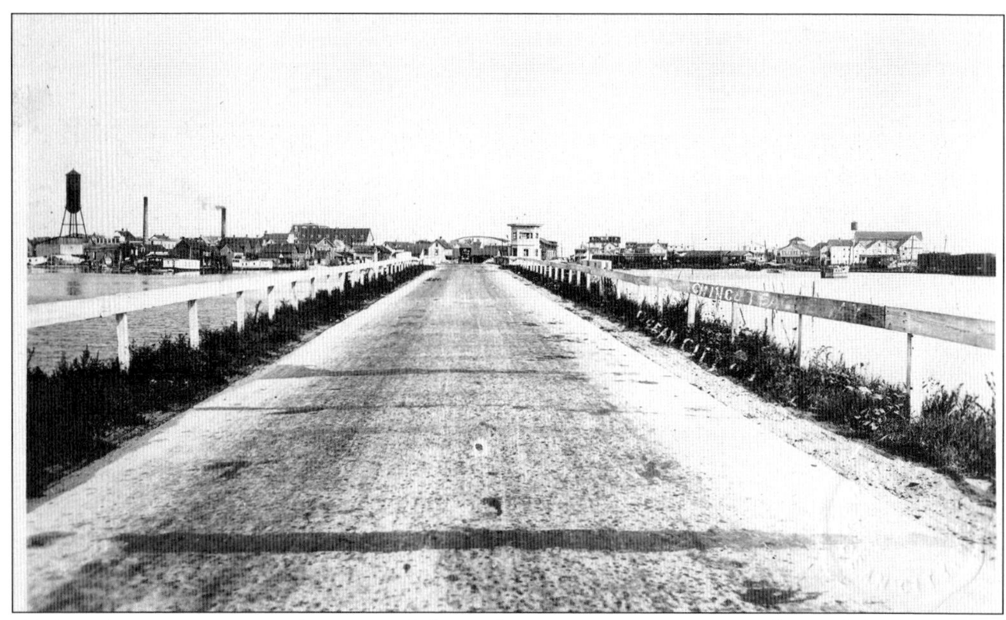

With an August 1923 note, this postcard shows the view east into town; just beyond the distant car, the road bends right to enter town on Worcester Street. On the road's barrier fence is painted the wrong identification of "Chincoteague Bay." On the horizon and directly above the letters, "teague" is the still extant merry-go-round building (with its broad polygonal cupola), which houses Trimper's carousel and several 1920s kiddie rides.

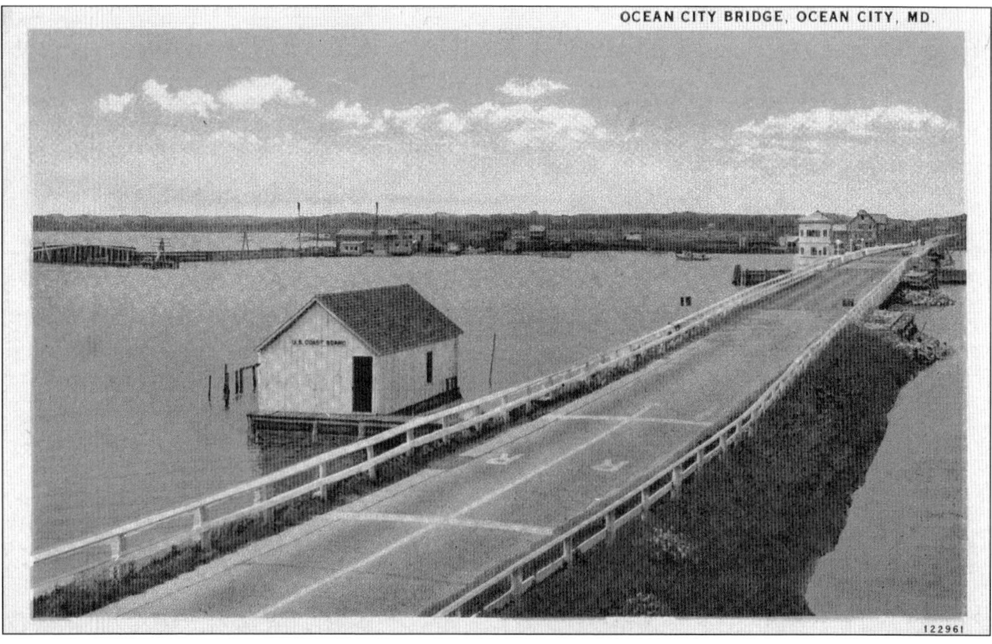

In this Louis Kaufmann postcard of the state road bridge, a US Coast Guard boathouse is seen adjacent. Above its roof is visible the railroad bridge. During the 1933 storm that cut through the Ocean City inlet, the railroad bridge was completely destroyed and the state road bridge damaged. Nine years later, the concrete "million dollar bridge," later named for Harry Kelley, opened (see opposite page).

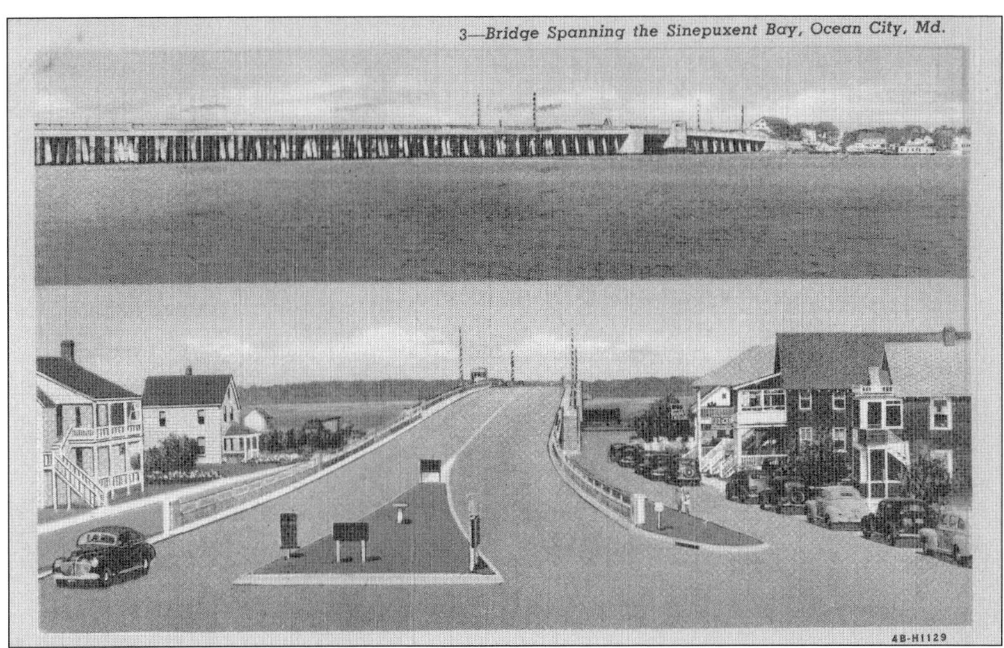

In this two-view Curt Teich postcard published in 1944, the new 1942 bridge is seen from the southwest (top) and looking west from North Division Street where the bridge enters town (bottom). The tower-like form at the bridge span is the bridge tender's station overlooking the channel; four upright poles are lowered to block auto traffic prior to the lifting of the drawbridge's metal roadbed. In the image below, the road divides as it enters town, directing incoming traffic (car, bottom left) via the right (south) fork onto (one-way east) Caroline Street, while departing traffic from (one-way west) Division Street entered the bridge via the north fork. Today, the direction of traffic on Division and Caroline Streets is reversed with all traffic entering town onto North Division Street. The Harry Cann postcard below shows the raised drawbridge from the northeast.

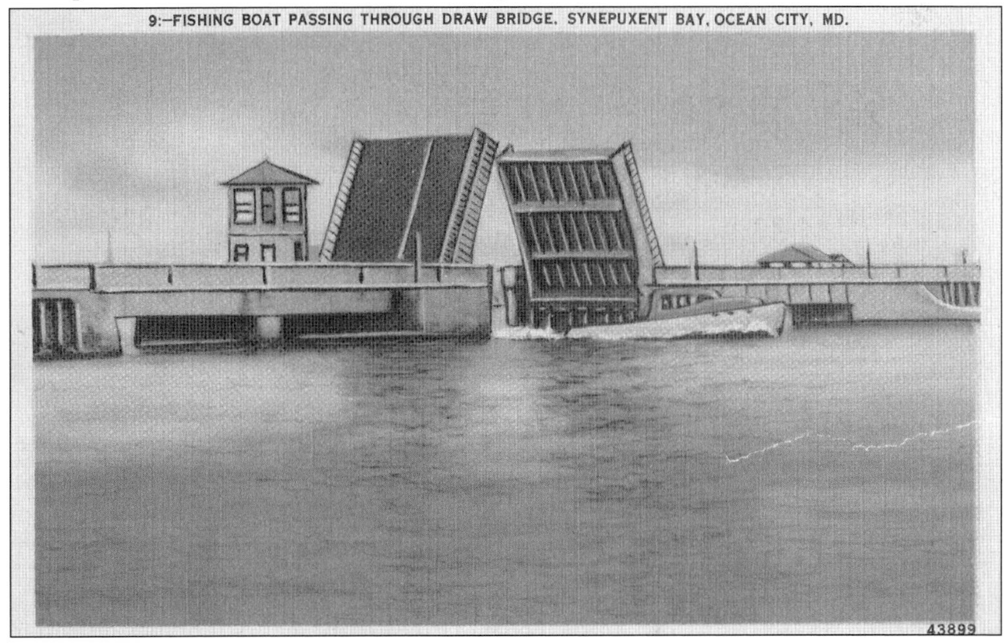

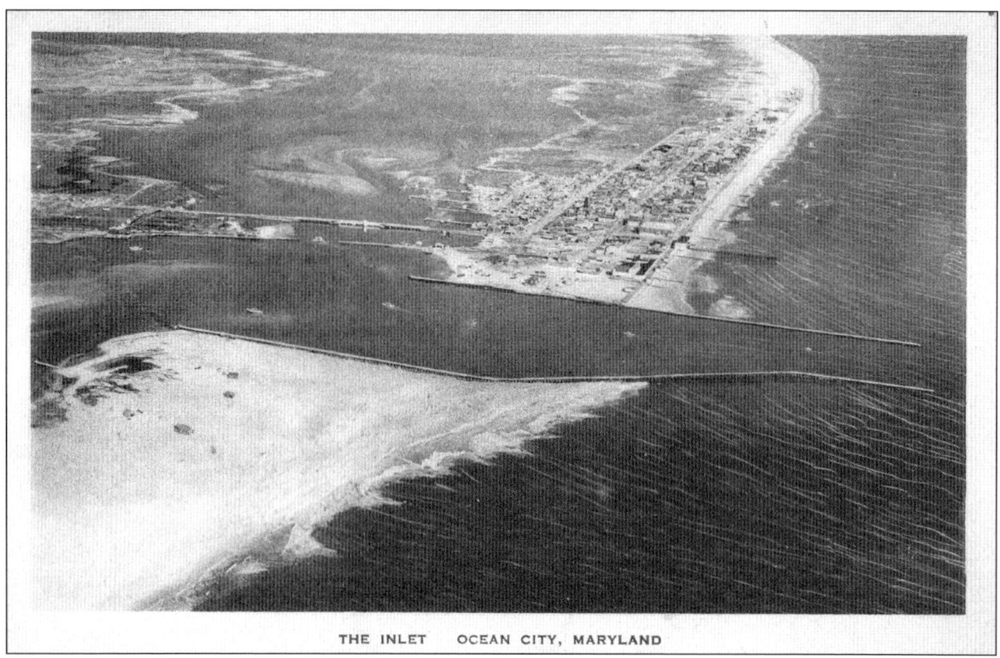

An aerial Albertype postcard postmarked 1937, four years after the great storm, shows the rapidly built jetties edging both north and south boundaries of the new inlet waterway. The two bridges to the mainland are visible as follows: the bridge below, in ruin, is the railroad bridge destroyed in the 1933 storm (see pages 130 and 131); the bridge above is the state road bridge (see pages 133 and 134), replaced in 1942 (just north of both bridges but not yet built) by the still used "million dollar bridge," later dedicated to Harry Kelley (see page 135). The pre-1942 view below shows the rapid westward shift of Assateague Island (bottom edge below jetty). The natural flow from the northeast of wind and waves would build up the town's beach north of the inlet, while the sands of Assateague Island below would erode and shift the island westward.

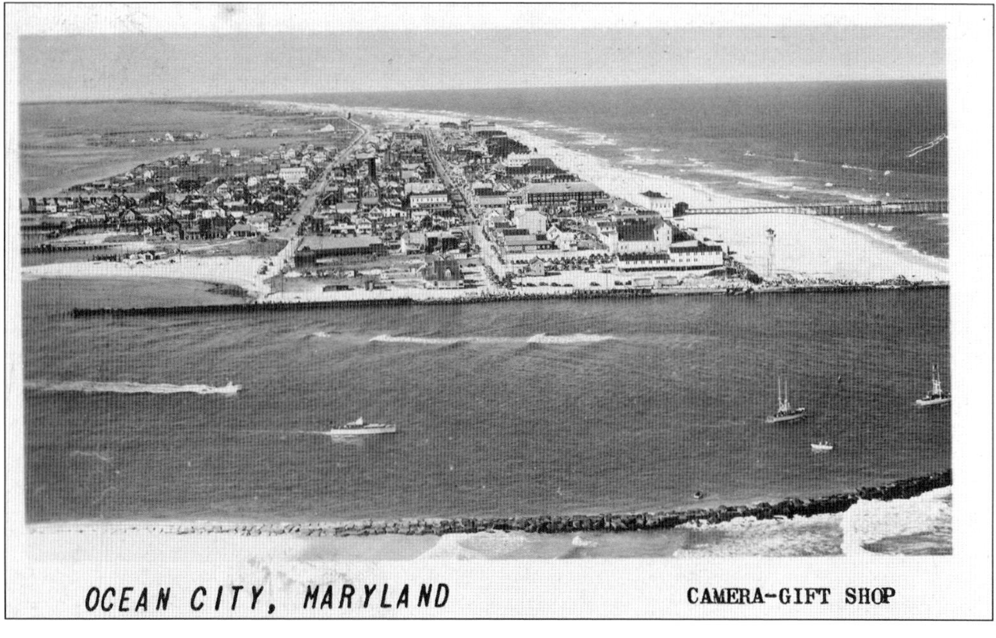

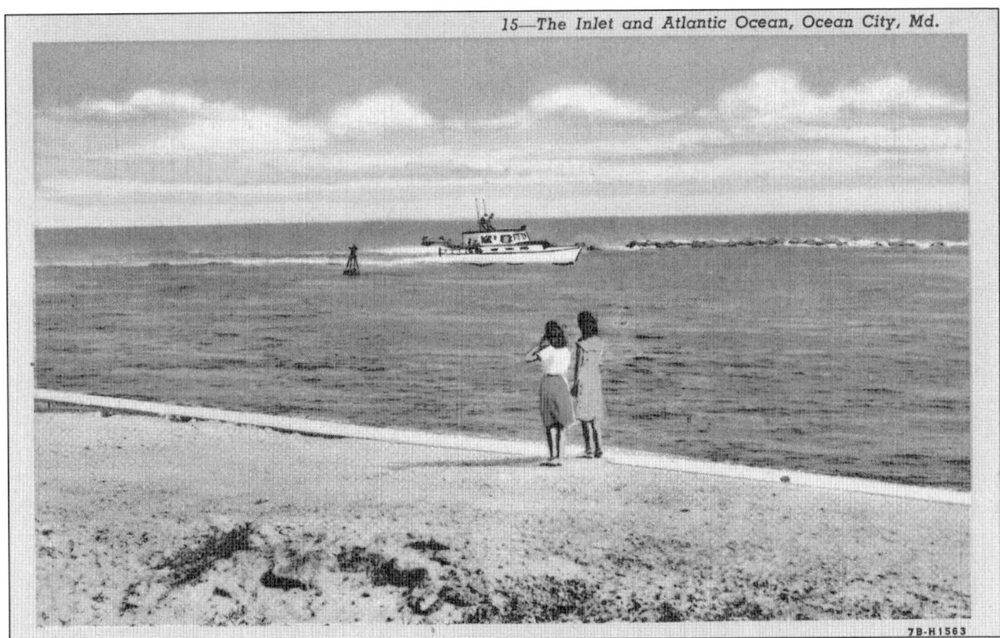

Two girls observe a deep-sea fishing boat returning through the new inlet to the safe harbor docks bayside where the day's catch will be unloaded. The Curt Teich Art Colortone postcard is coded 1947 and was distributed by Harry B. Cann Bro. Company, Baltimore. In the identifying code (bottom right), the "B" indicates 1940s decade; the 7 denotes 1947.

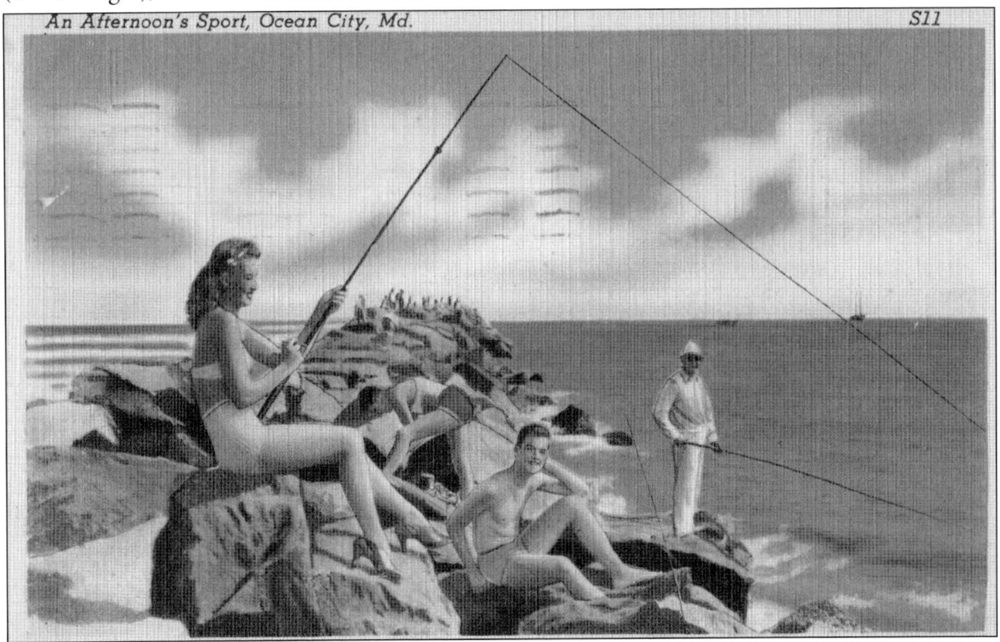

The inlet rock jetty provided a popular, although slippery, fishing venue for "an afternoon's sport." Despite its irregular and potentially dangerous footing, the east end of the rock pile has long been a favorite "lover's lane," and during storms, it provides picturesque scenes of crashing high waves. The posed fishing scene appears ludicrous when one notices the high heels worn by the "model." They are hardly suitable foot attire for the rock jetty.

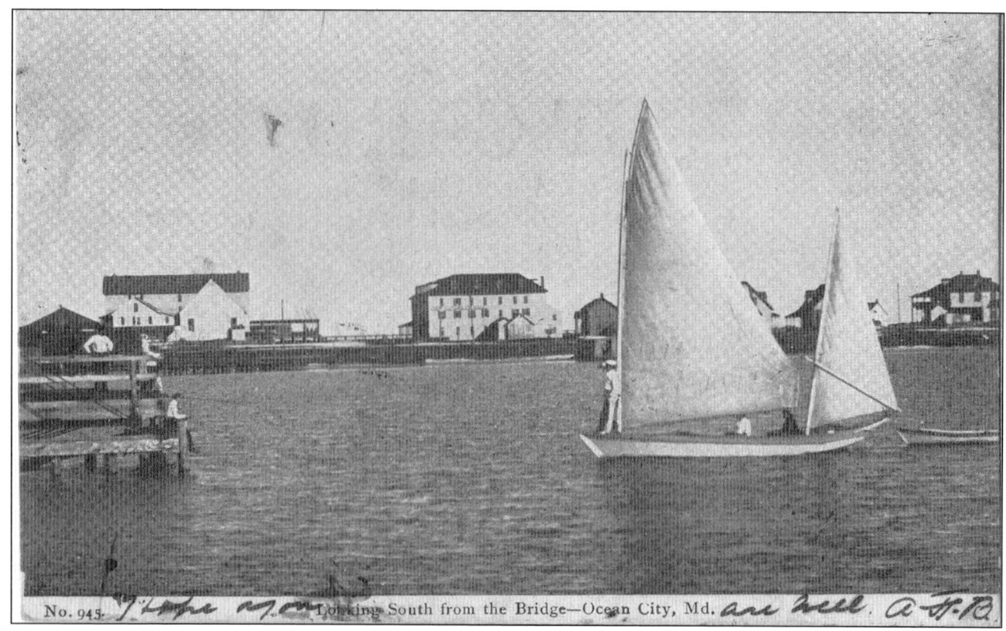

A two-masted cat ketch pulling a dinghy is viewed in this 1906-postmarked postcard, captioned "looking south from the bridge." The sender uses the bottom margin to write "Hope you are well," signing only her/his initials; beginning the following year, March 1907, messages were allowed to be written on the reverse (address) side, which, by then, featured a divided back.

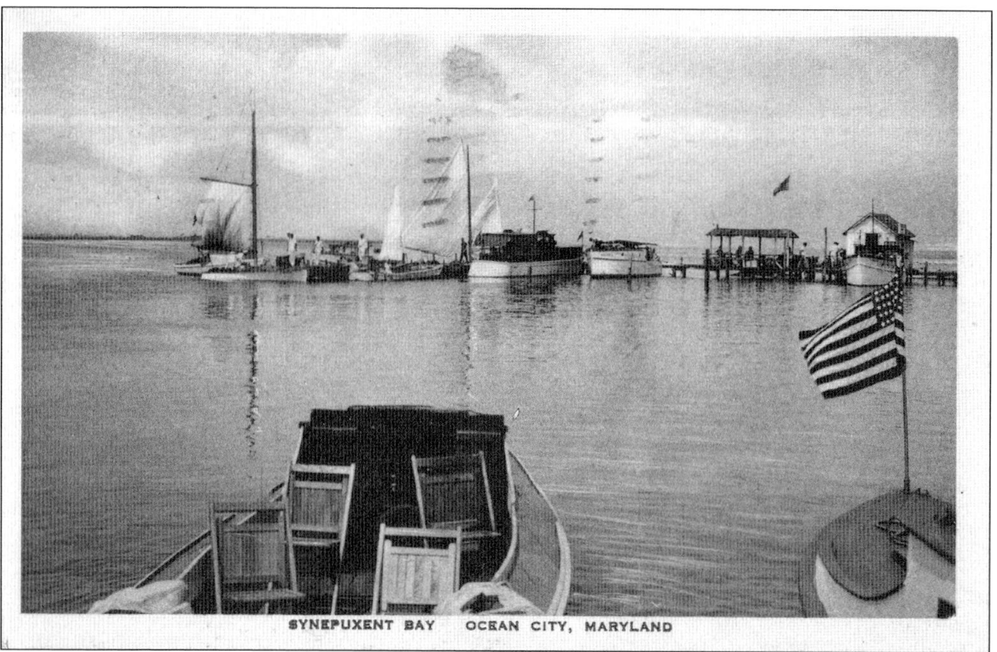

Although postmarked 1936, this R.D. Driscoll Boardwalk postcard of Sinepuxent Bay docks features an earlier photograph. Sailboats and motorboats offered sightseeing excursions around the bay departing from docks along the west waterside of town. Fishing in the bay was also popular, while short cruises and romantic outings by sail became favorite postcard subjects (see pages 156–159).

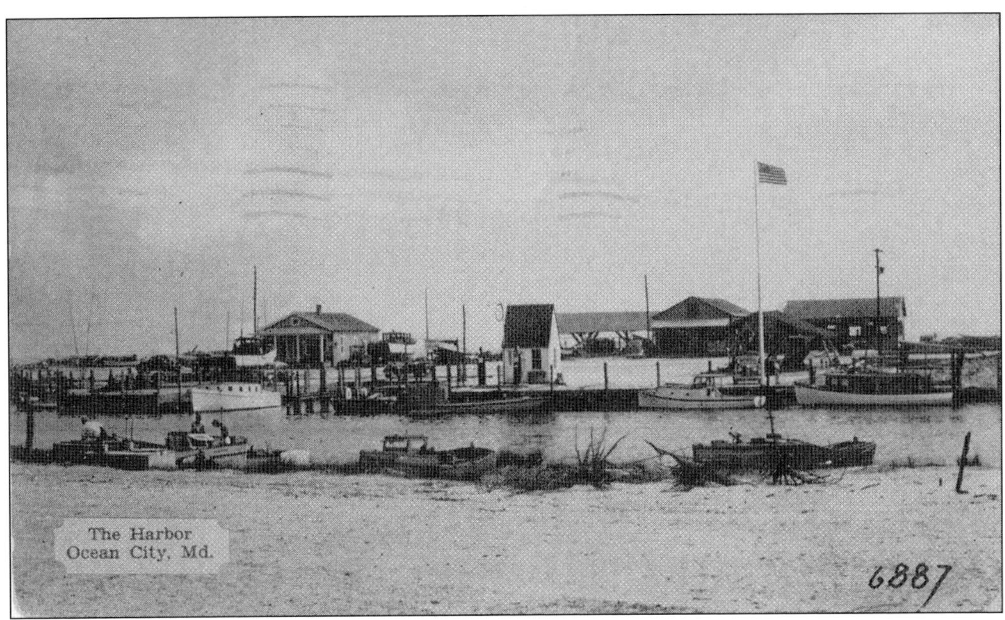

The West Ocean City harbor and docks developed on the west bank of the Sinepuxent opposite the south end of town. This 1944-postmarked postcard shows bulwarks providing docking for boats, while a small gabled gas station and pumps provided fuel. The gas station was later moved to Shantytown Village (1976–2003). Behind are various marine storage and repair buildings. This area today is home to the town's commercial fishing industry and several dockside seafood restaurants.

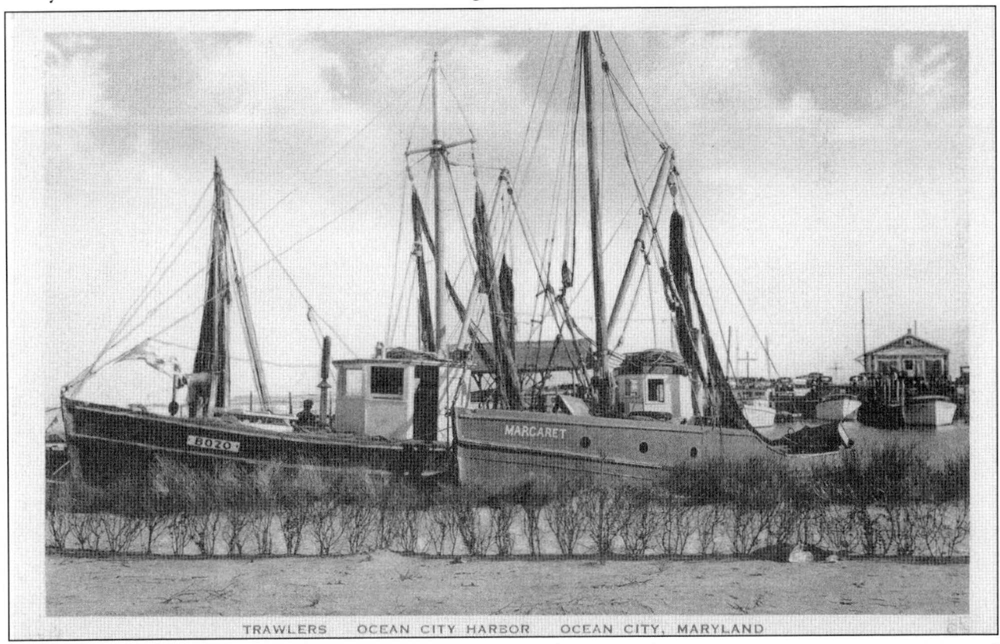

The trawlers *Bozo* and *Margaret* are beached overnight, providing a picturesque composition of masts, rigging, and nets at the West Ocean City harbor. These commercial wood-hulled (and later steel) fishing boats set their nets a mile or two offshore, then dragged the nets scooping up a variety of fish (flounder, striped bass, croaker, sharks, and bluefish) and whatever else is in the path (squid, rays, and horseshoe crabs).

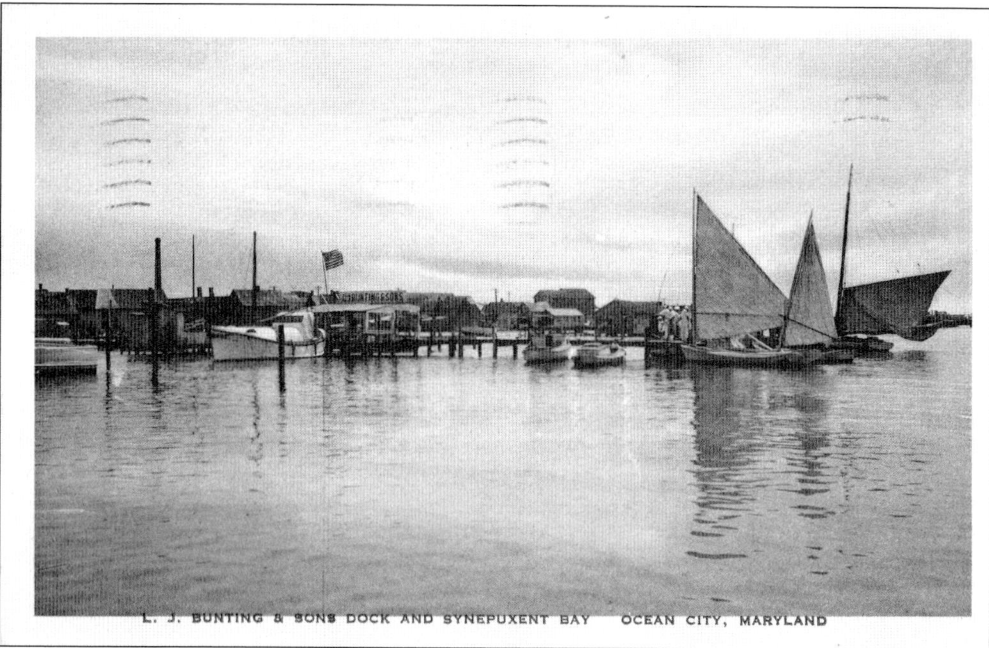

Ocean City's barrier island docks took on the street name, such as the Talbot Street docks, or ship captain's name, such as the "L.J. Bunting & Sons Dock," shown here (looking southeast) with piers and slips for sailboats and fishing boats. This white-border postcard is postmarked four years after the inlet broke through, joining bay to ocean and opening the way for deep-sea recreational fishing.

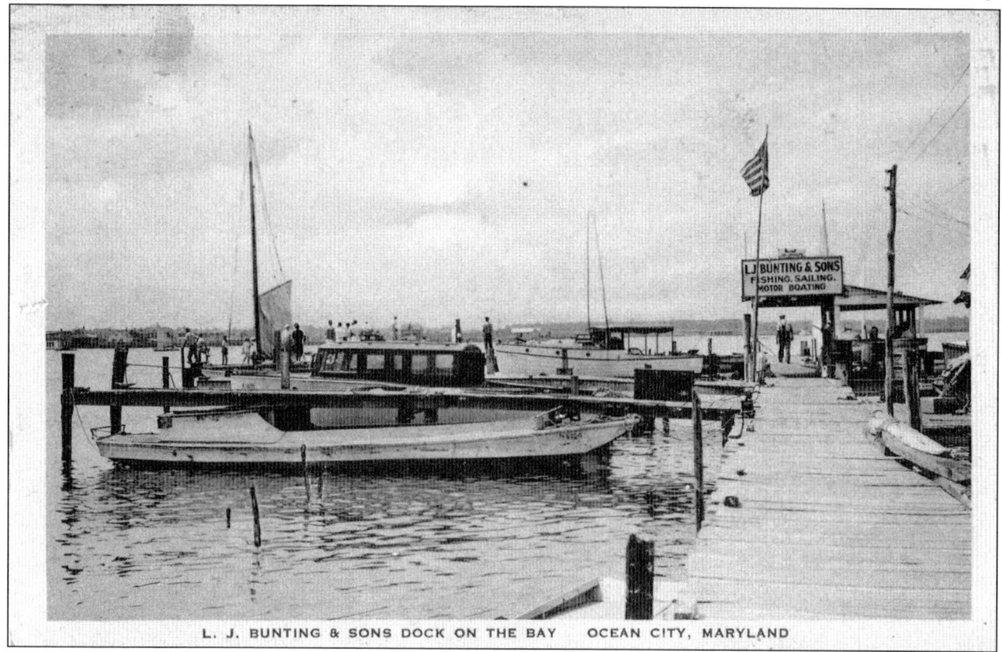

Postmarked the following year (1938), this view of the Bunting docks (looking west) shows Bunting's sign, which advertised fishing, sailing, and motorboating. At the time the photograph was taken (likely several years before the postmark and pre-1933 storm), such recreational activities were limited to the bay. Locals engaged in clamming and crabbing on the bay's sandbars and tidewater shores.

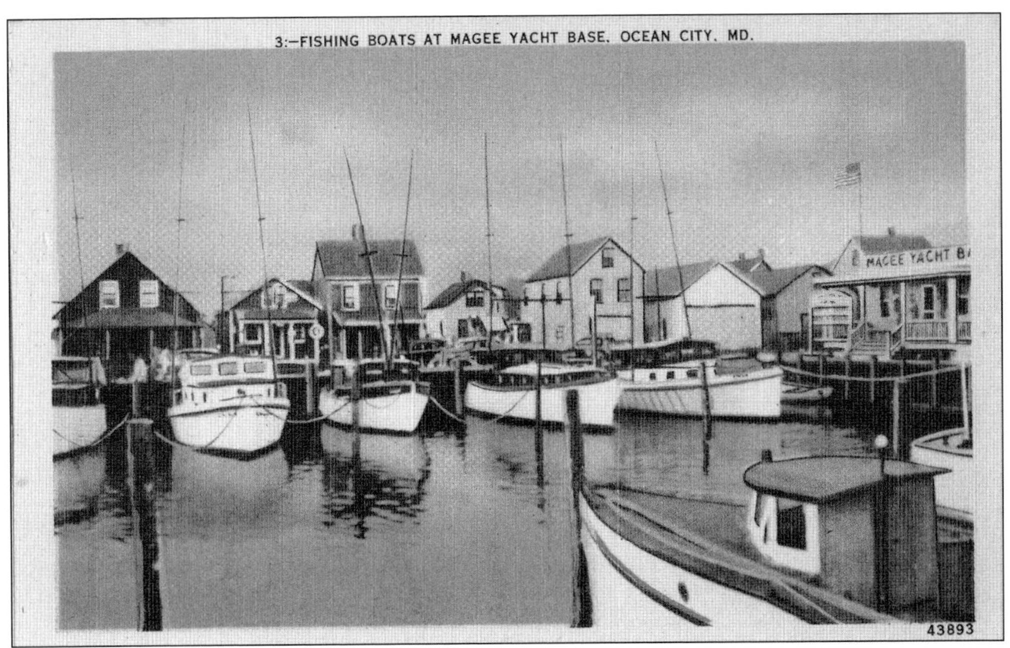

The tall outrigging on the boats docked at the Magee Yacht Basin indicate a fleet of ocean fishing boats whose objective was to land large tuna, marlin, sailfish, and other offshore marine trophies. Some of the day's catch (below) were likely sent to the taxidermist to be stuffed and mounted on restaurant walls or over fireplaces in private homes. Rewards for record catches became far more than bragging rights after the Annual White Marlin Open tournament was established in 1974. Today, the event is the "largest billfishing tournament" in the world. In 2022, the tournament drew 408 boats and over 3,500 contestants and awarded over $8.6 million in prize money. The first-place white marlin winner, as mentioned in the chapter introduction, landed a 77.5-pound white marlin and collected $4,536,926, a world record payout for a fish.

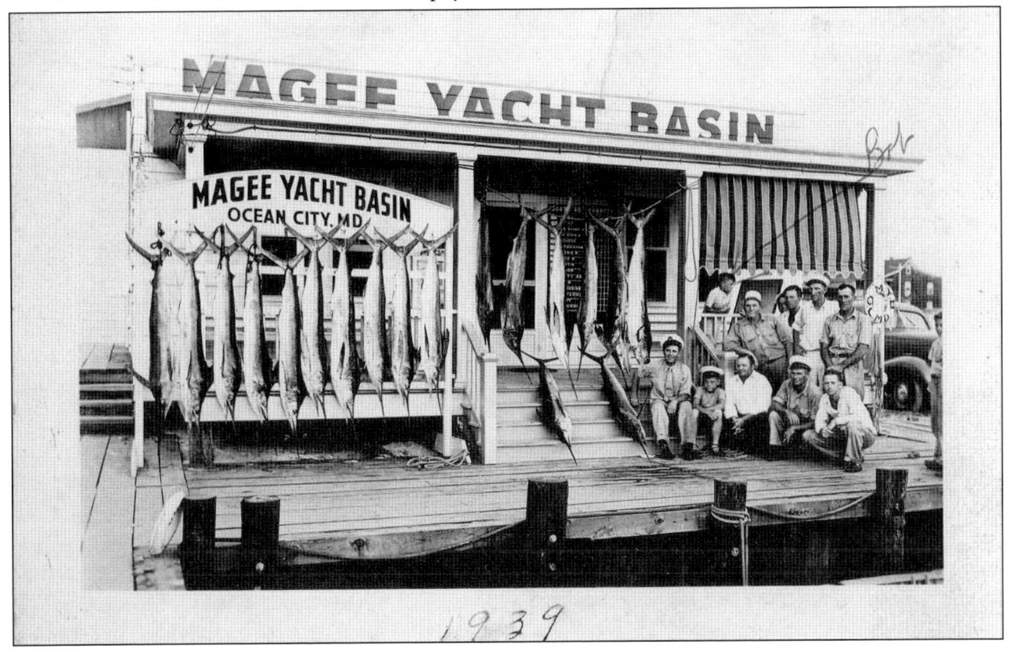

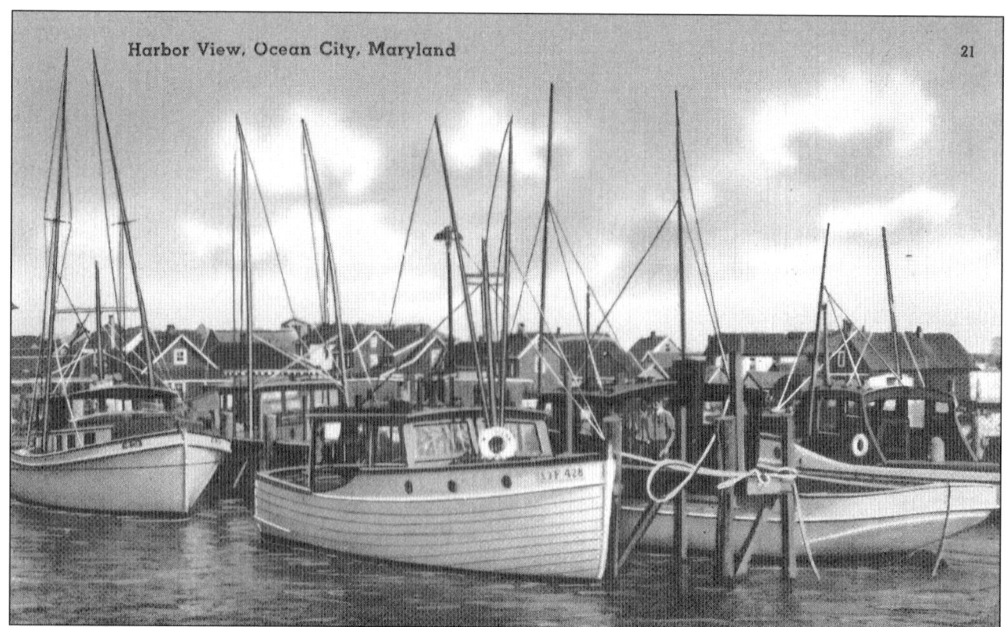

Postcard photographers often sought to create artistic compositions and used the air brush to add fluffy clouds. In some scenes, distracting elements were erased, and figures were sketched in to enhance the relationships among the picture's formal elements. Here, the photographer is attracted by the abstract lines of vertical masts and rigging, while the background horizontal cluster of rooftops conveys a town more crowded than was likely the case.

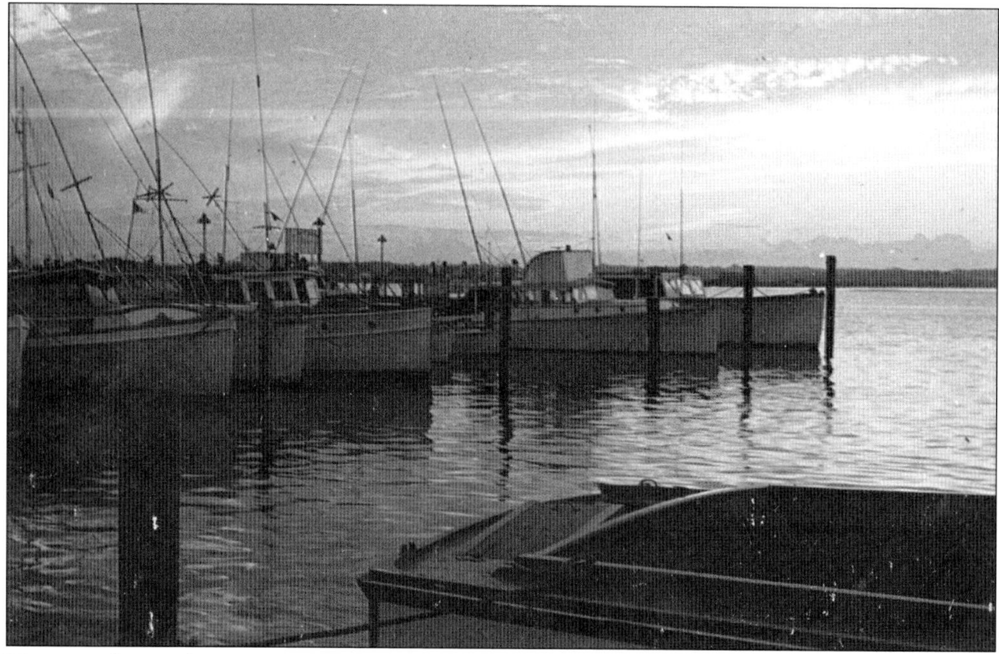

Photographer Walter H. Miller captured moored boats against a Sinepuxent Bay sunset in this undated postcard. The dock is located just south of the 1942 road bridge into town. Thus, already on the inlet side of the draw bridge, charter boats departed daily for deep-sea fishing without having to wait the twice hourly raising of the bridge (see page 135).

Robert S. Craig, whose photographs were published in *Popular Photography* and *U.S. Camera* (later retitled *Travel + Leisure*) magazines, contributed images for Ocean City postcards produced in the 1950s and 1960s by the Tingle Printing Company, headquartered in Pittsville, Maryland (see pages 119 and 122). He, too, found the bayside docks an attractive subject for sunset photography. Here, he captured the dramatically contrasting light and shade of the sun, highlighting darkened twilight clouds and spotlighting brilliant and glittering reflections on the bay. Originally printed in sepia, these photographs provide the following contrasting artistic qualities of light: the atmospheric tonal qualities of the water and sky in the sailboat photograph, and the dramatic backlighting of clouds in the charter boats image. (Photographs by Robert S. Craig.)

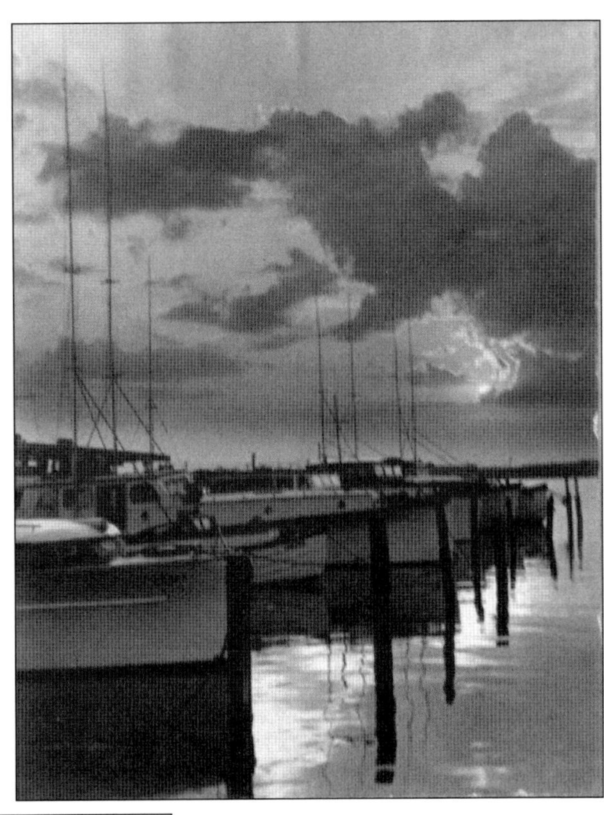

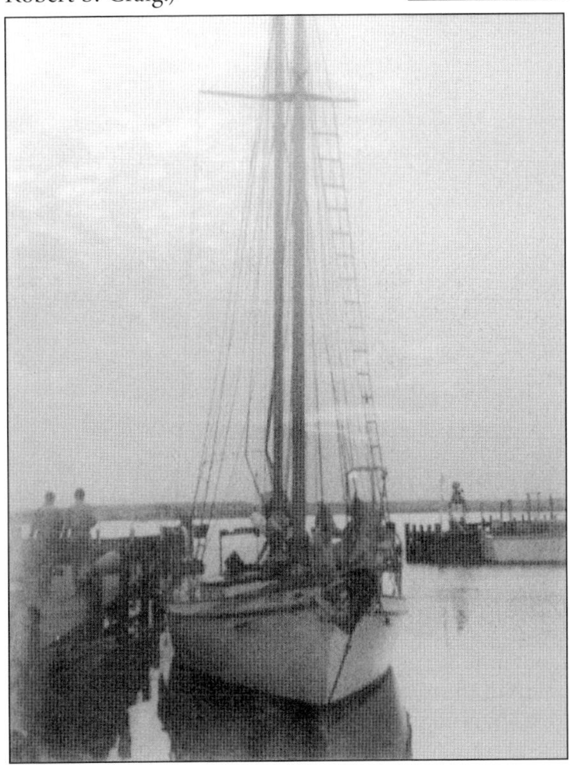

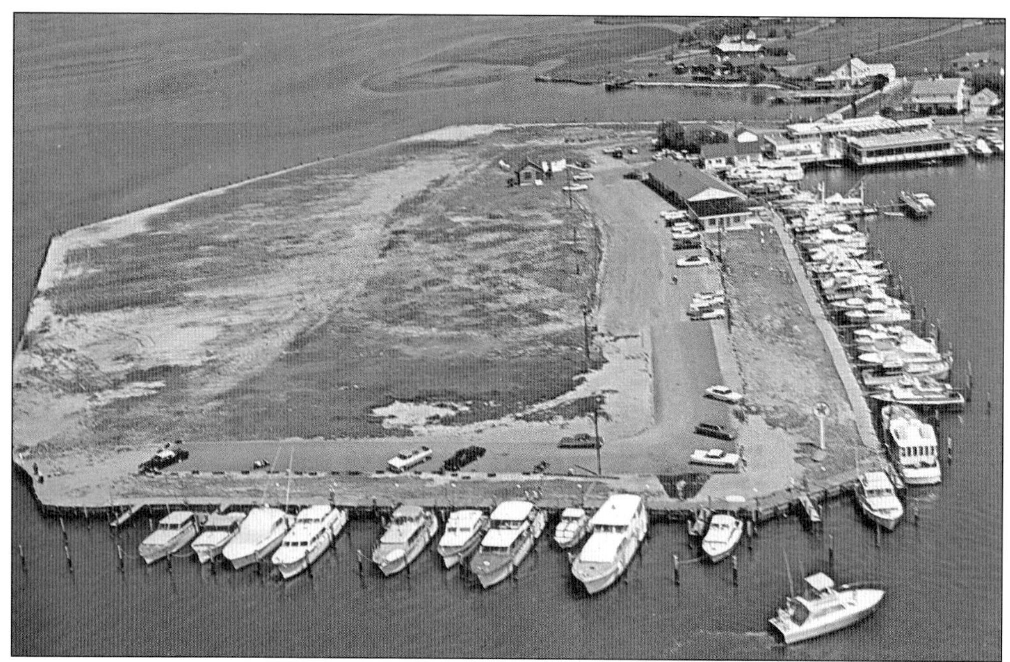

A second popular bayside dock was developed off Fourteenth Street at the Ship Café Marina whose deep harbor attracted yachts from up and down the East Coast. This early aerial view shows undeveloped portions of what was built in the 1930s as the Ocean City Yacht Club, which, later, included a small airstrip on the property. At the top of the image is Mallard Island with only a few early houses in evidence at its southern tip. The postcard below features the restaurant, appearing like a houseboat; owned by William and Ethel Ahtes, the Ship Café was later developed by owner Pete Boinis as the Gazebo Niteclub, a popular disco featuring music by the Admirals, one of the region's most versatile and popular bands.

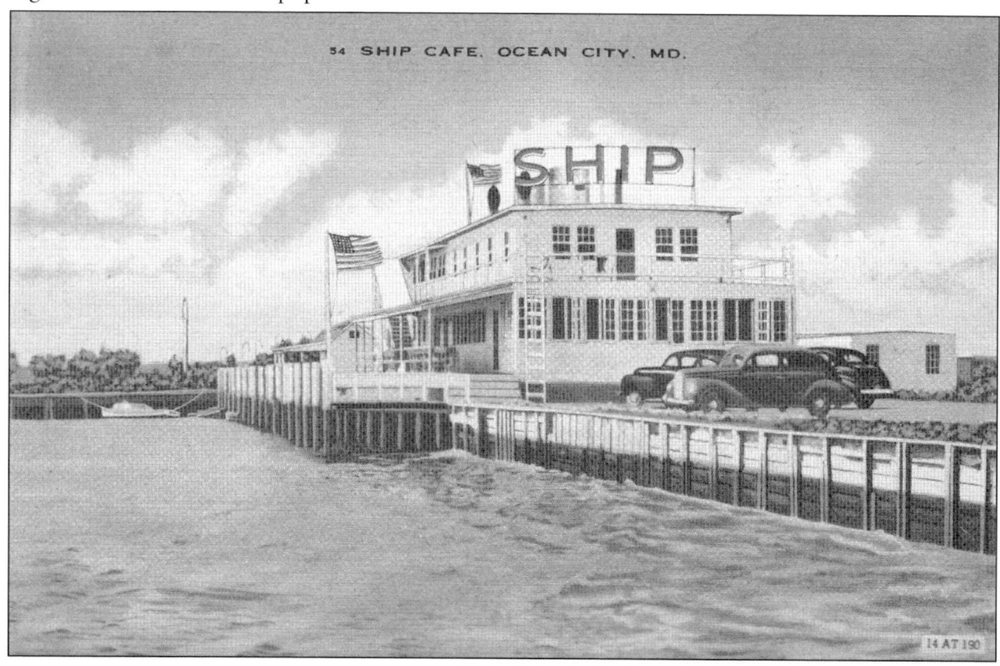

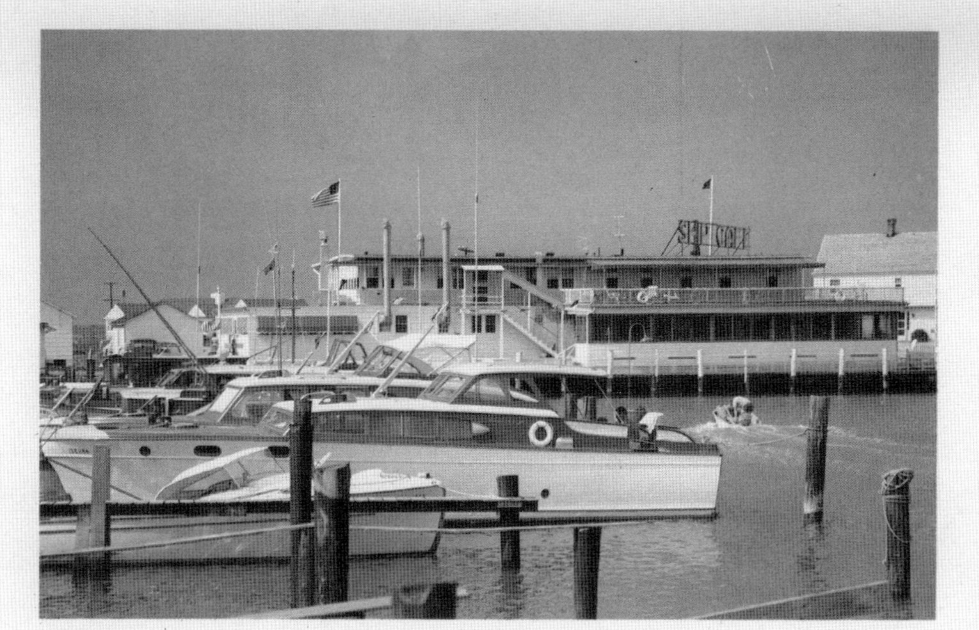

Yacht Club Island, privately owned yachts docked at one of Maryland's finest yacht basin and resort centers.

A devastating fire destroyed the Ship Café in May 1977 and ended the three-decade history of one of Ocean City's premier bayside restaurants and dance band venues. As the aerial photograph opposite shows, the Ship Café site is a peninsula connected to the barrier island by the Fourteenth Street neck. Offering almost 360 degrees of waterfront property, the site has since been developed as Harbour Island, a gated community of townhouses and mid-rise condo buildings (photograph below). Harbour Island's amenities include tennis courts, a swimming pool, boat slips, a fuel dock, a boardwalk, and the Reel Inn Restaurant and Dock Bar. Harbour Island is also home to the annual White Marlin Open fishing tournament, hosting the weigh-ins each August (see pages 127, 128, and 141). (Below, photograph by Robert M. Craig.)

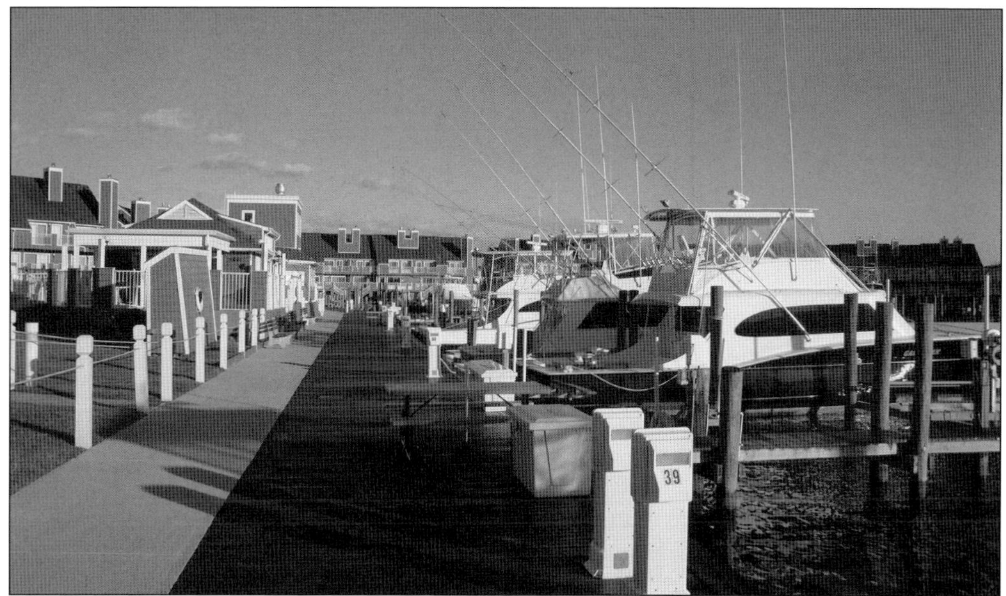

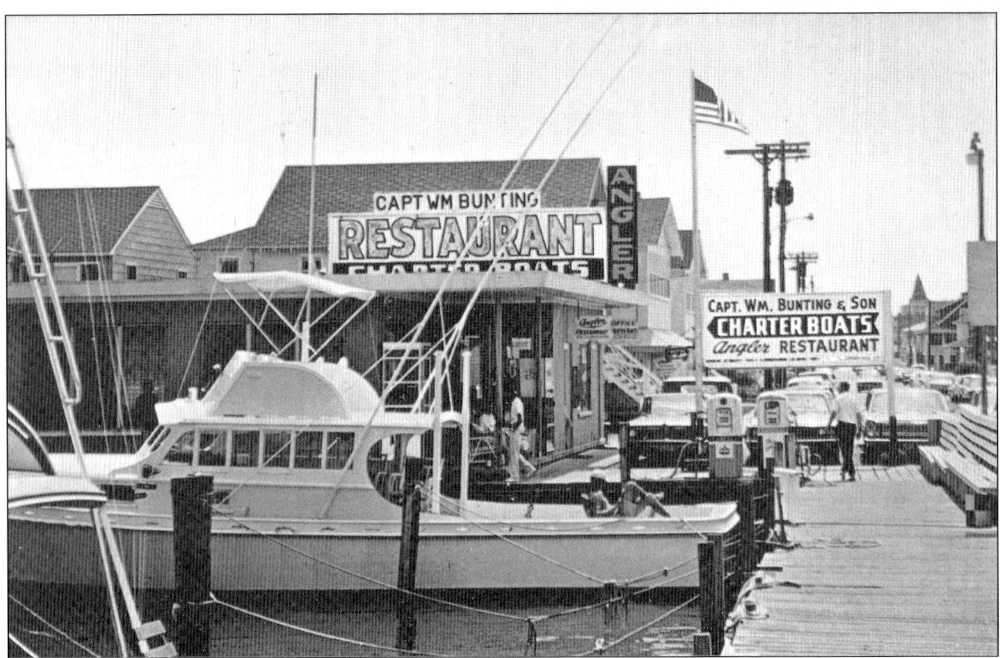

When Charles Rollins Bunting purchased this property around the turn of the 20th century, there was no inlet and only marsh grass bordered the shore of the bay through which Bunting's rowboats and sail bateaux were dragged ashore. Working the ocean pound nets, the elder Bunting's pound boat was beached nightly on the ocean side of the barrier island (see pages 28–31). Bunting's five sons began a fishing business bayside and were issued the town's first dock permit (see page 140 bottom), a dock rebuilt in 1945. William Bunting ultimately settled permanently here, and he and his sons ran charter fishing boats and opened the Angler Restaurant at the Talbot Street docks, and for years, the (now fifth-generation) Buntings have offered dinner guests evening ocean cruises aboard the *Angler*. The postcard below, postmarked 1976, was published by "B" of Salisbury, Maryland.

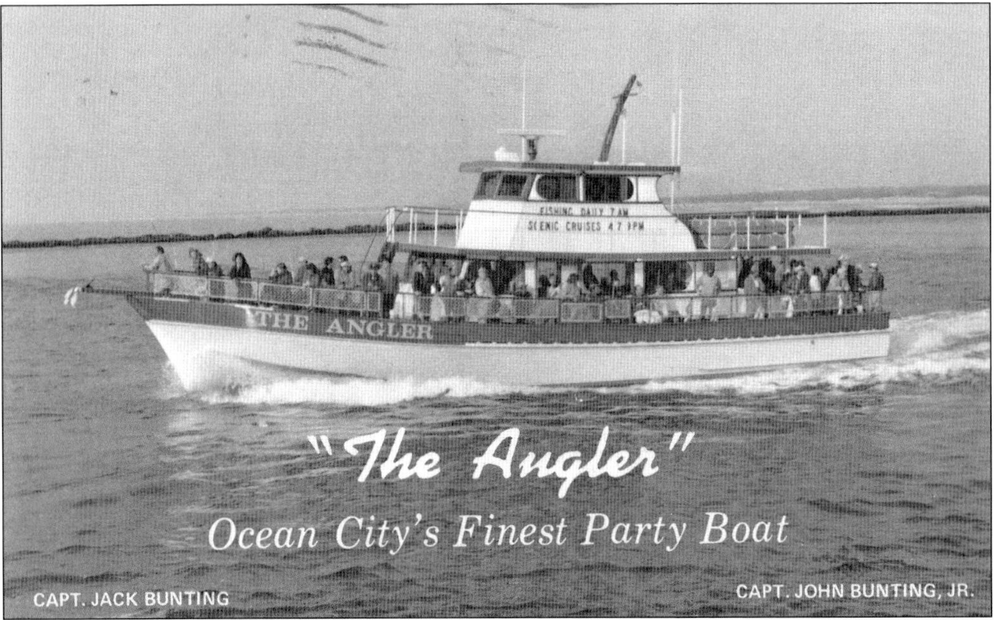

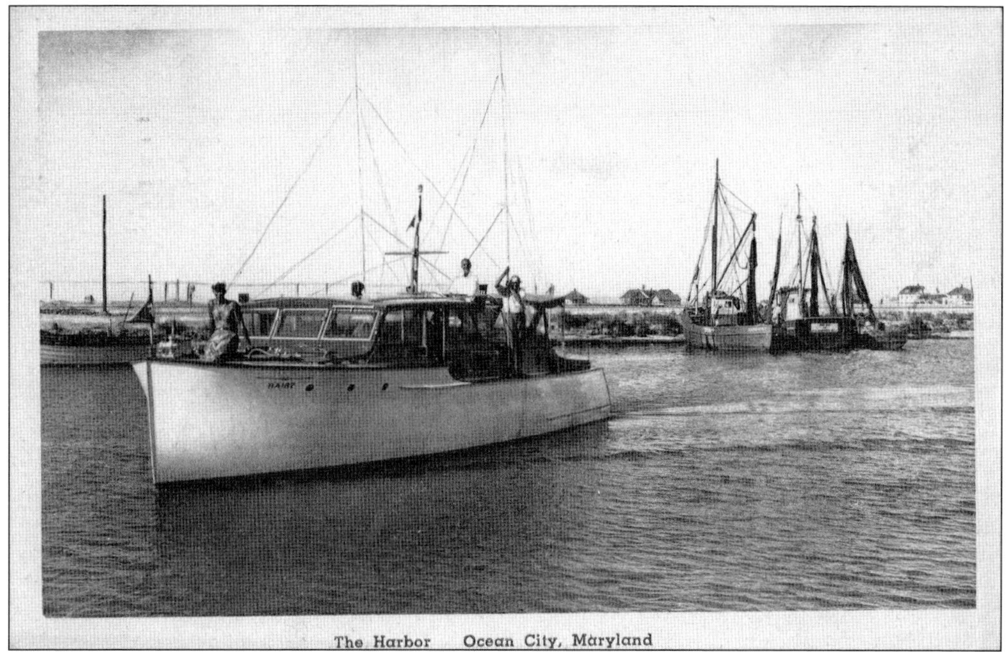

The *Angler* (see page 146 below) was built to serve as a head boat, a vessel that carries 50 to 80 passengers and anchors over a wreck or known fishing area for day-tripper fishermen to engage in a few hours of sport. The boat pictured above, however, was a private yacht. Rigged with outriggers for deep-sea fishing, the boat is shown leaving the harbor with trawlers moored in the background.

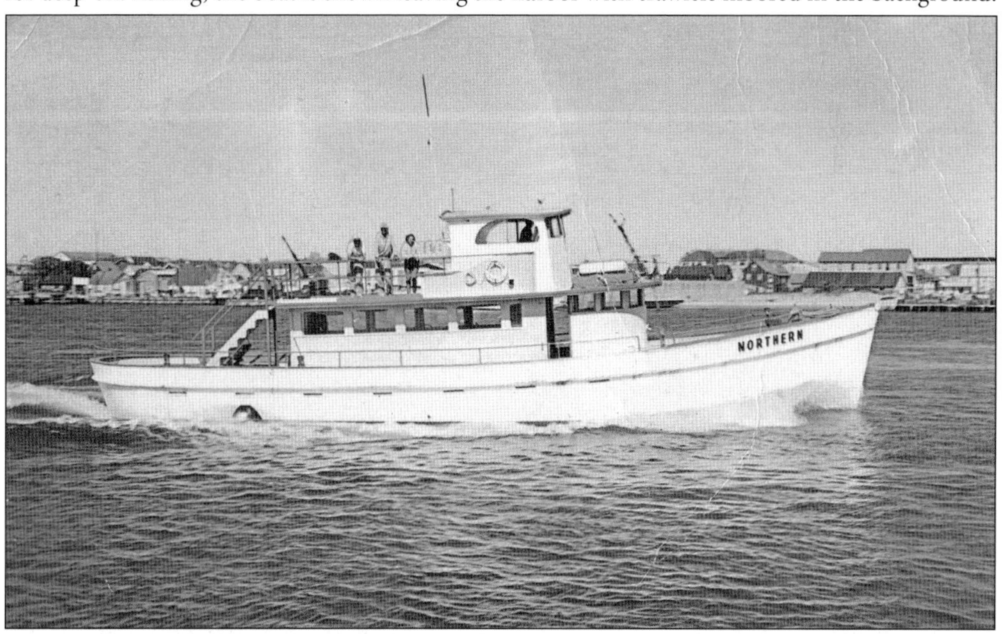

The *Northern* is captured in a photograph by Fred Brueckmann, owner of the Tingle Printing Company and frequent producer of postcard images in the decades after World War II (see pages 41 below and 98 below). This card is postmarked 1965. The *Northern* offered large groups deep-sea fishing excursions, but here, three cruising vacationers are shown admiring the view of the bay from the *Northern*'s upper deck.

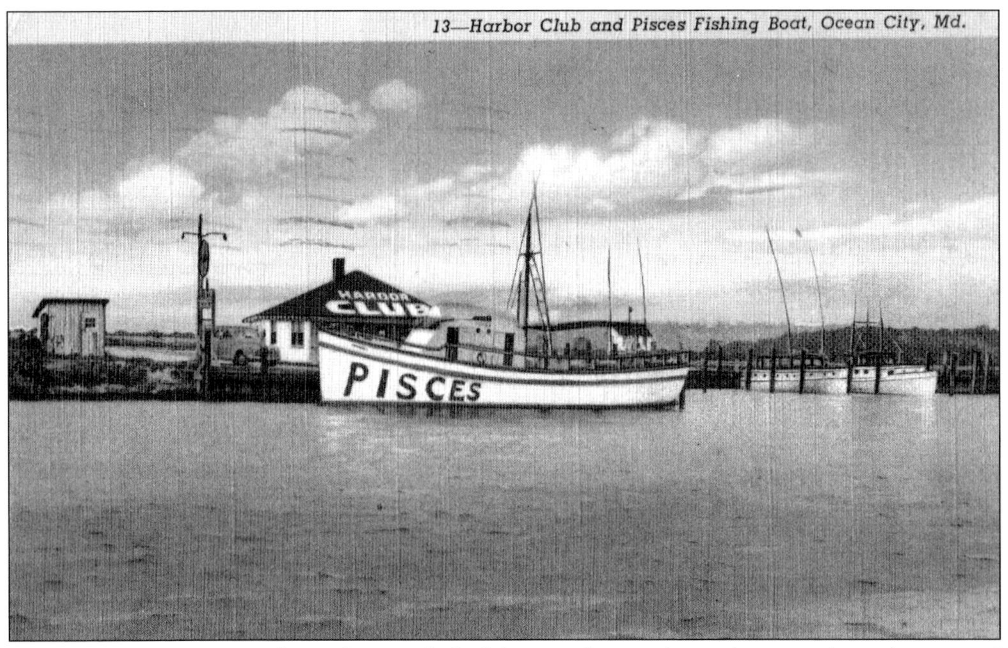

The head boat *Pisces* was a better-known daily fishing and cruise boat, shown in the 1941 postcard above, docked at the Harbor Club. She was brought to Ocean City by Ed Brex and initially operated at the end of Somerset Street at the White Marlin Marina (Ocean City Yacht Basin). Brex purchased property in West Ocean City, which, at the time, included Bob Ching's restaurant. He renamed the restaurant the Mast (see page 149), moving the *Pisces* there. However, following Brex's acquisition of the *Taurus*, he sold the *Pisces* to Gordon Patton who intended to outfit her as a treasure-hunting boat. On the maiden Caribbean voyage of Gordon's revamped *Pisces*, Gordon miscalculated navigation data and ran her aground at the east end of Cuba, where Gordon was captured by Fidel Castro, held for a few days, and finally released.

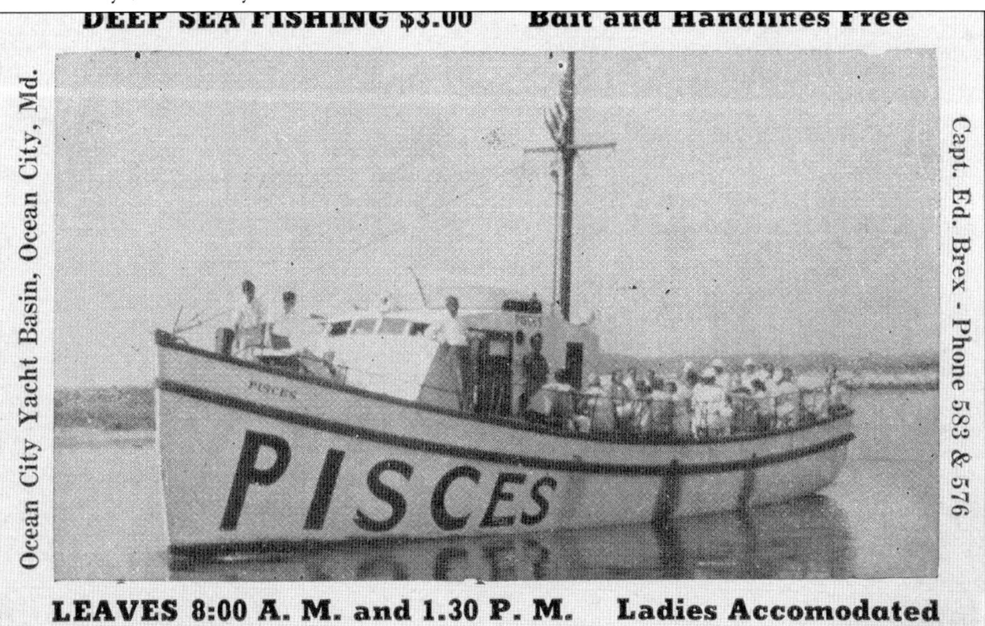

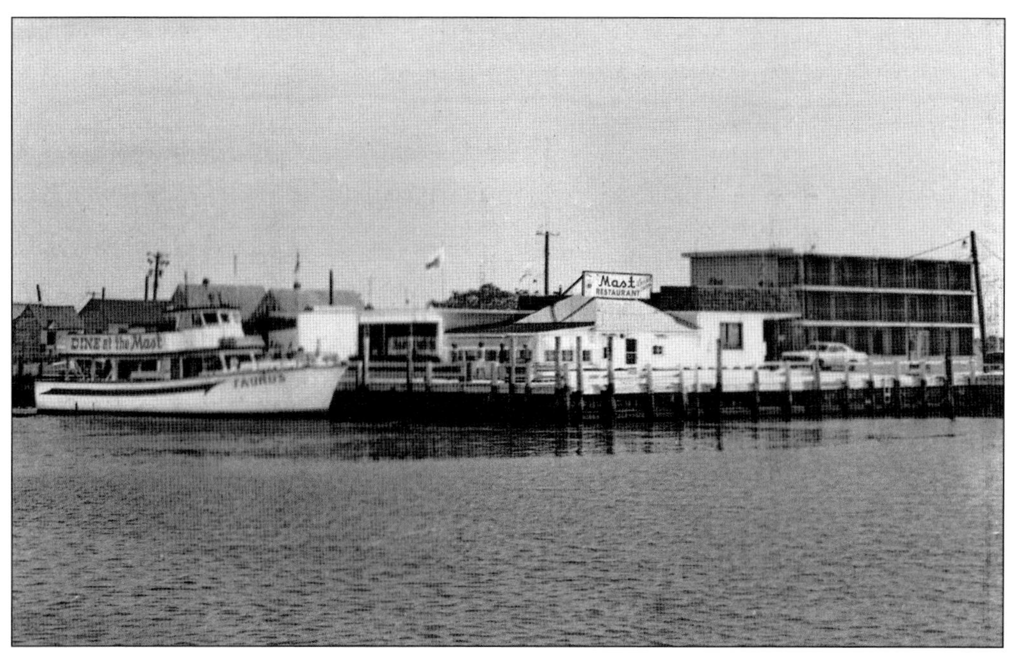

Bayfront dockside restaurants were increasingly popular in Ocean City following the 1933 creation of the inlet with its direct access from ocean to safe bayside harbor and docks. In the postcard above, Captain Brex's *Taurus* advertises the Mast restaurant along the boat's upper deck and is shown docked at the restaurant. Serving by day as a head boat, *Taurus* carried scores of fishermen (with "ladies accommodated") through the inlet to promising deep-sea fishing sites where red snapper, grouper, and amberjack were plentiful. *Taurus* then returned to port about 4:00 p.m. to offer free twilight cruises to patrons of the Mast restaurant. (See also page 146.)

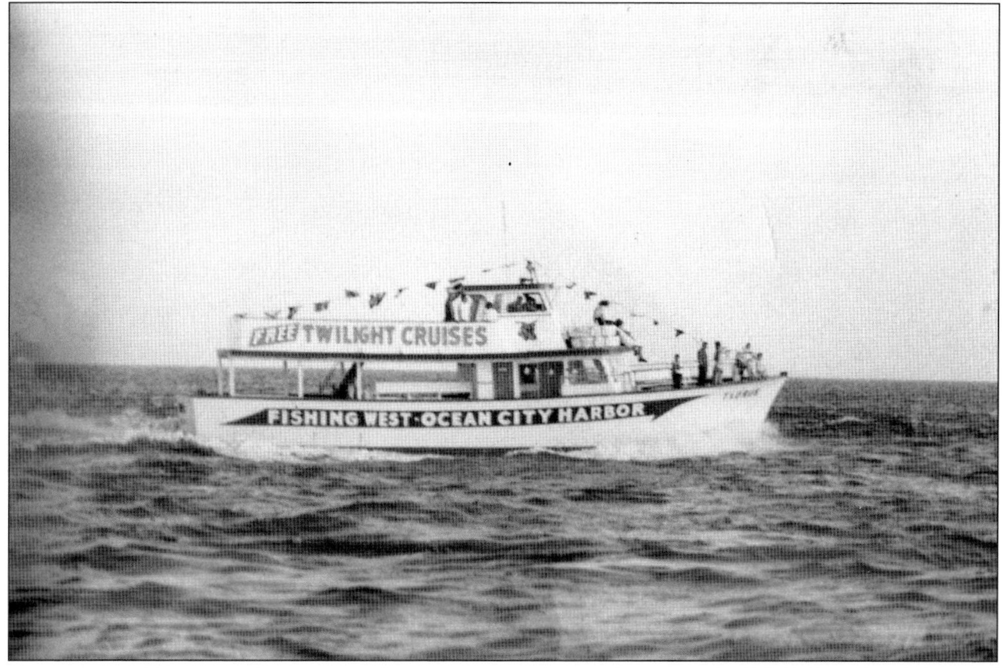

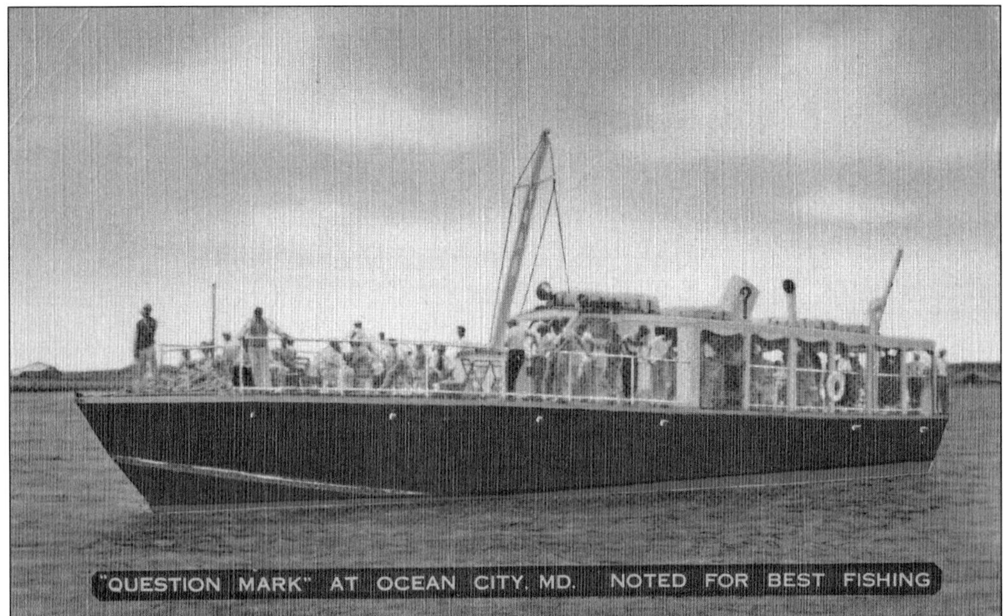

The 83-foot-long *Question Mark*, shown here in two paint schemes, was a converted PT (patrol torpedo) boat of the kind made famous by John F. Kennedy. The future president's first PT-109 sank in 1943; Kennedy was rescued and, subsequently, took command of PT-59. *Pee Tee* was another PT fishing boat that operated out of Indian River. The *Question Mark* was owned by Gordon Patton (see page 148) and operated as a head boat from the foot of Wicomico Street. Patton replaced the three original Packard gas engines with two diesels. Throughout the summer season, Patton took two trips daily to the wrecks off Fenwick Island (north end of Ocean City). When Patton sold the *Question Mark*, new owners sliced her in two and loaded her onto trucks with the intention to rebuild the boat—nothing more is known of her fate.

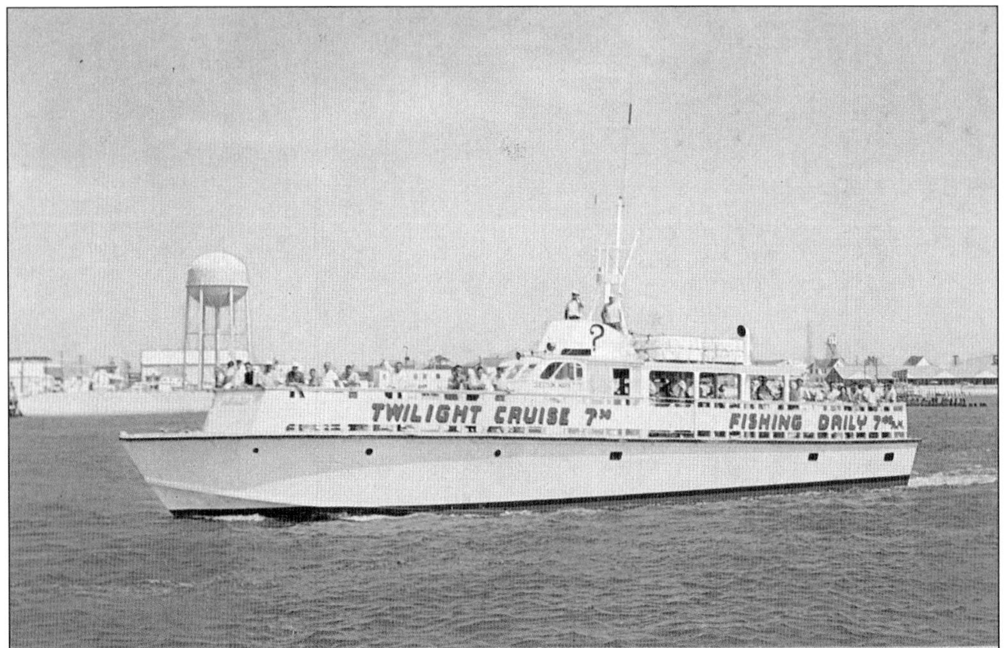

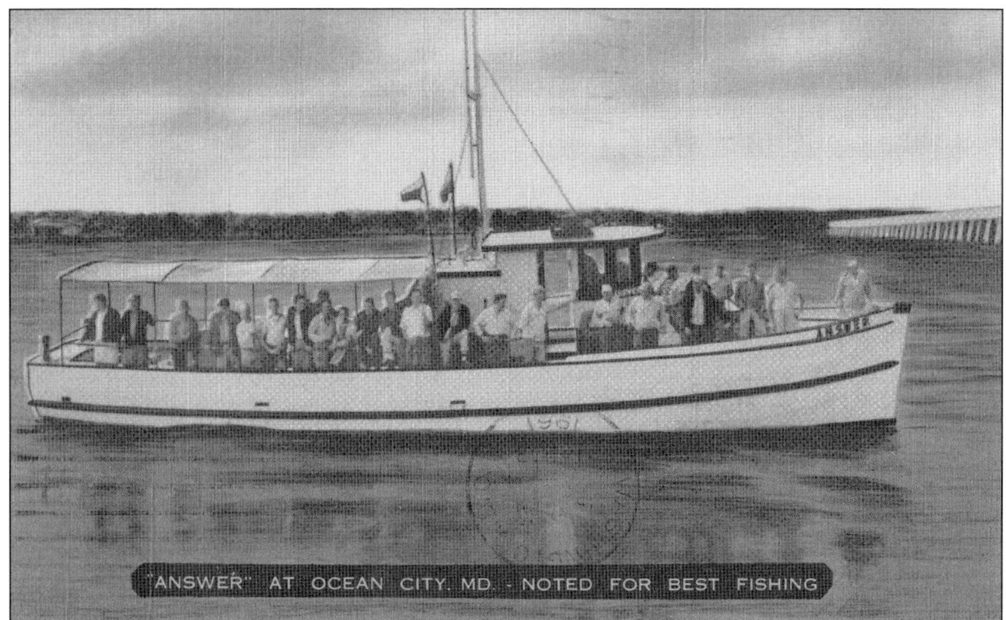

This linen Teknatone postcard of the head boat the *Answer* was printed by E.B. Thomas of Cambridge, Maryland. Captained by Paul Russell, the *Answer* offered daily "Porgy and Bass" fishing trips but cautioned that whisky and beer could not be brought aboard—although the latter was on sale once underway. *Answer* was first operated by Bill Patton, Gordon Patton's son (hence the boat's name); Bill later founded Frontier Town.

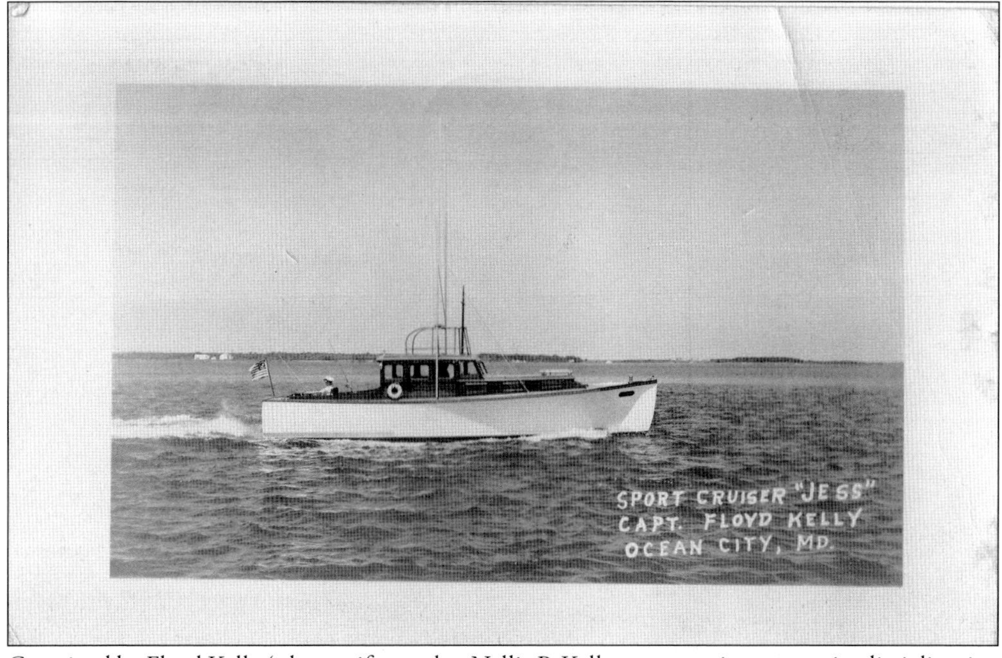

Captained by Floyd Kelly (whose wife, teacher Nellie P. Kelly, was notorious as a strict disciplinarian at the local Ocean City school), the *Jess* was later sold to Howard Merritt from Chincoteague who ran her as a charter boat during the 1950s. The 1962 storm may well have ended her days, as Merritt operated a different boat, the *Peggy*, from that date until he retired.

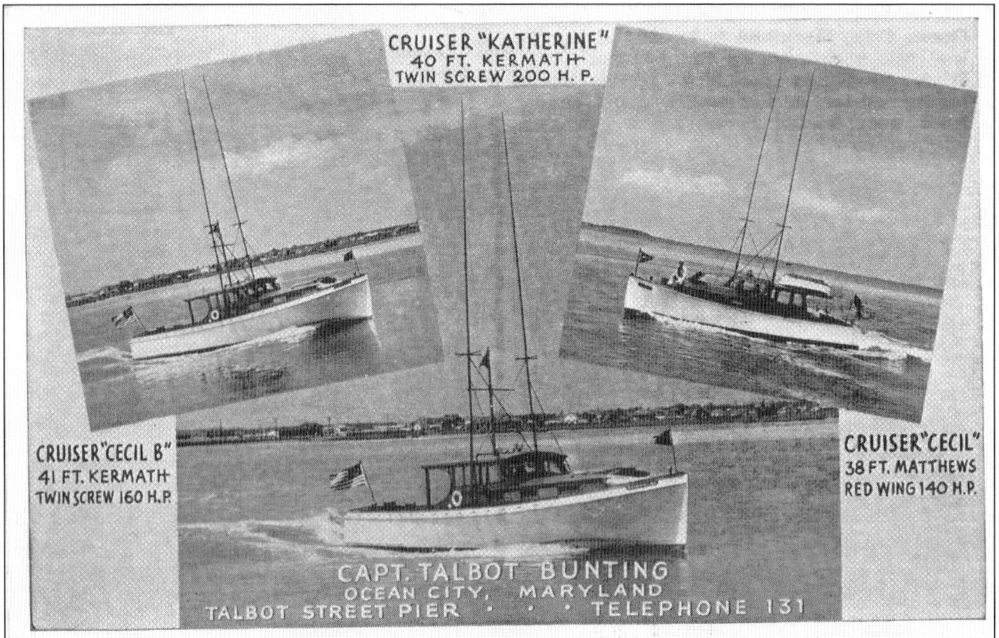

Three cruisers owned by Talbot Bunting are featured on a postcard advertising his Talbot Street dock charters. The *Katherine* (above at center and below) was a 40-foot, twin-screw charter boat with a reliable 200-horsepower Kermath engine; the engine manufacturer's slogan was "A Kermath Always Runs." Both the *Katherine* and *Cecil B* were built in Chincoteague in the early 1930s; *Katherine* was older and with a lower bow. By the late 1950s, *Katherine* was owned by Bunting but was sold in the 1960s. Slightly longer at 41 feet, *Cecil B* operated with a twin-screw, 160-horsepower Kermath. The 38-foot Mathews cruiser *Cecil,* built in Port Clinton, Ohio, in 1929, featured a 140-horsepower Red Wing engine. *Cecil* was later bought by Ricks Savage who put a bay clam rig on her.

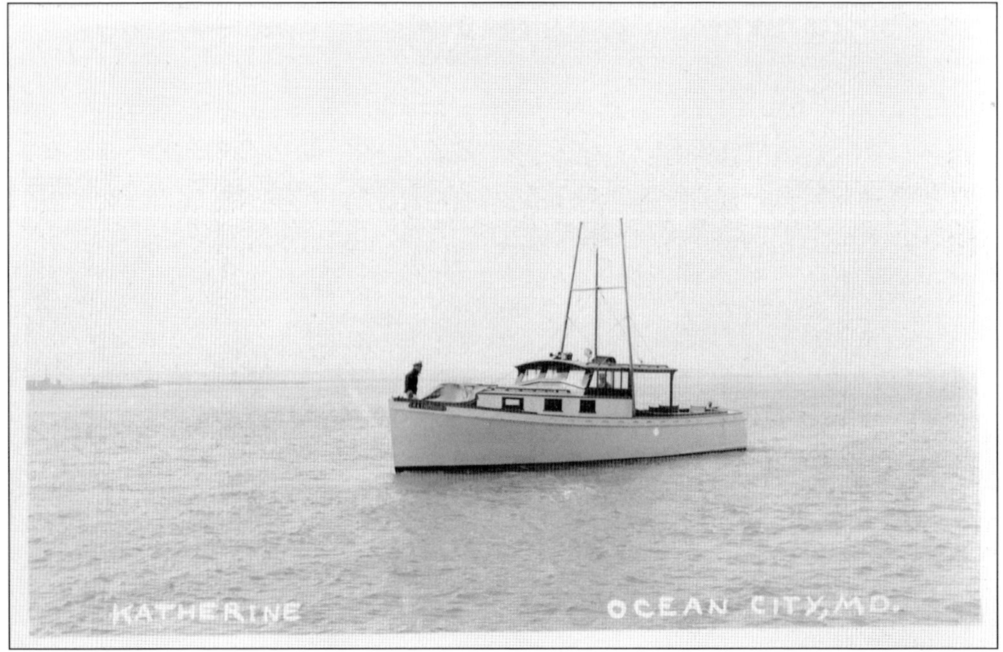

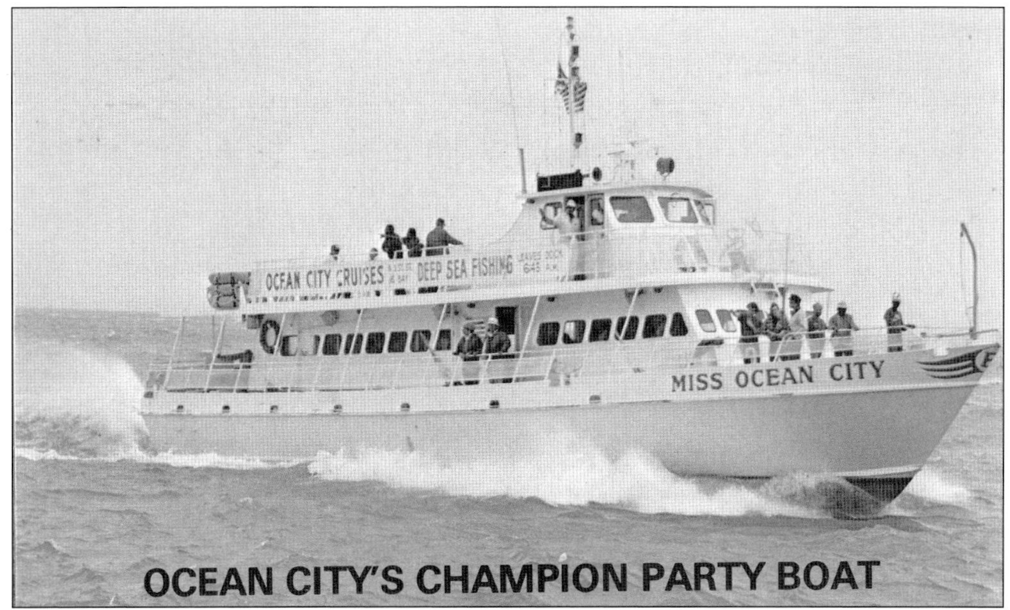

Built in the Gulf region (possibly Mobile, Alabama) for Rudy Thomas of Tangier, *Miss Ocean City* began life as a Chesapeake Bay passenger ferry christened *Steven Thomas* that transported passengers between Crisfield and Tangier Island. The boat was purchased by Jack Bunting to replace the *Angler*. Like other head boats, *Miss Ocean City* offered daily deep-sea fishing excursions and evening cruises from the North First Street dock.

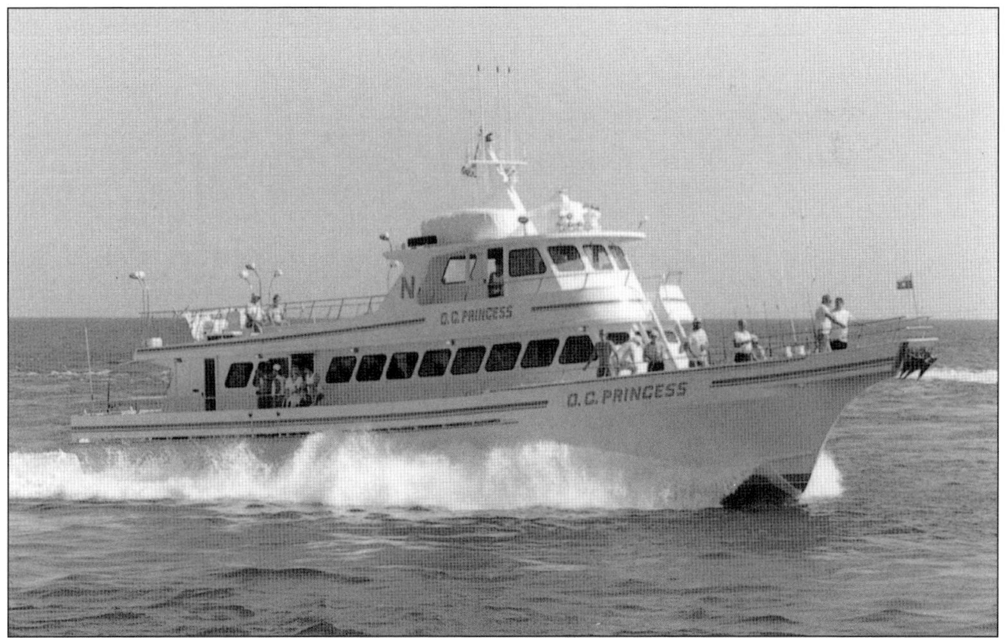

The *O.C. Princess* was a sleek vessel operated by Ray Nichols out of Shanty Town, a mock village of vernacular shacks containing gift/souvenir shops and located on the west shore of the bay, just south of the Route 50 bridge. Today, the property contains multi-million-dollar homes. Like Shanty Town's, the commercial success of *O.C. Princess* was short-lived; Nichols sold his head boat after just a couple of years.

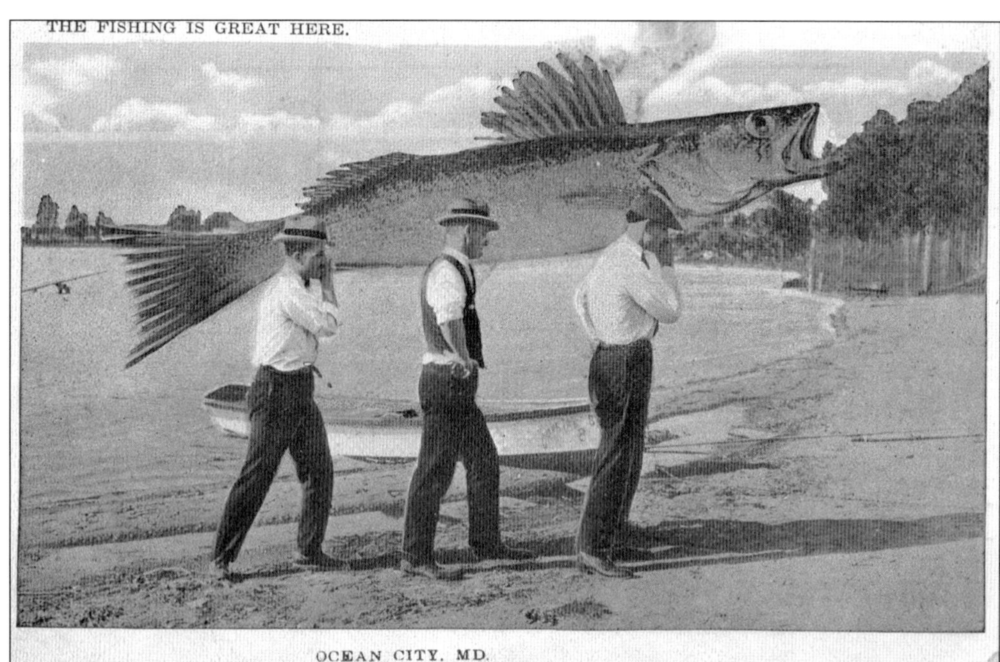

Fishing as an activity was ripe for novelty card fun, because everyone loves a good "fish story," and who hasn't exaggerated the size of the afternoon's catch? The appeal was so universal that a generalized scene (appearing here more lake-side than bayfront) could be localized by merely stamping the town's name on the postcard border. This "The Fishing Is Great Here" card is postmarked 1927.

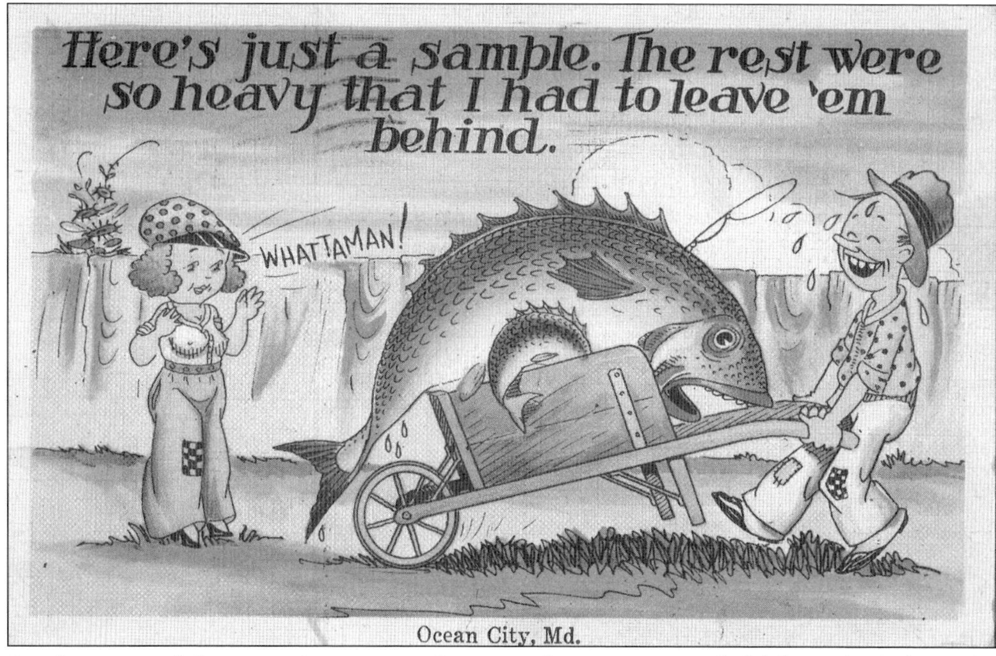

Another generic fish story utilizes cartoon figures to depict a mammoth fish being hauled away by wheel barrow. While the struggling and perspiring male brings home the catch, the admiring female declares, "WhattaMan!" Again, the generic message is localized with a town name in the lower border, while the card was otherwise sold in multiple locations. The postmark is 1937.

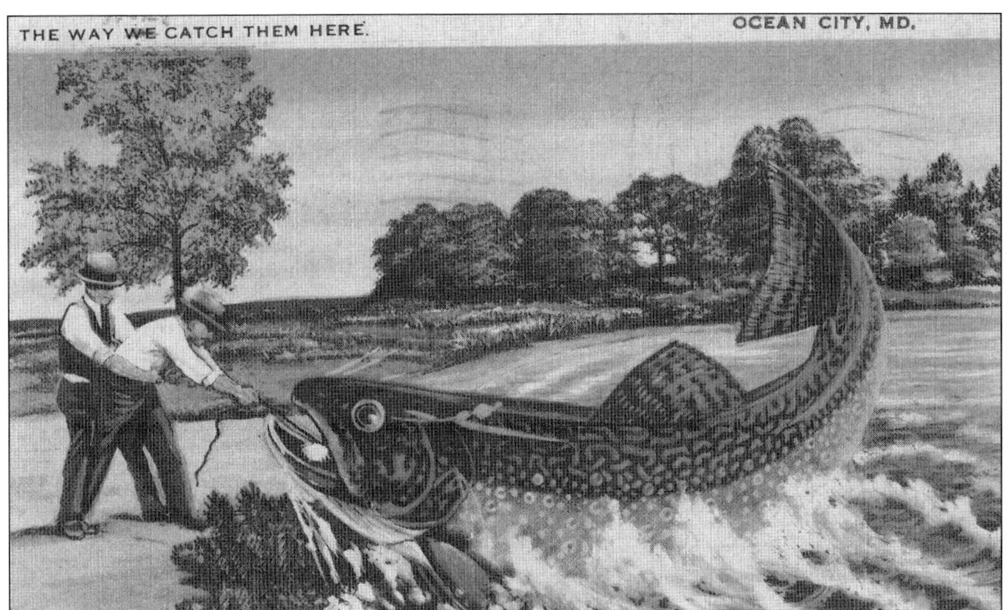

In this novelty card postmarked 1943, another giant fish is hauled ashore by two men. No fishing rod is in evidence; indeed, donned in top hat, vest, white shirt, and tie, the men appear dressed instead for their clerical office jobs rather than for recreational fishing. The caption "The Way We Catch Them Here" is trumped by the equally witty correspondent's quip, "Suppose You Had to Clean This, Mom?"

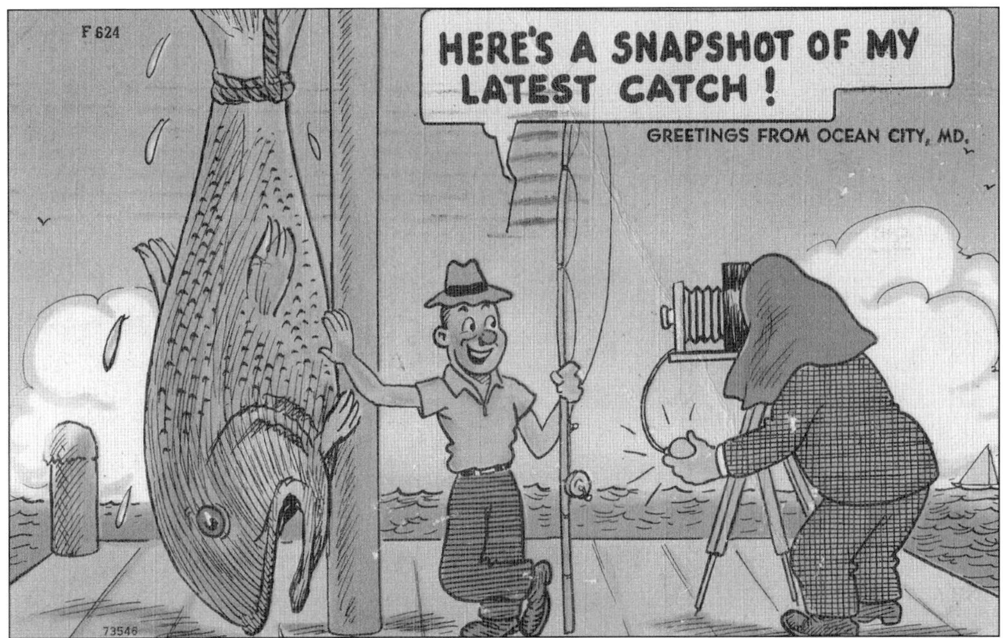

A cartoon card, postmarked 1950, depicts a fish some 10 to 12 feet in length, hanging from a dockside support, while a photographer records the improbable catch. A quarter century later, Ocean City would begin to sponsor its annual White Marlin Open Tournament where "weigh-in" scenes, such as this (see pages 127, 128, 141, and 145), would record white marlins weighing 50 to 70 pounds and blue marlins tipping the scales at half a ton.

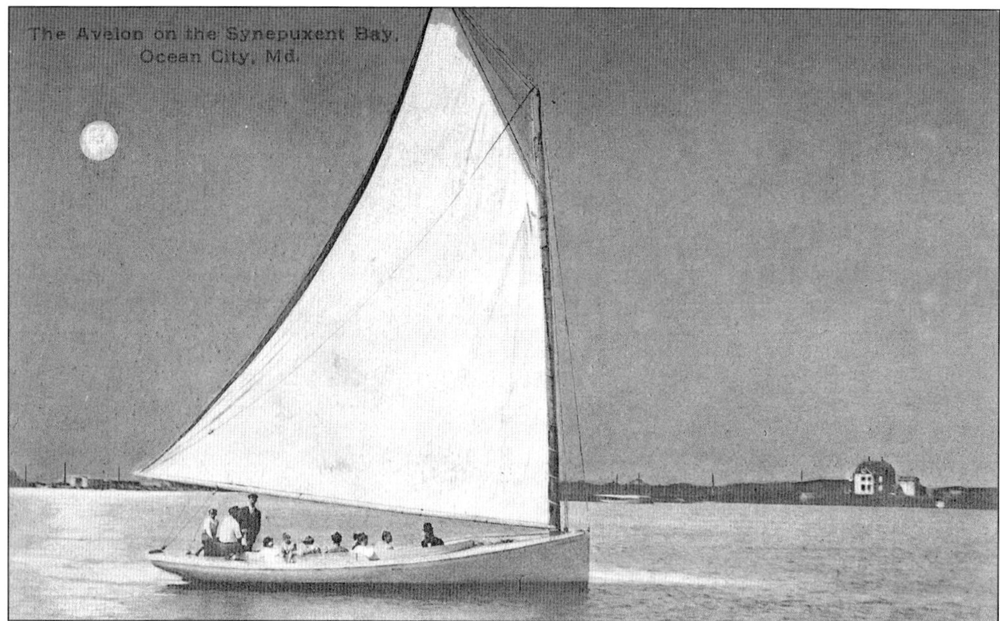

In this 1909-postmarked card, the *Avelon*, pictured above, is a larger catboat of the type available for rent along the Sinepuxent Bay both before and after the inlet was cut through. A catboat mast is positioned forward at the bow and here features a gaff (the short pole here running from three-fourths of the way up the mast to the top of the sail), which was later replaced on sailboats by the more manageable Marconi rig in which the luff (mast edge) of the sail extends straight up the mast. This same postcard but without the caption or moon and with airbrushed clouds was being printed by the Albertype Co. and sold by R.D. Driscoll in the 1940s. Also postmarked 1909 is the romantic image of "Moonlight Sail on the Synepuxent [*sic*] Bay." It depicts a large catboat sailing east toward a rising moon.

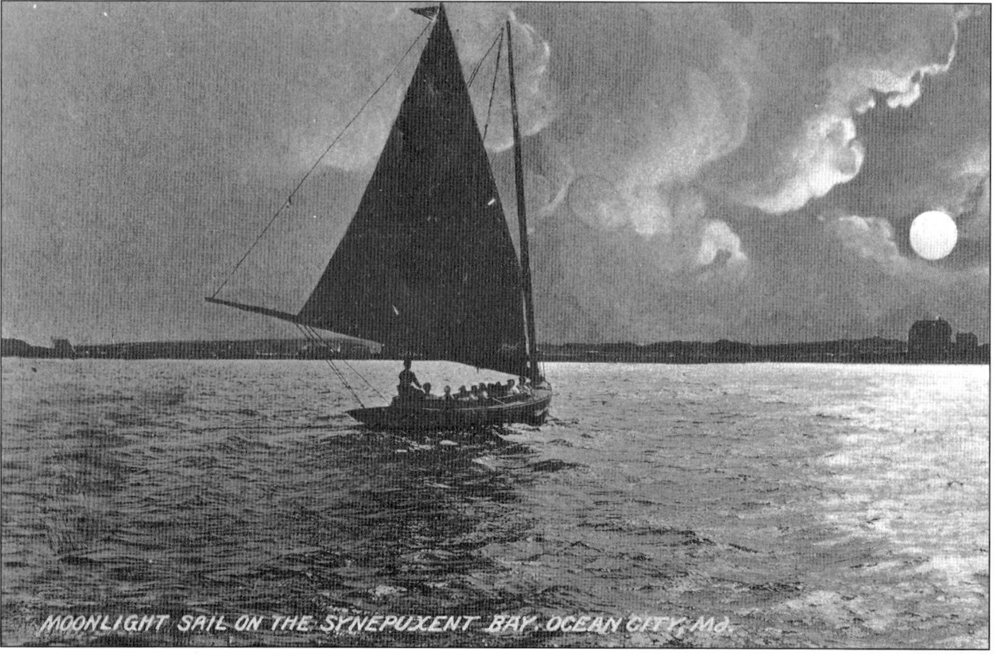

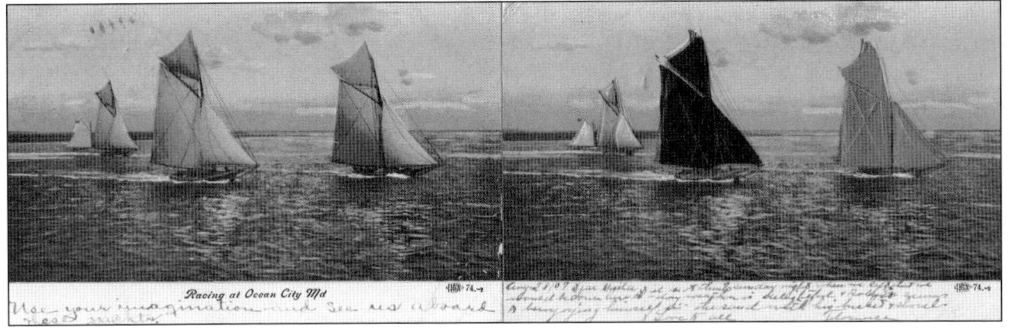

The same scene is featured in two Postal Card Distributing Co. postcards, both postmarked 1907 but with different hand coloring of sails and other details. This practice of duplication was followed by many postcard companies who may airbrush different cloud formations or adjust other elements but most often simply colorized the cards with different tones. The scene is of racing sloops, single mast boats with foresail (jib) and topsail.

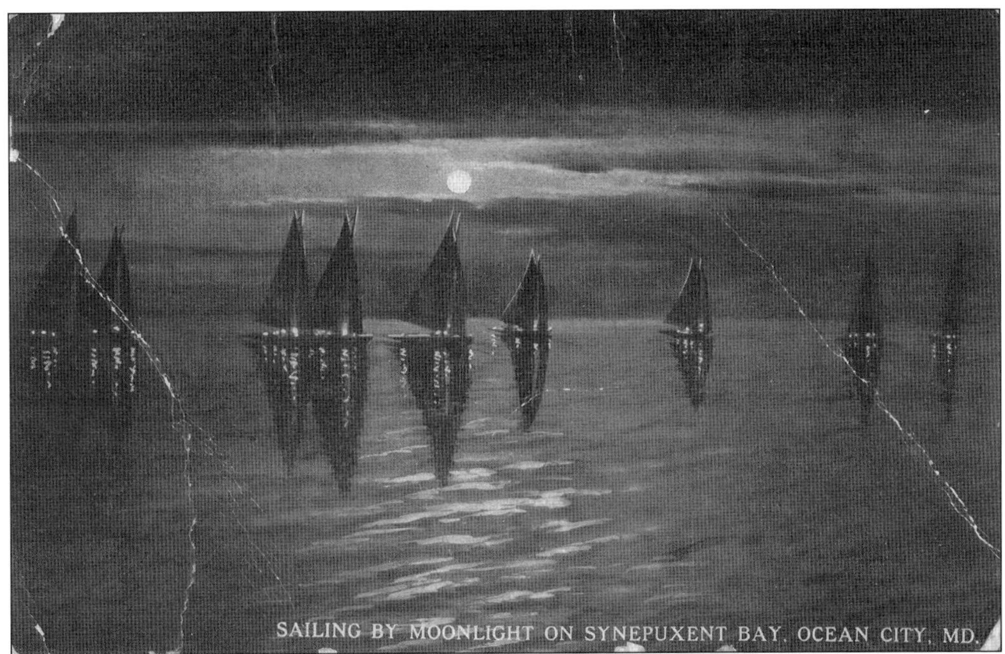

In the caption "Sailing by Moonlight on Synepuxent [*sic*] Bay, Ocean City, MD," Louis Kauffman & Sons of Baltimore only slightly altered the wording of their 1913 romantic image of a "moonlight sail" on the bay (page 156 below). However, note here that a virtual fleet of sloops is silhouetted in the moonlight. The authenticity of so many sloops on Ocean City's back bays is questionable (see caption page 158 below).

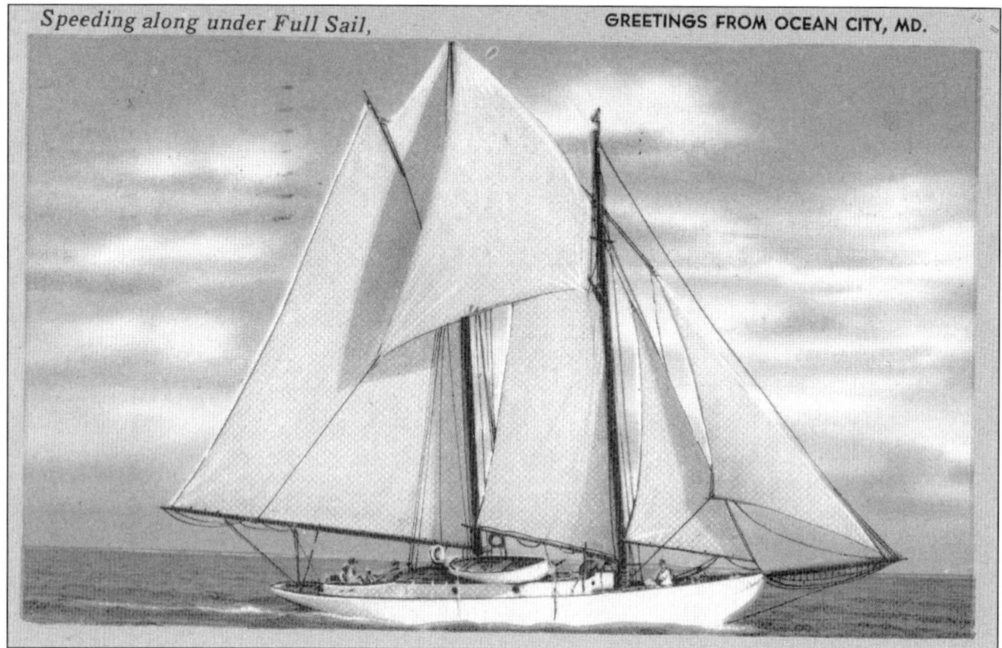

"Speeding along under Full Sail," this two-masted schooner was likely 45 to 50 feet in length; although schooners could be up to 85 feet long and could also have three to six masts (one was even built with seven masts). Main sail and foresails are carried on a gaff. This postcard was postmarked 1957, when such schooners plied the Eastern Shore waters from the Chesapeake to Sinepuxent and Isle of Wight Bays.

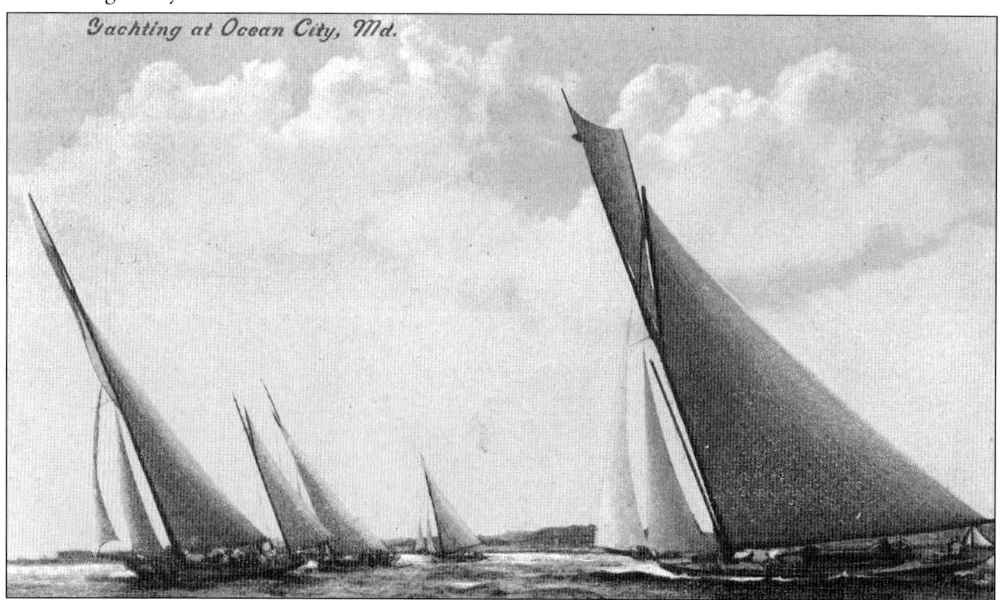

This early and generic Postal Card Distributing Co. card, postmarked 1909, is captioned "Yachting at Ocean City, Md." However, such single-masted ocean racing sloops were not found here and would be more at home racing off Newport, Rhode Island. They drew 10 to 12 feet of water and certainly would not be sailing the bay. Nonetheless, as enticements to draw vacationing public to town, such generic cards were widely sold.

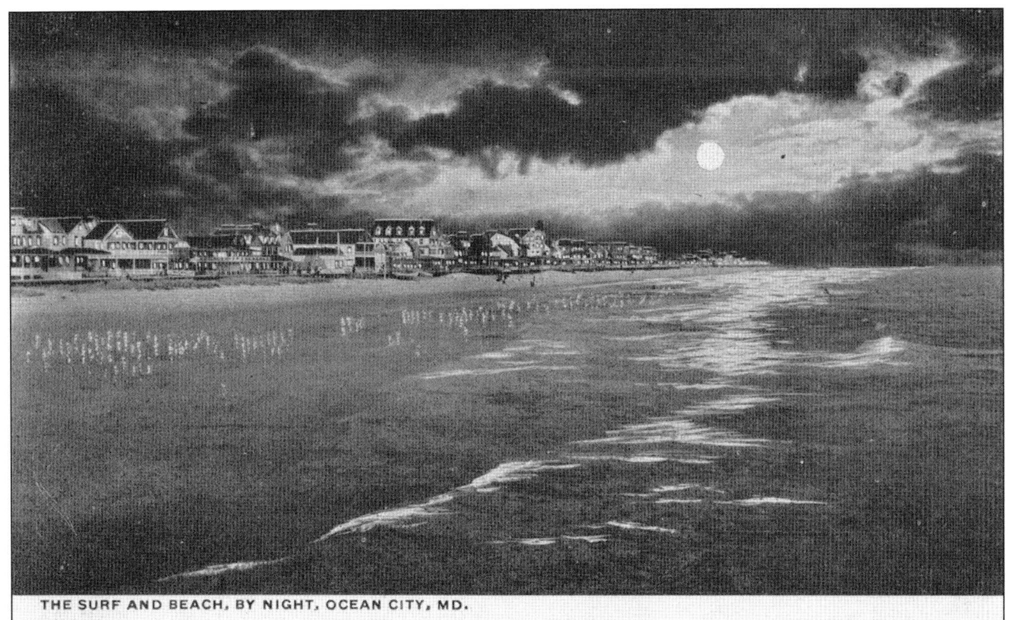

The images on this closing page of *Ocean City's Historic Boardwalk, Beach, and Bay: The Fisher Collection* involve noticeable poetic license. In the 1917-postmarked Louis Kaufmann postcard above, the photographer's image of the boardwalk and beachfront looking north from the ocean fishing pier is accurate enough, but the artistic addition of a full moon rising north-northeast could only make this image close to accurate in the dead of winter.

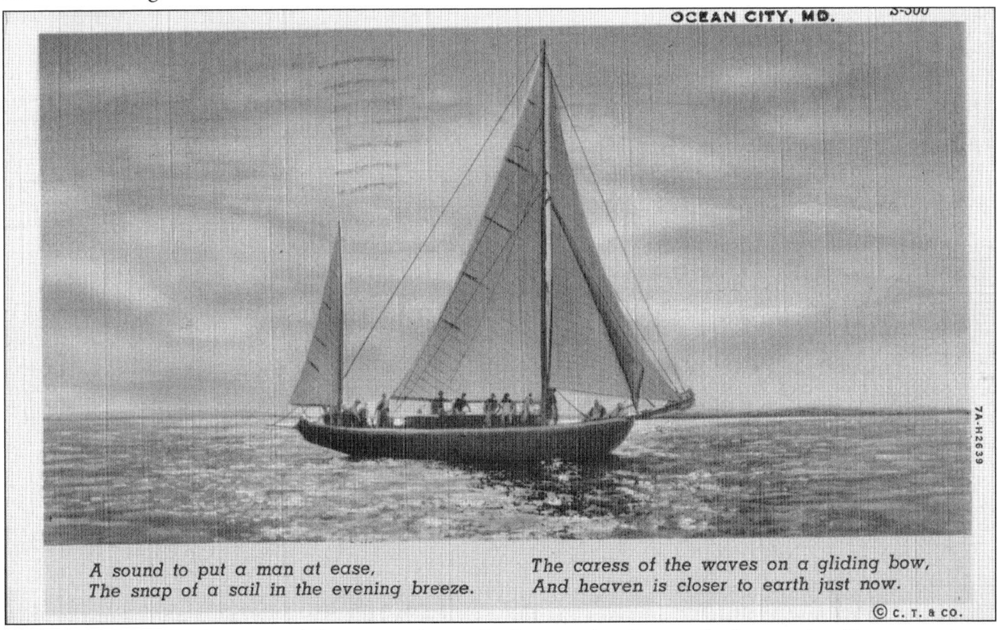

This 1937 Curt Teich postcard features a 40-to-45-foot yawl, a fore-and-aft rigged sailboat carrying a mainsail (here a Marconi rig) and one or more jibs (two here) with a mizzenmast aft, and is stamped Ocean City, Maryland, but it is unlikely such a yawl sailed these waters. However, the following sentiment is universal: "The caress of the waves on a gliding bow / And heaven is closer to earth just now."